J.F.Kennedy
and
Presidential
Power

Edited and with an introduction by

EARL LATHAM
AMHERST COLLEGE

D. C. HEATH AND COMPANY
Lexington, Massachusetts Toronto London

Contents

Contents

Introduction

Three threads of thought weave through the text and readings of this book about the presidential leadership of John F. Kennedy: the nature of political power; the powers of the president of the United States generally; and the exercise of those powers by President Kennedy specifically—whether he used them wisely, with knowledge or out of impulse, for the improvement of his own public image or the promotion of the public interest, for beneficial results or not. The unspoken question implied in each of the sections of the book is whether the president should have more or less power, or if this question cannot be decided in any easy yes or no fashion, the respects, then, in which one would wish that the powers of the president be expanded or curtailed.

In modern times, the power of the state—and the president of the United States is the chief of state—is the mightiest concentration of force in the society. In fact, the state (behavioral political scientists prefer to speak of the "political system") has a monopoly of all legitimate force and the officers of the state therefore hold in their hands controls of silk and steel that reach every member of the society. No other social organization—not the churches, the unions, the corporations, business or fraternal associations—can command all members of the society, deprive them of their property (taxes), or send them to death in war or prison. So dangerous did the framers of the Constitution think this power of the state that they divided it into separate elements—the states and the federal government, among three more or less independent branches—in order to prevent its fusion into one mass, under the control of one person or faction, whether a majority or a minority. And then the Bill of Rights was added to limit the exercise of the powers already granted, in order to protect further the liberties and security of the people from certain gross forms of arbitrariness and caprice.

Although the power of the state is commonly perceived to be vivid, dramatic, intimidating, incomprehensible, and even murderous—

and it *is* spectacular—power relations appear in all the activities of mankind, not merely in the decree of public authority. It may be appropriate here to look briefly at the phenomenon of political power in its broadest range. We have all heard of office politics, faculty politics, fraternity politics, and the like, and are familiar with the strife and scuffle for prestige, advantage, position, domination, and influence that takes place in the most ordinary social, family, and professional relations. Kurt Vonnegut has even mentioned marriage as a nation of two people, which is an interesting political idea; and Women's Liberation advocates speak of the domination of men in society as "sexual politics." All such relations are power relations.

There is a considerable body of literature on the subject of power in human relations, and there is considerable disagreement about the subject because it is often taken out of the category of ordinary human activity—like work and play, buying and selling, creating and cherishing—invested with magic and mystery and often discussed in words and treated with feelings more appropriate to religious, superstitious, and other emotive engagements of self. This is especially true of the power of the state. But the concept of power (including that of the state) in all its synonyms—authority, force, influence, prestige, domination, mastery, leadership, supremacy, tutelage, control, hegemony, sovereignty, pull, drag, and clout—basically means nothing more mysterious than the ability to act. If every man were a nation of one, like Robinson Crusoe, the limitations on his ability to act would be environmental, physical, and, perhaps, psychological. The ability to act, that is, would not depend upon the cooperation or consent of others, nor would it be limited by it. In such a case the ability to act would not be "political," for political power is a relationship among people, not between people and things, nor between things and things. It is a human event. When such an event occurs, tensions between superiority and subordination operate, tending to settle in various modes of equilibrium, of which equality is one. But it cannot be said that history has often shown distributions of power in exact and constant measure to every man. The most constant spur to social change has been, rather, the unequal distribution of power in political systems. It could with truth be said that if economics is the science of scarcity, politics is the science of disparity.

Although political power is basically the ability to act, nevertheless it is no more a single thing in its applications and appearances than is the concept of power in physics, mechanics, electronics, or hydraulics. For example, at the highest levels of abstraction there are broad philosophies, like that of pragmatism, and utopian creeds, like that

of the millenarians, that are also, as Arthur Schlesinger, Jr., has
pointed out, theories of power as well as theories of truth and of faith.
In the more obviously political theories of elitism and anarchism,
the crux of the matter is whether power is and should be the right of
the few or whether it should be abolished altogether.

However, not all theories about power have to be as imperial
in their reach and meaning as those just mentioned, extending as
they do into all aspects of society and governance. There are many
special concepts of power and ways in which it is or should be
exercised. For example, in the opinion of John Cogley, a writer in the
Catholic journal *Commonweal,* there is a Protestant conception of
power and a Catholic conception of power. The latter, he believes,
is more hospitable to the full use and range of influences than the
former, which he has held to be more narrow and restricted and
invested somehow with an aura of sin for which moral justification
is the only countervailance. Max Weber, one of the most influential
German sociologists of this century, also thought there were different
modes in the conception and exercise of power, and he classified
three principal ones—the traditional, associated with tribal and
primitive societies; the rational-legal, the characteristic form in all
mature developed systems of governance in Western countries; and
the charismatic, which is the special mode in revolutionary and
religious movements. But these are ideal types, rarely found in
unmixed purity. Even where the prevailing mode is rational-legal,
there are traditional elements (for example, there were no Catholics
among the thirty-four presidents before Kennedy), and there are
expressive variations in style that originate in the personality
characteristics of the leaders. Presidents may wish to concentrate
authority in themselves, evident in their reluctance to delegate it; or
they may wish to appeal to the people directly (plebiscitary power),
as a way of bypassing the requirement of the rational-legal mode that
they integrate their procedures with those of the elected representatives.
Both Franklin D. Roosevelt and President Eisenhower did this on
occasion.

Still one other variation in the exercise of power, even in well-
established, rational-legal administrative systems, is the difference
between the managerial and the idiosyncratic or personal approaches,
the former being the more bureaucratic, dependent for its results upon
the work of others according to established and stable routines; and
the latter being less routinized, given more to improvisation and
hunch, always conscious of the subjective and personal equations in
human affairs. The virtue of the first style is its predictable
dependability, and its vice is slowness, caution, lack of imagination,

and rigidity. The virtue of the second is flair and flexibility, and its vice is eccentricity, unpredictability, and avoidable risk. No president uses one to the exclusion of the other, but Eisenhower tended to be rather more managerial and Kennedy rather more idiosyncratic and personal in the exercise of their authorities. Symbols (to be discussed presently) are also important in any appreciation of the complexity of power, for they both evoke and stimulate behavior, and presidents are both artists and icons, more or less knowingly, in the establishment of symbolic meanings in political and social life.

This book of readings is about John F. Kennedy, but it is important to understand what it is not. It is not a biographical collection, and it is not a contribution to the hagiography that has grown up around one whose life was so tragically shortened. Nor is the book a rendering of the pluses and minuses of his administration, the costs and benefits—an accountant's summary of achievements —because the years since his death are still too short for fully accurate valuations, although this fact has not stayed some from casting up trial balance sheets. Tom Wicker, for example, has concluded that John Kennedy was a Golden Figure but that his administration was not a Golden Age, and some may remember the slain president more because he represented to us what we wanted to be than what we are. In January 1971, *The New York Times* correspondent Anthony Lewis, reported Lord Harlech, a friend of Kennedy's, as saying: "The Kennedy period was the last in which there was a feeling of optimism abroad in the world. From 1961 to 1963 we were all of good cheer." This may or may not be so. It is just too soon to venture these large judgments, and any temptation to do so should be discouraged by the contrariety of judgments already available. For example, "Was Kennedy another Lincoln?" The answers vary. Tom Wicker in an essay titled *Kennedy Without Tears* says that Kennedy will be remembered with Lincoln. On the other hand, William Carleton, who is reprinted below says that Kennedy will *not* be remembered with Lincoln.

The scope of this work is somewhat smaller but perhaps more important in content than the construction of obituary notices, however deserved the praise, or nostalgic and poignant the recollection. It is centered on Kennedy's exercise of presidential power. In the spring of 1963, a public opinion poll rated Kennedy highest as a family man and as a personality, and lowest as a philosopher, legislator, and military strategist. No one was asked in the poll, conducted by the Opinion Research Corporation, how Kennedy rated as the commander of the vast powers reposed in him as President of the United States, and yet it was to him that the people by a narrow

vote in 1960 gave control of the most coercive force in the country.
Indeed, within the scope of his constitutional authorities, the President
of the United States may be the most powerful single public officer
in the world, certainly so in the world of the representative
democracies.

How did President Kennedy use all this power in his few years
of office? Before the election, when asked why he wanted to be
president, Kennedy said because "that is where the action is." But
the action was not always manageable. In a television interview
in December 1962 (according to Wicker in *Kennedy Without Tears*),
Kennedy seemed to feel that most human effort is futile, and to show
a sense of the limitations of his office after two years in it. But he did
believe in action, especially when done with style and precision,
and looked upon politics as a game, with admiration even for those
who used sharp practice.

How did he play it? Despite his relish for the game, and the
possibility that in two terms of eight years he would have achieved
Olympic form, there were skeptical judgments like that made by the
Atlantic magazine in July 1963 that he had not actually played it very
well. It was reported that liberals in Congress were saying that
Kennedy as president had been too hesitant. The admonition of the
inaugural address—"And so, my fellow Americans, ask not what your
country can do for you; ask what you can do for your country"—
was embarrassing because, once installed, Kennedy had been vague
and unclear about almost everything except the Peace Corps, whose
earlier advocates had been Congressman Henry S. Reuss of Wisconsin
and Senator Hubert H. Humphrey of Minnesota. Robert Kennedy
was complaining that blacks were too militant. Kennedy had no
record at all on civil rights. In the economic field it was felt that he
was too inclined first to sound a high note and then a low note, and
then to compromise. In the field of foreign policy, it was felt that
he had done nothing to slow down the arms race. In fact, his
inaugural address was a Cold War speech. "Let every nation know,"
he said, "whether it wishes us well or ill, that we shall pay any price,
bear any burden, meet any hardship, support any friend, oppose
any foe to assure the survival and the success of liberty."

In many respects, these criticisms may have been premature for
there were signs of change even as they were in press. Two-and-one-
half years after taking office, on June 10, 1963, President Kennedy,
in a speech at American University, spoke of peace and disarmament
and urged the development of mutual interests with the Soviet
Union. The next day in a speech on national television after George
Wallace had symbolically resisted the enforcement of federal law at

the University of Alabama, President Kennedy spoke emotionally about questions of race. "We preach freedom around the world, and we mean it, and we cherish our freedom here at home, but are we to say to the world," he asked, "and more importantly to each other— that this is the land of the free, except for Negroes; that we have no second-class citizens, except Negroes; that we have no class or caste system, no ghettos, no master race, except with respect to Negroes?" Shortly thereafter, he proposed to Congress the adoption of the most comprehensive civil rights bill since Reconstruction.

There is evidence, then, that Kennedy did change in office as he found his way more surely. In 1966, three years after the assassination, a knowing political specialist, Clayton Fritchey, in a piece in *Harper's* said that Kennedy had started as a conservative in 1961 and became a liberal. At the beginning of his term he appointed Republicans to office, trusted the establishment more than he trusted intellectuals, and took a hard line on Communism. In view of this change one wonders whether actions taken in the early period would have been the same had Kennedy had in 1961 the experience he was to acquire by 1963. This is not a question of hindsight, but of qualifications.

For example, the Pentagon Papers show that in the spring of 1961 the President ordered 400 Special Forces troops and 100 other American military advisers to Vietnam without public notice of the action. These are small numbers when compared with the more than half-million American troops who were eventually sent to Vietnam. According to the Pentagon study, this commitment "signaled a willingness to go beyond the 685-man limit on the size of the U.S. [military] mission in Saigon, which if it were done openly, would be the first formal breach of the Geneva agreement." Under that agreement the United States was limited to the indicated number of advisers in Vietnam, and although the United States had not actually signed the agreement, it had pledged itself not to violate it. On the same day that President Kennedy decided to send the Special Forces, he also ordered the start of a clandestine war against North Vietnam, to be conducted by the South Vietnamese after training by the Central Intelligence Agency. What had been a "gamble" in the Eisenhower years was converted by Kennedy into a "broad commitment," with consequences that were to poison every aspect of American life. Would these earlier steps have been taken with knowledge of where they were to lead? Doubtless not, although no one of course can tell whether President Kennedy would have escalated the war to the extent to which President Johnson took it, or escalated it at all, and there is no way ever to find out. But the broad commitment was certainly in force at the time of the assassination because there were close to 16,000 American advisers in South Vietnam and Diem, the head of the state in South Vietnam, had been assassinated only the week before, with the acquiescence of the American government, if not through its clandestine participation.

The central concept of this collection of readings, as indicated above, is power, and especially the uses of presidential power by John F. Kennedy. Robert Frost hailed the accession of Kennedy as the beginning of an Augustan Age, but the essays below are concerned with certain trials and conditions and limitations in the American political process with which Caesar Augustus never had to strive. The materials are organized under four headings, each of which presents policies, problems, and concepts involving the use of presidential power to which the specific contributions that follow provide some understanding. Each of the sections is introduced by commentary on the specifics that follow, tying them in with the general themes of this introduction.

The title of the first part of this book is "Political Art and Presidential Mastery," and the problem it presents is the nature of the office of the president as seen by the president, and the ways in which the office can be conducted and *was* conducted by President Kennedy. There are many roles the president has to play, as the late Professor Clinton L. Rossiter showed in his work on *The American Presidency,* and many styles through which the power of the presidential office is wielded. A president's style is most often a function of his experience and temperament. His personality and the work habits of his life determine the modes of access to him of the many people with whom he has to cooperate, and through whom he comes to effect policy. For example, President Eisenhower's long career in the military service accustomed him to work with and through a highly structured and hierarchic organization of subordinates. A high military commander normally relies upon completed staff work by subordinates for the identification of issues, the development of alternatives, the rejection of some options and the retention of others, the consideration of various courses of action, and the case for and against the adoption of those to be recommended. A chief commander does not normally involve himself in this staff work but relies upon others to do it for him.

This procedure does spare a chief commander the burden of responsibility for the preliminaries, and it does free him from detail, but it also has several disadvantages when transferred from the military to the political and executive realms. For example, since the selection and sifting of issues is in the hands of others, it is *they* who get to determine what it is the president will see and hear, and by such selection, in fact, limit his choices. In so acting, subordinates get to wield some of the power of the president himself, although they are not responsible to the people for the choices that they have made, and there is only an indirect way (through the electoral process) for bringing the president to account for what they, in effect, have done. As the comments to come will show, President Kennedy's more idiosyncratic and personal style also had its advantages and disadvantages.

Part Two of the book considers the problem of power and purpose in domestic affairs during the Kennedy administration; and Part Three carries the inquiry into the area of foreign affairs. There is a considerable difference in the scope and autonomy of the president's powers in the two areas. In domestic matters, the separation of powers that is built into the Constitution gives to Congress ultimate authority to decide what legislation will be put on the books, and the president is unable to command these decisions. In foreign affairs, the scope of the president's power is very broad indeed and much of it is independent of the wish of Congress. In the comments that head both Parts Two and Three, these distinctions will be examined further.

In Part Two, attention is given to three examples of policy and public concern where the concept of power was and is especially important. That is to say, the problems involved were not mere issues to be decided this way or that within a framework of agreed assumptions, in which the outcome was merely a choice of one tactic or another; but alternatives of choice embodying philosophical conceptions about the use and distribution of power in the society. The first of the three examples is the conversion of Kennedy to the economic ideas of John Maynard Keynes; the second is the Big Steel crisis; and the third is Kennedy's conversion to civil rights. The concept of power involved in the first of these philosophical choices is the responsibility of the state for the economy, and the extent and width of the intervention it should undertake. Under the doctrines of Keynes, the state is a necessary mechanism in the operation of the economy, providing it with corrective balances in the interest of full employment. The older view was that the economy was self-correcting, that if left alone by government, it would somehow organize, allocate, and distribute the resources of the society most efficiently through the mechanism of price. To repeat, at stake in the two opposing views is the very political question of power—who is to make what decisions about the distribution of material goods in the society. To accept Keynes is to accept the primacy of politics over economics. Although the line between politics and economics is extremely difficult to draw, and although what the United States has had for fifty years is neither capitalism nor welfarism but a society in which both elements coexist, it is a fact that in a crisis of the economy, it is the political element that will prevail over the economic. It is not the businessman who will bail out the government, as J. Pierpont Morgan, August Belmont, and the Rothschilds did in the panic year 1893 when President Cleveland sold them bonds for gold, but the government that will bail out the businessman and control the rate of growth in the economy.

The second example, which illustrates a special aspect of the nature of power and the force with which the president can wield it, is the Big Steel Case in which the influence of the presidential office was such that the principal steel companies, which had increased their prices under circumstances that seemed to suggest uncandor, were pressured by President Kennedy into rolling them back to their original levels. Such intervention is not entirely novel—as long ago as 1902 President Theodore Roosevelt acted to avert a crisis in the anthracite coal industry—but it does represent one of the roles, that of guardian of the economy, that the people now expect the president to perform.

And the third example of power—civil rights—has many dimensions. First, it involves the interests of some twenty-four million people who, although not yet voting in the strength their numbers could mass, constitute nevertheless a substantial bloc of potential voting support which could be decisive in presidential elections. Since 1940 the proportion of the black vote that has been given to the Democratic Party has ranged as high as 98 percent in national elections, although this identification with the Democratic Party, strengthened by the Kennedy civil rights proposals that President Lyndon Johnson was able to get through Congress after the assassination, may not be enduring as blacks come to develop viable political institutions of their own. Second, and certainly at a higher level of philosophy and political sensitiveness, is the question whether democratic power is to be rationed to some and denied to others, or whether equality—one man's vote to represent the same quantum as that of any other—is to be the rule. And by extension, there is the question whether each man should not have equal access to facilities that theoretically are open and available to everybody. It is one of the axioms of democratic belief that every man should have the same share as every other of the formal power represented by the ballot to decide such questions of public policy as are presented to the electorate for determination.

There is a real sense in which the president may be regarded as the representative of all the people since he is the only officer of the government (along with the vice-president) who is in fact elected by a national constituency. The authority of the president and the force of his power in domestic affairs depend in great part upon the extent to which he is perceived to be the active spokesman for all the citizenry. Congressmen represent minorities (no Congressional district and no state of the United States comprises a majority of the people); it is therefore the president who symbolizes the whole, and the alienation of any substantial segment of the population diminishes thereby the force that the president is able to bring to bear in the enactment of legislation and the conduct of domestic policy.

Part Three concerns an aspect of the president's power that is widely misunderstood by the press and by the people at large and which recently has come under attack in the Congress and in the activities of citizens' groups opposed to the Vietnam war. This is the nature and extent of the authority of the president to conduct international affairs about which there has been disagreement between the Congress and the White House since the time of George Washington. The tension was especially acute in the period after the Second World War (although strong even in the early years of Franklin Roosevelt), and endured through the administrations of Presidents Truman, Eisenhower, and Kennedy; and after Kennedy, in the administrations of Presidents Johnson and Nixon. Presidents from Roosevelt through Johnson, as Senator Frank Church has pointed out, have tended to believe that it is only the president and his experts who can have the knowledge necessary to conduct international affairs in our time; and one might add that this seems to have been the view of President Nixon also. These were the presidents, according to common argument, with memory of a Congress that destroyed the League of Nations and hampered Franklin Roosevelt's quest for alliances against Germany and Japan. But the issue of presidential power in foreign affairs was litigated as early as March 1796 when the House of Representatives adopted a motion calling upon the president to submit all of the papers dealing with the Jay Treaty. Washington rejected the assumption of the House that it had any share in the treaty-making power, although Madison managed to get through a resolution asserting that the House did have both a constitutional right and duty to deliberate on the expediency or inexpediency of carrying any treaty into effect.

Thus from the earliest beginnings, the White House and the Congress have been in tension over the division of authority to conduct foreign relations. The view that has generally come to pre-

vail is that stated by John Marshall, and affirmed by Mr. Justice
Sutherland in 1936, that the president is the sole representative of the
United States in international affairs. However, since the end of the
Second World War various members of the United States Senate have
sought to establish claim to a share in the power, with greater
plausibility perhaps (the Senate *is* supposed to advise as well as consent
to treaties), but with no more success than the House. As the sole
representative of the United States in international affairs, the
president is empowered to commit the country to courses of policy
that, to paraphrase Fisher Ames, begin as seed wheat, to be sown
again, and to swell, almost beyond calculation, a future harvest of
tragedy. Such was the way in which the United States became involved
in Vietnam.

Foreign affairs, then, is the greatest free area under the
Constitution for the exercise of presidential leadership, and Part
Three presents material on three aspects of this leadership during
President Kennedy's term, the Cold War, Cuba twice, and Vietnam.
Central to the president's conduct of international affairs is his
understanding of the nature of the international world and its
principal parts, for from this definition of reality stem a thousand
subsidiary and corollary determinations and discriminations of policy,
much as the trunk fixes the location and direction of the branches,
twigs, and leaves which radiate from it and are nourished and
sustained by it. Despite the development of international "law" in
the last three hundred years, there is no international law that can
be enforced by due processes and nonviolently against refusing states
in the international community. All nations reserve to themselves
the final determination as to which of the rules for the civil conduct
of international affairs they will accept. Ultimately, each state
decides international policy in terms of its own interest; and the
course of international policy is most often determined by domestic
exigency. That is to say, if nations abroad take a strong anti-American
line, it is probably less because there is a general, abstract, and
free-floating hostility to the United States than because domestic
policy requires this international stance. The same is true of those
nations we regard as friends. Interest, not affection, is the knot in
international ties.

These concepts are illustrated by the three indicated aspects of
foreign policy developed in the Kennedy years. The first is the fact
that Kennedy started out on a Cold War note in his inaugural
address and then came to modify his view of the stance America
should take with respect to the Soviet Union. There is reason to
believe, however, that the early position had baleful consequences

and that Kennedy was not in office long enough to realize himself much national advantage or benefit from his change of view. At least one writer is of the opinion that Kennedy overreacted to Khrushchev repeatedly. One of the consequences of this overreaction, it is thought, was the Cuban missile crisis in which the two super-powers temporarily were, as the saying of the time had it, "eyeball to eyeball" and the threat of nuclear war was more imminent than at any time since Hiroshima.

But why does one say the "super-powers," as though the adversaries were abstract entities, or strangers, or impersonal institutions to whose confrontation the American people were merely passive witness, without personal peril or even involvement? The adversaries in confrontation were two individuals, Kennedy and Khrushchev, and if massive incineration were indeed the gage of the controversy, it was the American population that was about to be incinerated. Where was the power to decide, who had the authority to say yes or no, in whose hands did the fate of the country rest, perhaps precariously during the few days of the crisis? The answer, of course, is in the hands of the two men, one the spokesman for a totalitarian power and the other the leader of a representative democracy. And who could tell the difference between the two kinds of power at the time? There was no difference. The scope of presidential power is illustrated also by the earlier effort to topple Castro by the invasion of Cuba. It was the *president's* decision alone to invade the Bay of Pigs.

The war in Vietnam is a third example of the immensity of the power of the president in foreign relations. It illustrates also, however, the importance of knowledge and experience in the one man who can change a "gamble" into a "broad commitment" and, in the absence of personal knowledge, his dependence upon the "experts" and the "intellectuals" who presume to advise him. It seems to be true that when Kennedy came to the White House he had no position on Vietnam but developed one on the advice, among others, of General Maxwell D. Taylor. One of the tragic ironies of this broad commitment was that it took place at the same time Kennedy was ruing the fiasco of the Bay of Pigs. Theodore Sorensen is the authority for Kennedy's judgment about himself. Sorensen said, quoting Kennedy, "How could I have been so far off base? . . . All my life I've known better than to depend on the experts. How could I have been so stupid, to let them go ahead?"

Although it is true that in the field of foreign affairs the president's power is the greatest, it is only variably and contingently effective. It is only variably and contingently effective because the

other nations to whom he represents the United States follow courses
of their own, as dictated by their own perceptions of their needs.
As Stewart Alsop pointed out in a *Saturday Evening Post* article
in April 1963, President Kennedy hoped to promote an Atlantic
alliance that would have political, economic, and military features.
In the first part of the design, it was supposed that Britain would
enter the Common Market, and that this would lead to a United
Europe into which the United Kingdom would be tied politically and
economically, and to which the United States could relate itself
in an Atlantic partnership. On the military side, the United States
would contribute to the Atlantic partnership a centrally controlled
atomic deterrent, and the European nations would build the troop
strength of NATO up to thirty divisions. The philosophy behind
this plan was that Europe could thus withstand attack by conventional
weapons and the United States could thus avoid the risks of mortal
confrontation with the Soviet Union implied in reliance upon
nuclear weapons alone. But this was not to come to pass—certainly
not in Kennedy's time. Charles de Gaulle decided that France had
to have nuclear weapons of its own without the dependence upon the
United States that the Kennedy proposal entailed; and he decided
also to veto the admission of Britain to the Common Market. Indeed,
in the military realm, he went even farther and required the
United States to move NATO headquarters out of France. Thus
in the area of foreign affairs where—to repeat—the power of the
president is greatest, he must reckon with the vagaries of the men in
control of the other states in the international community, and the
way to harmonious and beneficial policies must be pursued along
a thousand confusing tracks.

But even so, the powers of the president in the world of foreign
affairs are very great indeed. The power of the executive to make
secret decisions, as Kennedy did in the two Cuban episodes and
in fixing American foreign policy in Vietnam—decisions that involved
or threatened war—is thought by supporters of strong executive
power to be necessary to the national security in an age of nuclear
arms. Arguments over the Pentagon Papers ultimately reduce
themselves to how broad this secret power should be, with the
advocates of strong executive power taking the position that it should
be as broad as possible because the state of international armaments
is such that instant action by the White House must be made possible.
Critics of executive power argue that somewhat less secrecy might
avert those very situations in which catastrophic war threatens.

The fourth part of the collection is titled "Power as Knowledge and Symbol," and there are two major themes. The first is the relation between Kennedy and the intellectuals whose articulate knowledgeability was both a source of ideas and, who, at the same time, were a symbol of style and status for him. The second theme is the idea that symbols are both representative and creative and, in both aspects, help to shape the meaning of a president for the multiform multitude and constitute, in this reference, one of the ingredients of presidential power.

Intellectuals in our society and in our time do wield a special kind of power, less traditional (one can scarcely imagine President Grant or President Harding making use of men who lacked credentials in business or the world of elective politics) but more imaginative, resourceful, learned, literary, knowledgeable, and, at best, free of ulteriority. Andrew Jackson had a "kitchen cabinet" to assist his judgment. Woodrow Wilson had his friend Colonel House, who served often as a special emissary and as an alter ego, and Franklin Roosevelt had a "brain trust." Since the New Deal, the conduct of governmental affairs has become almost incomprehensibly complex with both a proportionate and an absolute increase in the amount and variety of knowledge that any man, and certainly any president, must have in order to deal with the manifold problems of a highly organized and technologized industrial society. The burden of governance demands more and more expertness and the skillful president must know how to attract and use special talents.

A special characteristic of the specialist who qualifies as an "intellectual" is that he is also a critic. If he is free to judge policy without regard to mundane consequences, it is also true that he is free to criticize it. And the intellectual community is often in the van of public opinion. It is also a characteristic of "intellectuals" that, in America, at least, they have tended to be alienated from politics and that they have shown an affinity for solutions that allegedly more "practical" men find unworldly, although, to use the phrase of C. Wright Mills, the superior practicality of practical men is often a kind of "crackpot realism." Intellectuals are also likely to be highly articulate and freely expressive, and they often create difficulties for men in office in the exercise of their independence. Even in the Soviet Union the leaders of a totalitarian state have found that poets and other writers are pretty difficult to contend with. Finally, intellectuals in the United States most often have seemed to favor a liberal or left persuasion (there are also intellectuals of the right but they have been less venturesome); and they are inclined to push policy to lengths beyond the margins thought to be popular by politicians who, after all, must rely upon the electoral support of large numbers of voters who are skeptical of what they consider to be panaceas and utopias.

The problem for a Democratic president like John Kennedy in dealing with intellectuals was more difficult than it has been for Republican presidents because intellectuals when they have acted within the two-party system generally have allied themselves with what they perceive to be the reform elements of a party of reform. They cannot be ignored by a Democratic president because they represent votes, either their own, or those of followers; but they cannot be fully identified with too closely because to do so would alienate many others, perhaps even more numerous, whose support is essential to victory at the polls. President Kennedy's relations with the intellectual community were ambivalent, and the selections in Part Four discuss various aspects of this relationship.

John Kennedy was a man of ideas but he was also a very successful practicing politician. He was attractive to intellectuals because of the high style that he and Mrs. Kennedy brought to the White House, but many in the intellectual community were suspicious of him as a practicing politician. At the outset of his administration he was a conservative, as has been said. He had not taken a public position on Senator Joseph R. McCarthy, who was a friend of his father and for whom his brother Robert Kennedy had served as counsel on the Subcommittee on Permanent Investigations of the Senate Committee on Government Operations. It is possible, as Joseph Alsop has said, that Kennedy neither liked nor admired most leading liberal intellectuals and it is possible that he used them for clear political purposes, such as money and votes, as Joseph Kraft has remarked. The intellectuals in John Kennedy's administration, then, both as agents and as sources of presidential power, were at the same time an asset and a liability. The reader will have an opportunity to judge for himself what the relation was between Kennedy and the intellectuals and to determine whether on the whole they were one or the other, an asset or a liability.

In turning from power as knowledge to power as symbol we shift from reality to appearance, although it must be said that to speak dogmatically of a distinction between reality and appearance is to make too clear what philosophers have made too confusing since the time of Plato. It may be noted, however, that all Presidents have an unnatural existence. That is to say, few people in ordinary life act as though they expected that every word, gesture, and act, public and private, will be aggressively scrutinized. Presidents assume the burden of maintaining a variety of public roles, speaking lines and

striking attitudes appropriate to those roles. They are forced to
maintain a stage presence constantly when in the public view. For
presidents there is relatively little privacy.

Some, however, do manage to maintain some privacy. The
public was never witness to the poker playing of President Warren
Gamaliel Harding; or the meetings of President Franklin D. Roosevelt
with Mrs. Rutherford. It never heard President Harry S Truman
swear; or sit in with President Dwight D. Eisenhower at one of his
bridge games; or go with President John F. Kennedy to California
for the occasional quiet weekend he took. Now it is true that even in
the life of the ordinary man, as well as of presidents, there is a public
aspect and a private aspect, and it is just as well that not everybody
knows what everybody is doing all of the time. Every man plays
many roles in the course of the day, even in his public and social life,
and social psychologists have written books treating the presentation
of self in everyday life as if it were theater. And it *is* theater, for
much of social life is the manufacture and production of images of
self formed and shaped by a sense of self, much as the actor plays
various parts.

How much more so this is for a president of the United States
who is representing not only himself by trying to behave in such a
way that he fulfills expectations for him held by millions of people.
He adopts a public persona that strikes a balance between his inner
self and his public self, between reality and the appearance he
wishes to create. If the distance between the two is not broad he can
presumably be an integrated person. If the distance is great, the
tension between the two increases. All know that the manufacture
of appearances for candidates for office has become one of the heavy
industries of Madison Avenue and other places where advertising
techniques are celebrated. Many candidates spend a good deal of
money attempting to find the right formulas that will appeal to the
most voters, and they conform their behavior to the advice of
the ad-men. Most will not neglect the development of tones and
expressions of the most intense sincerity and devotion to morality.
The modern day has no monopoly on political artifice, however. The
Whigs in the election of 1840 did a persuasive job of convincing a
popular majority that the rich were just like the common man,
being different only in that they had more money. But modern
technology and the dominating influence of television have enhanced
the complexity and subtlety of the symbolism of office.

It is neither hypocrisy nor deception that is in question. As
Murray Edelman in *The Symbolic Uses of Politics* has pointed out,
the crux of leadership is not really what the leader does, but what

the following does. "Leadership" may even be the wrong word to describe what a principal person in authority provides. The word suggests that others acquiesce or conform because of his superior gifts of mind, capability, or personality. If one looks at the matter from the point of view of the follower, however, as Chester I. Barnard did in his influential work on *The Functions of the Executive,* it is clear that the executive really has only those authorities that those over whom he exercises presumptive command allow him. In fact, there is no innate pattern of personal characteristics guaranteed to sustain leadership, since leadership is, in the main, a social product. The leader must conform to the expectations of those over whom he has been set to preside, or he forfeits his office.

Leadership in the modern state, like all leadership, has symbolic aspects that in themselves are components of power. The president is perceived as one with a capacity, by his every act, to affect significantly the lives and material fortunes of large numbers of people. Tenure in large part depends upon the degree to which the president can convey the impression that helpful, beneficial, rewarding, and cherishing things are being done for large numbers of people, whether this is so, in fact, or not. After all, it was not President Franklin Roosevelt who cured the unemployment malaise of the Great Depression but Adolf Hitler, whose activities abroad put Americans back to work. President Roosevelt, however, was able to get four terms of office out of the assurance that he gave enough voters that he was for them. The president, in Edelman's formulation, personifies and reifies the process of government—he symbolizes the unknowable and incomprehensible, because it "is apparently intolerable for men to admit the key role of accident, of ignorance, and of unplanned processes in their affairs." It is also his belief that the basic condition for the "displacement of political leadership is the leader's inability or lack of opportunity to convey the impression of coping with an opposition that can be identified and personified." That is, even the process of election and reelection is the manipulation of symbols, a competition of value biases. Both the leader and the followers provide psychological benefits for each other.

As it is on the stage, even the setting of politics is symbolic. The White House is more or less the same building it has been since its reconstruction after the British burned it in the War of 1812, but its tone has varied with the quality and the personality of the occupants whom the people have put in it. During the incumbency of President Eisenhower, the guest lists were filled with the names of businessmen, football coaches, lawyers, and others from the world of practical affairs and sports. At the White House wedding of the younger daughter of President Nixon, notable guests included the television and movie comedian Red Skelton, the Reverend Billy Graham, and J. Edgar Hoover, director of the Federal Bureau of Investigation. In the administration of John F. Kennedy, great public notice was given to the appearances of Pablo Casals and other cultural luminaries, and the poet Robert Frost also appeared and spoke at the Inauguration. The Eisenhower symbolism was quiet no-nonsense and down-to-earth practicality; that of Nixon was "just folks"; and that of Kennedy was high-style culture, although his own personal tastes ran more to musical comedies than to chamber music.

Perhaps there should be a long essay written sometime on what may be called "political mimesis." "Mimesis" is the representation of reality, and a notable work was done by Erich Auerbach under the title *Mimesis,* in which he discussed the representation of reality in Western literature. He found, for example, that the expression of great themes, like love and death, war and peace, and revenge and compassion, was reserved for a high style of expression in which the actors were all upper class. Comedy and farce were the domain and province of the low style in which the actors were lower class. In Shakespeare's *Henry V* the great themes are stated by nobles, and the low comedy is provided by lower class soldiers. One could think of political mimesis, however, in some less literary and class-structured way. Mimesis is imitation, and the president who invokes the name of Lincoln is inviting his audience to see him in shawl and stovepipe hat brooding over the fate of the Union. For FDR, Truman, and Eisenhower, their presidencies were extensions of their pasts. That is to say, they, by reason of such elements as geography, economic status, religion, ethnic origin, and social mobility, had developed central identifications rooted in family and preprofessional experiences, coherent and inescapable personality patterns that enabled them to see a world organized around a unified and consistent set of perceptions. But it can be argued that President Kennedy was not merely an extension of an integrated past, but a rootless extrusion into the future, in which he made a restless search for and adaptation to other social models than those he inherited from Irish Boston.

In three major elements of this inheritance he showed adaptation and change in his political life, beginning with his first term as a Congressman, the three elements being religion, the distinction between new money and old money, and social verticality. As a Congressman Kennedy tended to follow the example of his father as a Boston Catholic conservative, pushing for extensive aid to parochial schools and his constituency's interest in bread-and-butter projects of social reform. But as president it was Kennedy who told those who resented the Supreme Court's decision outlawing nonsectarian prayers that prayer was internal and personal and did not depend upon public rituals in the schools.

As to the second element of adaptation and imitation, Kennedy was of course a wealthy man because his father had made a fortune in liquor, real estate, and stock-market speculation. But there was a hankering for identification with Yankee Boston as well as Irish Boston, and John Kennedy, therefore, went to Choate and to Harvard. More so than the brothers who survived his death, John Kennedy's models seemed to be people like the Saltonstalls, with whom he was often in closer sympathy than with the politicians who ran the Democratic Party in Massachusetts. When he was married to Jacqueline Bouvier, the wedding was set for Newport, watering place of the nineteenth-century rich, and Harvard University was represented along with other symbols of Yankee culture. As to the third element, social verticality, it has already been said that old Boston was the paragon, and Kennedy became a fusion of Yankee-Protestant and Irish-Catholic elements. John Kennedy as symbol in the White House therefore stood for many things. In fact, Norman Mailer has said that he was the epitome of the American movie culture, always changing roles and personalities. It is with assessments of the complex symbolism of John F. Kennedy by Norman Mailer and William Carleton that this collection of essays comes to a close.

1
Political Art
and
Presidential
Mastery

To become president of the United States is to assume responsibility for the supervision of vast material and manpower resources. When President Kennedy took office in January 1961, he became the head of an executive establishment of 2,382,000 civilian employees (it was 2,527,000 three years later) and a military manpower pool of 1,010,000 which was to increase to 1,610,000 by 1963. Budget expenditures for the fiscal year 1961 were $81,500,000,000, his first year in office; they were $92,589,000,000 in his last year in office. The national debt at the end of fiscal 1961 was $288,861,000,000 and in fiscal 1963 was $306,098,000,000. In October 1961 the United Nations had a membership of 103 nations, twice the number of original members. In December 1963 it had 111 members. The increase in the number of the world's nations in the period after the Second World War had slowed down obviously in the three years of Kennedy's term, but the decay of empire was even then still adding to the number of world states with respect to which he was, by the United States Constitution, the sole spokesman for and representative of America.

At the same time, the president was the head of the Democratic Party, as every presidential candidate is the head of his party. The loser in a presidential election is sometimes called the titular head of his party, and Adlai Stevenson once remarked after his loss to Eisenhower in 1952 that there was no one more titular than he. But it must be remembered that Kennedy was a minority president, that is to say, he had been elected by a majority of the votes of the Electoral College as the Constitution requires, but he had actually received only a plurality, not a majority, of the popular votes. Kennedy received 34,227,096 popular votes and Nixon, 34,108,546, out of a total of 68,838,005. This margin was less than one vote in each of the 166,064 voting precincts in the nation in 1960. Kennedy's first Congress —the 87th, which was elected with him—had 261 Democrats and 176 Republicans, a large majority of his party in power, many of whom had run ahead of him in their respective districts. In the Senate, there were 64 Democrats and 36 Republicans, which was another sizable majority for the president's party. In the 88th Congress, elected in 1962, the Democrats had 258 members and the Republicans, 176; while in the Senate the Democrats had 67 and the Republicans, 33.

The precariously small margin by which Kennedy won the presidency left him in a position of weakness in his relations with a Congress in which the Democratic margins were so robust, for two reasons. The first reason was the fact that they had won big, and he had not. The second was the geographical pattern of the seats held by Democrats. Northern and Western Democrats who tended to agree with the president were fewer in numbers than the combination of Southern Democrats and conservative Republicans which had done so much to wreck President Truman's domestic programs. The president therefore lacked effective and predictable legislative support based on party membership.

In these circumstances, what then should the presidential style have been? Richard Neustadt, a presidential assistant to President Truman, published a book in 1960 titled *Presidential Leadership* (based largely on observations of Truman and Eisenhower), in which he argued for a personal rather than a managerial control of the presidential office—that is, the president should always guard his own power and let policy serve it, to the end that he amass enough to prevent its dissipation, since his problem usually is that he rarely has sufficient control of the necessary variables to make a "command." In this view, the United States Government is not really a separation of powers but a separation of institutions with shared powers and the job of the president is to try to persuade those with whom he shares power (the Congress) that to act in his way is to act in their own interests. According to this argument, it is important then for the president to personalize his power and to augment his personal influence. One of the ways to do this is to have several sources of information on the same thing. The managerial mode as was said in the Introduction is to rely upon the staff work of subordinates who in the extreme case simplify and reduce complex issues to questions of yes and no.

Schlesinger says that Neustadt's opinions supported Kennedy's predilections toward a fluid presidency, but Sorensen says that Kennedy was annoyed by the fuss that newspapers made over the Neustadt essay and Kennedy's interest in it. Not that President Kennedy rejected the conception of personalized power. To the contrary, he knew well the nature of political power, rejected the managerial conception, and maintained many advisers of different outlooks and opinions. In the essays that follow, Louis Koenig reviews the personal style of Kennedy as president in which Kennedy was his own chief of staff, and Douglass Cater criticizes the personal approach and finds faults and dangers in it. Readers may want to make a judgment about the two approaches and apply it to specific events discussed later in the book, like the Bay of Pigs disaster and the Cuban missile confrontation.

The piece by Fletcher Knebel views Kennedy as a politician and although it concentrates upon campaign politics and not presidential politics, it displays Kennedy's remarkable acuity in the power struggle that any campaign for the office of president becomes, and the many sides to Kennedy's political art. Kennedy, for example, is presented as the wary politician; the nimble politician; the courageous politician; the instinctive politician; the lucky politician; the political strategist and tactician; and the clinical political critic. Ted Lewis, however, finds these very skills to be a fault when it comes to dealing with Congress since some of the president's supporters gained the impression that Kennedy was without ideology, that he was merely a technician, employing inferior arts in the negotiation of his programs in Congress, overlooking the value of the great stroke, the plebiscitary tactic that Franklin Roosevelt and even Dwight Eisenhower employed with good effect, an appeal to the people over the heads of their elected representatives.

Henry Pachter says also that Kennedy's conception of his office was manipulative and not ideological, that the president detested bureaucratic proceduralism and sought to go around it. He is of the opinion that this practice was responsible for the Bay of Pigs fiasco and for the involvement of the United States in Vietnam, although, if true, one should also say that it was responsible for a more benign kind of foreign policy, such, for example, as a new attitude toward nations of the Third World and the establishment of the Peace Corps.

Tom Wicker summarizes Kennedy's political accounts at the time of his death and notes the opinion of James Reston that Kennedy's problem was not how to get elected, but how to govern.

Louis W. Koenig

Kennedy's Personal Management

John F. Kennedy's administrative method veered decidedly toward Roosevelt's. Like Roosevelt, Kennedy aimed to carve out a maximum personal role in the conduct of the Presidency but without some of the more jagged methods and much of the turmoil of the Rooseveltian model. Kennedy clearly visualized his Presidential role when he declared in his 1960 campaign that as President he would want to be "in the thick of things." Kennedy the President was true to the promise of Kennedy the candidate. He put in abundant hours at desk-side conferences and on the telephone, pursuing details well down the line of departmental hierarchy, and took a constant hand in coordination, its weight laid not merely upon top-level endeavor but upon minor affairs as well.

Kennedy's intensive involvement was more than an applied philosophy of the Presidency. It was a reflection of his personality, aptitude, and body chemistry. Kennedy personally comprised a bundle of restless curiosity, a high quotient of vigor, and an extraordinary spongelike capacity to absorb the daily torrent of governmental data.

To carry forward his administrative view of the Presidency, Kennedy relied upon several operating principles and expedients. Unlike Eisenhower, who stressed institutional structure, Kennedy placed great store in personal relationships. The person—his talent, perception, and reliability—counted more than his organization. Kennedy's person-centered approach reflected his pre-Presidential career, passed chiefly in legislative politics and in political campaigning, in both of which working relationships are highly personal. Accordingly, in dealing with department Secretaries and White House staff members Kennedy insisted upon direct relationships, unhampered by organization and hierarchy. He, for his part, remained highly accessible to a large circle of colleagues.

Kennedy, dealing with the departments, did not stop with the department head but reached down the hierarchy to lesser levels. A loud, clear hint of this practice was sounded in the preinaugural period in the manner of the President-elect's selection of his foreign policy aides. He designated an Assistant Secretary and an Undersecretary of

From The Chief Executive, *New Revised Edition, by Louis W. Koenig,* © *1964, 1968, by Harcourt Brace Jovanovich, Inc., and reprinted with their permission.*

State and the ambassador to the United Nations before selecting his Secretary of State. To underscore the principle implied in the sequence of these appointments, of direct Presidential superintendency of foreign affairs, Kennedy for his first three foreign affairs nominees, and for others after them, accompanied the public announcement of their selection with a phrase hailing the "post" as "second to none in importance." The President-elect's pointed tribute signified his intention to deal directly with second- and third-echelon subordinates. Kennedy's own assessment of his experience in the Presidency affirmed the wisdom of this tactic. In a year-end television interview in 1962, he was asked, "Is it true that during your first year, sir, you would get on the phone personally to the State Department and try to get a response to some inquiry that had been made?" "Yes," Kennedy replied, "I still do that when I can, because I think there is a great tendency in government to have papers stay on desks too long. . . . After all, the President can't administer a department, but at least he can be a stimulant."

Kennedy injected himself at any point along the decision-making spectrum from problem-selection to final judgment. Whereas Eisenhower wanted decisions brought to him for approval, Kennedy wanted problems brought to him for decision. Eisenhower preferred a consensus to be laid before him, stated briefly and in general terms. Kennedy eschewed consensus; he wanted to know a problem's facets and alternative answers, keeping decision for himself in consultation or "dialogue," as the administration called it, with advisers. Kennedy's keen nose for detail took him far into the interior of problems. Although interested in general principles, he was essentially a pragmatist and had, as a colleague said, "a highly operational mind." Policy separated from operations, in his view, was meaningless. His desk, not surprisingly, was piled high with reports and memoranda which he read closely. Conferring with an official, he would reach into the pile, pull out a memorandum, and resort instantaneously to a paragraph to make a point or raise a question. "President Kennedy," a colleague said, "is a desk officer at the highest level."

Kennedy entertained well-defined views of the proper role of the individual department. His tactic was to devolve upon individual department heads and on identified subordinates the responsibility for recommending policy initiatives and overseeing the execution of decisions. He took a stern view of a luxuriant bureaucratic phenomenon, the interdepartmental committee, beholding it as an intruder upon departmental responsibility and therefore something inherently bad, to be extirpated if at all possible. After several months in office he abolished a lengthy list of interdepartmental committees and reassigned many of their functions to department Secretaries and other officials.

Committees, being hardy administrative plants because they serve vital purposes, cannot be eliminated by mere Presidential prescription. They are an inevitable bureaucratic routine for establishing interdepartmental collaboration at the working levels. Seldom do problems of any significance appear that are not interdepartmental in their contours. The committees that Kennedy killed, not surprisingly, did not stay dead. Many on his list resumed a more or less surreptitious existence after a decent interval.

In lieu of committees the Kennedy administration resorted to "task forces," a name appropriately suggestive of vigor and purpose. Task forces, which consisted of departmental representatives and usually one or more White House staffers, were not merely committees by another name. "They operate with a consciousness of having a mandate, often from the President himself," a participant explained. Task forces carried a sense of the importance of getting things done, which often stirred bureaucracy to faster, more constructive effort. The attendant White House staff member was a powerful reminder of the Chief Executive's need and interest, a bearer of his influence upon decision, not merely in the moment of final choice but along much of the journey of its formation. Departmental participants in the task forces were not altogether enthusiastic about the contribution of their White House colleagues. "When the President's man says something, you don't know whether he is speaking for himself or for his boss," a department man exclaimed, "The effect can be, and often is, to cut off discussion too soon."

Kennedy, like Roosevelt, viewed the White House staff as a personal rather than an institutional staff, a vehicle for maximizing his influence rather than its influence throughout the executive branch. Impressed that the larger a staff is the more apt it is to become institutional, Kennedy tried heroically to cut back the sizable staff he had inherited from the Eisenhower administration, but with small success. In meting out staff assignments, Kennedy put his staff on action-forcing rather than program tasks and gave it a mixture of fixed and general-purpose responsibilities. These expedients likewise were intended to reduce the advance of institutionalization and to keep the staff personal.

Kennedy's White House staff, unlike Eisenhower's, was not organized by hierarchy or pyramid but like a wheel whose hub was the President and whose spokes connected him with individual aides. Five aides occupied major functional posts. The staff assistant to the President, Kenneth O'Donnell, handled appointments and Presidential travels and was an omnibus "chief White House official for party politics," in touch with the Democratic National Committee and local party figures. The special counsel, Theodore C. Sorensen of Nebraska, whose association harked back to Kennedy's Senate days in 1953, had responsibilities running across the board. His office, comprising two assistants, focused Presidential objectives, planned programs, broke impasses, and passed judgment on timing. Sorensen drafted Presidential messages and speeches with high artistry and a capacity that Richard Nixon once hailed as "the rare gift of being an intellectual who can completely sublimate his style to another intellectual." Sorensen sat with department Secretaries formulating their budget and legislative programs and attended the President's meetings with legislative leaders and prepress conference briefings. Sorensen had an acquisitive, cosmopolitan intelligence, which, as a colleague put it, "can understand anything from sugar subsidies to bomb shelters."

McGeorge Bundy, a former Harvard graduate dean, was special assistant for national security affairs. Bundy, aided by a small band of assistants ("the Bundy group"), kept watch for weakness and trouble in defense and foreign policy administration and saw to remedies and repairs. In the President's behalf he occupied a central place in the stream of intelligence. He received copies of virtually all the incoming cables to the Secretaries of State and Defense and the Director of the CIA. He sorted these out and put the most important before the President. Other key aides were the assistant for Congressional relations, Lawrence F. O'Brien, and the press secretary, Pierre Salinger.

There were other important aides not so involved in the major daily tasks of the President. Ralph Dungan, who was responsible for personnel, or "head-hunting," as he put it, maintained a permanent list of talent available for government posts, checked job recommendations from legislators, the Democratic National Committee, and the departments. Beyond this, Dungan took on roving assignments—he was Presidential overseer of foreign aid and of African and Latin-American policy. The assignments of Arthur M. Schlesinger, Jr., the historian, were even more diverse—he acted as a liaison between the President and United Nations Ambassador Adlai Stevenson and between the White House and the State Department on Latin-American policy, and he occasionally gave assistance with Presidential speeches.

The White House staff reaped a steady harvest of influence from Kennedy's habit of entrusting important responsibilities to individuals in whom he had confidence. Staff members, therefore, oftentimes performed functions traditionally handled by departments and diplomatic representatives. Schlesinger—not high-level State Department officials—traveled through Latin America to survey the area's requirements, gathering data and impressions that became the basis of the future aid program. Press Secretary Salinger—not the State Department or the United States Information Agency—negotiated in Moscow an agreement for the exchange of information. The attendant publicity of such assignments stripped many of the White House staff posts of their traditional anonymity.

Kennedy deployed his White House staff as critics of departmental performance and as emergency repair crews when departmental undertakings went awry. He restored direct work-flows between departments and himself and made his staff responsible for "monitoring," but not "obstructing," departmental access to him personally. A key function of the White House staff was to spot political and policy weaknesses in departmental proposals. Staff members played a decisive part in heading off a tax increase that may have made sense economically but not politically during the Berlin crisis of July 1961; they delighted liberals by implanting several public-ownership features into the communications satellite bill; they knocked down a State Department proposal that action on the trade bill be postponed for more than a year, until 1963. There was wide agreement that a large advantage of the Sorensen-Bundy service was penetrating analysis. "When Sorensen gets into something," a Bureau of the Budget career man said, "it gets a thorough scrubbing." It was also the lack of such a scrubbing that plunged the staff to the far depths of its worst failure, the abortive Cuban invasion in the young administration's fourth month. The staff was admittedly timid about raising questions that should have been asked. "At that point," a White House aide confessed, "we just didn't have the confidence to tell the veterans of the bureaucracy, 'Look, you're crazy.'"

In another blow at the institutionalized Presidency, Kennedy performed drastic surgery on the most advanced expression of that phenomenon, the National Security Council. He abolished the NSC's nerve- and work-center, the Planning Board, and its organ for implementing decision, the Operations Coordinating Board. Most important of all, he shunned the NSC by seldom bringing it into session. He sought counsel for major crises like Berlin of 1961 and Cuba of 1962 by bringing together an *ad hoc* group of advisers in whom he had special confidence. In lieu of the Planning Board and the OCB was the Bundy office, which greatly scaled down the former mountainous paper work.

Kennedy also largely dispensed with cabinet meetings, holding that the entire body of Secretaries should be assembled only for matters of full breadth and significance. He saw no reason for the entire cabinet to ponder matters affecting only three or four departments. The cabinet, consequently, met infrequently. In the summer of 1962 various department heads, then occupied with the political campaign, happened to converge upon Chicago. There they laughingly acknowledged that what had not transpired in Washington for some months was at last happening in the Middle West, a cabinet "meeting"!

The Kennedy technique clearly maximized the President's involvement and imprint upon policy, breathed vitality into sluggish bureaucracy, and extended the reach of a highly knowledgeable President and his staff into the departments. Yet there were also disadvantages. There was feeling that Kennedy was too accessible to operating personnel, too much "in the thick of things," overimmersed in minor policy and small detail, with too little time for major business. Or again, that Kennedy's emphasis on swiftness—terse statement, quick strides from one problem to the next—resulted at times in inadequate consideration of alternatives. Much public business, like reducing the arms race or overhauling the tax system, does not permit quick, concise expression. "The system now," a frequent participant said, "favors people who know exactly what they want to do. It is tough on people who have dim misgivings—even if those misgivings happen to be very important."

One strength of the Kennedy system may also have been a weakness. His method rested upon the realistic view that the executive branch, lacking the apparatus of collective responsibility found in Great Britain, depended heavily, for action and decision, upon the President's judgment. Yet what ordinarily was plausibly realistic may have caused at times an overdependence upon the time, energy, and talent of the President. The great risk of the Kennedy method is that no single mind, even a Presidential mind, can absorb the information or muster the wisdom necessary for sound judgment of many intricate issues pouring upon the President.

The problems with which American statesmanship must deal have acquired a complexity that renders them no longer fit for individual insight and judgment, no matter how perceptive. To be dealt with adequately, they must at some stage be subjected to collective study involving diverse technical skills, specialized knowledge, and organizational viewpoints. Decision without collective study is apt to be founded on inadequate information and to lack roundness of judgment.

Douglass Cater

The Do-It-Yourself Nature
of Presidential Power

As a people, we continually apply yardsticks to our Presidents and call out the measurements. Even while the man is fresh in office we commence solemn deliberations about what his rating will be according to the Gallup poll of history. We have established all sorts of indices for determining, of an instant, whether a President is "strong" or "weak," "great" or "mediocre." We seldom bother about contradictions; it is an old American tradition to accuse one of being despot and weakling in the same breath.

The trouble is that we have never been very precise about defining what we expect of the President. It is extraordinarily difficult to describe his job. We know from reading our newspaper that the man residing at 1600 Pennsylvania Avenue gets a great volume of mail, meets politician and miscellaneous publicity seekers, approves or vetoes laws, commands millions of military personnel along with countless tanks, planes, and missiles, and generally "runs the government." He is expected also to boss his party, inspect floods and other disasters, greet kings and sundry heads of state, and occasionally pay visits abroad. He is the nation's top strategist and its chief public relations man.

Theodore Roosevelt once described the President as "almost . . . a king and prime minister rolled into one." Certainly he suffers the adversities of both. His every move outside the White House stirs a public celebration, more impromptu but scarcely less regal than the British monarch's. On the other hand, his every act receives scrutiny in Congress more persistent and critical than a prime minister might expect in Parliament. A President cannot resolve his differences by dissolving Congress, nor can Congress, except by use of the unlikely weapon of impeachment, dismiss him.

Political scientists are accustomed to breaking down the Presidency into neat functions—referring colloquially to the hats the man in that office wears. But this, too, deals inadequately with the complex and overlapping nature of his job. The President does not always recognize when he takes off one hat and puts on another.

Not all the professional measurers apply the same yardstick. Some talk about the President in managerial terms, others in charismatic, still others in purely aesthetic. Sidney Hyman has described one role of the President as that of "an artist"—certainly an important perspective. But all the yardsticks have had one thing in common: they were outsiders' standards for taking the measure of the man in the White House. It remained for Richard Neustadt, a professor at Columbia University who once served as President Truman's assistant, to try to look at the job through a President's eyes. His book, *Presidential Power: The Politics of Leadership,* which delves into the official lives of Roosevelt, Truman, and Eisenhower, is an intriguing exercise in scholarly transmigration.

To begin with, Neustadt remarks on a paradox of Presidential leadership in recent times:

> We tend to measure Truman's predecessors as though "leadership" consisted of initiatives in economics, or diplomacy, or legislation, or in mass communication. If we measured him and his successors so, they would be leaders automatically. A striking feature of our recent past has been the transformation into routine practice of the actions we once treated as exceptional. A President may retain liberty, in Woodrow Wilson's phrase, "to be as big a man as he can." But nowadays he cannot be as small as he might like.

> The paradox is that the growth of the President's role as the central agent of government is by no means the same thing as leadership. His role has grown largely because no one else—neither Congress nor the courts nor the bureaucracy—can supply the services he is called on to provide. The White House is the only place where the competing claims on government can be brought into some sort of adjustment.

"In form, all Presidents are leaders nowadays. In fact, this guarantees no more than that they will be clerks." Neustadt's study of power is in reality a penetrating examination of the chronic weakness afflicting the modern President. Truman summed it up as well as any when he remarked, "I sit here all day trying to persuade people to do the things they ought to have sense enough to do without my persuading them. . . . That's all the powers of the President amount to." Kennedy echoed the theme when, in response to a query whether he had encountered any problem he had not anticipated, he mentioned the difficulty of getting decisions carried out effectively, "It's easier to sit with a map and talk about what ought to be done than to see it done," he said.

A President has to have an acute awareness of the resistances that exist to any step he takes. The elements of his essential knowledge can be picayune: that he must communicate with a certain committee chairman in the mornings because he is too drunk by afternoon—any afternoon—to be coherent; that a certain bureaucrat is so buttressed by interest-group support that he can regularly defy the occupant of the White House, Democrat or Republican; that a certain issue has grown so mired in lobbyist intrigue that it is irredeemable. If he is to be any good, a President must have a mental catalogue of the movers and shakers in the Washington community, their habits and habitats. He needs to know the crotchets of M. De Gaulle of France, Mr. Meany of AFL-CIO, Mr. Reston of *The New York Times,* and many, many others.

How does the President save himself from merely serving as clerk to other people's priorities? The "commands" he can give with reasonable expectation that they will be carried out are fairly few and limited in scope. Neustadt delves particularly into three instances of the power to command: Truman's firing of General MacArthur, his seizure of the steel mills, and Eisenhower's dispatch of troops to Little Rock. All three were self-executing in the sense that the President's order was obeyed—though the Supreme Court later reversed the steel seizure. But all three were forced on a President as acts of last resort. Whatever their necessity, they represented failures rather than successes in Presidential leadership. The consequences flowing from them were a severe drain on the President's power.

For a graphic description of a President's dilemma, it is useful to read the Inter-University Case Study, *The Steel Seizure of 1952.* Its conclusion is that, ". . . while the White House was convicted by public opinion of the crime of grasping for unchecked power, its troubles in the steel crisis had come from its lack of influence—over public opinion, over labor and industry, and, in the critical early stages of the controversy, over some of its own stabilization agencies." A decade later, President Kennedy resorted to persuasion rather than command when confronted by a sudden price rise in the steel industry.

Persuading people to do things, as Truman remarked, is the principal way Presidents get things done. Truman's own experience with the inception of the Marshall Plan offers vivid evidence of how Presidential persuasion really works. Viewed in the context of the times—Truman being otherwise engaged in bitter warfare with the Republican Eightieth Congress—it was a miraculous venture. It required skillful use of Presidential power, but it also required borrowing on the power and prestige of everyone in sight. One wonders whether it would have been possible at all except for the cast of supporting actors: General Marshall, Senator Vandenberg, Under Secretary Acheson, the Harriman Committee, Bevin and Bidault, and finally Joseph Stalin himself. Each provided help—Stalin, by opposition—which a politically embattled President could not provide. The result of the successful venture undoubtedly added to the President's power to deal with foreign policy.

The President has certain advantages in the game of persuasion. He commands publicity as does no other politician. He acquires added persuasiveness from the awesome elevation of his office and because few politicians wish to offend him unnecessarily. He has indirect ways of punishing offenders which, though cumbersome, can be cruel. It is necessarily a subtle business.

"The essence of a President's persuasive task with congressmen and everybody else," Neustadt writes, "is to induce them to believe that what he wants of them is what their own appraisal of their own responsibilities requires them to do in their own interest, not his. . . . That task is bound to be more like collective bargaining than like a reasoned argument among philosopher kings." This interpretation runs counter to widely held views about Presidential power. A good many Americans seem to think that only folly or knavery on the part of the President prevents him from getting his views accepted. President Eisenhower paid indirect lip service to such an idea at the time he announced his intention, despite ill health, to run for a second term. Because there had been a "public clarification" of a number of important issues during his first term, Eisenhower argued, he could now safely delegate them to close associates. Four years later, Eisenhower was still working hard to clarify those issues and, if anything, was delegating less.

The press adds to the mythology of Presidential leadership when it suggests a process by which all the business of government, on reaching the stage at which a decision must be made, passes through the White House "in" and "out" baskets. In reality, nothing could be further from the truth. Even assuming that the government's business could be channeled so rigidly, there are finite limits to a President's time—to the number of associates he can see, the documents he can read, the decisions he has the physical endurance to make. Decision-making goes on at all stages and levels of government; important policies and programs bloom or wither often without a deliberate act by the President.

The chief executive must try to impose his will by more selective means. He does it, consciously or unconsciously, by his "choices"—a word more precise than "decisions": the choice at his press conference of the appropriate words to stimulate or squelch someone else's decision; the choice of whether to shortcut channels and reach down through officialdom to grasp a problem requiring attention; and, most important, the occasional choice not to make a difficult choice.

Neustadt's thesis is that a President builds up or tears down his power by the choices he makes. He should make them with a constant awareness of his personal power stakes, for building power through his choices is the only way he can find to make his job operable. This is the unique contribution he must offer to policy-making after his experts have offered their contributions. A President must be an expert in building power.

We have been accustomed for so long to thinking about Presidents in the more lofty concepts of nation-building that the above thesis comes as a rude shock. This argument for a shrewd and power-conscious President seems Machiavellian. But, in the tradition of Machiavelli, Neustadt is convinced that only an expert in power can bring together the princely states of American government. He also believes that such an expert can best assure a "viable" public policy. In the decade ahead, comprised of a "snarly sort of politics with unstable parties and unruly issues," the Presidency will be no place for political amateurs.

By such a yardstick, Neustadt rated the three Presidents: Roosevelt, high; Truman, medium; Eisenhower, low. It remains to apply that measure to Kennedy, who completed less than three years in office.

President Kennedy's early career offered few indications of that zestful love of power which Roosevelt exhibited. The eldest son, Joseph Kennedy, Jr., was slated to be the politician in the family. Only after Joe Jr.'s death in World War Two did the second son, as his father has noted, feel obliged to take over the legacy. Kennedy's record in both the House of Representatives and the Senate showed him to be a tough campaigner, but not one of the power-conscious elite of those two bodies. He neither sought nor was invited to join the so-called inner clubs. Until near the end of his career in Congress, he did not exhibit much concern for legislative achievement.

Close friends differ about the origins of Kennedy's Presidential ambition. As late as 1956, he was remarkably indifferent to the efforts of his associates to promote him for Vice-President on the Democratic ticket. He took stoically his narrow defeat at the Chicago Convention in 1956. Three years later, when he had already commenced the sustained drive for first place, he still managed to convey a certain dispassion about his high ambition. Asked bluntly by reporters why he *ought* to be President, he answered simply that he thought he could do as good a job as anyone else available. To the question of why he should *want* to be President, he quoted an ancient Greek proverb he had learned from Dean Acheson: "Happiness lies in the exercise of vital powers along lines of excellence in a life affording them scope." Kennedy admitted he found in politics, as in no other pursuit, a purely personal happiness. This seemed hardly a driving motivation for seeking power.

Kennedy's writings provide a few clues to his notions about leadership. His first book, *Why England Slept,* an expansion of his college thesis written in 1940, gave an impressive analysis of the British government's failure to keep pace with German rearmament. The chief villains were not the politicians but the unthinking British public which, he felt, refused to support forthright leadership and then sought "to make scapegoats for its own weaknesses."

Fifteen years later, while recuperating from an operation, Kennedy drafted his *Profiles in Courage* which took quite a different approach to the problem of leadership. This time he paid glowing tribute to the politician who, in time of crisis, stood staunchly against the prevailing sentiment of colleagues and public. The book was a testament to a leadership prepared to sacrifice power for the keeping of conscience.

There were to be further shifts in Kennedy's perspective. Almost a year before his inauguration, he delivered a speech to the National Press Club which drew heavily on the charismatic school of Presidential interpretation. (A short time before the speech, one of his aides had borrowed Sidney Hyman's book.) "In the decade that lies ahead," Kennedy declared, "the challenging, revolutionary Sixties, the American Presidency will demand more than ringing manifestos issued from the rear of the battle. It will demand that the President place himself in the very thick of the fight, that he care passionately about the fate of the people he leads, that he be willing to serve them at the risk of incurring their momentary displeasure." Referring to Woodrow Wilson's assertion that a President is at liberty to be as big a man as he can, Kennedy argued, "But President Wilson discovered that to be a big man in the White House inevitably brings cries of dictatorship. So did Lincoln and Jackson and the two Roosevelts. And so may the next occupant of that office, if he is the man the times demand."

During the spring or summer of 1960, Kennedy read Neustadt's book. That it struck a responsive chord is evident from the thinly veiled account of its author's experience as reported by Richard Rovere in *The New Yorker* a month after the election:

> About a month ago, the President-elect asked a man from an eastern university to advise him on a wide but clearly defined range of current problems and to give him the name of people

competent to deal with them in the new administration. A day or
two earlier, the newspapers had reported that Mr. Kennedy had
asked another man—one whose background was more practical
than theoretical—to do a job that sounded to the new recruit
very much like, if not identical with, the one he was being asked
to undertake. The scholar, who has a fluent command of the local
patois, asked Mr. Kennedy how he should "relate" to the other
appointee. The answer was crisp and categorical: "Don't." The
President-elect went on to say that it would suit him down to the
ground if the two men never saw each other; he supposed, though,
that they would have to confer, and he only hoped that they
would do as little conferring as possible before they reported, as
he wished each of them to do, directly to him. With his eyes on
the ceiling and the merest hint of apology in the voice that is
noted for its rather narrow emotional range, he said, "I simply
cannot afford to have just one set of advisers." Far from being
offended, the scholar left with a spring in his step and a firmer
conviction than he had had up to then that the republic was in
good hands. . . .

Mr. Kennedy, he felt, had already mastered the beginning of
Presidential wisdom. "If he had not made that remark," he said,
"I should have gone directly to my hotel room and got to work on
a memorandum pointing out the weaknesses of the command system and urging him not to be afraid of a little administrative un-
tidiness. If a President has only one set of advisers, the advisers
take over the Presidency."

The attempt to measure Kennedy leadership presents a number
of bafflements. At times there appeared to be a conflict between the
"passionate" President of the Press Club speech and the power-conscious President of Neustadtian analysis. Or, using Kennedy's earlier
writing, there was a tension between the politician of conscience depicted in his second book and the politician constrained by an apa-
thetic public of his first.

Critics have found evidence of this conflict on all sides. The
politics of foreign aid provides a clear example. In the first Inaugural
Address, the Alliance for Progress proposals, and numerous other pro-
nouncements, the President promised eloquently to assist the underdeveloped countries along the road to progress. Foreign aid was to be
rescued from its former stereotype as simply a way of supporting the
defense effort. Impact programs to stimulate basic growth in Latin
America, Africa, and Asia were to be given the highest priority.

The results were hardly in accord with all these high hopes. The
progress of the new AID agency was frustrated by frequent delays as
well as a rapid succession of three directors during its first three years.

The President's legislative proposal to finance development aid on a long-term basis finished with a hastily negotiated compromise which left power intact in the hands of the obstinate lords of the congressional appropriation subcommittees. With foreign aid subjected to ever increasing re-examination, its political future looked increasingly dark. Members of Congress who have sought to fight for the program, complained bitterly of being abandoned by the White House.

On other foreign fronts, critics have also pointed to a dualism between "vigorous" and "realistic" Presidential leadership:

Laos: The President held a televised press conference to emphasize, with use of maps, the threat to southeast Asia of a communist takeover of this little country. The settlement in Laos, negotiated not long afterward, promised at best that if the communists kept their word the country would remain neutral;

Berlin: Kennedy voiced repeated determination not to yield Allied rights. Yet he did not make a passionate protest when the Soviets erected a wall dividing that beleaguered city, and lesser officials tried to characterize "the Wall" as a psychological defeat for the Soviets;

Cuba: Kennedy accepted the "tunnel vision" of his CIA advisers by agreeing to the ill-fated invasion in the Bay of Pigs. Yet a cautious concept of power caused him to eliminate plans for U.S. air "cover" of the refugee invasion force which was sadly under strength for such a mission. Only a year and a half later, with Soviet missile sites under construction in Cuba, did he pick up the challenge.

On the domestic front, there were similar contrasts between courageous expectations and cautious operations. In Congress, President Kennedy offered quiet support to Speaker Sam Rayburn in the fight to enlarge the House Rules Committee. But enlargement was a timid and, in retrospect, not wholly effectual way of trying to tame that recalcitrant group, and when Rayburn died, Kennedy remained fastidiously aloof from any show of preference in the short-lived struggle for leadership in the House. There was little evidence that the President was willing to take risks to obtain congressional reforms that might lessen the legislative stalemate. The very narrowness of the margins of defeat—on Medicare, on the Administration farm bill, on the Urban Affairs Department—revealed a discouraging inability to supply the necessary inducement to shift the balance.

The legislative struggle took on a quite different character from the trailblazing of the New Deal era. It is more reminiscent of the dogged trench warfare of the First World War than of the swift panzer movements of the Second. The item-by-item fight on Kennedy's tax reform proposals was more typical of the massed confrontation of forces that frustrated spectacular gains.

In a number of major battles Kennedy appeared to make a display more for the record than for anticipated results. There was the frantic and futile effort to push the Urban Affairs plan through the Senate before it received an inevitable veto in the House. Similarly, Medicare was hurried before the senators in hopes of diverting attention from the slow strangulation it was receiving in the House Ways and Means Committee. Bills for federal aid to lower and higher education went down to defeat in a way that obscured party responsibility.

Despite his campaign promises to "get America moving," Kennedy's actions in the economic field created the image of a President whose primary role was to adjust and balance the delicate mechanisms of the economy instead of stoutly exhorting it to new furies of movement. The effort to stem the gold flow, to correct the adverse balance of payments, and to spur industry through sizable tax concessions gave evidence of this cautious preoccupation with balance and adjustment. As he declared somewhat impatiently to criticism, "What we need is not more labels and more clichés but more basic discussion of the sophisticated and technical questions involved in keeping our mighty economic machine moving steadily ahead."

The President was equally impatient with criticisms that his policies in the foreign field appeared to lack a "grand design." After one background session, *The New York Times* reported that "President Kennedy believes that the grand design of his Administration's foreign policies derives from what he thinks has been a generally consistent United States course since 1945. As he sees it, the long-range purpose of himself and the nation is to work toward a world in which free states can develop sufficient internal resources to maintain their independence." Of course, the critic could respond that this was a concept so grand that it was entirely lacking in design.

It must be admitted that the vantage point of a Washington reporter is not the best for gauging leadership. Trevelyan wrote of the first Queen Elizabeth, "Her bold decisions were few and can be numbered, but each of them began an epoch." Yet a scribe attending Elizabeth's court might well have had difficulty perceiving which ones were epochal. The press corps in Lincoln's capital did not discern greatness in the President's often irresolute behavior. Hindsight tends to etch deeply the sharp lines of leadership that appeared blurry close at hand.

Unlike Queen Elizabeth, a modern President must feel content not to begin any epoch if only he can maintain prosperity and avoid a war. Conceding his many difficulties, Kennedy enthusiasts found promising portent in three decisive acts during his early years in office: the challenge and rebuff to the steel industry's attempt to raise prices; the dispatch of federal deputies and troops to enforce the court-ordered enrollment of a Negro, James Meredith, in the University of Mississippi; and the confrontation of Khrushchev with the "quarantine" of Cuba. All three were successful in accomplishing short-term objectives. Steel reduced its prices; Meredith was enrolled; Khrushchev withdrew his missiles and bombers from Cuba.

In staging the showdowns, the President displayed a capacity to mobilize the strength of his office speedily and efficiently. Particularly in the second Cuban crisis, he acted in such a way that sustaining strength was drawn from other holders of power, at home and abroad. By Neustadtian analysis, he showed keen awareness of the stakes and came through these crises with his personal power not only intact but enhanced.

Yet, it must be pointed out that the three episodes had other factors in common. None started as acts of the President's own volition, but were forced upon him—by U.S. Steel President Roger Blough, by Mississippi Governor Ross Barnett, and by Soviet Premier Nikita Khrushchev. All three had been attempts to call the President's bluff; he had to respond or be counted a coward. In each case, his opponents grossly overplayed their strength. Blough lacked the economic conditions to sustain a price rise; Barnett had no troops to back him up once the President federalized the National Guard; and Khrushchev was without conventional military capacity to break a blockade.

Those who participated most intimately with the President during the Cuban crisis—dramatically described as the prototype war of the thermonuclear age—are cautious about drawing lessons from it. One White House participant has pointed out privately that certain conditions made the situation unique. First, for nearly a week the government had possession of documented intelligence—evidence of the missile sites—about which no one in the press knew, or knew that the government knew. This permitted remarkable facility in planning the response, catching the enemy by surprise, and forewarning friendly allies. In marked contrast, for example, the building of the Berlin Wall was known simultaneously to government and press and was accomplished before government officials could confer with one another or consult the Allied powers in Berlin.

Secondly, the military phase of the Cuban quarantine was directed, quite literally, from a telephone on Secretary McNamara's desk, providing tight control against the accidental or the unexpected. The chief anxiety in Washington was whether Soviet communications were as foolproof as those of the U.S. Doubt on this matter prompted the decision to allow the first Soviet ship, the tanker *Bucharest*, to pass through the blockade uninspected.

A third condition set the course of the Cuban crisis. In responses to questions at his press conference the previous month, the President had flatly committed himself to act in the event of aggressive buildup in Cuba. Would he have acted had he not made that public commit-ment? Having experienced the awful loneliness of the decision to risk cataclysmic war, the White House assistant was unwilling to make that assumption lightly. He reported that not a single member of the inner council really believed that the quarantine alone would accomplish Soviet withdrawal. The terror of total war was a living reality.

Success in Cuba clearly resulted as much from the flaws in Khrushchev's strategy as from Kennedy's counter strategy. Once the quarantine had been evoked, the only options left to the Soviet leader were to launch a thermonuclear attack against the U.S., or to back down. Evidently he had not even made plans for staging a diversionary aggression elsewhere in the event of being challenged in Cuba. Kennedy, on the other hand, guarded his options by preparing for a swift escalation of force if the Soviets failed to withdraw the missiles. But he left the terrible choice of nuclear retaliation entirely up to Khrushchev.

After more than two years in office, the President's Special Counsel, Theodore C. Sorensen, a long-time aide, gave two lectures at Columbia University soberly reassessing the business of decision-making in the White House; both his words and mood were a far cry from Kennedy's exuberant Press Club speech of 1960 which Sorensen had helped draft. Now the deputy chose to stress the perplexities of leadership: ". . . too often a President finds that events or the decisions of others have limited his freedom of maneuver—that, as he makes a choice, that door closes behind him. And he knows that, once that door is closed, it may never open again—and he may then find himself in a one-way tunnel, or in a baffling maze, or descending a slippery slope. He cannot count on turning back—yet he cannot see his way ahead. He knows that if he is to act, some eggs must be broken to make the omelet, as the old saying goes. But he also knows that an omelet cannot lay any more eggs." Sorensen also underlined five limitations that encumber a President. "He is free to choose only within the limits of permissibility, within the limits of available resources, within the limits of available time, within the limits of previous commitments, and within the limits of available information."

As President Johnson suddenly took over the reins, the totting up of success and failure made judgment difficult. Successful negotiation of a nuclear test ban had marked an easing of tension, even if momentary, with the Soviets. On the other hand, the Western Alliance, so carefully woven together since the war, had begun to show signs of unraveling. Despite the successful passage of the President's mutual trade bill in Congress, U.S. negotiations with the Common Market had reached a state of mutual recriminations. Domestically, the economic indicators were showing advancing prosperity while the political indicators continued to reveal deep pockets of poverty. On the racial front, the late President had been making a try with tardy haste to provide equal citizenship and opportunity for Negroes before pent-up frustrations boiled over. Yet the very effort was threatening to rouse bitter opposition from powerful sectors of the white community.

Amid such perplexities, it is hard to decide on a yardstick for measuring a President, much less on how to apply it. Even while pondering Neustadt's brilliant analysis of Presidential muscle structure, one instinctively comes to feel certain reservations. Like Machiavelli's earlier anatomy of power, it is susceptible to misreading. A President preoccupied with his personal stakes can make all the wrong choices—for the nation if not for himself. Taken too literally, preoccupation with power could result in a "what's-in-it-for-me?" attitude compounding caution with caution. Or, contrarily, preoccupation with power can produce a cynicism about its usage. Presidential leadership has other ingredients, including some as difficult to define as "intuition," "vision," "conviction," and—to borrow from Kennedy—"courage." In any diagnosis, these ingredients contribute much to the health or ills of the body politic. There is danger that by overly concentrating on the muscle the body culturist ignores what moves the muscle.

This is merely to conclude, contrary to Lord Bryce, that Presidents *ought* to be great men and that a prime characteristic of greatness is the ability to employ power consciously but never too self-consciously. History reveals that great Presidents must show a capacity not only to conserve power but to risk squandering it when the occasion demands. The nation has profited from such philanthropy.

Fletcher Knebel

The Unknown JFK

"Pol" is to politician as cop is to policeman. The word's origins are lost in the sawdust and acrid odors of the saloons and ward clubs of big-city politics back when bosses were bosses. The pol first flourished while Bath House John and Hinky Dink ran Chicago's first ward and James Michael Curley held intermittent sway amid the benign corruption of Boston.

Edwin A. Lahey, chief of the Washington Bureau of the Knight Newspapers, who learned the word when he covered Chicago in the days of Al Capone, says "it was always a term of affectionate contempt." But there is no contempt on the lips of the Kennedy men when they refer to their slain leader as a "pol." With them, it is a term of affectionate admiration, a tribute to a professional who excelled at his trade. "Jack was a real pol," says White House Assistant Lawrence F. O'Brien, the organizing pol of the great Kennedy Senate and White House victories, and when O'Brien says it, there is pride in his voice and the memory of many campaigns in his eyes.

Some of the Massachusetts politicians who were close to Kennedy are resentful of the deification of their friend in one short year. They intend to write a history of him as a fellow pol, lest the real John F. Kennedy be lost forever in the gathering myths of martyrdom. "The real man is being swept away by legend," protests one of them, "and there's danger that soon there'll be only a demigod, instead of the man we knew. Jack Kennedy was first and last a pol."

It is difficult to remember this core of truth in the complete Kennedy, for the man was so many other things: the lover of poetry, the sailor, the historian, writer, wit, consumer of fish chowder, frolicking father, speed reader, companion of the arts, fastidious dresser, champion of excellence, amateur painter, patron of intellectuals, a man who revered courage and bore searing pain for most of his adult life—the radiant knight of Camelot.

The elegance, the quip, the wispy smile and the casual restraint live on in memory, obscuring the workaday Kennedy, the man who plied the trade of politics for the last seventeen years of his short life. He first ran for the House of Representatives from Boston in 1946, and he never stopped running. He was still campaigning that brilliant

Reprinted from Look, *November 17, 1964* © Look *magazine.*

day in Dallas when his open convertible passed below the Texas School
Book Depository building.

Those who saw Kennedy the pol in action will never forget the
sight. There was the wary politician. One day in 1959, when his as-
yet-unannounced quest for the Presidency obsessed him, he was talking
of his prospects in his Senate office in Washington when a telephone
call came from a Democrat in Massachusetts. The man sought Senator
Kennedy's endorsement for a state office of fleeting consequence. Kennedy tensed as he listened. His pale eyelashes narrowed, his smile faded,
and his pencil-slim cigar, clamped by a jaw, worked rhythmically. Did
the man have the backing of the state committee? Kennedy asked. The
caller claimed he did. Then why did he need Kennedy's help? To sew
it up.

"I don't believe you. You're asking me to risk my national prestige
for a two-bit job up there," said Kennedy. The voice came out like
dry ice. "If you lose, the word goes out that Kennedy hasn't got any
influence in his own state."

The man pleaded. Kennedy resisted, cussing as his fury pressed
against the throttle. Finally, it was agreed the man would come down
on the night train from Boston, bringing with him a checklist of the
committee. Only if he had a clear and provable majority would Kennedy add his endorsement.

"He's got one hell of a nerve," said Kennedy when he hung up.
"He never helped me when I ran for the Senate the first time."

There was the nimble politician, eager to exploit any opening.
One day in 1960, when his Catholicism was becoming a boiling issue,
Kennedy stopped the Rev. Frederick Brown Harris, a Methodist and
the chaplain of the U.S. Senate. Kennedy wanted to know whether the
cleric thought his religion would hurt him. Dr. Harris said he wasn't
sure, but he didn't mind saying that he, for one, believed that Kennedy
would always put "country before Church and self."

The next day, Kennedy sent an assistant to the chaplain with a
request that he put the comment in writing. Dr. Harris declined, fear-
ing to mix in politics. For a time, Kennedy spoke bitterly of the chaplain's refusal, but later, animosity faded. When he became President,
Kennedy treated Dr. Harris most graciously. Kennedy harbored several famous grudges, but most of them eroded before reason.

There was the courageous politician. Once, while a member of
the Senate committee investigating Teamster and other union rackets,
Kennedy was visited by two prominent Democrats whose backing could
prove significant in gaining the support of the Illinois delegation for
his Presidential nomination. They wanted him to use his influence
to kill a phase of the investigation that would embarrass a company

they represented. The Senator told them the decision was up to his brother Bobby, who was then counsel of the committee. He advised them to take their plea to Bobby, whose office was in the basement of the same Senate Office Building. When the men left, Kennedy called his brother, said the mission "smelled" and told him to deal with the men as he saw fit. Result: Bobby refused to suppress the probe. When the two Democrats hinted at political retaliation, he ordered them out of his office.

There was the instinctive politician. During the closing days of the 1960 campaign, Martin Luther King, Jr., was jailed in Georgia for his part in an Atlanta department-store sit-in. Kennedy's brother-in-law, Sargent Shriver, who was with the candidate at the O'Hare Inn near Chicago, urged him to call Mrs. King. Kennedy immediately phoned her in Georgia to express his concern and regrets. He did it without consulting the advisers milling about his suite, and several, when they learned what he had done, moaned that he'd committed a prime tactical error. Kennedy brushed the complaints aside. He was right. The call created a sensation among Negroes. President Eisenhower later complained that a "couple of phone calls" won the close election for Kennedy because of the late attraction of Negro voters.

There was the lucky politician. Two crucial episodes led to Kennedy's amazing White House victory as the first Roman Catholic and the youngest man ever elected President. In 1956, he narrowly lost the Vice-Presidential nomination. Four years later, he won a primary victory over Sen. Hubert H. Humphrey in heavily Protestant West Virginia. In both cases, Kennedy made the right decision—but he made it for the wrong reasons.

Kennedy went to Chicago in 1956 with the backing of the New England states for the Vice-Presidential nomination. It was a courtesy gesture only, for all hands assumed nominee Adlai E. Stevenson would pick his own running mate. Instead, Stevenson ordered an "open" convention contest for Vice-President. The delegates received the news with the joyful ferocity of caged wild animals at feeding time. Kennedy called his father, former Ambassador Joseph P. Kennedy, a constant political adviser, who was then vacationing on the French Riviera. Should he jump into the free-for-all?

Old Joe Kennedy said no. He argued that Jack's national ambitions might be destroyed forever. There could be but two results, counseled the father. One, Jack would win the nomination. But Stevenson was sure to lose the election to President Dwight D. Eisenhower, and in the sour aftermath of defeat among Democrats, Kennedy's Catholicism would be blamed for Stevenson's rout. Two, Jack would take a beating on the convention floor and thus wreck any future hopes for the White House. A Kennedy friend who was in the hotel room during this conversation recalls that Kennedy turned from the phone to say that he knew his father was right. But after a few minutes, he decided to make the race anyway. "Jack's decision was based on two things," the friend remembers. "First, he had many commitments of support, and to refuse now would be to reveal himself as a man who ran from a fight. Second, Jack Kennedy loved combat, and he just couldn't stay out of this open battle."

The next day, Kennedy lost the nomination by a sliver-thin margin to Sen. Estes Kefauver of Tennessee in a wild, surging floor battle. Millions of televiewers got their first glimpse of the handsome, graceful Senator from Massachusetts with the boyish smile and the rich thatch of chestnut hair. Kefauver had won the nomination, but Kennedy, by his near miss, had won the sympathy of countless Democrats. From the day of the Stevenson-Kefauver defeat in the 1956 election, Kennedy took a lead in the 1960 Presidential polls that he was never to lose. Jack the pol had been right—for the wrong reasons.

In 1960, Kennedy entered the West Virginia primary because early polls by his friend Lou Harris showed that he had a wide lead over his probable opponent, Senator Humphrey. Also, Kennedy believed he would first trounce Humphrey in Wisconsin and that Humphrey would then withdraw, handing West Virginia to Kennedy uncontested. Instead, Kennedy's win over Humphrey in Wisconsin was inconclusive, and when they both moved on to West Virginia, the polls suddenly showed Humphrey in the lead. The private pollsters explained that the West Virginia voters, overwhelmingly Protestant, had learned by now that Kennedy was a Catholic, and they recoiled at the idea of a Catholic President. This forced Kennedy to take the offensive on the religious issue, until then a muted subject, and he did it with candor, sincerity, and an oratorical fervor that turned the tide. Humphrey was helpless before the late swing, for the Kennedy men made West Virginians believe that a vote against Kennedy was a vote for bigotry. Kennedy buried a forlorn Humphrey on election night in a vote of landslide proportions. Again, he was right—for the wrong reasons. A good pol has to be a lucky pol.

There was the politician who thrived on crisis. "If you can't take the heat, stay out of the kitchen," said Harry Truman. Kennedy could take the heat. During the labor-reform bill fight of 1959, he proved himself a skillful maneuverer amid the intense, conflicting pressures of business and organized labor. Again, in the fall of 1960, as he approached the election day of final decision, Kennedy grew calmer, more poised and self-contained, while his opponent, Vice-President Richard M. Nixon, seemed to fray under the pressure.

There was the political tactician. After his election as President, Kennedy talked one day with Rep. Stewart Udall at the Hotel Carlyle in New York after naming the Arizonan his Secretary of the Interior. Udall suggested that Kennedy add a cultural sheen to the inaugural ceremonies by asking the poet Robert Frost to speak. "Great idea," said Kennedy. "We'll do it." Then, with a grin, he added quickly, "But with Frost's skill with words, people would remember his speech instead of mine. I think we'd better have him read a poem."

There was the restrained politician. Kennedy would not be made to look the fool. He had an instinctive abhorrence of the campaign sideshows in which candidates appear as freak attractions. He would not kiss babies, pose in ridiculous situations or wear outlandish headgear. Not once did he don any of the hundreds of exotic headpieces, from Indian warbonnets to construction workers' hard hats, that were thrust upon him. Even on the morning of his death, in Texas, he declined to wear a ten-gallon sombrero. He inspected the gift, fingered it and brought it near his head, as if measuring the fit. But he never actually put it on.

There was the politician whose combative urge was honed to a knife edge. "The Presidential nomination won't be handed to anybody," he said in the winter of 1958–59. "I may not win, but if I'm beaten, the winner will know he's been through the fight of his life."

There was the politician of strategy. Kennedy was his own best strategist, as he was his own best public-relations expert and his own best humorist. He planned the grand design of his upset victory over Sen. Henry Cabot Lodge in 1952 and the outline of his hairline capture of the Presidency in 1960. Early in his drive for the White House, Kennedy began going after the big-city leaders who would control delegates at the Democratic convention. Long before other candidates made their first move, Kennedy had Rep. Charles A. Buckley, the aging boss of the Bronx, in his corner, largely through the efforts of his father, Joe Kennedy.

Kennedy told a friend in those days that he would not repeat the mistake of Franklin D. Roosevelt, Jr., who lost the Democratic nomination for governor of New York in 1954 because he failed to get the New York City bosses on his side. "If Frank had gotten the New York leaders," said Kennedy, "he'd still be governor today, and he'd be the one running for President instead of me." Kennedy made his pitch for every boss, although it took his West Virginia primary victory to convince some of them that a Catholic could win after all.

There was the politician who analyzed his rivals with clinical dispassion. Thirteen days before he won the Democratic nomination at Los Angeles, Kennedy spoke in an interview of the man he was to pick as his running mate, Lyndon B. Johnson. He thought Johnson could have won the Presidential nomination.

"But Lyndon made one grave error," Kennedy said. "He should have entered a Northern primary and won it. West Virginia, perhaps. I think he could have beaten Hubert and me there if he'd made a fight out of it. Johnson had to prove that a Southerner could win in the North, just as I had to prove a Catholic could win in heavily Protestant states. Could you imagine me, having entered no primaries, trying to tell the leaders that being a Catholic was no handicap? They would have laughed me out of the room. In the same way, when Lyndon said he could win in the North, but could offer no concrete evidence, his claims couldn't be taken seriously. I suppose he made the mistake because he took a flippant view of the primaries, like Harry Truman. For some men, such as Lyndon and myself, primaries are not only good, they are absolutely vital."

If his fellow pols were to fault Kennedy at all, it would be on his reckless use of his own body, energy, and resources. He drove himself without mercy, despite the multiple ailments nagging his lean frame. Democratic Chairman John Bailey recalls arriving in Washington, D.C., late one night with Kennedy. Both men were worn out and disheveled from a prenomination tour. Bailey said bed would look good. Not for him, replied Kennedy with a wry smile, for he was taking another plane to keep a speaking date—in Alaska.

During the Nixon campaign, Kennedy treated his fragile backbone with disdain. Despite two delicate operations that almost killed him, Kennedy would vault out of a convertible without opening the door or walk from hood to hood across parked automobiles. Once, he transferred from the rear deck of one car to the hood of another while both were in motion.

During the 1952 campaign against Senator Lodge in Massachusetts, an aide waited outside while Kennedy shook hands with firemen in a firehouse. When Kennedy came out, he was dragging a leg and wincing with pain. He had, he confessed, accepted the firemen's challenge and slid down their pole, only to land hard on his feet and rock his injured spine. Kennedy was smuggled to Washington, where he visited a doctor and spent several days recuperating. All this was done in secret, for the Lodge people were openly questioning young Kennedy's health and stamina.

As a pol, Kennedy was skilled in all the usual arts of deception, strategy, maneuver, timing, and pressure. But from the outset, there was something that set him apart—a flair, an elegance, a detachment, a self-deprecatory humor and a rippling intellect. He was a pol with class. His "nuts-and-bolts" organization man, Larry O'Brien, recognized it the first time he talked with Kennedy sixteen years ago. "It was 1948, and he was a kid congressman," recalls O'Brien. "He had just talked to a state labor convention. Eddie Boland [now Rep. Edward P. Boland, Dem., Mass.] and I had breakfast with Kennedy. Eddie and I were impressed, and I remember we sat and talked after he left. We agreed that the guy had what it took. In fact, if he got the breaks, we agreed, Jack Kennedy would be President someday."

His time came, then flashed by like a streaking star in the hush of dusk. President Kennedy is mourned by millions, but none remember him with more clarity and poignancy than his fellow craftsmen, the American pols.

Ted Lewis

Kennedy: Profile of a Technician

For two years now, President Kennedy has been an activist, displaying his managerial and manipulation techniques in almost every facet of government. As a result, the public knows a lot about the President's techniques of leadership and yet paradoxically little about the direction in which he is moving or how he will act when obstacles confront him.

Normally our Presidents, after two years in office, become more or less stereotyped in the public mind; it has always been fairly clear how they would act in any given situation. It is uniquely different today as Kennedy enters his third year in office. It should be possible, but it isn't, to say that he is a strong President, or that he is developing into one; or, perhaps, that he is an energetic President who applies his energies unpredictably. With Kennedy, all such estimates are hazardous, at best. His record shows that he displays power, sometimes ruthlessly, in facing up to one problem, and then meets another with caution and uncertainty.

Any examination of his operations to date suggests the basic reason for the fog over the Kennedy image. His methods and style vary, and the unfortunate impression is left that they vary with the economic, political, and global climate. This flexibility suggests to some

From The Nation, *February 2, 1963. Reprinted by permission.*

the lack of deep-rooted political ideals and purposefulness in connection with domestic policy. More serious is the effect of his apparent opportunism in the foreign-affairs arena. Even the simplest pronouncement by the President on a cold-war policy problem raises doubts abroad whether it carries the conviction of real intentions.

This is the price that Kennedy is paying for his manipulation techniques—some of them devious.

The Cuba crisis operation certainly showed that the President could move with power and daring. But the real significance of this grave crisis has never been properly emphasized. This centers on one fact—that in twenty-one previous months of dealing with Nikita Khrushchev, the President had failed to convince Moscow that he would stand firm when the issue of a nuclear war was posed starkly.

Could it be that Kennedy's flexible style in handling his Presidential responsibilities both on the home front and in dealings with our own allies contributed to Khrushchev's need to try to solve the Kennedy enigma? Why else were the Soviet missiles and bombers placed in full view in Cuba? By forcing the issue, Khrushchev was finding out what he wanted to know about Kennedy—and, incidentally, what the American people were even more desirous of knowing.

Cuba provided solid evidence, then, as to how the President would act in a grave international emergency. There are few sound clues to be found in his record as to how he will respond in any particular domestic home crisis, big or minor. His rhetoric—inspirational as it often is—is of scant help, for too often he has followed tough talk by accepting compromise. At various times, and under varying conditions, he has displayed great impetuosity, an excess of caution and both impatience and admirable perseverance.

One of the keenest inquirers into the Kennedy *modus operandi* is probably James MacGregor Burns of Williams College. In his friendly but penetrating 1960 political biography, *John Kennedy: A Political Profile,* Burns predicted that Kennedy, if elected, would

> . . . mobilize traditional tools of Presidential power and use them with force, astuteness and tenacity. He would show a flair for personal influence and manipulation, perhaps some of the flair Roosevelt had. He would drive hard bargains, forming alliances with Republicans when necessary, but compromising too, when he lacked the votes.

This was perspicacious forecasting. Yet it is not so much the President's personalized methods of operating as it is the complex nature of his personality and the uncertainty as to his goals that disturb the American people, even those—and they are in the majority—who admire and support him. His motives, in any given situation, are becoming more and more suspect. This is already developing as a political problem, although it is clearly one the Democratic Party is going to have to live with as long as Kennedy is in office.

Consider, for example, the questions being raised around the country: Why is the President unwilling to take on Congress and go to the people for support of the social-reform and other "forward looking" domestic measures he once considered vitally needed? Is there still something about the Cuba crisis we haven't been told about? Have we been playing British politics with the Skybolt missile? Will Kennedy really make a fight to get the new Congress to act on medicare and education aid? Or will he go all out only to get passage of his tax-cut–tax-reform program?

This questioning state of mind often breeds ugly suspicions. Hence, for example, the whispers that the President and his brother, Attorney General Robert F. Kennedy, are pursuing a personal vendetta against Jimmy Hoffa, the Teamster boss. Hence the suspicion that the President, while appearing the essence of frankness, is actually quite a conniver, *vide* the Adlai Stevenson affair. Hence the Republican-fed report that Kennedy timed the Cuban missile crisis for just before the November elections.

The examples could be multiplied many times. The President, however, appears impervious to these widely aired suspicions. He obviously remains supremely confident of his standing with the American public.

In the view of some liberals, the fairly widespread wonder as to what really goes on in Washington is founded on loss of faith in the President's political philosophy. Kennedy won the election in 1960 as a liberal. He has since performed as a middle-of-the-road progressive. The view of the Democratic Party expressed by White House aide and historian Arthur Schlesinger, Jr., probably comes closest to revealing what the party is up to as it functions here under Kennedy. The party, wrote Schlesinger in *The Politics of Hope,* is "humane, skeptical and pragmatic . . . has no dogma, no sense of Messianic mission, no belief that mortal man can attain Utopia, no faith that fundamental problems have final solutions."

A President subscribing generally to that belief would operate about as Kennedy has. He has Republicans high in his Administration like Treasury Secretary Dillon and Defense Secretary McNamara, on whom he counts for advice. He keeps on friendly terms with those in

Congress, like Senator Harry F. Byrd (D., Va.), who oppose virtually all bills embodying the party's national economic and social philosophy as espoused by Kennedy in the 1960 campaign.

The liberal disillusionment with Kennedy of 1963 is, of course, one factor responsible for the questions constantly raised as to the President's motivations. In this connection, there is an interesting off-beat estimate which suggests that, under Kennedy, a vacuum on Democratic Party issues exists in Washington. It comes from Maurice Rosenblatt, chairman of the Board of Advisers of the National Committee for an Effective Congress. Rosenblatt had this to say about the President:

> One of the accepted generalities or clichés of our time is that he [Kennedy] is a master politician. He certainly is a master at election politics, at getting elected. But what we say is that he needs to use more of the arts of persuasion and more of the arts of politics to get his program through [Congress].

Rosenblatt said that while historically the Democratic Party was able to create issues very well, it has been a long time since it did so. He credited Eisenhower with making the last two big issues—that of the balanced budget and inflation. And he did so by carrying his cause to the people; as a result, his "message" got through to Congress.

Kennedy's refusal to use his popular leadership to put national pressures on Congress rankles with the reformist element in his party. But in true pragmatist fashion, Kennedy says he is convinced he can fare better working with Congress than by fighting it. This wheeling and dealing with the legislators is one of Kennedy's most intricate techniques. His wheel horse in this operation is his legislative lieutenant, Lawrence O'Brien; but the Chief Executive is always battle-available, making personal phone calls to Capitol Hill as he practices the soft art of persuasion.

The dealing is occasionally of precinct-politics character: a suggestion that defense contracts may be at stake, or that patronage may be frozen; or a reminder that the President is most likely to find time to campaign in behalf of a Senator or Representative who votes "right."

Not all of the pressures come from the White House; they can come from the Administration's leaders in Congress. But with the President and the White House staff in the thick of the operations, one assumes that the pressures originate with the Chief Executive.

This manipulating method of dealing with Congress is the basis for the suspicion that the President moves in similar devious ways in all other affairs of state. The reasoning is unfortunate. Dealing with a recalcitrant Congress, particularly one dominated by one's own party, presents a problem wholly different from that posed by world and domestic issues not subject to the legislative mill.

When a critical decision must be reached at his own official family level, the President's technique is something else again, although the technique may vary from issue to issue. On cold-war problems, he is an inveterate brain-picker, using those whose grasp of the situation, and willingness to propose and defend effectively the solution they favor, he has learned to respect. It would be almost axiomatic, therefore, should a crisis of the order of Cuba develop again, that he would move toward his own decision by listening to men like Dean Acheson, Secretary McNamara, Secretary Dillon, Chief of Staff General Maxwell Taylor, his brother Robert and, of course, his own national security adviser, McGeorge Bundy. Secretary of State Dean Rusk's absence from this list should be noted. What Rusk thinks, he would keep to himself, as he wants to be in a position to carry out loyally whatever decision Kennedy makes.

Sometimes, of course, a major issue involves the jurisdiction of both the Executive Branch and of Congress. This, in the past, has called for a different managerial technique. Kennedy has shown himself at his most skillful in this type of operation. In the last Congress, Kennedy succeeded in bringing about passage of the important tariff-reduction act aimed at fitting the United States into the trade pattern of the developing European Community. Name Republicans like former Secretary of State Christian Herter were called in as high-level lobbyists. Key public-relations men from private industry were "loaned" to the White House to make the build-up effective.

The same sort of elaborate selling job will be done on the new Congress to get the tax-cut program through, with Republican talent carefully brought into the act along with respected business leaders.

Where the White House technique has fumbled—and is likely to do so again—will be generally in actions taken on the domestic scene in which the President and the Attorney General find themselves involved together. This has been particularly true in the Administration's attempt to "manage" the news. It is natural, of course, for the Administration to be open and aboveboard with the communications media when it has nothing to hide, i.e., when the White House considers that it has handled a problem adroitly and successfully. But when there has been a failure, the trap door on "authoritative" information is slammed shut, as after the Cuban invasion fiasco of April, 1961. Or, as in the University of Mississippi story, the media are used to cover mistakes.

In Mississippi, there had been pre-crisis negotiations by telephone with Governor Ross Barnett of a nature suggesting that Attorney General Kennedy actually thought that he could persuade the arch-segregationist to fall in line—and stay there. There was also the highly questionable final decision to send federal marshals into Oxford first, not troops.

Except in the South, the whole nasty episode receded in public interest with the Cuban crisis of late October. But last month it was revived in an "authoritative" *Look* magazine article that carried the imprint of helping Administration hands. Why? News management again: to convince the public that the Barnett-Bobby Kennedy phone talks made sense—which they never did and never will.

The Administration's management of the news *after* the Cuban crisis was more disturbing to many people than the controls exercised during the crisis itself. This involved "authoritative" revelations of what supposedly went on in the secret sessions of the National Security Council. And more recently there has been the questionable news management of the Cuban prisoner-ransom deal. Once the prisoners had been returned and American reaction was highly favorable, it suddenly developed that the deal had been masterminded by Robert F. Kennedy, not lawyer James B. Donovan, though that certainly had not been the impression given the public earlier.

Undeniably, the President's overall handling of his office has been unusually controversial. On the other hand, few Presidents in our history have been subjected to so close a day-in, day-out scrutiny. This was in part because of Kennedy's comparative youth and the great national interest in how he would sail the ship of state. But there was something more. Kennedy followed Eisenhower and whipped Nixon to gain office. The man he succeeded in the White House had occupied the Presidency for eight years. Eisenhower was a most undevious character; his every move was easily comprehended, almost predictable. Those who know him say that he had neither the capacity nor the inclination for intrigue. Then, in 1960, Kennedy campaigned against Nixon, who had already established a reputation for deviousness— "Tricky Dick," many people called him. By comparison Kennedy, despite his admitted mental ability, seemed simple and disarming— ironically, more in the mold of Eisenhower than was Nixon.

So, once elected, Kennedy's frequent use of intricate, usually skillful but occasionally devious, techniques came as a surprise to his supporters and was disconcerting to many of them. James MacGregor Burns, in his new book, *The Deadlock of Democracy*, cautiously implies a little disillusionment on his own part. Referring to the trouble met by the Administration's proposals in the 1962 Congress, he said the difficulties "aroused complaints by some liberals that the Administration lacked a central purpose of vision or grand design, that it had bent before every gust of public opinion instead of coming to grips with its enemies, that the Augustan age of poetry and power forecast by Robert Frost had become a managerial age of empty rhetoric and manipulation." Burns somewhat softly gives it as his opinion that these critics underestimate the "centrifugal forces operating on the President and the sheer intractability of the operational problems." But he still thinks there is something to their point of view.

An estimate of the Kennedy operation in the future based on the past still must be highly tenuous. About all that can be guaranteed is that life in these United States, as long as Kennedy is in the White House, is likely to be exciting—and somewhat insecure.

Henry Pachter

JFK as an Equestrian Statue: On Myth and Mythmakers

Pointing to Theodore White's book on the campaign of 1960, President Kennedy remarked to Arthur Schlesinger: "When I read your Roosevelt books, I thought what towering figures those men around Roosevelt were—Moley, Tugwell and Berle. Then I read Teddy's book and realized they were just Sorensen and Goodwin and you." [1] Kennedy's court chronicler is well aware of the historian's temptation to draw his hero big; but in relating this anecdote he also hints that perhaps the perspective may be reversed: since FDR and his associates *were* giants who made history, then perhaps in the eyes of History people may be striding ten feet tall though with our own eyes we see them walking around the campus with wrinkled pants. The way this anecdote turns upon itself is both a measure of Schlesinger's sophistication and an example of the mood which pervaded the Kennedy years. If Schlesinger's account of *A Thousand Days* (a perhaps involuntary but characteristic counterpoint of other people's millennia) has been called monumental, it is so by a strange inversion of the muralist's technique: he paints small to obtain the effect of bigness, and to this end Schlesin-

From Salmagundi, *Vol. I, No. 3, 1966. Reprinted by permission.*

1 Arthur Schlesinger, Jr., *A Thousand Days* (Boston: The Houghton Mifflin Company, 1965).

ger does not spare himself: he readily admits where he and his friends were wrong; he even admits, as a good historian, that occasionally they won by mistake rather than by foresight. Kennedy himself set the tone in his self-deprecating humor: "I became a hero involuntarily; they sank my boat." The disclaimer only underlines the claim; the modesty emphasizes the pride. It is the "Tiny Alice" technique: looking through the right end of a telescope, we know that we see a magnified view and therefore assume that the object is small; but if the same object is shown through the wrong end of the telescope, we are ready to believe that it is really very big.

Eisenhower's memoirs produce the impression that their author was of small stature; he never seemed to doubt that his course was right. Kennedy vowed that "the memoirs of our Administration will be written differently," and he gave his assistants concrete instructions to that effect. The President who more than any other before him tried to endow his office with a sense of history also was concerned about his own image for posterity. He has been well served by Arthur Schlesinger, Jr., and Theodore Sorensen,[2] both of whom were witnesses to his actions, recipients of his confidences, and partisans of his effort. Both also were predestined by training, inclination, and talent to do for Kennedy what one of them already had done for Jackson and F. D. Roosevelt. As was to be expected, both books are considerably above the level of memoirs; they are interpretations of Kennedy the man and of his meaning for his contemporaries, or maybe for the future. In this endeavor they are naturally partisan and occasionally they have to be consciously personal; but then Schlesinger had never claimed that his earlier histories (or those of Macaulay or Beard or Mommsen for that matter) had not been partisan. Every historian is a mythmaker, and those who don't know it are poor historians. A point of view has never hampered good history writing; only prejudice does.

The art of mythmaking is, of course, not new; Cromwell wished to be portrayed "warts and all." The test of the myth is precisely that it stands up to evidence and survives the efforts of the debunkers. Far from concealing Kennedy's shortcomings, Schlesinger quotes pages of critical comment. Nor does he need to pretend that his hero sprang

---

[2] Theodore Sorensen, *Kennedy* (New York: Harper and Row, 1965).

Since I am going to criticize certain aspects which both books have in common, it is only fair to state here that each in its own right is a superb, engrossing, and informative work. Schlesinger's has more historical sweep and perhaps more philosophical perspective; Sorensen's is the book of a political scientist with his typically static analysis. Hence my own prejudices run in favor of Schlesinger, and as a historian I can sympathize more with the problems he was facing than with Sorensen's. Hence I am going to quarrel with him more than with Sorensen; but I want it understood that my criticism is a left-handed compliment to the achievement.

from Jupiter's head wise as Minerva and cunning as Mercury. Both books, on the contrary, rest their case on Kennedy's astonishing capacity for growth. He had been a pragmatic, opportunistic politician, they admit, and not very seriously committed to any idea. When he was shown how historians had rated the American presidents, he wondered why Wilson and Theodore Roosevelt should rank above Polk and Truman. He much preferred the doers to the visionaries, those who carried legislation through Congress to those who had agitated for new conceptions. Yet ironically, his own fame was to rest, in Sorensen's words, on the things he started rather than those he completed, on what he stood for rather than what he achieved.

Kennedy started out indeed by raising people's hopes almost "involuntarily"; he hardly understood how much they really were waiting for a new voice. When Stevenson tried to impress on him that our disarmament plan could not be effective unless we meant it, Kennedy remarked that he understood the propaganda value of such slogans. Stevenson was "stung," the report goes, and to Kennedy's annoyance used the word "faith." Harlan Cleveland had to reconcile the two men by a truly diplomatic suggestion: that we adopt "general and complete disarmament" as a goal but present our program in terms of "next steps." This procedure, which was likely to hand the Old Maid back to the Russians, pleased Kennedy, and he even adopted as his slogan a book title by Seymour Melman: let us challenge the Russians to a "peace race," he said. He was, in his own words, "an idealist without illusions," and his general outlook on politics cannot be defined more precisely than in his instructions on the defense of Berlin: "Our objectives are carefully limited, but our commitment to defend them is unlimited." It is no mean feat of mythmaking that Kennedy emerges from this tale as a hero capable of inspiring a world with hope.

Kennedy was committed only to total commitment, but to no particular idea; whatever ideology he needed was developed out of the possibilities as they presented themselves. As both Schlesinger and Sorensen make clear, he made a virtue out of his disdain for ideologies. It was his skepticism rather than love of peace which allowed him to envision the end of the cold war. A man like Dulles needed to believe that the enemy was vicious, or he could not have fought; Kennedy fought when he had satisfied himself that the enemy had a motive for fighting, whether ideological or practical. The New Dealers, too, had been committed to ideologies and therefore believed in America's mission to police the world for democracy. Schlesinger and Sorensen probably quote Kennedy when they heap scorn and ridicule on Chester Bowles's long-windedness, George Ball's sentimentality, Stevenson's indecisiveness, all New Dealers' desire to fight for lost causes and grand designs. The terms "liberal" and "conservative" had no meaning for Kennedy, a disciple of Castlereagh and Talleyrand for whom ideologies were right if and when they worked. Again it is ironical that this man should have become the idol of the committed Left—a myth based on a misunderstanding, enhanced by his tragic death.

What distinguished Kennedy from the New Dealers was his conviction that the problems of modern society are not so much based on conflicts of interests as on questions of management; he refused to believe that there is one key to all problems and he never understood why people could get excited over all the problems and issues which had aroused their feelings under Roosevelt; nor was he persuaded that the democratic way of life was destined to prevail inevitably. To ideologies or "myths" he opposed "reality," which meant the technological, administrative means to attain accepted ends. Above all he feared "passion." What is at stake, he said at Yale, was "not some grand warfare of rival ideologies which will sweep the country with passion, but the practical management of a modern economy." (It is the measure of America's backwardness that Kennedy was right as against his audience on that occasion.) He was above all a political operator, and he tried to persuade others that he was neither a capitalist nor a socialist, neither a reactionary nor a progressive, but a pragmatist. He was slightly offended when businessmen refused to understand this approach. Sensing that he was "not one of theirs" (Schlesinger) they took his many gifts—a liberal depreciation allowance, a generous investment tax credit, a heavy tax cut—as a Christian Scientist would take vaccination. "I go to the Chamber of Commerce and talk about what we are doing for business—and they sit on their hands. I go to the UAW and warn them about the necessity for restraint—and they cheer every word. . . . It's all political and emotional."

Politics has to do with emotions, indeed, but Kennedy took a long time to understand what that meant. As Sorensen tells us with disarming frankness, he voted for civil rights legislation first not out of conviction but because he counted the voters in his constituency. But gradually during his tenure of office the problem took hold of him, and the better he knew it the more did he become truly engaged in its solution, until Martin Luther King felt moved to acknowledge his great ability to "respond to creative pressure." I am afraid this is the right word, and in its own way this is a moving story. But let us be clear about the nature of Kennedy's "response": it was the response of the practicing statesman, neither to the call of an idea nor to the call of people, but to the call of a job at hand; something threatened to get out of control and had better be managed well than hesitantly. In this same spirit Schlesinger and Sorensen define the philosophy of the "New

Frontier." They describe the "New Frontiersman" as an activist, a man open to ideas of whatever kind, ready to change his mind, too; he was an officer in World War II, is duly "cool," laconic in tone and grim of humor, distrustful of evangelism, but zestful and purposeful, versatile and unconcerned with protocol; above all he is completely committed to "Modernity."[3] Whereas the New Dealers had been "philosophizers" who believed in power and rationality, the New Frontiersman would do things "because they were necessary rather than because they were just and right."

A shattering experience for both sides was Kennedy's meeting with Negro leaders before the March on Washington. He felt their attempt to bring pressure on Congress might alienate votes which were so necessary to pass the civil rights bill. He could not understand that the March was necessary, not so much for the sake of legislation but as an assertion of the Negro movement's maturity. Kennedy did not understand movements and he did not build a popular coalition, as Roosevelt had done. He kept saying: "A good many programs I [!] care about may go down the drain as a result of this; we may all go down the drain as a result of this." And Martin Luther King kept saying: "It may be ill-timed, but I have never been in any action that was not ill-timed." Kennedy wanted to do everything *for* the people but nothing *through* the people, and he could not understand that no one can do anything for the people unless he first has called them to do it for themselves. Roosevelt understood this, but Kennedy did not have it in him to fight for a popular program and to lead the people in a fight for it. Schlesinger reports that he urged Kennedy to "stage a knock-down-drag-out fight over federal aid to education or Medicare"; but Kennedy made his top legislative priority the trade extension bill. Perhaps Kennedy was right and people were not ready to build a people's party; maybe it was his tragedy that as a born leader he had nobody to lead and no cause to fight for. The New Frontier was the end of Populism and the end of ideology. Instead of causes the Kennedy Administration had problems of better management.[4]

So Kennedy had to make *himself* the cause, building the future of America on his own and his wife's charm, on his better understanding and greater courage, last not least on the excellence of his advisers. There is a moving passage in Schlesinger's book about the conversion of that very disheartened man, Ed Murrow, from a doubter into a believer: "At last he had found someone since Churchill[!] in whose intelligence and purpose he could wholeheartedly believe." Other mem-

[3] Schlesinger takes a full chapter *not* to explain what that term means, but he explains very well that it does not mean "left of center."

[4] A similar view has been expressed by Karl E. Meyer in *Progressive* (January 1966).

bers of the group are equally devoted to Kennedy, and in turn receive the encomiums of Schlesinger and Sorensen. This group, often referred to as "the Charles River crowd"—or by others as the Harvard intellectuals—was the new elite of modernity which proposed to make the American government over, but since they had nothing behind them, they had to rely on the brilliance of their leader, JFK, and his myth. Most of the new men, including Kennedy, were poor administrators; but this is just the point of the Kennedy myth: the New Frontiersmen claimed that the enemy was not American society but the Administration itself. The most amusing and engrossing parts of Schlesinger's book are his thumbnail sketches of pompous bureaucrats and the colorful lays of his bouts with them. Other members of the group, above all the President himself, also suffered from their inability to move the cumbersome apparatus of government or to bend it to the purposes of Modernity (and the only redeeming feature is the evidence that in Moscow something very similar, or worse, was hampering Khrushchev). The image which results is that of a government of Rhodes scholars rolling up their sleeves to prod the sprawling departments into action, forcing them to rethink all their assumptions and to respond quickly to the manifold initiatives coming from the rejuvenated White House.

Every revolution (as of all people Schlesinger, the historian of the New Deal, knows best) will bog down in the problems of yesterday unless it can supersede the established administrative machinery or, as in Roosevelt's case, has the good fortune to step into a vacuum. But Kennedy wanted to be a Danton without September, or even without a Bastille; no wonder that the fighting took place inside the Bastille. Schlesinger is very eloquent in describing what went wrong with the *Alianza para el Progreso*. First, of course, he duly mentions the desperate economic conditions and the frustrating political environment in the Latin countries: weak or undemocratic or demagogic governments, more interested in the dollars that were to come forth than in the projects that were to be financed, and not interested at all in Kennedy's reform suggestions; and on the American side, no one who dared to say "or else." Sarcastically Schlesinger notes that "the A.I.D. bureaucracy was not accustomed to running revolutions and crusades." While Hamilton Fowler was too busy reorganizing, recruiting, and selling the idea, and hence "had no time to worry about the substance of the A.I.D.'s work," the idealistic Moscoso was "always a little at sea in Washington." Indeed, why should any bureaucracy "run" the Latin American revolution? Arturo Morales-Carrion put the finger on the spot: "The Latins don't understand the lingo of technocracy; they expect to hear the language of nationalism. Unless the *Alianza* is able to marry itself to nationalism, it will be pouring money into a psychological void." No device of "multilateralization" (Schlesinger manfully fought for literacy in government, but here he succumbs) could wrench the program loose from its bilateral Yankee image, and no amount of prodding from the White House could make the agency work better, for in "implementing" its objectives it had to rely on its opposite numbers abroad. What Schlesinger derisively calls "the permanent government" was international, too.

To the world problems, so the legend goes, Kennedy would have sought "political solutions" everywhere, avoiding ideological warfare and eschewing military commitments—if only the holdovers in the State and Defense Departments had let him! The most persistent of all the Kennedy myths, willfully and artfully perpetuated, expanded and documented by Schlesinger and Sorensen, is that of the young idealistic President bogged down in the quicksands of bureaucratic proceduralism, the vested interests of departmental baronies, and the habits of thought acquired by the Defense, Intelligence, and Diplomatic communities in long years of hard and disappointing experience.

By this King Arthur's side, of course, there were the young shining paladins: Schlesinger, Sorensen, Goodwin, Harriman, Chester Bowles, McNamara, Udall, Taylor, Stevenson, Martin, Moscoso, and others, each in quest of a problem in distress, raring to cut through the thickets of bureaucratic rule and to make policy according to new principles, with new methods, and by personal initiative. (I can testify that they made a good job of it, for I had to listen to the wails of State Department officials who spent their nights reviewing and rethinking every position paper they had written in the previous Administrations, or straightening out the effects of "White House interloping.") No love was lost between the Young Turks on Pennsylvania Avenue and the mossheads of Foggy Bottom; though biological age was not necessarily the difference between them, the "image" of the White House crowd certainly was that of "youth." Here is Schlesinger's portrait of Dean Rusk, his *bête noire:*

> He rejoiced in the role of tedium. . . . Concepts like national sovereignty and self-determination seemed to have the same reality for him as mountains for Udall or wheatfields for Freeman. The stereotypes of diplomacy were his native tongue. . . . As he would talk on and on in his even, low voice, a Georgian drawl sounding distantly under the professional tones of a foundation executive, the world itself seemed to lose reality and to dissolve into a montage of platitudes.

It must be admitted that Schlesinger also praises the intelligence and other qualities of Dean Rusk, and that the whole controversy has been much overplayed in the press. Moreover, Sorensen does not confirm, but specifically denies Schlesinger's report that Kennedy had decided to let his Secretary of State go—and in fact, why should he? Not any more than Roosevelt wished to be rid of Hull. Both presidents wanted to be policy-makers themselves, but needed by their side a firm, well-informed, reliable administrator and diplomat who was capable of handling the daily business. Schlesinger himself says that Kennedy liked to take advice from all sides but left no doubt that Rusk was his principal adviser and the coordinator of all foreign policy. Rusk, who reciprocated Schlesinger's feelings about him, often remained quiet in meetings, held back, and did not fight for the view of his department. He said he would not participate in discussion when underlings or gossips were around, and neither Schlesinger nor Sorensen informs us how often the Secretary of State saw the President privately after meetings with the National Security staff and others. Since Schlesinger is a great historian, I hesitate to raise the question: how good a source is he?

The sculptor of an equestrian statue takes the risk that grooms and veterinarians will pose as art critics. A professional historian wonders whether Schlesinger does not blur the borderline between testimony and gossip when he repeats Kennedy's outburst: "Bundy and I get more done in a day than the whole State Department in six months." Any of us could have said that; if Kennedy did so in a moment of anger, Schlesinger does not tell us what the occasion was; hence we cannot weigh the importance of his testimony. In another instance we can; if Kennedy indeed intended to fire Rusk "after the elections," i.e. presumably some time after his second inaugural, that left sixteen to eighteen months between the moment of anger and the possible cabinet change—he cannot really have been exceedingly dissatisfied if he expected to live with Rusk for another year and a half.

Schlesinger the pamphletist here has done a disservice to the historian; since the former disagreed with the policy of the State Department, the latter must insist that Rusk also was a drip and did not really count very much. The truth probably is that Kennedy's policies were much closer to Rusk's than Sorensen and Schlesinger were able to see, since from where they were sitting, they became most conscious of the many instances where their personal intervention or the use Kennedy made of their special talents did shift things a little their way. In all humility I submit that Schlesinger can take credit for his contribution, but in speaking of it, he is not speaking as a historian but as a witness. Rusk had been recommended to Kennedy by Lovett, a distinguished and ardent Cold War man, and the most superficial inquiry must have made Kennedy aware that as Assistant Secretary of State for

Far Eastern Affairs, Rusk had advocated and announced the policy of non-recognition against the Peking government. The attempt ever so subtly to suggest a divergence between Kennedy and his Secretary of State must fail. Stevenson, Chester Bowles, and other liberals were available for Rusk's job, but Kennedy passed them by.[5]

There is no doubt that Rusk represented "The Department" in the specific sense that it resisted Bundy's demand to re-enact the Berlin and Geneva and Camp David conferences all over again, that it insisted on using the doctrines it had formed, and that it spent time checking every new move with the proven allies. Schlesinger is rather unfair in complaining that the State Department was slow on the pick-up; sometimes, of course, that was its way of proving that a problem about which the White House had a "sense of urgency" needed neither urgency nor solution. Understandably, the Young Turks were exasperated, but the key perhaps is to be found in this passage of Sorensen's: "State Department aides grumbled privately that their prestige suffered if they were not present at key decisions." Indeed, Kennedy did not even take his Secretary of State along to Nassau when he met with Macmillan.

To move the "permanent government" at all, the White House staged periodical bursts of inroads into the towers of expertise, organized parallel sources of information, or even gave direct orders to the lower echelons. This "White House despotism" soon led to an administrative chaos unknown since the time of Roosevelt. But the difference was this: despotic governments which eventually unhinge the Establishment and create new institutions are related to a new idea or to a popular movement. Kennedy had no intention of giving the country new institutions; he only wanted to improve the results of the old, to inspire it with his own "sense of urgency." His revolution was one of methods only, and hence the "meddling" of the White House crowd was resented. In an aside to a seemingly unrelated subject, Schlesinger draws the conclusion: Kennedy was skeptical about the United Nations as an institution; he rather looked at it as an instrument for political action because "if developments did not generate institutions, no amount of institution-building can control developments." That, I assume, also expresses Schlesinger's philosophy of history.

Since the White House crowd was not interested in new institutions and did not represent a popular movement, its despotism had to

---

[5] For all the interesting detail which Schlesinger tells us about the resignation of Chester Bowles, he avoids probing into its political meaning. Here Sorensen is more candid, but it is Schlesinger who quotes Kennedy saying, after the Belgrade Conference: "You know who the real losers were? Stevenson and Bowles!" The neutrals' collapse before Khrushchev's 50-megaton bomb defeated their views.

be personal, and its justification had to be the image of the charismatic leader whose personal style itself was a message. How true this was we did not know until we saw the resentment against his successor who lacks style, charisma, and mystique; who can ride a hundred horses without every appearing to be a Man On Horseback, and who can tell the guild of artists, writers, and critics "how much we are doing for their business" without moving a hand. Even after the Bay of Pigs, intellectuals did not decline an invitation to the White House (but Schlesinger is honestly surprised that Alfred Kazin should have published a critical article after he had been invited to Hyannisport). Johnson, on the contrary, was suspect even before he had a chance to try. It is a necessary part of the King Arthur myth that Kennedy did not want Johnson; but after reading both books carefully I have concluded that three things are certain: *Robert* Kennedy did not want Johnson; John F. Kennedy knew from the beginning that he needed Johnson and was afraid that Johnson might not make himself available; thirdly, Kennedy mocked Johnson's eager acceptance. Schlesinger has been attacked for publishing this episode. I do not feel that it hurts Johnson, as may have been intended; it was just a mischievous story told by an exuberant winner about the loser. A historian, of course, must use merry anecdotes to enliven his story, but if all the merry anecdotes tend to aggrandize the figure of Kennedy and to reduce the stature of others, one wonders whether there is a purpose in the method.

Sorensen makes no secret of his intent; his book is admittedly a monument to Kennedy's achievements and his conclusion is that "the man was greater than the legend." He summarizes: "[Kennedy] stood for excellence in an era of indifference—for hope in an era of doubt—for placing public service ahead of private interests—for reconciliation[!] between East and West, black and white, labor and management." One wonders whether this is the same Sorensen to whose collaboration Kennedy credited so many thrilling, tinkling, stately, or antithetical phrases. Here is not Kennedy's intensity but only his rhetoric; it is not Kennedy's painful awareness of conflicts but his helplessness before them. If Kennedy knew a thing, it was that conflicts are not settled by "reconciliation" but can possibly be made manageable. In contrast to Morgenthau and others, I do not believe that there was nothing to Kennedy but the rhetoric of his aides; on the contrary, it appears that Sorensen was able to produce the famous Kennedy style only when Kennedy himself was around. He had identified so completely with the master that he knew what Kennedy wanted, what he thought, and how he would say it. But it is not correct to say that he has written the book which Kennedy himself would have written. In some respects he did better and above all, more; he provides accurate information on a number of details which he did not dare to leave out but which Kennedy might have. In another sense, he gives us less than we could have expected from Kennedy, because as the quoted passage has shown, Sorensen can only give us the empty shell, the Kennedy of Madame Tussaud.

The man Kennedy was too intelligent to write himself up as a myth; but his memorialists, of course, can produce a waxen image which can be placed right beside the George Washington who could not tell a lie. Thus, Kennedy gave all his government income to charities and never wore either ring or jewelry; he never asked but "searchingly" or "pointedly," he never talked but either "sagaciously" or "wittily," never answered unless he "quips" or "snapped back" (sic), never acted except "prudently," "decisively," or "boldly" and never stated but "sincerely." Needless to say, the more one knew him, the better one liked him, and the higher he rose, the more did he relish "to get back to the people." No President had "ever[!] seen so often and known so well the people and the problems of every part of the country." And to top it all, this must be quoted verbatim: "His only brushes with the law arose from his tendency to ignore traffic signs." Truly, no Eagle Scout ever was more fit to be President.

Where one finds this sort of thing, one is bound to ask whether the memorialist may not have slightly touched up the monument here and there to give the warts a little more style, and whether one's memory of the recent past is intimate enough and reliable enough to be trusted when it responds to the memorialist's vocation of events with consenting recognition.[6] The easiest check, for this writer, was a comparison of the two books, and the finding is that they do not agree on all points, some of them minor, but some of them important. The greatest divergences concern precisely questions which have received widest publicity: whether Kennedy wanted Johnson or had only teased him; whether he planned to dismiss his Secretary of State or valued him; whether the dismissal of Chester Bowles was just a matter of in-

---

[6] An instance where everybody's memory might be helpful is the day after the Bay of Pigs disaster, when Kennedy ran for cover to Gettysburg. The newspapers and the newsreels showed him together with Eisenhower in a demonstration of national unity in a moment of distress. In Schlesinger's book the episode looks like this: "he called in Nixon . . . and by the weekend he had talked to Eisenhower, Rockefeller and Goldwater." This is not history but *Geschichtsklitterung*.

Another instance is Schlesinger's report that "Rostow and Bell managed to insert a little of the new philosophy into the [foreign aid] message before it was delivered"; this underground message said that the task was "not negatively to fight Communism [but] to help make a demonstration that economic growth and democracy can develop hand in hand." I have found similar formulations in every one of Eisenhower's State of the Union messages.

compatibility between him and Rusk, or whether there were political reasons as well. There are differences about policy, too; one gets a different impression of Kennedy's plans in Vietnam from Sorensen and from Schlesinger, and there are even different details on the Bay of Pigs adventure, though one might guess that the episode had been amply discussed in the White House. Part of the differences may be due to the simple fact we already have pointed out—that neither of the two writers was a witness to all transactions, and their errors may be a warning to all historians that even the most expert and professionally careful memorialist may not be safe as a source.[7]

To bolster their own adulation, the memorialists quote witnesses. They get testimonials from African leaders, specifically from Gabon and Nigeria but not from Ghana where it would count, on Kennedy's leadership in the race question; and here is a testimonial to Kennedy's administrative ability: Shortly after his nomination he asked Clark Clifford for some background information on the setup in the White House. "If I am elected," he said to the astounded Truman aide, "I don't want to wake up on November 9 and have to ask myself, what do I do now?" Clifford, continues Schlesinger, *"impressed by Kennedy's foresight,* promptly accepted the assignment." No fifth-grade reader could tell French children a more convincing anecdote about the foresight of Pepin the Short! Yet we are constantly assured that this is not the story of Pepin the Short: Kennedy would not stoop to the corny tricks which came so easily to Nixon, such as opening a speech with a "Pat and I" greeting (p. 65); "Never a Jackie and I" (p. 115). Who was it that met the reporters in Paris saying: "I am the guy who accompanied Jacqueline"? Of course, the gambit is much more sophisticated, the wit is graceful, and the occasion is not *cherché.* But there are other books on Kennedy's wit, and proof that he was not vulgar is not acceptable as an introduction to his greatness.

I hope that I am not carping, for I really admire both Schlesinger's and Sorensen's books; I also am aware that in a 1000-page volume the professionals are bound to find a few mistakes of fact. Yet one has the uncomfortable feeling that all the mistakes are friendly to Kennedy. Speaking of the President's address to the U.N., Schlesinger claims that "the momentum of his words, sustained by Stevenson's effective leadership, continued through the 16th General Assembly. The *troika* [Khrushchev's demand for reorganization] was defeated and U Thant became Secretary General *with unaltered authority."* The italicized words are an unfortunate exaggeration, for the Russians accepted U

---

7 It is interesting, e.g., that Schlesinger, whose assignments were mainly in the field of foreign policy, knew nothing of the private correspondence between Kennedy and Khrushchev, and of the latter's exotic means of transmittal.

Thant only after the entire power structure in his office had been dismantled and his cabinet had been reconstructed along the lines of the troika. Likewise in the U.N.—"Because of the cogency of our arguments and the basic confidence in Kennedy's purposes, our refusal to support sanctions [against South Africa] was readily accepted by the Africans." They accepted in the sense that they had no choice, but certainly not "readily." Schlesinger also calls it "a brilliant stroke" that Kennedy promised to stop arms shipments to South Africa within five months—the Africans had been very insistent that he do so at once. Finally—was Kennedy really such a small man that his own fame can shine only if Eisenhower's is diminished? It is somewhat less than generous to deny that Eisenhower enjoyed great prestige in Africa: Lumumba did not appeal to the U.N. (as Sorensen thinks) but to Eisenhower, who told him to turn to the United Nations. Also, the Volta project had been approved by Dulles, and it is not true that Herter refused to see Nkrumah. In general there was much more continuity in our African policy than either Sorensen or Schlesinger admits. Though Kennedy was the first Senator publicly to call for an end of the Algerian war, the French then accused Dulles of seeking a secret understanding with the F.L.N.

Perhaps the least candid treatment has been accorded the Bay of Pigs disaster. During the electoral campaign, Schlesinger says on p. 72, underlings published a statement on Cuba which Kennedy unfortunately had not seen: "We must strengthen all anti-Batista, anti-Castro democratic forces in exile and in Cuba. These fighters for freedom have not received any support from our government." Sorensen attributes the "outline" of this statement to Kennedy himself (p. 205). I remember that I felt apprehension, because it was rumored that somewhere Cuban exiles were training, I cannot believe that Kennedy, with his excellent press relations, was unaware of these rumors, and therefore I believe Schlesinger when he writes that Kennedy's campaign writers "dropped Cuba." Yet he was unable to "drop" the issue, because Nixon raised it in the T.V. debate: with the reckless demagoguery of which he was capable, he attacked Kennedy for advocating an invasion plan which he knew was Eisenhower's—and Kennedy failed to answer. On p. 224 Schlesinger dismisses as "campaign oratory" a speech in which Kennedy accused the State Department of ignoring the advice of Ambassador Earl T. Smith, a crony of old Joe Kennedy and Batista who had known all the time that Castro was nothing but a Communist. The particular target of the hundredpercenters then was Assistant Secretary of State Rubottom, whose wait-and-see attitude toward the 26th of July Movement was considered subversive. Maybe this is the reason why Schlesinger, who otherwise is bubbling over with background information, introduces Rubottom, when he finally met Kennedy, merely as "a foreign service officer of temperate but cautious views." According to Schlesinger, Dulles informed Kennedy, ten days after his election, of the training center in Guatemala. Sorensen withholds this information but is satisfied to tell us that on Inauguration Day Kennedy "inherited" the invasion plan. Just shortly before the election, the plan had been expanded, from a mere guerilla operation, to a military invasion. But Kennedy told Dulles to "go on." Although he had "grave doubts" and was "amazed at the magnitude and daring" of the plan, he probably did not perceive at that time that the problem was not technical feasibility but political justification.

Sorensen then argues that the CIA placed the new President before the unpleasant choice of liquidating well-laid preparations and disbanding an army which had been training for nearly a year, or of escalating the planned operation. Schlesinger, too, names two arguments as decisive: the U.S. might appear as a paper tiger and Castro might triumph if the plan was scuttled; secondly, we had "the disposal problem": what to do with the exiles once they had been trained. The escalation, it seems, was urged on the President by all experts; admittedly it increased the political risk, but it limited the military risk. Reading the two books jointly, one cannot doubt that Kennedy was constantly concerned to limit the U.S. *political* involvement and therefore insisted on staging silly "cover stories," but never intended to cancel the invasion. Yet, from November 18, 1960, and thereafter he had not one and not some but at least a dozen opportunities to decide whether the operation should be minimized or maximized, turned back into a guerilla drop or expanded into a beachhead invasion. The two arguments therefore have holes as wide as a hangar: if the world was to interpret cancellation of the plan as a sign of weakness, then it must have known about it; if, on the other hand, the plan developed a dynamism of its own and was blown up to its eventual proportions only in the course of constant pressure, then it is difficult to see why it could not be canceled while it was small or scaled down when it threatened to get out of hand. Sorensen tells us that the President knew what was at stake: he had to disengage the U.S. morally and politically from the operation, but the Chiefs of Staff had misled him: they assured him that the invasion could succeed without American involvement and even without an uprising behind Castro's lines. This, according to Schlesinger, is a lie. The Chiefs of Staff had attached very precise conditions on their prediction of success: there must be an uprising in Cuba; Castro's air force must be destroyed and the beachhead must be covered by airplanes. Neither of these conditions were fulfilled, and it must be said in Kennedy's honor that the invasion failed mainly because of his anxiousness to keep the U.S. from overt participation.

Schlesinger contributes two pieces of important information to the story. On March 11, more than five weeks before the invasion, he was assigned to write a White Book explaining its aims to the world. He also testifies that he made Kennedy aware that a first-class observer had shown serious doubts that the Cuban underground was ready to overthrow Castro. It is surprising, therefore, that both memorialists blame "the experts" and quote Kennedy as blaming the Chiefs of Staff, the CIA, Rusk, and the entire establishment: "How could I be so stupid? All my life I have known not to rely on experts." This story lays the ground for the later buildup: when Kennedy freed himself from the advice of the experts but followed his own instincts, then he was successful, brilliant, and virtuous. It might be more correct to say that Kennedy would have canceled the invasion order if he had taken more seriously his experts' advice that the success depended on U.S. involvement. Too late did he recognize that the question was not whether the invasion could succeed, but whether, as indicated, he could justify it politically. The moment he understood this, he nobly took all the blame on himself, and rightly so, because thereby he laid the ground for the confidence which he earned among other statesmen.[8]

Sorensen knows that Kennedy would not want to be absolved and Schlesinger knows that he cannot be absolved. Both memorialists, however, try it, because they are now serving the myth. Kennedy the man had the capacity to learn and to grow. An equestrian statue cannot grow. Kennedy the myth cannot have made a terrible blunder; he was misled by the experts, or rather the wrong kind of experts. In this way the image of the knight in shining armor is preserved, and Kennedy emerges as the leader of a projected new world order. He was credited with ideas on peace which he probably did not have, or at least for which no more valid quotations can be cited than from other con-

---

[8] Clifton Daniel, of *The New York Times,* told the World Press Institute that Kennedy could not have been "misled." As reported in his paper on June 2, 1966, Mr. Daniel depicted President Kennedy as apparently torn in two directions. Meeting with a group of editors after the incident, Kennedy "ran down a list of what he called premature disclosures of security information." While he scolded *The New York Times,* the President said in an aside to Mr. Catledge, "If you had printed more about the operation you would have saved us from a colossal mistake." Mr. Daniel recalled that in both a television interview on Meet the Press and in his own book *A Thousand Days* Arthur M. Schlesinger, Jr., said that *The Times* had suppressed an article giving "a fairly accurate account of the invasion plans." Holding up a copy of the April 7, 1961, edition in which the article appeared, Mr. Daniel said: "Mr. Schlesinger was mistaken, both in his book and in his appearance on Meet the Press."

temporary statesmen. In that connection he has been bracketed with Khrushchev and John XXIII as a trinity of peace.

Particularly in Europe, it seems, people went overboard from the beginning. After the Bay of Pigs, R.H.S. Crossman, the British Labor M.P., told Schlesinger: "Had this happened under Eisenhower, they would have staged mass meetings in Trafalgar Square and hung Dulles in effigy." (They did march eighteen months later against the blockade in the missile crisis.) The Socialist Professor André Philip, writing in *Preuves,* castigates Johnson for intervening against "Juan Bosch, the friend of Kennedy," quite forgetting that Kennedy did nothing to save his "friend" from plotters who clearly had found encouragement in his Defense establishment. But earlier, Kennedy had stated his preferences in this order: a decent democratic regime, a continuation of the Trujillo regime, a Castro regime: "we cannot renounce the second until we are sure that we can avoid the third." Likewise, Chet Huntley reflected the opinion in a special NBC report on Vietnam, that the Peace Movement derived from Kennedy's death; it seems that he manfully averted war, whereas his successor joyfully skidded into it. Let's be fair: Kennedy greased the rails on which Johnson launched us into war; when Kennedy's career was cut short we had as many thousand "advisers" in Vietnam as we had hundreds when it began. His own view of their role broke through unexpectedly in a humorous reference to his brother's campaign in Massachusetts: "No Presidential aide will take part in that political war, except as a training mission." He also created and sent the now infamous "Green Berets." Schlesinger reports that the President believed in what now is derisively called the domino theory: "For us to withdraw from that effort would mean the collapse not only of South Vietnam but of South East Asia." And it was behind his back that Lodge allowed the overthrow of Diem! Finally, here is Schlesinger's summary of Kennedy's reasoning: "Neutralization was the correct policy, but the matter was not that simple any longer. The effort had been made, American prestige was deeply involved, extrication would not be easy. To strive for neutralization, it was essential to convince the enemy that they could not win. . . . The U.S. had no choice but to stiffen its position, whether in preparation for negotiation or for resistance."

It so happens that the country in question is not Vietnam but Laos, and Kennedy has generally been credited with winning peace there through a wise policy of neutralization. But Johnson seems to have applied his arguments verbatim to Vietnam—to "honor our commitments" and to defend on the shores of the Mekong River "the safety of us all." The comparison is the more striking as the Pathet Lao then was much stronger than the Viet Cong are now. But fortunately

for Kennedy, the Chinese and North Vietnamese then were not ready
to sustain a prolonged war, Khrushchev was less interested to get into
Laos than to get the Chinese out, and above all, a strong neutralist
Premier was available in the person of Prince Souvana Phouma. Kennedy also took military steps and used military threats to attain agreement on Laos: when the Communists attacked, he did not hesitate to
send two air squadrons to Thailand, despite the warning of all military
men—"experts," I assume—to avoid land war in Asia.

To no one's surprise Schlesinger tells all this with a certain
relish; for it will be remembered that he was the Government's speaker
at the great Washington teach-in. He is much more reticent when he
has to speak about Vietnam directly, and here I wonder whether the
friend did not get in the way of the historian, and the memorialist
defeat the memoir-writer. He exonerates Kennedy from any responsibility for the mess he left to Johnson, on the strange ground that
Kennedy "had never really given it his full attention." He gave it
enough thought to send General Maxwell Taylor there, not once but
several times, and incidentally, an American President just could not
afford to ignore a country where people were setting themselves aflame.
While Schlesinger is far from counting Kennedy among the peace
demonstrators, he shields him from their charges; according to Sorensen, the fault lay entirely with Rusk who failed to resist the Pentagon's
view that "you can't carry out land reform while the local peasant
leaders are being murdered." This charge is misleading, for it was Rusk
who recommended Lodge, the most decided spokesman of a "political
approach" to Vietnam; we have seen that the memorialists have a
tendency to blame either the military or Foggy Bottom for every failure. It is all the more surprising that the Dominican affair has not
stimulated their curiosity. Kennedy's "friend" Bosch was overthrown
by a Junta which could not have acted without the consent of some
American officials; yet the memorialists remain silent and dismiss Bosch
as "a literary figure"—was that Kennedy's expression?

It seems to me that the attack on Rusk's abilities as a Secretary
of State has its foundation in a deeper aversion to his policies. Rusk
had inherited the NATO orientation from Acheson; he still was a
"cold warrior." Schlesinger and Sorensen on the other hand sympathize with that group of foreign policy critics who would rather put
up with a deterioration of NATO than lose an opportunity to talk to
the Russians; as a corollary, they would exploit and emphasize the
Sino-Soviet split; they also take a more tolerant view of neutralism and
generally approach the "third world" in a more liberal, more intelligent, and more sympathetic spirit. Until the archives are opened,
Schlesinger's fascinating account of the in-fighting between the "Euro-

peanists" and the multiple-optionalists will be a major source for students of American foreign policy and its formulation. Schlesinger makes it abundantly clear that Kennedy considered MLF (the now defunct project of a multilateral nuclear fleet) as a "fake" to be dangled before German eyes as long as de Gaulle tempted them with other false alternatives—a deception as reckless as the whole swindle of German reunification which has plagued American policy since 1948.

Yet Kennedy remained convinced that the German defense contribution was essential, and the more he gained experience the firmer did this conviction engrave itself into his mind. He was enthusiastic about his reception in Germany; Mrs. Kennedy told Mayor Brandt that he had the film of his Berlin visit played for his household again and again, and Sorensen reports that he playfully suggested leaving a note to his successor "to be opened at some time of discouragement" with the words "Go to Germany." NATO-critics like Morgenthau have observed that Kennedy's German policy was incompatible with his American University speech. Morgenthau draws the conclusion that Kennedy was not sincere in either but merely was swayed by his own rhetoric—which only goes to show that Professor Morgenthau does not understand diplomacy. Here is a basic dilemma of American foreign policy the "resolution" of which may not be in the interest of the United States for a long time. Kennedy understood that it was better to leave things in suspense, make believe that we were prepared to negotiate with the Russians about Berlin while assuring the Germans that we would not give it away, placating the critics at home and abroad by serious attempts to liquidate the Cold War while knowing that the Russians would agree only to their own terms.

It is a pity that the Truman and Eisenhower Administrations have not produced as splendid a historian as the Roosevelt and Kennedy administrations were fortunate to have in Professor Schlesinger. In that case we would see that every president started out with messages of goodwill, feelers for a settlement, and vows to negotiate, but ended in disappointment, frustration, and restricted options. Kennedy not only was well advanced along this road when he was shot; in one respect he had gone further than any of his predecessors. After the Cuban Missile Crisis he behaved like the owner of the NATO alliance; while he was talking about partnership and interdependence, he blandly assumed that the allies had to subordinate their defense policy to American dictates. He humiliated Macmillan by scuttling the Skybolt project and he advertised to the world public what he was going to do to de Gaulle.[9] Assuming these decisions were wise and that they

---

[9] I have expressed both my admiration for Kennedy's handling of the Missile Crisis

were dictates of the political reality rather than of an imperialistic whim, it still is true that Acheson pressed his recommendations to the allies with infinitely more tact, and that even Dulles never claimed superior wisdom for Washington.

The "old European hands" in State were appalled at the rough treatment which their wards received at the hands of the young despots in the White House, and they understood it even less as this Administration constantly exhorted everybody to spare the sensibilities of third parties—but that applied only to the "Third World," neutrals and underdeveloped areas, not to allies. The "Grand Design" was undermined by the President's own attitude to his partners. Schlesinger can praise Kennedy for his contribution to the ouster of France from Africa, and yet sympathize with his "anger at the clandestine French campaign against the U.S. in Asia and Africa"; he can display a historian's understanding for de Gaulle's attack on the military and economic foundations of Kennedy's European policies, and yet as a friend join in his sigh of desperation: "What can you do with such a man?" He can rejoice that the European Left preferred America's nuclear monopoly to any partnership arrangement, but neither he nor Kennedy understood that it was the Grand Design itself which the Europeans resented. They scolded Dulles for considering nonalignment a sin where the "Third World" was concerned, but they took it for granted that Europe's interests were best known to Washington and they were blind to Europe's craving for self-respect. The Young Turks in the White House considered Europe an American protectorate to an extent that they did not permit themselves in the Third World any more.

Kennedy's true claim to fame in matters of foreign policy is his genuine reversal of American attitudes to the Third World. Here, as in other fields, the promises were greater than the achievements, but more than in other fields we must grant that the difficulties were both enormous and inherent, and that the new approach was a long-range program. Kennedy used all his charm and best efforts to change the image of the U.S. in the eyes of the Southern Hemisphere, and he used all his persuasive powers to re-educate the American public on our responsibilities toward the underdeveloped countries. He taught Amer-

and my criticism of his follow-up in *Collision Course* (New York: Praeger, 1963). At that time no one could have guessed how soon the "Grand Design" would be shattered. No one can tell now whether Kennedy, had he lived, would have let this come to pass nor, had it happened, whether he would then have followed the line of a more active coexistence policy, a line suggested by the Kennedy myth. Kennedy's basic pragmatism makes it impossible to affirm that he would have striven for such an approach under all circumstances, and equally impossible to deny that, had the need for such a policy arisen, he would have turned it into an opportunity.

ica to adopt a different attitude, first to the "neutralism" of under-developed countries, second to their "socialism." He also taught the American public that the problems of underdeveloped countries are basically different from ours, and that our aid should be tied to stern suggestions for structural reforms. Of course the *Alianza para el Progreso* bogged down from its beginning, and Latin American experts had warned that to make it work the reforms would have to be much deeper than requested. But a beginning had been made to attach the right kind of "strings" to foreign aid, and as with the Peace Corps, our people learned more than the beneficiaries from the experience. The main change was in the approach, generally characterized as a switch from "project-oriented" to "area-oriented" aid, the latter implying a certain amount of planning. What Kennedy did may be illuminated by Schlesinger's example of food shipments to needy countries. Eisenhower had treated Public Law 480 as a program to dispose of surpluses, and even liberal Senators had been unable to make the idea attractive to farmers and constructive for our foreign policy. Kennedy "thrilled a farm audience" by turning the problem around: "I don't regard farm surpluses as a problem. . . . I regard them as an opportunity."

Schlesinger, of course, is able to repeat here the insight he gained in his studies of the New Deal. Eugene Lyons had shown that every single measure for which FDR became famous had been initiated by Herbert Hoover, including the controversial A.A.A. But Schlesinger showed that there is all the difference in the world between grudgingly yielding to necessity and enthusiastically embracing an opportunity: the same measure in a different context is the difference between despair and hope. Taken out of context certain bits of Schlesinger's information are misleading: it must be news to some of the people involved that the world waited for Chester Bowles to suggest that foreign aid should "concentrate on countries which could make effective use of assistance"; the area approach had been the philosophy of U.N. development aid under American leadership and with predominantly American funds, complementing and often underpinning U.S. bilateral aid. Yet the Kennedy Administration convinced other governments that it believed what Eisenhower had merely conceded. No doubt, vested departmental interests resisted this new philosophy; they had found it easier to use foreign aid as a bribe for friendly governments and as a prop for shaky friends. But as the budget figures and the *Congressional Record* show, this kind of aid is on the way out anyway, not so much because it is disreputable but because it has become, in computerese, "counter-productive." It is easy to overestimate the actual change where the change was mostly in the ideology, or the importance of a particular decision and the influence of a particular personality where the trend already was pointing in the same direction.

Marshall Shulman has remarked about recent Soviet policies that moves "undertaken for short-term, expediential purposes have tended to elongate in time and become imbedded in doctrine and political strategy." This theorem, which the Kennedy Administration put to good use in dealing with the Kremlin, may also be true of our own State Department. Its most remarkable application, however, became possible in the Afro-Asian world. Kennedy took long shots on Sukarno, Ben Bella, Nkrumah, and other unsafe leaders, just hoping that their problems would outlive their ideologies. It may have been foolish to hand West Iran over to Sukarno, but there was hardly anything else to do, and one just had to pray that Sukarno's grip on power would slip before the Communists were ready to take over or before the officers of the army had forgotten our services. In that case Kennedy's gamble paid off. Likewise, Kennedy was right to trust Souvana Phouma. But he lost Brazzaville and came near to losing Leopoldville, and no matter how many Africans Kennedy was able to charm, he did not break the distrust of Nyerere, Cheddi Jagan, and other ideological anti-imperialists. Ben Bella declared himself thrilled by Kennedy— and went to Havana; Nkrumah wrote him a moving letter—and went to Peking. Would historian Schlesinger allow one of his students to weigh "charm" against political reality? Or to believe words where action pointed the other way? Dulles too had recognized India's neutrality, while Kennedy was delighted to provide her with arms. He also hoped, of course, that the neutrals would always be neutral on our side. The difference was that Kennedy was bold and had confidence, while Dulles was anxious. Therefore, the one was inspiring, the other forbidding.

Yet I cannot discover in all this any new policy. For Wilson's famous war aims formula, Kennedy substituted the slogan "a world safe for diversity." He recognized that democracy was not for everyone; it was a luxury rich countries like the U.S. could afford. The dichotomy "here Freedom, there Communism," was a simplistic cliché of the fifties; instead of the "unitary dogma [which had] dismayed our allies," he looked forward—in the Berkeley Speech co-authored by Schlesinger and Sorensen—to "this emerging world of independence and diversity [which] is incompatible with the Communist world order." One may quarrel with such formulations on two grounds. As a conception, diversity is not on the same level as democracy. Democracy is a substantive ideal, diversity a formal, almost procedural matter. One can call on people to sacrifice their lives for democracy, not for diversity, democracy being one of those concrete ideals which diversity permits. In practice, the diversity will not be one of various ideologies but one of many nationalisms, and of this Schlesinger says that it excludes the idea of a Communist world order—which brings us back to the blessed alternatives of Communism and Freedom, and the entire exercise reveals itself as mere rhetoric, the substitution of a tactical device, diversity, for a material idea, democracy.

Moreover, to abandon old-fashioned American progressivism for newly remodeled multi-nationalism is a step backward. We may not have lived up to our ideals of progressivism but at least we professed them. The New Frontier placed the progressive measures in the framework of "rationality" and substituted the dynamism of a technocratic elite for the movement of people. It represented the new *"style"* of the postwar generation rather than a new *idea* for all nations. It fought the old "experts" in the bureaucracy only to replace them by a new form of expertise; it was imperial and pragmatic rather than democratic and ideological. Instead of an idea it had a dynamism and instead of a movement it had the magic power of a charismatic leader. Norman Mailer said of him that Kennedy would "deliver American idealism from the stereotyped responses of the past." Others were merely satisfied to enjoy the beautiful picture of a handsome couple in the White House. Still others were gratified by Kennedy's prose and his sense of urgency or were beguiled by the intensity which he put behind everything he did. But literacy itself is no sign of greatness, nor does brilliant rhetoric guarantee the substance of what is being said, and a dynamism toward unidentified goals is no proof that the goals have been well defined in the head of the leader.

Yet myths have a way of verifying themselves: if enough people believe them, they act with the belief that other people too act on the same assumptions, and that makes the myths come true. So the prediction of Kennedy's ultimate vindication must be believed in since so many people drank hope from his promises—or did they? Was it not rather his tragic death which seemed to confirm dire forebodings? Few people can bear to see a young man die in vain; Kennedy's life acquired significance through his death. The romantic imagination now endowed him with the ideas he must have died for. Most ironically, the crime of Dallas vindicated Kennedy in the eyes of his critics, and many who had been impervious to the charm of the living Kennedy now appropriated his corpse. He became a culture hero against whose stature they measure the reality of American civilization, or an apostle of peace against whose myth they measure the realities of American policy. Particularly in Europe the myth of Kennedy has taken ineradicable roots, precisely because it seems to justify European superiority feelings vis-à-vis Dallas. It is almost necessary for America's

critics to have an American martyr who was killed by Americans—
and of course, no serious writer in Europe believes the Oswald theory.
It is significant that the first serious challenge of the Warren Report
should have been written by M. Léo Sauvage, correspondent of *Le
Figaro,* not by any American.[10] Sorensen explicitly endorses the Warren Report, while Schlesinger is singularly silent or remains ambiguous
enough to imply his failure to be impressed. The death of the hero, of
course, is part of the classical myth, and we would deprive ourselves
of significance if that death were nothing but the error of a madman.

The death of Kennedy also ended the reign of the Charles River
team, the intellectual elite which had turned technocrats and managers.
The myth is that it deprived America of the opportunity to be inspired
by ideas. It is not the vocation of the idea-man to rule, it is his business to stand by, critically or encouragingly, but independently. He
must not be identified with power, or else he loses contact with the
sources of his ideas. Since men of power must always betray the ideas
while they realize them, men of ideas must remain critics of power.
This is how the mythmaker has betrayed the myth, and Schlesinger
has forsaken Liberalism for Modernity.

10 *February 1968.* I wrote this essay before publication of Edward Jay Epstein's
study of the Commission's work.

Tom Wicker

*Lyndon Johnson vs.
the Ghost of Jack Kennedy*

The fact of the matter is that it was not one of the better months of
the Kennedy years in Washington—that November of 1963. It was
good football weather most of the time, as I recall it, and a lot of
things happened that made good copy, but most of us felt we were
marking time. We were on the edge of an election year and if there
was anyone in town who believed President Kennedy would be defeated, he was brooding in silence, not speaking out. The real question,
the deep thinkers said, was whether Kennedy could win a big victory

and turn it into the kind of accomplishment he had promised in 1960 but hadn't been able to deliver.

People talked a great deal about Barry Goldwater, who obviously was getting ready to run and who was beginning to be taken as a serious candidate in a town accustomed to thinking of him as pretty far out. Kennedy, however, was doing nothing to build up Goldwater and still was dealing with him lightly.

"Senator Goldwater," he told the A.F.L.-C.I.O. convention in New York, "asked for labor's support before two thousand cheering Illinois businessmen." And at a news conference, he sharpened the needle. He would not criticize the Senator just then, he said, because "he himself has had a busy week selling T.V.A. and . . . suggesting that military commanders overseas be permitted to use nuclear weapons, attacking the President of Bolivia while he was here in the United States, involving himself in the Greek elections. So I thought it really would not be fair for me this week to reply to him."

The Diem government was overthrown in Saigon and both Ngo Dinh Diem and Ngo Dinh Nhu were assassinated. Duong Van Minh, a general known as Big Minh, took over the South Vietnamese government and both the State Department and the White House made it plain that, while they regretted the deaths, they thought the new regime would be better able to prosecute the guerrilla war.

Nevertheless, the downfall of the Diems seemed one more indication that the high hopes with which the Kennedy Administration had got under way three years earlier were somewhat threadbare. Kennedy had put his bets down on Diem, and the increased American commitment to the South Vietnamese government that he had made in 1961 had been his first real show of muscle in the Cold War. Now, if there was a sense of starting over again in Vietnam, the death of Diem still was a tacit admission that Kennedy either had backed the wrong horse and stayed with him too long, or else had abandoned an ally under pressure. No one seriously doubted that the coup had been acquiesced in and perhaps aided by the United States. Such knowledge runs against the American sense of righteousness.

That November, Kennedy had plenty of other troubles besides the Goldwater boom and a baffling, faraway war that no one liked.

The Soviets had copped a Yale professor, Frederick G. Barghoorn, in Moscow and jailed him for spying. Nikita Khrushchev said convoy incidents at Berlin had increased the threat of war. The sale of American wheat to the Russians was blocked on the question of whether it should be for cash or on the cuff.

The Administration put new restrictions on Red diplomats' travel here, probably in retaliation for Barghoorn's incarceration (the Soviets turned him loose late in the month still insisting he was a spy). Kennedy was forced to admit he couldn't pull as many troops out of Vietnam as he had promised earlier that he would. Treasury experts met with representatives of nine nations to worry over liquidity and the monetary system and announced the possibility of a new unit of international currency. And in case anyone should forget the Caribbean, a Cuban refugee entered the White House in the tourist line, picked up one of Mrs. Kennedy's Greek urns, and threw it through one of her antique mirrors.

The balance-of-payments deficit was down to a six-year low in the third quarter, but there was no political mileage in that. Labor announced a $750,000 kitty to register Democrats for an all-out fight against what George Meany called Goldwater "reaction," but Labor is always with the Democrats. Congress upped the Peace Corps budget to $102,000,000 from $59,000,000, but there were few other legislative victories in sight.

Kennedy gave up publicly on getting his civil-rights and tax-cut bills enacted in 1963, although he predicted an "eighteen-month delivery" for 1964. "Westward look, the land is bright," he quipped about this prospect, sounding as if he were trying to cheer himself up. Foreign aid, he also conceded, was under the hardest attack since the Marshall Plan; he managed to salvage the program, but it was badly cut and tied his hands in dealing with Eastern Europe.

Southern reporters wrote that Kennedy's popularity was at a low ebb in Dixie, due to his civil-rights program, Brother Bobby's Justice Department agitators and Senator Goldwater's availability. The Fed raised the margin requirement for the first time in five years, from 50 to 70 percent, and Wall Street grumbled. John Kennedy went to Florida and denied he was soaking the rich. But after the steel crisis a year and a half earlier, the fat cats seemed to have had enough of Joe Kennedy's son.

In Philadelphia, analysts were discovering the white backlash as Mayor James H. J. Tate, an unimpressive party pol, squeaked back into office in a municipal election in which the Italian wards barely gave him a majority. A backlash like that against the President, the analysts said, could throw the 1964 election to Goldwater.

Congress was in a mess. It was not just that the narrow Democratic majorities and the Administration's political problems had bogged down the Kennedy program. The whole institution was under fire as an anachronism and Senator Thomas Dodd of Connecticut rose on the Senate floor to charge Majority Leader Mike Mansfield with adopting a "Wall Street attitude" and bankers' hours. The Republicans, he said, were doing nothing, not even providing effective opposition. Everett Dirksen rumbled that Dodd was a victim of "cerebral incoherence." To complete the picture of leaderless chaos, Senator Richard Russell, the South's head coach in Congress, accused his old ally, Charles Halleck of Indiana, of being "adorned in the leather shirt and tasseled moccasins" of the New Frontier because he was backing the civil-rights bill.

For the first time in the Kennedy Administration, the smell of scandal—a familiar odor in Washington—was in the air. Senator John McClellan, the righteous Arkansan who had helped Bob Kennedy pursue Jimmy Hoffa, lambasted Deputy Under Secretary of Defense Roswell L. Gilpatric for an alleged conflict of interest on the TFX. Billie Sol Estes, the Texas free enterpriser, appeared before a Senate hearing and took the Fifth. Secretary of the Navy Fred Korth—another Texan—had resigned and it soon was learned that he had been using Navy stationery for indiscreet private business correspondence. The headwaiter of the House of Representatives, one Ernest Petinaud, was taken on a Congressmen's junket to Paris for no apparent legislative purpose. None of this touched President Kennedy directly, but at a news conference he was forced to defend the moral climate of Washington in his time as being no worse than it was anywhere else.

The biggest scandal was the sudden emergence of a South Carolinian named Robert G. Baker, whom almost everyone in Washington knew, as something more than a good source on Senate affairs and a protégé of Vice-President Lyndon B. Johnson. People who weren't talking politics and Barry Goldwater were either talking about Bobby Baker or burning their files. Some did both.

Johnson had other troubles. The reports from the South were that the Vice-President, who had taken a strong stand behind the President's civil-rights bill, was in worse shape there than Mr. Kennedy himself. Johnson spent part of the month in the Benelux countries, making Atlantic Partnership speeches, but in his home state of Texas, he needed partnership more. There, Governor John Connally, another Johnson associate, and Senator Ralph Yarborough, an anti-Johnson Texas liberal, were locked in the kind of ideological feuding that makes Texas politics unique. The split was so bitter that it threatened to throw Texas' twenty-five electoral votes to Goldwater—and Johnson's main claim on the Kennedy Administration had been his ability to carry Texas and some of the South for the Democrats.

Robert Kennedy, moreover, had not wanted Johnson on the ticket even in 1960, recalling with resentment the Texan's sharp campaign remarks about John Kennedy and, worse, Joseph P. Kennedy. He had ignored the Vice-President for three years, as did many other Administration officials. Johnson, after all, was not in the spirit of the New

Frontier; Washington laughed at the story that he had gone to the unveiling of the Mona Lisa at the National Gallery in white tie and tails when the crowd was in black tie. The camel driver and the Texas bellow in the Taj Mahal had made Georgetown party-goers cringe with embarrassment, and everybody clucked in sympathy when Konrad Adenauer was shipped off to spend a weekend at the LBJ ranch. Where in God's name was *that*?

So there was talk, that November, of "dumping" Johnson in 1964. But one man did not ignore or treat Lyndon Johnson coolly. John Kennedy had a quietly effective relationship with his proud and difficult Vice-President. It was a direct relationship, strictly between two men; the Kennedy staff had to be circumvented since it tended to take the "Bobby line" on Johnson. The President listened to Johnson's advice on politics, though he did not always take it. He did not, for instance, follow through on a Johnson suggestion of a Southern speaking tour to pave the way for the 1964 civil-rights act. Nor was Johnson's advice often proffered unless sought. He would sit silently through high-level meetings, rarely injecting himself into them, absorbing information.

Kennedy gave him useful assignments—civil rights and Congressional liaison at home, goodwill trips abroad. Johnson was sent to deliver a major address in Berlin during the crisis of 1961. He was provided ample office space, staff, perquisites. There were frequent evidences of Kennedy's personal sensitivity to Johnson's feelings. When the White House Correspondents' Association, at an annual banquet, gave the President two silver carriage lamps, his response was notable for courtesy as well as for wit.

"Lyndon Johnson and I," he said, "will hang these in the White House—one for Everett Dirksen and two for Charley Halleck."

Johnson often praised Kennedy in private and he never tired of recalling the President's campaign defense of his religion before the Greater Houston Ministerial Association. Frequently, he added: "I was never so proud of an American as I was of Jack that night."

Kennedy may have recalled that it was Lyndon Johnson who had put him on the Senate Foreign Relations Committee—a breakthrough toward national stature. And at the 1956 Democratic National Convention, in the breakneck Kennedy-Kefauver fight for the vice-presidential nomination, Johnson as chairman of his delegation had cast "fifty-six votes for the fighting sailor who wears the scars of battle. . . ."

Above all, Kennedy had kept Johnson informed. The Vice-President was "in" in that sense, if not socially. He participated in most of the meetings on the Cuban missile crisis, for instance. No major government operations were going on anywhere that he did not have some knowledge of—unlike Harry Truman, who entered the White House and only then learned that he had an atom bomb ready to explode.

In return, Johnson appreciated the President's deference to him. He never violated the unofficial canon that vice-presidents ought to be seen and not heard; he never got out front with a news conference or an unguarded statement: I do not know of any reporter who got a "leak" from Johnson that damaged or denigrated the President. In fact, Johnson leaks of any kind were few and far between throughout his vice-presidency.

Moreover, vice-presidents—as presidents have allowed them more stature and responsibility—have come more and more to be regarded as important administration officials. To cast Johnson aside for 1964 would be politically embarrassing. Besides, Kennedy had said in 1960, when the two men were racing each other for the Democratic nomination:

"If I didn't want this job myself, I'd get behind Lyndon. He's the ablest man I know in American politics and he really cares about this country as I want a president to care."

Kennedy's entire treatment of Johnson suggests that he considered the Texan as a man who could take over the presidency capably, if need be, and there was nothing more important than that.

So he tried to scotch the "dump" rumors at a news conference. Johnson would be on the ticket again, he said, "of course he will, no question he will." But the capital was more impressed by the White House social office's announcement that Jacqueline Kennedy soon would accompany her husband to Texas on a political trip designed to help Johnson mend his home fences. Mrs. Kennedy, it was agreed, would be a powerful asset in Texas and if she campaigned for the ticket in 1964.

That month, there was of course the usual flow of Washington minutiae. President Kennedy interceded and saved Mrs. Kennedy's childhood home, Merrywood Estate on the Potomac, from being sold by her family to a high-rise apartment developer. He and the First Lady moved into their new $100,000 weekend house on Rattlesnake Mountain in Virginia. The Department of Labor added the high cost of dying to the price index. Norman Thomas turned seventy-nine and said he did not choose to run again. Earl Warren rejected a proposal by Representative Robert Ashmore of South Carolina and Judge Howard Smith of Virginia that "In God We Trust" be carved in stone above the Supreme Court bench.

The President watched a Polaris missile fired at Cape Canaveral. He also cut a ribbon above the Mason-Dixon line and opened the last link of an interstate highway that made it possible to drive from Washington to New York without hitting a traffic light, at a cost in tolls of $4.55. Then he went on to New York City and entered Manhattan without a police escort, adding eight minutes to the drive from the airport to the Carlyle Hotel, and causing a police official to remind him that he had taken "the most unnecessary risks." Earlier in the month, Kennedy had laid a wreath on the Tomb of the Unknown Soldier at the Arlington National Cemetery.

But what I recall mostly was the sense of trouble in the air—probably not irreparable trouble, but serious enough for worry. Goldwater, the backlash, Vietnam, hatred in the South—these were ominous portents, and we marked time until their meaning could be read. Questions at Kennedy news conferences frequently suggested that the President was in trouble. How did he feel about it?

That November, he told the reporters he still liked being President because "it's rewarding and I've given before the definition of happiness of the Greeks . . . the full use of your powers along lines of excellence. I find that, therefore, the presidency provides some happiness."

But James Reston of *The New York Times* made a swing around the country and came back to write:

> There is a vague feeling of doubt and disappointment in the country about President Kennedy's first term. . . . One has the distinct impression that the American people are going to reelect him, probably by a wide margin, but don't quite believe in him. . . . Accordingly, his problem is probably not how to get elected but how to govern. He is admired, but he has not made the people feel as he feels, or lifted them beyond their private purposes to see the larger purposes he has in mind.
>
> He is simply better known than anybody else, and this will probably be enough to assure his reelection, but this is a far cry from the atmosphere he promised when he ran for the presidency in 1960.

Then John Fitzgerald Kennedy went to Dallas and was murdered. The troubled and involuted Texan, Lyndon Johnson, became President and many people believe that at that moment—2:39 P.M., November 22, 1963—a Golden Age ended.

I sat in a stuffy, cramped room in the Baker Hotel in Dallas on the morning of November 23, when the great plane had borne its burden of mortality back to Washington, and the fact of death was palpable and fearful in every heart, and Lee Harvey Oswald was snarl-

ing his tiny pathetic defiance a few blocks away in the Dallas jail.
I wrote that morning what I thought about the way things were, and
would be.

Perhaps only at the death of a President does it come fully
clear how nearly the national life—the basic expression of what
John F. Kennedy loved to call "the great republic"—has become
centralized and symbolized in the White House and the man who
lives there. What is most certain today, as Lyndon Johnson ends
his first twenty-four hours as President, is that there will be little
change, yet there will be great change.

There will be little change because the national life and a
nation's course are not irrelevant affairs, swinging wildly like a
weather vane in any gale. A national life and course spring
fundamentally from an almost algebraic total of all the people,
their areas, the interests, the activities, the ideas, that are contained within it. And the death of a man, even of a President,
will not much change these matters. The harsh fact of death is
that life goes on about as it did before.

Nor is the Presidency an office of whim and inclination. Great
imperatives always act upon it. The necessities pile up. The limitations remain. Wheels in motion are hard to stop; not easily
slowed or speeded. The world in which a nation exists, no less
than the nation itself, spins remorselessly upon its axis—diminished by all deaths, altered by few.

Yet, the accession of Lyndon Johnson to the office of John
Kennedy will bring great change, too. For if the Presidency imposes upon its occupant its own inescapable requirements, yet
the manner and style in which he makes what may even be inevitable responses are vital ingredients of those responses.

Now it is two years later and there has been little change—yet
there *has* been great change. The issues and problems are much the
same and if there is greater concern over the situation abroad there
is demonstrably more achievement at home. But men say the Golden
Age is gone—implying, perhaps believing, that the Kennedy years were
a period of higher heart and broader spirit, a sort of Instant Greece,
when everything from art to athletics flowered, and the people rose
above themselves.

It is a peculiar and gripping notion. Johnson fans—in whom, if
not in their champion, a spirit of resignation is becoming evident—
may argue all they wish but to no avail that their man is the one who
is getting things done.

It is generally conceded here that Johnson has unsurpassed gifts
of political leadership, and that he has a remarkable knowledge of the

government's intricate and cumbersome machinery, soaked up in thirty years of getting things done in Washington. His is not the professional political manager's encyclopedic knowledge of every courthouse hack and precinct boss in the country and his reliance is not upon a vast network of operatives turning the country into a "Johnson machine." Rather, Mr. Johnson's supreme gift is an eerie and entirely personal instinct for the place where the power lies—whether it be the crucial votes needed to swing a controversial measure in the House, or the powerful national interest that must be mollified or persuaded, or the appointment or proposal that will produce the maximum effect on the populace.

Scarcely less awe-inspiring is the Johnson sense of timing. He can be forced—as the Reverend Martin Luther King showed when he used the Selma crisis to speed presentation of a voting-rights bill. But he can resist forcing, too—as when he refused, last summer, to be pushed into surrendering the United States' position on financing the United Nations before he had the ground prepared. Usually, his timing is precisely his own—as when he presented his Vietnam resolution to Congress the day after the Gulf of Tonkin crisis. He had been carrying it around in his pocket for weeks waiting for the moment.

Because of these gifts, and his titanic ability to persuade—or overwhelm—it was Lyndon Johnson who pushed through the tax-cut and civil-rights bills, who settled the rail strike, who took charge of Congress and got it moving again even with the same narrow Democratic majorities that plagued Kennedy, who neutralized Otto Passman's depredations on the aid program, cut the fat out of the budget, and overcame the religious deadlock on Federal aid to education. It was Johnson who smashed Barry Goldwater and won the Big Landslide. It was he—not Kennedy—who cut most eloquently to the heart of the "Negro problem" with his monumental commencement address to the Howard University Class of 1965, and it was he—not Kennedy—who achieved medical care for the aged.

He has kept prosperity booming along, really attacked the balance-of-payments deficit, and proclaimed goals in his Great Society program that may be more specific and desirable than any comparable outline ever given us in the Golden Age.

Yet, when Lyndon Johnson turned the White House over to a national festival of the arts, the artists replied by attacking his foreign policy and snickering, in some cases, at the cultural effort. The Negro leaders remain suspicious of his Southern accent, heritage and Congressional voting record. The liberal intellectuals bemoan his manners, impugn his sincerity, and head for the universities. His regulatory appointments, although so far they have been excellent, are searched microscopically for traces of oil and gas, and his new man in the anti-trust department, Donald Turner, is watched to make sure he does not turn the economy over to Big Business—although no one was less prominent than the trustbusters in Kennedy's time.

It is a sad and terrible likelihood that Lyndon Johnson will not live down the fact that he followed John Kennedy. "It seems I have been waiting all my life for this moment," Johnson said, the night before he won the greatest political victory in American history. But the shadow of Kennedy will fall on him all his days.

One suspects he knows it and struggles against it. He reflects the unfairness of it in small telling ways—an insistence to visitors, for instance, that *his* staff is better than Kennedy's. The prime ministers of two countries, he once confided, had come to him for information on how he had handled poverty and medicare legislation—and "these are *sophisticated* people with real *style.*" The country boy who went to Southwest State Teachers' College, he will say slyly, is putting through legislation the intellectuals from Harvard couldn't pass. The impression Johnson frequently leaves is that Kennedy mismanaged Congress, botched some tough problems, and turned too many "kids" loose on men's work.

Yet, he once brought tears to Bob Kennedy's eyes at a White House memorial service and he can speak movingly and with obvious sincerity of the man who helped him keep his self-respect in the obscurity of the vice-presidency. It is not John Kennedy himself that Lyndon Johnson resents; it is Washington's unwillingness to let each claim his own greatness without comparison to the other.

Most of Washington's unhappiness with Lyndon Johnson rises subtly from just such a comparison. There is, first, the famous matter of style. It is a commonplace nowadays to say that Johnson has none. In fact, he has a more identifiable style than Kennedy had but it is the outsize and outgoing style of the West. He is an imperious range boss, with expansive notions that everything is possible, an earthy turn of phrase, and the occasional crudities and intensities of a background rooted in poverty, social bitterness, a lack of amenities, and a fierce determination to overcome these influences. He sets a lot of store by size, like his state and the West generally, and as a result his moods and everything about him—including the derogatory stories and the claims of his followers—tend to be out of proportion and overblown, just as the old Western tales of gunmen, cowpokes, and Indians have grown into romantic legends that obscure the hard, dusty, monotonous, lonely, and exploited lives of the early Western men.

Johnson's worst problem is this excess. It is reflected, first, in his own personality, all of whose components are outsize—his vanity and his guile, his personal impulsiveness and his public caution, his rages and his joys, his drive and his compulsive need for people around him, his ruthlessness and his warmth, the transparence of the "image" he seeks in public and the sincerity he can convey in private.

In turn each of these magnified proportions of Johnson is magnified again—enormously—by the constant play of publicity and attention on the man in the White House. A vastly human—not superhuman—man whose strength is essentially private, cast by fate into the most public place on earth, Johnson's every burst of anger seems a tantrum, and his slightest act of pettiness, his most casual slip of tongue or manners, is escalated into the cruelties of Caligula.

It is another commonplace to say that Johnson is just a politician —and nothing can be said about a public man in America that is more damning. Somehow, we want our leaders to rise above politics, like Dwight Eisenhower, and we can be unforgiving of those who don't. Johnson's struggle for existence in the jungle of Texas politics, his slick maneuvering in the Senate, his accumulated wealth, his lack of simon-pure liberal history, and his genius for compromise—hated word! upon which the Republic is founded—make up a record that brings enduring suspicion on his head from a people passionately convinced that politics is a dirty business with which Presidents ought not to trifle.

The living and breathing reminders, the flesh-and-blood heirs of the Golden Age, moreover, are right here with us. Nothing perpetuates the memory of what was, nor heightens the sense of it, like the presence and voices of Robert and Ted Kennedy in the United States Senate. The strong physical resemblances, the close association of Bob Kennedy with every act and attitude of the Kennedy Administration, the known facts that he opposed his brother's selection of Lyndon Johnson as his running mate and that Johnson scratched Bobby Kennedy from *his* vice-presidential list last year—all these embellish the conclusion taken for granted in Washington that Robert Kennedy himself will run for President some day. The net effect here is that the unspoken attitude toward Lyndon Johnson of many people in Washington is that he is somehow a Constitutional usurper who does not belong where he is.

All these themes reached crescendo when Johnson loosed the bombers on North Vietnam and intervened in the Dominican Republic. History, says the old saw, must judge these actions, but meanwhile much of Washington has assumed the task. The crude politician in the White House, it is asserted, doesn't understand foreign affairs (as Kennedy did and Bobby would), believes in throwing American weight around overseas, and is dangerously willing to use the Armed Forces to get his way. Johnson did not start the Vietnamese war, of course, and no one knows how John Kennedy, who would have been surrounded by virtually the same advisors, might have reacted in 1964 and 1965 to the same circumstances; nevertheless, there are those who are convinced that they voted against Goldwater and got him anyway.

Thus, it is here, in this self-transfixed company town of the American people, that the Golden Age counts its most passionate believers, and it is here that the Johnson Administration is at its nadir of esteem. Yet, that is only half the story. For if Washington is not happy about Johnson and lifts its Martini glass nightly to the Golden Age, yet no one seriously disputes that Lyndon Johnson is in charge here now and that what his adherents say is true: things *are* being done. The pace, if anything, has quickened and unless one buried his capacity for excitement with John Kennedy on the slope at Arlington, one still finds here the fascination of action and challenge and of men responding to their world.

This is a paradox that invites study. The Golden Age has passed and is mourned, yet its works continue and are in many ways improved. Perhaps Pat Moynihan, the brilliant and perceptive former Assistant Secretary of Labor who now is running for office in New York City, put his finger on it a few days after John Kennedy's death. "We'll laugh again," he said, "but we'll never be young again."

I think that gets at the truth because it fixes the real difference in the Golden Age and the present time where it belongs—on us. I believe the Golden Age actually was the Age of a Golden Figure. And we have erected that figure into such a towering symbol ("Towering," Lyndon Johnson recently told a speechwriter, "is a Kennedy word. Take it out.") that it diminishes all else. We remember John Kennedy for what we wanted to be and we do not like to admit that Lyndon Johnson takes us for what we are.

Here was this handsome young man of wit and elegance and wealth and education, this Irishman who like so many other Americans had come unscathed and affluent from the melting pot, this earnest and perceptive thinker who could deal familiarly with the baffling complexities of the world, this tough competitor in whom we sensed the steel that is as inevitably a part of the American tradition as Daniel Boone's rifle, Andrew Carnegie's forge, and Franklin Roosevelt's leg braces.

Like Adlai Stevenson, Kennedy was a public leader who could give eloquent voice to what he believed, who seemed to embody in public behavior and appearance the flowering of a civilization. For that reason, primarily, he could attract first-rate men to his service (many of them old Stevensonians). And when he had the power to do it, he was unafraid to move in new directions and to defend his decisions; it was Kennedy who adopted the new economics and who, having faced down Khrushchev in the Cuban missile crisis, sought the test ban treaty and a détente in the Cold War.

Beyond all that, he was obviously a hell of a guy. ("He's a swinger," a teen-age girl told me during the 1960 campaign.) Kennedy had beaten the odds on death as a war hero. He had beaten the odds on life by being born rich and marrying a beauty who could charm de Gaulle, redecorate the White House, and ride to hounds. And he had beaten the odds on history, despite his Catholicism and his inexperience, by winning the Democratic nomination and edging Nixon.

He was reported to be a sharp golfer when his back was right, roamed with the jet set, welcomed longhairs to the White House, hobnobbed with movie stars, had cute kids, and spent his weekends in glamour at Hyannis Port, Palm Beach, and Palm Springs. During his time in the White House, it was an article of faith with red-blooded American males (and not a few women) that the President was a lady killer who had won the favors of every eager beauty between Hollywood and the Via Veneto.

After he reached for the presidency and won it, Kennedy was seldom called "just a politician." He was certainly no snake-oil artist. He made demands, preached sacrifice, spoke of difficult days ahead, even questioned whether the Republic could endure. To the people he addressed, he said, "you must." Above all—from the day he decided it was possible that a Catholic could be elected until the day he died, when he refused to put on a big Texas hat and two six-guns—he challenged the American myths. He rejected posturing and dogma and shibboleths, and to many Americans, particularly the young, he offered the hope that a new generation could cast aside the past and handle its own problems in its own way—that it could be itself. He was the Holden Caulfield of American politics.

To idealistic young people, to skeptical intellectuals, to Americans weary of the materialism and mass culture of their society, he struck all the right notes. They listened to his eloquence, were fascinated by his style, and approved of his distinction. He became their symbol and their ideal, the Golden Figure, the proof in himself that America could have learning and urbanity and elegance and wealth and pleasure and beauty—and still have its strength and vigor and idealism.

Lyndon Johnson would have been no such Golden Figure had John Kennedy never lived. The essence of *his* leadership is not public and his weapon is not the word, nor the symbol. Instead he plays upon men's ambitions and interests and weaknesses and beliefs as if he were an artist at the yellowing keyboard of human nature.

If John Kennedy seemed, to a romantic and doggedly idealistic people, bogged down in a materialism they both desire and despise, the symbol of the civilization America was destined to produce, then Lyndon Johnson is the masterpiece, the perfect instrument, of the politics America did produce. And a political system that works reflects a people.

For some, that is what is too much, too hard to take—not Johnson's style, not his foreign policy, not his political maneuvers, but the fact that somehow he makes the wheels go around and the country move.

To admit that is to admit that we need politicians and politics, we need manipulation, we do have ambitions and interests and weaknesses and beliefs that can ensnarl or release us—we are not golden but human.

For my part, I am glad to have lived in the age of John Kennedy and Lyndon Johnson. I don't count that other time more glorious than this. I am not concerned with which was the greater. Kennedy gave us a vision and Johnson is giving us reality and I say we need both. We have too seldom had either.

2
Power and Purpose in Domestic Affairs: Economic Policy, Big Steel, Civil Rights

It was said earlier that the American system is not one of separated powers but of separated institutions with shared powers—that is to say, both the president and Congress participate in the making of laws and strong presidents have strong programs. A president's philosophy obviously determines the direction and the force of policies he chooses, but his leadership requires the acquiescence of Congress since it enacts the laws. In economic matters President Kennedy's philosophy was rather conservative when he assumed office, but by January 1963 he had become an economic liberal, meaning he had accepted the main outlines of the economic views of Keynes, as discussed in the Introduction.

Three converging forces influenced this change: an unstable economy, a Congress that was skeptical about increased spending programs, and a group of advisers—intellectuals, that is—comprising the Council of Economic Advisers. A recovery in the economy which had begun in 1961 failed to sustain itself and began to slow down and splutter, with signs of the onset of a mild recession and a diminishing rate of economic growth. In May 1962 the stock market fell and the spring of 1962 was, according to Edward S. Flash, one of gloom and discontent. Theodore Sorensen does not go so far but admits that the consensus among the advisers was that "unemployment was too high, that Budget deficits at such times were both unavoidable and useful, and that consumer purchasing power should be more strongly supported by Federal actions than had been true under previous administrations." In general, President Kennedy was not very well informed in the study of economics (like many of us), but (unlike many of us) he did read, and he listened to advisers, and he learned from them.

As the Part One Commentary indicates, federal spending under Kennedy increased substantially from 1961 to 1963, but while his spending programs were geared in 1961 to produce specific benefits in specific programs, the spending and tax policies in 1963 were being fitted to general economic conditions. That is to say, by 1963, President Kennedy was proposing a tax cut, increased spending, and an increasing deficit as a combination of actions intended to produce sustained growth, increasing employment, and consumer welfare.

The decision to concentrate upon the improvement of the growth rate by the several indicated policies was a decision to improve the whole in the expectation that the parts would prosper. An active approach with a somewhat different emphasis, however, was that favored by John Kenneth Galbraith, who argued the benefits of more public spending. He was critical of the tax cut and thought, according to Sorensen, that a ten billion dollar increase in federal expenditures would do more good than a ten billion dollar tax cut. Others in the circle of President Kennedy's advisers urged heavily increased outlays for public works and other specific activities of benefit to special social and professional communities.

It will be remembered that effective control in the 87th Congress was in the hands of conservatives, although the Democratic Party had substantial majorities in both houses. The proponents of a cautious policy toward the prevention of recession argued that tax reform was the course to take, a reform that would close loopholes in the tax laws and eliminate the kinds of privilege that benefit the few. The tax base would thus be broadened but not at the expense of the smaller tax payers who necessarily have to spend most of their income, and increased revenues (deriving from tax reform) would be available for spending programs. The view came to prevail, however, that tax reduction rather than tax reform was the better policy for the problems of unemployment and economic stagnation because it would put money directly into the hands of those most likely to spend it (the small consumer), thereby sustaining demand and creating jobs that would reduce unemployment. Although Secretary of the Treasury Dillon preferred the cautious approach, President Kennedy took the bolder line and, as has been said, set it out in his budget message in January 1963; but the prospect of passage did not seem to be especially hopeful. The Congress had been unwilling to enact even a temporary tax cut in the summer of 1962, and the chance that it would enact one when the feared recession actually failed to materialize, and at a time when deficits were increasing, seemed to be remote. The tax bill was finally enacted, however, with the help of a television appearance by the president and the assistance of his successor in the White House.

It seems to be generally agreed that although President Kennedy took advice on economic matters from many people—J. Kenneth Galbraith, Paul Samuelson, and Seymour Harris, for example—his conversion from an economic conservative into an economic liberal is probably due to the influence of the Council of Economic Advisers, and especially its chairman, Walter Heller, of the University of Minnesota. The statements by Edward S. Flash and Herbert Stein, printed below, give credit to the CEA and Heller, and both suggest that the conversion is a good example of the influence of intellectuals, a thought that might be considered in connection with the selections in Part Four. Flash concentrates upon the changing of Kennedy from an economic conservative to a liberal Keynesian, and discusses the influence of experts (especially Heller) in bringing it about. Stein concentrates upon the tax cut and the relation between Kennedy and intellectuals, and on how decisions are made. Stein was later appointed to the Council of Economic Advisers himself when President Nixon assumed office, and eventually became its chairman.

In the course of the anxiety in 1962 about the state of the economy and the recession that never materialized, there occurred a controversy over a rise in the price of steel products, which supplies an example of another kind of presidential leadership more specific and coercive than the general education of the country and the Congress to which Kennedy devoted himself as he, at the same time, was learning some economics. The confrontation between President Kennedy and Roger Blough, head of United States Steel, over a proposed price increase shows the great range of influences that the

president has at his command; and in some cases, as in the activity
of his brother, Attorney General Robert Kennedy, how power may
possibly be misused to produce desired results. Hobart Rowan
discusses the Big Steel crisis and the cross-pull of pressures, public
and private, employed to force the United States Steel Corporation to
rescind its price increase.

It is possible, as some have suggested, that President Kennedy
overreacted in this crisis, an overreaction rooted not in the substantive
damage to the economy threatened by the proposed price increase,
but by the affront to Kennedy's image of himself as a leader. Readers
may wish to consider this suggestion in connection with the discussion
of symbol as power in the Introduction and in Part Four. It may be
noted also that William Carleton, in the piece set out in Part Three,
thought that Kennedy had overreacted on another occasion—the
Berlin crisis—and perhaps for the same suggested reason. David
Horowitz in Part Three intimates that President Kennedy's handling
of the Cuban missile crisis was motivated by considerations of prestige
and image. Success in all these encounters undoubtedly begets
prestige and prestige is an ingredient of presidential power. The
conjunction of public and personal values in the exercise of presidential power is doubtless inevitable although it would be a compromise
of the public trust if the second should dominate the first.

Effective presidential leadership requires the setting and ad-
vancement of clear national priorities, and today few would disagree
that one of the top priorities is the full restoration to the black
population of the rights that the Constitution of the United States
says is theirs. The record seems to indicate that President Kennedy
did not, until the summer of 1963, exhibit a really strong degree of
public commitment to this cause. As Walter Lippmann points out
in the short piece of his reprinted below, President Kennedy had no
initial major proposals on civil rights. He comments on Kennedy's
legislative strategy in going slow on civil rights in exchange for
Southern support on the tax bill. But President Kennedy came to
realize rather suddenly that the tokenism of a telephone call to the
wife of Martin Luther King, held in a Georgia jail during the
presidential election campaign of 1960, could hardly press forward the
cause of black civil rights, however much it might have benefited
Kennedy in the campaign. It was the fight to prevent the enrollment
of two blacks at the University of Alabama in 1963 that led him to
stake his personal prestige and all his power on the Negro cause.
T. George Harris discusses in some detail the influence that the
activities of Martin Luther King had in producing the progressive

civil rights policy to which President Kennedy eventually committed himself, and which his successor had enacted into law.

Perhaps there are three lessons about presidential leadership in the material in Part Two. The first is that a president's conceptual limitations will reflect themselves in the policies he advocates and opposes, as in the case of Kennedy's economic conservatism and his imperfect perception of the vital significance of the civil rights movement. Second, presidential leadership often must pay for benefits out of costs—to get a tax cut, it seemed to be necessary to compromise on basic civil rights. What you can afford to buy depends in large part on how much you want to pay, and upon whom you are willing to lay the sacrifice. And, third, the very prestige of the office of the president is enough to get him the immediate attention of all the media, as in the confrontation over the Big Steel price increase, and the resources of the White House for the harassment of private citizens and newspaper people are very great also. When the full powers of the executive are synchronized and raised in pitch and tempo, the blast is likely to be obliterating.

This section concludes with a judgment by Rexford Guy Tugwell (once a prominent New Dealer) on President Kennedy's domestic program, and it may seem to some to withhold generosity, beginning as it does with the assertion that "nothing of note was accomplished." But for the student of leadership the significance of the criticism may lie less in the verdict than in the oblique acknowledgments that presumably support it. Tugwell faults Kennedy for not fully appreciating the importance of the massive migration of people to the cities and the developing urban crisis with its racial complications, extending thereby the failures of Truman and Eisenhower who were neglectful in this respect. But Kennedy, he says, was not obsessed (as were his predecessors) with Communist designs; the Congress was in the hands of Northern and Southern conservatives and he had little power to move it; if he had lived he might have done all that President Johnson did, and better. And he might have avoided the agonies of an extended land war in Asia. These remarks, although speculative, have high value since they come from a critic.

Edward S. Flash

Conversion of Kennedy from Economic Conservative to Economic Liberal

If the delivery of the President's Special Message on Taxation completed the development of the proposals as proposals, what conclusions can be drawn regarding the contribution of the Heller Council to that development? In this specific case, what difference did the Council make? What does its contribution to tax revision as one area of economic policy suggest regarding the overall significance of its performance?

There seems little doubt that the Heller Council developed and gained acceptance for the economic philosophy upon which the tax program was built. The sterility of the five-year lag, the gap between progress and potential, the resistance to improvement of unemployment, and the drag of the wartime tax structure constituted the elements calling for change. Tax reduction, expansion of consumption relative to investment, deficit based upon full-employment surplus, and applications of both multiplier and accelerator concepts made up the countering elements on the basis of which answers to the call would be developed. Together the elements comprised a compelling leitmotif repeated throughout the development of the program. Based on a combination of Keynesian analysis, a Commons interest in human welfare, and a New Frontier sense of purpose, the resulting composition was given its first public try-out before the Joint Economic Committee in March, 1961. After its second presentation in the January, 1962, *Economic Report,* the piece was refined, expanded, and played with increasing frequency—both publicly and privately—throughout the year. Ignored at first, it gradually became acceptable and was then adopted as part of the Administration's repertoire with its most notable performance in the 1963 *Economic Report.*

As for the tax program itself, the Council had virtually no hand in the development of the reform proposals. The Council lost its battle for proposing a tax cut in the summer of 1962; it failed in its effort to avoid spacing the 1963 program reductions over three years and to have reduction proposals considered unencumbered by reform measures.

From Economic Advice and Presidential Leadership *by Edward S. Flash. New York: Columbia University Press, 1965, pp. 269–275. Reprinted by permission of the publisher.*

In short, the program was basically that of the Treasury. The Council, by its argument and education, however, sold the idea of tax reduction on its own merits and having brought the idea through the consideration of whether or not to seek cuts, the Council then shaded the contents of some of its specific aspects. The $10-billion net reduction approximates what Heller had in mind and although the reductions were spread over three years rather than concentrated in one, smaller initially than Heller had advocated, applicable later than he thought appropriate, and more tightly bound to reform than he thought wise, Heller's arguments very likely saved the reductions from being even more thoroughly compromised. This influence meant in turn that the Administration accepted a larger deficit than it originally had had in mind. Furthermore, the Council's persistent pressure for tax relief for the consumer probably caused the proportion of tax reduction to be larger for the individual than for the corporation and larger for the lower and middle brackets than for the upper brackets than originally had been envisaged.

In expounding its views, the Council educated not just the President, Congress, and the public, but also Treasury. It is reasonable to conclude that Treasury architects accepted the Council's viewpoint to the degree that they felt possible by the time the tax proposals had reached the final stage of ratification. It is also reasonable to assume that "liberals" within Treasury, such as Brazer, would not have been able to modify Treasury's stand without outside help from the Council. In other words, Treasury's final tax proposals represented a balance between Heller and Mills, between reduction and reform, that would not have been the same had there been no Heller. The sense of accomplishment that Heller and his associates may have had over the ultimate passage of a bill involving an $11.5-billion net reduction may have been tempered by both the delay in its passage and the fate of the reforms that the Council too had favored. But at least the Council's economic arguments on behalf of reduction appear to have won general political acceptance. To the reformers in Treasury went the bitter pill of seeing proposed structural reforms designed to increase revenues by $3.5 billion whittled down by the legislative process to reforms producing only an additional $300 million.

As demonstrated by the Administration's tax program, the primary significance of the Heller Council is that it was the most important single creative force in the development of a new approach to economic policy. As the Employment Act of 1946 ratified the government's responsibility for the nation's economic welfare (and hence its acceptance of Keynesian principles), the tax proposals of 1963 signaled the policy-maker's recognition that expenditure-revenue combinations leading to deficits can be a constructive force in economic growth. Policy thinking became more consistent with economic thinking. A new tradition was established. The Council analyzed, advocated, articulated, and gained acceptance for new economic values, new techniques of economic analysis, and new concepts of fiscal policy as a positive contributor to national economic well-being. As recognized in subsequent paragraphs, the Council's was not a solo performance, but among its peers the Council took a lead which it did not relinquish; it persuaded, cooperated, and competed with tact and effectiveness.

Of parallel significance is the fact that the Heller Council won Kennedy's acceptance of its views. It is quite a turnabout for a President to commit himself to a balanced budget one year and defend a voluntarily incurred deficit the next. Heller provided the President, who was above all else a pragmatic politician, with an economic force or model against which, on economic matters, political or noneconomic forces could be measured.

My own belief is that the Council, primarily in the person of its Chairman, encouraged Kennedy to develop a sophisticated economic philosophy which he had not previously possessed and, in so doing, transformed an instinctive conservative into a conscious liberal. It is impossible to say how much of this transformation was a matter of Heller's actually changing Kennedy's mind, that is, his convictions, on economic policy and how much was a matter of strengthening his willingness to champion publicly Keynesian full-employment economics that he may already have privately accepted, regardless of the political consequences. The first refers to his thinking and the second to his strategy; Heller apparently affected both. The conservatism that Kennedy preached in 1961 appears to have been synonymous with the conservatism he thought. The first half of 1962 was marked by a conflict between the public stance he felt obliged to take and the developing shift in his thinking. His espousal of tax reduction in the latter half of the year reflected a return to relative coincidence between his thinking and his public advocacy.

Correspondingly, in the beginning the Council was more tolerated than successful. Subsequently, it was more successful in principle than in practice, but ultimately it was successful on both counts. This progression in turn indicated a growing acceptance of the Council for its views and also for its competence. The Heller Council was part of an Administration that valued competence highly and penalized incompetence with exclusion. The Council made the grade with Kenneth O'Donnell and Lawrence O'Brien as well as with the President. Such acceptance was translated into generally harmonious relations with the Budget Bureau, the Treasury, the Federal Reserve, and the wide range of other agencies with which the Council dealt. Such disenchantment with the Council as there was appeared to come primarily from the antigovernment businessmen who thought the Council did too much and segments of the labor phalanx which objected to the Council's putting less emphasis upon larger expenditures than upon tax reduction and also to the Council's attempt to cultivate business groups.

The significant impact of the Heller Council is important in itself, but the explanations for it are no less important. At the risk of oversimplification, four separate but related reasons for the Council's impact emerge:

1. The faltering in early 1962 of a recovery started barely twelve months before, another in a series of postwar falterings, enhanced the Council's arguments with acceptance and urgency. The persistence of the balance-of-payments problem forced a close examination of cause and effect, to say nothing of a search for new approaches. The success of the "twist" policy of high, short-term and low, long-term interest rates gave an indication of what experimentation might accomplish. The postwar prosperity and relatively greater rate of economic growth of competing countries provided convenient and tempting examples of advantages to be derived from economic planning and liberal deficit policies. The refusal of Congress to accept expenditure increases, as initially favored by Heller, obliged both the Council and the Administration to turn their attention to tax reduction.

2. The Council had in Kennedy a remarkably receptive and educable President. He was at the time the first President of the United States and only world leader born in the twentieth century willing to grasp and work with modern economics. His concept of the Presidency, his style of political leadership, and the issues with which he was attempting to deal encouraged, even forced, him to make full use of the Council. Kennedy's pragmatic responsiveness to unfolding developments at home and abroad, his rapport with intellectuals, and his impatience with the pace of public affairs in general and of Congress in particular combined to yield a unique receptivity to the Council's views as well as harmonious working relationships.

3. As a Budget Bureau colleague remarked, "Heller was lucky in his Secretary of the Treasury." Despite the fundamental difference in orientations between Heller's emphasis on growth and Dillon's on stability, they were both able men in their respective roles. Each could understand and respect the views and responsibilities of the other. Each apparently had a very high regard for the ability of the other. Their differences, as important as they were in, for example, the tax proposals, were more in terms of emphasis than of principle, of timing than

of content. Heller was thought to be more ebullient than Dillon, who was known for his calm reserve, but each was able to communicate with the other, to cooperate on a broad variety of projects, to adjust to the views of one another and—more important—to those of the President. Such an association did not rule out competition, but it did mean competition in compromise rather than in divisive conflict. This creative variety of competitive relationship extended to the staff levels of the Council and Treasury and also to the other components of the Kennedy Administration led by men such as Bell and then Gordon of the Bureau of the Budget and Martin and his Federal Reserve. Between like-minded men of considerable ability there existed in their work a spirit of rapport and mutual assistance essential to the Council's achievement and to its assistance to others.

4. The Heller Council was in 1961 and 1962 a strong Council composed generally of very able, well-led, aggressive, amazingly hard-working, and productive professionals. The Council was able to capitalize on the experiences of its predecessors and from the developments in economic knowledge, in improved statistical data, and in advanced quantitative analysis. Under Heller's driving force, the Council became a round-the-clock scout on the New Frontier.

In short, the Heller Council was in harmony with its times. In an era of change, the Council advocated change, change that spanned economic, social, political, and technological developments, change that was as tidal as civil rights and as explosive as Cuba. The Council too was in a hurry; to be passive and conventional in public policy was to be out of tune.

Part of the anguish over Kennedy's assassination is the belief held by many that he was beginning to break out of the detached uncommitted approach to issues of which James MacGregor Burns had written only four years previously and of which some of his own lieutenants complained in the summer of 1962. "If we only knew what he really wanted," they would say. It is not too great a tribute to suggest that the Heller Council was one of the contributors to the emergent breakthrough. On November 22, Heller was part of a delegation led by Secretary of State Rusk en route to Japan to develop more effective economic arrangements with that nation. He was working with Dillon, Martin, George Ball, and McGeorge Bundy on promoting international monetary reforms. Heller had received permission to proceed with the development of the antipoverty program, upon which Robert Lampman of the Council staff had done the preliminary work. Although under attack, the Council's guides to wage rates were established as a major factor in labor-management wage negotiation. In part coincidental with, in part an outgrowth of the Council's contribution to the 1963 tax program, the guidelines represent a new breadth and depth of policy involvement achieved by the Council and encouraged by Kennedy.

After the assassination, Heller developed close working relationships with President Johnson. However, after almost four years of sixty-to-eighty-hour weeks, he resigned in November, 1964, to return to the University of Minnesota. The Council chairmanship was assumed by Gardner Ackley. To fill not only Ackley's place but also that of John P. Lewis, who had resigned earlier in the year to take a position with AID in India, Johnson appointed Arthur Okun of Yale and formerly of the Council staff and Otto Eckstein, a frequent consultant to the Council from Harvard. To these professionals and their colleagues has gone the responsibility of advising a far different President and an increasingly different Administration on ways to achieve "The Great Society."

Herbert Stein

Tax Cut in Camelot

Between the time of Herbert Hoover and the time of John F. Kennedy a revolution occurred in American fiscal policy. This revolution was the main ingredient in the transition to the "new economics," the coming of which was widely hailed in the early 1960's as the basis for confidence that full employment and steady growth would be maintained in the future.

The act which more than any other came to symbolize the fiscal revolution was the tax reduction of 1964. On John Kennedy's Inauguration Day in January, 1961, the stage was set for that act. The play had been written, a receptive or at least permissive audience was in its seats, and the actors were in the wings. However, the action was not to begin immediately.

The stage setting was the longest, most serious, period of unemployment since the War. It was almost three-and-a-half years since unemployment had been near the conventional 4 percent measure of high employment. After an abortive recovery from the 1958 recession, unemployment had risen again and was nearing 7 percent on Inauguration Day. Moreover, the recent experience led to the fear that the next recovery, when it came, would also stop short of high employment. Two other items were prominent in the scene. First, tax rates were so high, relative to expenditures, that they would yield a large surplus at high employment. There was room to cut taxes or raise expenditures and still retain the expectation that the budget would be in balance when high employment was regained. Second, the balance-of-payments deficit was believed to require high interest rates in the United States to curb the flow of United States funds to the rest of the world. This meant that the 1960 Democratic campaign formula of easy money with budget surpluses could not be relied upon to achieve high employment because that was a formula for low interest rates. The main, if not exclusive, reliance for economic stimulation would have to be placed on fiscal policy.

There were several possible routes to the conclusion that tax reduction was the appropriate act to be performed on this stage. According to conventional "functional finance" principles, the principles to be found in the textbooks of 1961, when unemployment is high the budget deficit should be increased. With the more cautious principles of the Committee for Economic Development, the 1949 Douglas Committee, and others of the postwar consensus, a large full-employment surplus should be reduced to more moderate size in the absence of strong evidence of inflationary danger. And even if fiscal policy was not to be used to manage the level of economic activity, a balance-of-payments deficit might call for a reduction of taxes, relative to expenditures, in order to raise interest rates and curb the flow of dollars abroad. This idea was commonly advanced in European financial circles. Certainly the combination of excessive unemployment, a large high employment surplus, and a balance-of-payments deficit wrote the script for expansive fiscal policy. And most of the informed audience would have agreed that if the play was to be a success, the main act would have to be tax reduction. Moreover, there were many who wanted taxes reduced.

How the country would receive this act—tax reduction—was more in question but should not have been. That part of the labor movement which expressed opinions on national economic policy, as distinguished from labor policy, had been for fiscal expansion for years. A considerable sector of the business and financial community had come to accept compensatory fiscal policy, if not in totally uninhibited form then in the form of balancing the budget at high employment or in some version of cyclical balancing. Even among those who had not come that far, the desire for tax reduction was so great that they were prepared to swallow its unorthodox fiscal trimmings. Much of the Republican national leadership—outside the Congress—accepted the role of expansionist tax reduction, and although they would not cheer a Democratic Administration for doing it they would not make a great issue of it either. Mr. Nixon's approval of tax reduction as an expansive measure had been clear in 1958 and 1960.

Of course, there would be opposition, especially in the Congress. Much of the opposition would be partisan and ritualistic, and would require a partisan and ritualistic response. Given their standing in Congress, the opponents could delay the outcome. But they could not prevent it, nor punish those who produced it. In the postwar period, there had been several cases in which Congress had tried, successfully and unsuccessfully, to cut taxes against the opposition of the President. There were no cases of Congressional resistance to tax reduction proposed by the administration.

The players who were to perform the tax reduction were President Kennedy and his advisers. We shall turn to them in a moment. But first it must be made clear that although the setting, the script, and the audience were prepared, the performance was not easy or inevitable. In 1492, it was known that the earth was round. Columbus had neither made it round nor discovered its shape. Others had made long ocean voyages before him, and some, it would appear, had been to America. But it was not inevitable that Columbus should go to America in 1492, and the fact that the times were ripe does not detract from the performance. Decisions still had to be made, and they required courage.

Did the Plot Call for a Tax Cut?

The Kennedy Administration could not be sure that the conditions called for a tax cut according to their own guidebook. By early 1961, the appraisal of the economic situation as one of persistent sluggishness, and not merely transitory recession, was a common one. But this was an economic forecast like many others, and it could be wrong. If it were wrong, a large tax cut might only open the way for the return of inflation. The idea that the balance-of-payments deficit called for reducing taxes rather than balancing the budget was also common. But there was an opposing view that the first essential was to reassure our foreign creditors by pursuing a sound fiscal policy.

Moreover, aside from its appraisal of the economic situation, the administration was not sure that tax-cutting was the role it had been chosen to play. Kennedy, in his inaugural address, had called upon the nation for sacrifice, and this seemed to him inconsistent with tax reduction. In other and perhaps less romantic terms, the administration had promised to improve the nation's educational system, to provide better medical care for the aged, to rebuild the cities, and to do many other things that would cost money. It had promised to accelerate growth, and the prevailing view was that more growth required budget surpluses. There was a long-standing Democratic interest in tax reform to close loopholes. All of these seemed incompatible with tax reduction. To start on the tax-reduction road might keep the administration from reaching more important goals.

Probably most important, the administration could not be sure of the political consequences of cutting taxes when the budget was in deficit. "Fiscal responsibility," symbolized by a balanced budget, had been a commonly used term in the 1960 election campaign, as in previous campaigns for thirty years. The fact that fiscal responsibility was considered to be the property of the Republicans had not prevented the Democrats from winning six of the last eight Presidential elections and thirteen of the last fifteen Congressional elections. Perhaps the public's affection for budget-balancing did not run very deep. But it was something for a President, especially a Democrat, to think about.

By 1961, thirty years of experience, analysis, and discussion had made a tax reduction in the conditions then prevailing not only an available course but a probable one. But the action still had to be taken, and knowing that it could and should be done was different from doing it.

The Pre-Inauguration Kennedy

The most important thing about Kennedy's ideas on fiscal policy before he became President is that they were lightly held. Kennedy has been called the first modern economist in the American Presidency. This may have been true in 1963, but it was not true on Inauguration Day. At that time, Kennedy's fiscal thinking was conventional. He believed in budget-balancing. Although he was aware of circumstances in which the budget could not or should not be balanced, he preferred a balanced budget, being in this respect like most other people but unlike modern economists. But if he brought into the White House no very sophisticated or systematic ideas about compensatory fiscal policy, neither did he bring with him any deep intellectual or emotional commitment to the old ideas. This was partly a matter of his youth. He was not the first Keynesian President on Inauguration Day, but he was the first who was not a pre-Keynesian—the first who had passed the majority of his life in the post-Keynesian world where the old orthodoxy was giving way to the new. This characteristic he shared with his contemporaries. But he had, in addition, special characteristics that helped prepare him to accept the new economics he did not yet know. The son of an extremely wealthy, urban, Catholic family was unlikely to confuse personal budget-balancing with financial acumen or financial acumen with moral virtue. Moreover, there was in his home enough familiarity with the banking and financial community to reveal that its financial precepts were not necessarily Holy Writ. His one course in economics at Harvard had been modern, i.e., post-Keynesian, and although it left no affirmative impression on him, it did nothing to inhibit him from later looking at fiscal policy in a functional way.

Men of an earlier generation of different background, like Eisenhower, could be taught not to make a fetish of balancing the budget, and with strong advice and in clear situations would make fiscal decisions that violated the traditional rules of sound finance. But they could never get over a feeling of discomfort about this, and when there was any reasonable economic case for doing so would lean toward balancing the budget. Moreover, their spontaneous talk, free of speechwriters, would have a much more conventional cast than their actions. Whatever their course, they would prefer to sail under the traditional colors, not simply as a political strategem but because they found those colors more congenial.

Kennedy Acts Quickly and Surely

Such a person in a position of responsibility would probably have come to tax reduction if confronted with the problems of 1961–1963. But a person like Kennedy, with less firm attachment to the older ideas, would come to the tax cut more surely and quickly.

Kennedy was also free of older ideas of a different kind—in this case traditional, liberal, Democratic ideas. He was not shocked by the fact that some people were very wealthy, or even by the fact that some of them managed, through various tax loopholes, to escape paying very much tax. He was not likely to let a functional fiscal policy for economic expansion get permanently entangled with antirich and anti-corporation reformism and thereby alienate the people whose testimony to the soundness of his policy he needed. Unlike Roosevelt, he would not make his program of recovery carry too much burden of reform.

Kennedy's record as a Congressman showed no firm ideas about national fiscal policy and little interest in the subject. When Senator Douglas made his first effort in 1958 to enact an antirecession tax cut, Senator Kennedy voted against it. A few months later, partly on the advice of Professor Seymour Harris of Harvard, he voted for Douglas' second tax-cut proposal—which also failed. Later in his term, Kennedy obtained appointment to the Joint Economic Committee, the Congress' great seminar on fiscal policy, but he did not attend its meetings.

Kennedy campaigned in 1960 as a fiscal conservative. He did not match Roosevelt's 1932 Pittsburgh speech in which the Democratic candidate attempted to take the mantle of sound finance away from Herbert Hoover, but at least he was careful not to arouse conservative sensibilities. In a debate during the West Virginia primary campaign, on May 4, 1960, Senator Humphrey came out for raising income-tax exemptions from $600 to $800 per person. Kennedy replied that he couldn't go around the country urging increased expenditure programs and also say that he was for reducing income taxes that year. "And I don't think, therefore, that at the present time until the economy is moved up, I think it's going to be impossible to reduce income taxes." This exchange prompted Arthur Krock to say, in *The New York Times,* "To those who have carefully noted the public records of the Senators there could have been no surprise in yesterday's evidence that Kennedy is more of a fiscal conservative and is less special-group minded than Humphrey."

The Democratic platform on which Kennedy ran was expansive in monetary policy and restrained in fiscal policy:

> We Democrats believe that our economy can and must grow at an average rate of 5 percent annually, almost twice as fast as our average rate since 1953. We pledge ourselves to policies that will achieve this goal without inflation.
>
> As the first step in speeding economic growth, a Democratic President will put an end to the present high-interest, tight-money policy.

Among the ways to assure that the goal would be achieved without inflation was "budget surpluses in times of high employment."

The campaign discussions on both sides were marked by confusion between the problem of growth, meaning the problem of the rate at which the potential output of the economy rises, and the problem of full employment, meaning the problem of keeping actual output close to its potential. The Democrats seemed to be promising not only to get actual output up to its potential but also to make the potential rise more rapidly than its historical average. That is what the 5 percent goal meant. But the statistics they used to demonstrate the poor performance of the Eisenhower Administration reflected failure to keep output at its potential level, and the remedies they proposed also related mainly to this problem.

In any case, neither the platform nor Kennedy's campaign

speeches suggested that Eisenhower's fiscal policy had been too restrictive, in the sense of having too large surpluses, or that the Democrats would behave differently in that respect. Their main fiscal promise was that they were going to spend more. But this spending had its intellectual rationale in Galbraith, rather than in Keynes. That is, it was spending that would divert a larger part of the national output to public purposes from private purposes—not spending that would be undertaken to compensate for a deficiency in private demand and to bring about full employment. Its motivation was not that private spending was inadequate in amount, but that much of it was unworthy in quality.

Both the platform and Kennedy were firm in declaring an intention to finance the enlarged government expenditures within the limits of a balanced budget. After pointing to the needs for larger public programs, the platform said, "We believe, moreover, that except in periods of recession or national emergency, these needs can be met with a balanced budget, with no increase in present tax rates, and with some surplus for the gradual reduction of our national debt." However, the Democrats said that they were prepared to raise taxes if necessary.

Kennedy was even more cautious about the conditions in which a deficit might be justified. They were not merely a "national emergency" but a "grave national emergency" and not merely a "recession" but a "serious recession." However, he held out no promise of debt reduction—at least not in 1961, 1962, or 1963.

The idea of reducing taxes in a recession came up in the October 7, 1960, television debate between the candidates. Mr. Nixon was asked his opinion about what to do in a recession. He mentioned credit expansion as the first move, and then said:

> In addition to that, if we do get into a recessionary period we should move on the part of the economy which is represented by the private sector—and I mean stimulate that part of the economy that can create jobs—the private sector of the economy. This means through tax reform and if necessary tax cuts that will stimulate more jobs.

Asked the same question, Kennedy took the opportunity to give his standard talk against hard money and then turned to fiscal policy:

> If we move into a recession in '61 then I would agree that we have to put more money into the economy, and it can be done by either of the two methods discussed. One is by a program such as aid to education, the other would be to make a judgment

of what's the more effective tax program to stimulate our economy.

Kennedy's most developed formulation of a fiscal policy was presented near the end of the campaign, on October 30, in a statement about the international position of the dollar. This statement was intended to assure foreign holders of dollars that the election of Kennedy would not lead to a depreciation of the currency, and also to assure the American business and financial community on the same point. He said:

> First, we are pledged to maintain a balanced budget except in times of national emergency or severe recession. Furthermore, we will seek to maintain a budget surplus in times of prosperity as a brake on inflationary forces. Through the vigorous use of fiscal policies to help control inflation we will be able to lessen reliance on restrictive monetary policies which hamper growth.
> Wherever we are certain that tax revision—including accelerated depreciation—will stimulate investment in new plant and equipment, without damage to our principles of equity, we will proceed with such revision.
> We will also carefully examine our entire tax structure in order to close loopholes which are unnecessarily depriving the Government of needed tax revenue, and in order to develop tax policies which will stimulate growth.

In a few words, the Kennedy economics of 1960 was increased expenditures for defense and for public services, financed within a budget that would be balanced in prosperity out of the growing yield of the existing tax system with higher taxes if necessary, and monetary expansion to keep the economy operating close to its rising potential.

Platforms and campaign speeches are notoriously poor indicators of what a candidate thinks or of what he will do if elected. The 1960 program might have been just an election tactic—easy money for the populists, balanced budgets for the conservatives, and more public benefits for everyone. But there is no reason to doubt the sincerity of his belief in the budget-balancing part of the program. And indeed, it would have been most surprising if he had thought anything different in 1960, because the program happened to be not only the old conventional wisdom of Democratic politicians but also the new conventional wisdom of the Democratic intellectuals. For several years, the Joint Economic Committee, on the advice of leading economists, had been promoting the idea of easier money to stimulate the economy, coupled with a budget surplus to prevent inflation and to add to the savings available. This was considered the path to more rapid growth. And the idea that the country badly needed more government spending had been given a new rationale in John Kenneth Galbraith's *The Affluent Society,* one of the most influential economics books of the postwar period.

Some of these ideas were already, during the campaign, in the process of changing. First, it was coming to be realized that the budget already had a very large implicit surplus—would yield a large surplus at high employment—so that there was no need to drive for more fiscal restraint. Second, the persistence of the balance-of-payments problem was suggesting that the easy-money part of the fiscal-monetary program was not timely. Third, the thought was spreading that we were not simply going through another recession but were in a period of persistent stagnation, so that the problem of getting our potential output converted into actual output took precedence over the problem of choosing between public and private use of the output. This appraisal of the situation was to be important when Kennedy took office, but it came too late to influence Kennedy before the election.

Supporting Players—The Kennedy Economists

Kennedy's economists did not dictate either his ideas or his actions in the field of fiscal policy. Nevertheless, he was more influenced by professional economists than his predecessors had been. In part, this was simply the continuation of a rising trend of influence that dated back to Roosevelt and his Brain Trust and ran through the Truman-Keyserling and Eisenhower-Burns relationships. The trend of economists' influence was rising anyway, but it made a leap upward with the Kennedy Administration. Kennedy was especially prepared to accept new ideas. Moreover, he had, for a President, an unusual interest in abstract thinking, read a great deal, enjoyed the company of intellectuals, and was for these reasons open to education by economists.

The economists in turn had exceptional qualities. They were, for one thing, extremely self-confident. Of course, anyone who becomes adviser to a President is likely to be self-confident, but there are degrees of this. The Kennedy economists were, in the main, of that generation which had been most moved intellectually and emotionally by Keynes' *General Theory.* They were neither so old as to have learned it grudgingly and with qualifications nor so young as to have first met it as an already well-established doctrine. They had enlisted as foot soldiers in the Keynesian army at the beginning and risen through the ranks to become marshals. The Keynesian movement had swept economics. Although the meaning of Keynesianism as a doctrine had changed substantially, the esprit de corps of the school remained. Now its leaders were coming to Washington, with this victory behind them, to practice what they had been teaching. They had no reason to doubt that they knew what to do.

This self-confidence helped to make them persuasive with the President. They did not regard their role, however, as merely advising the President. Their role was to bring about the policies they regarded as correct, as long as the issue had not been foreclosed by a decision of the President. They were assiduous in mobilizing support for their views, inside and outside the government, in order to increase the likelihood that the President's decision would be their decision. Once the President's decision was made they were equally vigorous in trying to sell it to the country. In these efforts they were assisted by the presence of like-minded economists in other government agencies, on the staffs of Congressional committees, and to some extent in the press and in organizations of labor and business.

Of course, a President may be influenced by his advisers, but he also chooses his advisers. There is, thus, always some uncertainty about how far the advisers are to be regarded as exerting an independent influence. One of Kennedy's most important advisers, Paul A. Samuelson, put the question this way: "The leaders of this world may seem to be led around through the nose by their economist advisers. But who is pulling and who is pushing? And note this: He who picks his own doctor from an array of competing doctors is in a real sense his own doctor. The Prince often gets to hear what he wants to hear."

The key words here are "array of competing doctors." As far as ideas on fiscal policy were concerned, Kennedy did not choose from an array of competing doctors; he chose from an array of doctors whose ideas were basically the same. If he had chosen six American economists at random, the odds were high that he would have obtained five with the ideas on fiscal policy that his advisers actually had, because those ideas were shared by almost all economists in 1960. As Walter W. Heller later said: "Thus the rationale of the 1964 tax-cut proposal came straight out of the country's postwar economics textbooks." His economic advisers were eminent expositors of the standard economics of their time. They had done much to make it the standard economics. For example, the man who might be regarded as their intellectual leader, Paul A. Samuelson, was also the author of the most popular economics textbook of the postwar period. Kennedy did not choose his advisers to advocate and practice a particular brand of fiscal policy upon which he had already determined. He chose them as representative of the economics of his time, and having done that, he exposed his policy to influence by the economics of that time.

In the fall of 1958, Senator Kennedy began to expand his staff in preparation for the race for the 1960 nomination. Theodore C. Sorensen wrote:

> At the same time, with the help of Professor Earl Latham of Amherst College and a graduate student in Cambridge, I initiated at the Senator's request and in his name an informal committee to tap the ideas and information of scholars and thinkers in Massachusetts and elsewhere. Drawn primarily from the Harvard and Massachusetts Institute of Technology faculties, with a smattering of names from other schools and professions, the members of our "Academic Advisory Committee" held their first organizational meeting with me at the Hotel Commander in Cambridge on December 3, 1958. The economists in this group who later became advisers on fiscal policy to President Kennedy were John Kenneth Galbraith and Seymour Harris, of Harvard, Paul A. Samuelson, of MIT, and James Tobin, of Yale.

Role of the Academic Advisory Committee

What was expected from this committee was more than information and ideas. As Sorensen wrote:

> No announcement was made at the time about the committee's formation, but its very existence, when known, helped recruit Kennedy supporters in the liberal intellectual "community" who had leaned to Stevenson or Humphrey. This was in part its purpose, for the liberal intellectuals, with few delegates but many prestigious and articulate voices, could be a formidable foe, as Barkley and Kefauver had learned. Suspicious of Kennedy's father, religion and supposed McCarthy history, they were in these pre-1960 days held in the Stevenson camp by Eleanor Roosevelt and others. Kennedy's "academic advisers" formed an important beachhead on this front.

The Kennedy economists, like most American economists of 1960, believed that the chief economic problem of the country was to achieve and maintain high and rapidly rising total output. That is, the problem was full employment and economic growth. The keys to the management of that problem were fiscal policy and monetary policy, with fiscal policy being the senior partner in the combination. Full employment, or economic stabilization, and economic growth were the main objectives and guides of fiscal policy; budget-balancing was an irrelevancy. The economy was not in need of any basic structural reform, of the character of the National Recovery Act, French planning, or nationalization of industry. In general, the "free market" worked well and was not to be tampered with, but particular issues of government intervention in the market must be considered on their merits and without prejudice. Steps to make the distribution of income more nearly equal were good but they were not the urgent need and not the main road to improving the economic condition of the mass of the population, and they had to be evaluated with due regard for their effects on economic growth.

This set of ideas, which not only justified the big tax cut but also made it the centerpiece of Kennedy's entire economic policy, was the standard economics of 1960. It was Keynesian, but much modified from the American Keynesianism of 1946. What Milton Friedman said in 1966 was already true in 1960: "We are all Keynesians now and nobody is any longer a Keynesian." What had produced this change was the agreement by all parties that both monetary policy and fiscal policy could increasingly affect total spending and the level of total money income. Increasingly after 1951, monetary policy had been reincorporated into Keynesian thinking. Once this happened, the distinction between Keynesians and non-Keynesians ceased to be significant.

Three Ways Kennedy Economic Cast Differed

Within this general consensus of economists there were, of course, differences of emphasis and of degree. Three points distinguished the Kennedy economists from the Eisenhower economists and from a probably small minority of economists in the 1960's.

1. The Kennedy economists were less concerned with the problem of inflation than the Eisenhower economists, to say nothing of Eisenhower himself. Samuelson had foreseen this in 1956 in discussing the economics of Eisenhower:

> I should like to put forward the hypothesis that the relatively minor economic differences between the Republicans and Democrats during 1953–56 has been in the nature of a lucky accident. For reasons that will not necessarily be relevant in the future, *we have been able since 1951 to have a very high degree of prosperity and also to have stable prices.* The drop in farm and other staple prices made this possible.
>
> In the future the dilemma between very high employment and stable prices is likely to reassert itself with increasing force. Then it will be found that the Republicans do differ from the Democrats in the greater weight that they will give to the goal of maintaining an honest dollar in comparison with the clashing goal of keeping unemployment extremely low.
>
> In this clash of ideologies, social welfare functions and not scientific economic principles must play the decisive role.

Samuelson states the choice in a Democratic way. There is also a scientific problem involved in calculating how much additional unemployment, and for how long, would result from "maintaining an honest dollar." Some who would opt for avoiding inflation would say that in the long run such a policy would cost little, if any, additional unemployment. Nevertheless, it was undoubtedly true that the Kennedy economists attached less value to the avoidance of inflation than the Eisenhower economists did.

2. The Kennedy economists were willing to supplement general fiscal-monetary policy with other measures to loosen the constraints under which these general policies operated in achieving high employment. Specifically, they were prepared to "intervene in the market" to a degree that more conservative economists would not have accepted. If confronted with the dilemma that high employment could not be achieved without inflation, they would not be content to choose one horn or the other of the dilemma. They would want to try to remove the dilemma and alter the terms of choice—in this case, by government action to influence the decisions of individuals, businesses, and labor unions in setting wages and prices. If they found that monetary expansion was limited by the need to keep U.S. interest rates high enough so that money would not flow abroad, they would wish to remove that inhibition also, by selective measures to alter the patterns of interest rates, by placing a tax on lending abroad, or by pressure on U.S. lenders.

This willingness to operate directly upon the market should not be exaggerated. In comparison with standard European or Japanese practice, the interventions the Kennedy economists were prepared to recommend were small. But they were prepared to go further than the Eisenhower economists. As Walter Heller later said, "It is hard to study the modern economics of relative prices, resource allocation, and distribution without developing a healthy respect for the market mechanisms. . . . But I do not carry respect to the point of reverence."

3. The Kennedy economists had a high degree of confidence in their ability to forecast economic fluctuations accurately and to adapt fiscal and monetary policy continuously on the basis of these forecasts in order to achieve economic stability within a narrow range. Lack of such confidence was a major element in the preference displayed in the earlier postwar period by the Committee for Economic Development and others to have a largely passive fiscal policy aimed at minimizing the risk of large errors but not at trying to counter forecast fluctuations unless they were large or foreseen with unusual clarity. Walter Heller's main writing on fiscal policy before he became chairman of the Council of Economic Advisers under Kennedy was an argument against this position. His view then, in 1957, was stated mildly:

No conclusive evidence is available to prove that forecasting techniques are now a thoroughly reliable basis for discretionary stabilization policy. But many new or improved forecasts of important segments of the economy, such as plant and equipment outlays, are now available. The Council of Economic Advisers does not hesitate to invoke "prospective economic conditions" as a basis for discretionary judgments to hold the line on federal taxes. Qualified observers judge our short-term forecasting record as having operated "not too unsuccessfully" in recent years. Guarded optimism as to the future of economic forecasting seems justified.

After his experience on the Council of Economic Advisers, Heller believed that his "guarded optimism" about forecasting had been confirmed:

In part, this shift from a more passive to a more active policy has been made possible by steady advances in fact-gathering, forecasting techniques, and business practice. Our statistical net is now spread wider and brings in its catch faster. Forecasting has the benefit of not only more refined, computer-assisted methods, but of improved surveys of consumer and investment intentions.

The Kennedy economists did not come to Washington in January, 1961, with a plan for a large permanent tax cut in their briefcases. This became their program only a year-and-a-half later and was their reaction to the developments and the frustrations of the intervening months. But it was the reaction of men who, because of the attitudes described here, were committed to expansionist policies. They were not afraid of overdoing things, because they were not very worried about inflation; they were willing, if necessary, to intervene in the market to control the consequences of inflation if it should come, and they had great confidence in their ability to foresee how much expansionary policy would be enough but not too much.

The effort to stimulate the economy by fiscal policy, culminating in the 1964 tax cut, was smaller and later than the Kennedy economists would have liked. But the fiscal stimulus would almost certainly have been smaller and later without them. Moreover, while the tax cut was being considered, and after it was adopted, they were the chief interpreters of its significance. If the tax cut was a lesson for the future, it was a lesson first seen through their eyes.

Hobart Rowan

The Big Steel Crisis:
Kennedy vs. Blough

The New York headquarters of the giant United States Steel Corporation are at 71 Broadway, overlooking the historic Trinity Church graveyard, peaceful and incongruous in the midst of the busy skyscrapers. On Wednesday afternoon, April 11, 1962, U. S. Steel Chairman Roger Miles Blough turned on the television set in his private 20th-floor office, and waited for President Kennedy's press conference to come on.

He knew that Kennedy was angry. That was clear enough after Blough had walked into the President's office the night before with the surprise announcement that U. S. Steel was raising prices $6 a ton. Several other big steel producers had since followed suit.

But he didn't realize just how infuriated the President was until he watched and listened to Kennedy, his voice taut with emotion, denounce in bitter language the willful group of men who had displayed "irresponsibile defiance" of the public interest.

It was an experience that comes to but few men. "Some time ago," said the President (in a reference to his Inaugural Address), "I asked each American to consider what he would do for his country, and I asked the steel companies. In the last twenty-four hours, we have had their answer."

Blough listened as Kennedy continued the tongue-lashing:

> The simultaneous and identical actions . . . constitute a wholly unjustifiable and irresponsible defiance of the public interest. In this serious hour in our nation's history, with grave crises in Berlin and Southeast Asia, when . . . restraint and sacrifice are being asked of every citizen, the American people will find it hard, as I do, to accept a situation in which a tiny handful of steel executives, whose pursuit of private power and profit exceeds their sense of public responsibility, can show such utter contempt for the interest of 185 million Americans.

It was an awesome indictment, unparalleled in bitterness and scope. As Blough watched the televised press conference—alone in his 20th-floor office—I was just one floor below with a dozen lesser steel corporation officials grouped around another TV set. They sat in grim silence, totally unprepared for—as one put it—the President's "barn-burner." As the picture tube showed Kennedy leaving the State Department auditorium stage, a company official snapped off the set and said: "Well, I thought he would have viewed the situation more in sorrow than in anger."

I had flown up to New York from Washington after phoning Blough and making a date for an interview that afternoon. It had been apparent that Kennedy, stunned by the steel price increase, would blast back, and I wanted to get Blough's story directly from him. I had suggested that we wait until after the JFK press conference, and Blough invited me to watch it in the company offices, then come up to see him.

For the real beginning of the fateful confrontation between Kennedy and Blough in the spring of 1962, one must go back to the devastating 116-day steel strike of 1959. This developed into the longest and costliest steel labor dispute on record because President Eisenhower pursued an incredible, nineteenth-century, hands-off attitude. It was ended only when Eisenhower's Secretary of Labor, James P. Mitchell, and Vice-President Nixon secretly—so that Eisenhower wouldn't find out—mediated the dispute.

During the 1960 campaign, and soon after he took office, Kennedy made it clear that *he* would not sit idly by, as Eisenhower had, and watch the economy slowly strangulate in the bind of a management-labor dispute. He adopted the philosophy of Arthur J. Goldberg, Mitchell's successor as Secretary of Labor, that there was a public interest to be considered as well. Goldberg, former counsel to the Steelworkers Union, assumed his new role with a determination to force a revision of old concepts of collective bargaining.

All too often, collective bargaining operated according to jungle law; the parties fought, struck a bargain determined by which side was stronger at the moment. And under the pattern established for years, where the Government did intervene to force a settlement, it usually was on the understanding that higher wage costs would simply be passed on to the consumer. "Ten years ago," Goldberg mused in a private conversation as he ended his term as Secretary of Labor, "I never even heard the term 'balance of payments.' Today, it has to be a consideration at every bargaining table." Indeed this was something new! To be "free," Goldberg liked to say, collective bargaining had to be responsible. This not only meant that the Kennedy Administration would not tolerate anything like the 1959 steel strike, but it would try to anticipate and head off such power struggles before they started.

On September 6, 1961, when rumors in the trade hinted at a steel price increase coincident with the final stage of the wage boost negotiated by Nixon and Mitchell, Kennedy wrote steel company presidents asking that they "forego a price increase," in which case it would "clearly then be the turn of the labor representatives to limit wage demands to a level consistent with continued price stability." On September 14, he wrote in the same vein to McDonald: "The Steelworkers Union can make a significant contribution to the public interest. . . . This implies a labor settlement within the limits of advances in productivity and price stability."

This was the "symmetrical" approach worked out by Goldberg and Economic Council Chairman Walter Heller. The plain meaning of Kennedy's letter to the steel companies was that if they played ball, he—the President—would turn the heat on labor. Of McDonald, he demanded statesmanship, and gave him a measure—productivity limits—of how far he could go. The companies did, in fact, pass up a price increase in the fall of 1961, but most of the executives resented the Kennedy letter and doubted that Kennedy would or could pressure McDonald.

Some of the responses to the Kennedy letter were unbelievably blunt, even rude. One dispensed with the usual "Dear Mr. President" salutation, and started out, simply: "Sir."

Nevertheless, the Administration was encouraged by the fact that prices had not been advanced, and Arthur Goldberg was put to work that fall and winter to apply the same heat to the union. Kennedy really was trying to make good on the "symmetrical" approach, but most observers weren't sanguine. Others were derisive: after all, wasn't Arthur Goldberg a former paid hand of the McDonald union?

The doubters didn't know Goldberg very well. Once the graying ex-labor lawyer stepped into the Kennedy Cabinet, he had only one client—John F. Kennedy. Day in and out, he insisted on "the greater exercise of government responsibility in the area of collective bargaining." In countless speeches and interviews Goldberg hammered away at the theme that the Government must more and more "provide guidelines to the parties to insure that settlements reached are right settlements—not only in the interests of the parties themselves, but which also take into account the public interest."

This was strong medicine for the ex-plumber who heads the AFL-CIO, burly George Meany. In Bal Harbour, Florida, where the AFL-CIO Executive Committee was enjoying a sun-drenched session, President Meany exploded that Goldberg was "infringing on the rights of a free people and a free society." But Goldberg's message came through loud and clear to his old boss, Dave McDonald, President of the United Steelworkers of America: Kennedy wouldn't help him get an excessive wage settlement.

In private talks with McDonald, Goldberg—for years the brains behind the steelworkers' many bargaining achievements—urged McDonald to agree to an unprecedented, ahead-of-schedule start on negotiations. If the situation deteriorated into a strike, Goldberg warned McDonald, the Kennedy Administration wouldn't hesitate to throw the book at the union.

On January 23, 1962, the President himself met secretly with Blough and McDonald at the White House, and urged that they start talking early and come up with a noninflationary pact. The upshot of this meeting, after further conversations in Pittsburgh, was agreement to start the talks on a new contract at the end of February, four months ahead of the June 30 expiration date. This seemed to be a victory for the President's public plea for "industrial statesmanship." The negotiations, between teams headed by McDonald for the union, and R. Conrad Cooper of U.S. Steel for the industry, broke down rather quickly, but Kennedy threw his personal prestige into the breach, and talks were resumed March 14.

During this hectic period, Goldberg kept up an unremitting pressure on both Blough and McDonald. In his Economic Message in January, Kennedy had said that the nation "must rely on the good sense and public spirit of our business and labor leaders to hold the line on the price level in 1962." In tougher phrases, Goldberg kept returning to that thought. He pointed to the productivity guidelines in the 1962 Economic Report, which implied a wage boost of no more than 3 percent, and said bluntly that a settlement in that framework was what the President wanted to see. And he wanted the matter settled quickly, to avoid the twist and pull on the economy occasioned by an inventory buildup in anticipation of a strike, followed by liquidation of excessive stocks later.

One of the secrets of Arthur Goldberg's success as Secretary of Labor was that having the President's full confidence, he never hesitated to speak in the name of the President. And if he felt it necessary to speak in the President's name, and let him know about it later, that was all right with Mr. Kennedy. Thus, Goldberg could and did express Kennedy's concerns and views in vigorous terms.

Kennedy's economists were convinced that if the possibility of a steel strike were out of the way without an inflationary settlement, it would be a tonic extending economic recovery. Thus, when word came

that a new contract had been signed on March 31, three months ahead
of schedule, for a modest 10-cent wage package, there was rejoicing in
Washington. Kennedy himself hastened to arrange a special tele-
phonic hookup to the Penn-Sheraton Hotel in Pittsburgh to con-
gratulate McDonald, Cooper, and their aides.

It was an amazingly cheap settlement, so much so that McDonald
gruffly refused to put an official value on the package. And none of it
was in actual hourly wage rates; all of the 10 cents—the industry's
estimate, verified quietly by union lawyers—was in fringe benefits
designed to improve pensions and to ameliorate the pain of the growing unemployment in the steel mills. The notion that the union needed
government help to win such a limited settlement from the industry
bothered some of the labor "pros." Just before the new contract was
initialed, one grumbled: "I sure wish Kennedy had put Goldberg
on the Court instead of White." He got his wish to have Goldberg
removed from the labor scene a few months later.

It was true, of course, that the economic climate was exactly
suited to Goldberg's drive for a quick and noninflationary settlement.
Rising unemployment and competition from other products for steel's
markets provided neither the union nor the industry with strong bargaining weapons. Common sense thus dictated a harmonious settlement. But in the steel industry, there has been a singular lack of
common sense; as Cooper pointed out, the 1962 contract was the first
that had been signed since 1954 without a strike.

And since it was the first time that the Government had plunged
into a steel collective bargaining situation, before a crisis, Kennedy
was entitled to feel that he had risked the prestige of the Presidency
and won a great home-front victory. In the week that followed, the
contract was universally hailed as "noninflationary," and the nation
settled down to assess the new influence the Kennedy Administration
had brought to bear by asserting "the public interest."

And then the bomb dropped. It was dropped by Roger Blough.

On Tuesday, April 10, 1962, or as soon as the last union had
signed the basic agreement of March 31, the Board of Directors of
U.S. Steel met in New York, and decided to raise prices an average of
$6 a ton, an increase of 3.5 percent, billed as a boost to enable the
company to "catch up" with earlier cost pressures.

Blough had a secretary call Presidential aide Kenny O'Donnell,
and request an appointment with Kennedy for about 5:45 P.M. Blough
took a company plane (one of the fleet U.S. Steel maintains) to Washington and proceeded to the White House.

Kennedy wondered what Blough had on his mind (as a matter

of fact, when he saw his name on the calendar, he checked with his secretary, Mrs. Evelyn Lincoln, to see if someone hadn't made a mistake). He didn't have to wait long to find out.

Ushered into the President's oval study, Blough said: "Perhaps the easiest way I can explain why I am here is to give you this and let you read it." Whereupon, Blough handed the President a four-page mimeographed statement which at the very moment was being given to the press in New York and Pittsburgh for A.M. release, Wednesday, April 11.

The President skimmed the mimeographed sheets, and his expression became grim. He reread the release slowly. "I think you have made a terrible mistake," he told Blough. The President rose, went to the door of his office and told Mrs. Lincoln to get Arthur Goldberg "immediately." Within minutes, the Secretary of Labor, who had been in his wood-paneled departmental office, was at the White House. The President told Goldberg that Blough had raised prices. It took a moment for it to sink in. Infuriated, Goldberg turned on Blough, and asked:

"Why did you bother to come, if the price increase is already decided on?"

Fiddling with his bifocals, Blough responded that it was a matter of courtesy. Scornfully, Goldberg said that it was hardly courteous to confront the President of the United States with a *fait accompli*. It was, Goldberg said, more like a double cross.

A few weeks before, on his way to a meeting in Washington's Sheraton-Park Hotel with Walter Heller and the Business Council's economists, Blough had told me that he saw a rough similarity between his job and the President's. "The President has a tough job," he said sympathetically. "He can't be liked by everybody." And, he continued, broadening the reference to include himself: "Sometimes, we have to take positions that are not quite popular."

That tense evening in the White House, lectured by Goldberg as the President sat by, silent and angry, Blough knew that he had taken a position that was "not quite popular" along the New Frontier. But he didn't yet know what he had touched off.

As soon as Blough left, a Presidential aide said later, Kennedy and Goldberg decided that "this is war." They sent for Heller, Special Counsel Ted Sorensen, brother Bobby, Council member Kermit Gordon, and O'Donnell. They were joined later by a few others, including Assistant Press Secretary Andrew Hatcher.

His fury slowly rising, the President strode up and down his office, blasting the stupidity and cupidity of Roger Blough and the U.S. Steel Corporation. It was then that he got off a bitter observation:

"My father always told me that all businessmen were sons of bitches, but I never believed it until now!"* This explosive bit of frustration, when it became public a few days later, helped to convince many that he was really anti-business, deep down. Businessmen, of course, often applied the same term, and worse, to the late President.

By the time Kennedy left his office that Tuesday evening to dress for a Congressional reception, some of the lines of attack were settled, and work was begun on a draft of a Presidential statement. The mood was one of gloom; no one was really hopeful of upending the price increase. But the President's order, meeting the challenge thrown down by Blough, was to mobilize every force within the Government. Truly, it was a cold-blooded campaign—the U.S. Government vs. U.S. Steel—and Cabinet officers, Congressmen, and personal friends were thrown into the battle. Among the weapons were antitrust subpoenas, a grand jury investigation, diversion of Pentagon business, threats of hostile legislation, personal appeals to smaller steel companies, and above all—the unique power of the Presidency.

As I walked the flight of stairs to Blough's private office in New York that Wednesday afternoon, I wondered how a man just excoriated by the President of the United States before the entire nation would react. I was prepared for almost anything except Blough's unbelievable aplomb.

A high government official once described Blough to me as a "cold fish." This may be unkind, but it is accurate. Calm and unruffled, Blough walked into the board room adjoining his own office, and sat down with me and Phelps Adams, U.S. Steel vice-president for public relations. His greeting was matter-of-fact, and while he clearly didn't like the idea of being condemned as a power-hungry tycoon, he wasn't visibly upset. This was a tough, unemotional businessman, insensitive, I think, to public reaction.

The basic justification for a price increase, Blough said, was that U.S. Steel, like any other company, must have enough revenues to continue in business. "The President feels that we acted contrary

* The version quoted here was published by *The New York Times* on April 23, 1962. The first published version was reported by *Newsweek*, some days ahead of the *Times* story, without reference to the phrase "sons of bitches." It is the recollection of some who were present that the President said "S.O.B.'s." In any event, at a later press conference, when asked about the *Times* version, the President didn't deny he had used the phrase, but smilingly noted that he was talking about steel executives, not all businessmen.

Kennedy was annoyed that this story had leaked out of his private conference with his advisers. He tried to track down the source of the "leak" to *Newsweek*, whose version was on the newsstands (and read at the White House) on Monday, April 16.

to the public interest," he said in a monotone. "Well, I feel that a lack of proper cost and price relationships is one of the most damaging things to the public interest."

This was the essence of the case: steel was caught in a cost-price squeeze. The industry needed extensive modernization that could be financed only by building up internal reserves. Blough claimed that with no price increase in four years, U.S. Steel's profits as a percentage of sales had slipped from 9.5 percent in 1957 to 5.7 percent in 1961. And even though the 1962 wage agreement was conceded to be modest, the industry felt that it exceeded productivity gains, and thus would accentuate the squeeze on profits.

Blough scoffed at the idea that Kennedy had been double-crossed. He cited his September 13 response to the President's September 6, 1961, letter requesting that the steel companies hold the price line. "If anybody thought that U.S. Steel would not at some time raise prices, they must not have been reading the English language," he told me.

The Blough letter—which U.S. Steel proudly had printed up as a classic explanation of its case—said that "the pressures of the market place are inexorable, and cannot be disregarded by a steel company or any other company, or for that matter, cannot be disregarded by any nation which wishes to maintain its position in a competitive world."

This kind of generality didn't answer the double-cross charge. It was quite true, as Blough reiterated, that he had made "no commitment" to anyone with respect to prices. But this was a thin semantic reed. The fact was that Blough had also done nothing to counter the impression that there was a quid pro quo: no inflationary wage boost, no price increase.

I put it to Blough directly. Didn't you, I asked, let this impression get around? Blough offers the world an impassive expression most of the time, and his voice is restrained. But he summoned some feeling to say: "Certainly not!"

Why was it assumed in Pittsburgh, in Washington, in business circles everywhere, that there would be no steel price increase? Tapping a yellow pencil on a conference table, Blough answered:

> That didn't result from anything I've said. I suspect, perhaps, that the impression was a by-product of the Government's economic guidelines, which led some people to think that all past [wage] increases might just be forgotten.

But that was not the general belief then—or now, in retrospect. As the London *Economist* observed:

Earlier . . . the steel companies . . . had welcomed the Administration's help in bringing the steel workers to the bargaining table to negotiate a new labour contract well in advance of the expiry of the old one, and in pressing them to moderate their demands. But as soon as the contract was signed, Mr. Blough broke what everyone had presumed, although it had not been stated specifically, was his side of a bargain.

Mr. Kennedy may have overreacted—but if he did, it was because he felt he had been deceived, or "sandbagged." (A year later, when the steel companies announced selected price increases on some products, it was on the anniversary of the 1962 imbroglio. It may have been a coincidence of dates, but Kennedy didn't think so.) To complicate things, the trickery, as JFK saw it, deprived him of a substantial achievement that he had staked much to win. And no Kennedy has ever liked to lose, or to see the fruits of victory vaporize.

Bobby Kennedy later put it this way:

Mr. Blough sat in on a number of conferences with the President, and with Secretary of Labor Goldberg where efforts were made—which he applauded—to keep David McDonald and the steel union from asking for a large increase in wages. That effort was made on the basis that there wouldn't be any rise in the price of steel. Mr. Blough never said during that time: "Well, no matter what happens, I'm going to have to raise the price of steel.". . . So when the rise was announced, it came as a complete surprise to us.

What Blough didn't sense was that many business and financial experts would conclude that he pulled a boner. Typical was the feeling of Per Jacobsson, late Managing Director of the International Monetary Fund. Returning to Washington on the Eastern Airlines shuttle, I had the good fortune to bump into this financial wizard, confidant of statesmen. It soon became apparent that Jacobsson, on the last lap of a trip back to Washington from Switzerland, hadn't heard of the steel news.

"Mr. Jacobsson," I asked, "did you know that Roger Blough raised steel prices six dollars a ton last night?"

A big, friendly bear of a man, Jacobsson was stunned. "He did what?"

I repeated the news, and filled him in on the day's developments, including the President's denunciation of Blough, and the beginnings of the rollback effort.

"But that's incredible," Jacobsson finally said. "Why, I've just been all over Europe, and they were happy with the wage settlement because they assumed that it meant there would be no price increase. And I told them they were right!"

That was the assumption here, too, coupled with a belief that a new interpretation of the "national interest" was taking hold—one that would somehow temper the demands of labor or management. But such a broad interpretation of the national interest isn't accepted by Blough. He told me, during that private session in April 1962, that steel should not be considered a bellwether industry. "You hear the argument," he continued, "that steel is different because we have more impact on the economy. I just don't agree with that. We must have enough profit to do the things that have to be done."

But what Blough had difficulty in explaining then or later was how a price increase would help the domestic steel industry meet already vigorous inroads being made by cheaper foreign steel, or competition from other materials like aluminum, concrete, and plastics. He conceded that a higher price for domestic steel might temporarily add to the competitive problem, but insisted: "If we're going to be able to compete in the long run, we need better plants, and to get those, we need higher profits that will permit reinvestment of capital. That's why we raised prices."

The Administration's position, of course, was that the higher-price route was neither a necessary nor desirable way of financing capital improvements. An analysis by Walter Heller's Council observed on this point:

> Neither economic principle nor the actual experience of the steel companies affords a justification for the view that prices should be set at levels permitting 100 percent internal financing of investment capital. Capital improvements increase the value of the assets owned by stockholders; increasing prices to pay for them amounts to taxing steel users for the benefit of the stockholders.

But neither the Administration's counterarguments nor its overall concern about the economy carried much weight with Roger Blough. What came through very clearly was that the President of the United States had his job to do, and Roger Blough had his own to do, and he didn't understand why people just couldn't see it that way. I asked: "In making a difficult decision like a price increase in steel, what weight would you say you gave to the Administration's reiteration of the need for price stability?"

His answer, in measured tones, was most revealing: "Against the background of thinking in terms of costs—which is the background I think in—the Government's position was one of the factors that was weighed very heavily, along with all the others we have to contend with."

Thus, Roger Blough, as he put it so well himself, is a man who thinks "in terms of costs." To such a man, the national urgency, as expressed by the President of the United States, was only "one of the factors" that received consideration. But it was just *one* factor, weighed along with others—say, the cost of scrap or pig iron. In the world of the Roger Bloughs, costs and prices and profits are the big determinants. Something as fuzzy as a sense of responsibility—the Goldbergian "national interest" concept—is not very high on the list. After all, how do you show the "national interest" on a balance sheet?

Blough's bid for a price increase was at once bold and imprudent, worsened by overtones of bad faith. It betrayed an insensitivity to the larger issues involved. The company was aware that the President had a press conference scheduled the next day, and didn't even think its timing was bad, in a public relations sense. The fact is that Blough expected fully to get away with it. At worst, he expected a slap on the wrist, not a sock on the jaw. His misassessment of how Kennedy would respond was an incredible gaffe, which could be made only by a man who thinks exclusively in terms of costs and prices. Now, he had been labeled profit-and-power hungry by a popular young President, and the question was, as that event-packed Wednesday came to a close, could Blough resist the Presidential onslaught?

He couldn't as it turned out, but at that juncture, the results were not visible. The Presidential press conference blast over, Blough, unruffled and unmoved, didn't think his price increase was at all jeopardized.

On Wednesday morning Bethlehem Steel, No. 2 in the industry, announced a price increase. So did the other big companies: Republic, Youngstown, Jones and Laughlin, and some smaller ones like Wheeling. By the time the President strode into the State Department auditorium at 3:30 P.M. to deliver his blistering denunciation, the follow-the-leader bandwagon, so typical of the steel industry, seemed to have begun, inexorably, to roll over the Kennedy Administration.

However, as night fell in Washington that Wednesday, there were still five small companies, representing 14 percent of the industry's capacity, that had not raised prices. These were Inland Steel, Armco, Kaiser Steel, Colorado Fuel & Iron, and McLouth Steel. Immediately, the Administration pursued a "divide and conquer" strategy.

Perhaps the key role, ultimately, was played by Joseph L. Block, Inland Steel Co. chairman, who at the time was vacationing in Japan. Block was no stranger to Washington: during the early 1940's, he was one of the heads of the War Production Board Steel Division. **More** recently, he had accepted membership on Kennedy's 21-man Labor-Management Advisory Committe created at Goldberg's suggestion.

When George Meany a few months before denounced Goldberg's insistence that the public interest had to be considered paramount, it was Block who came to his defense with this public statement: "A contest of strength where the stronger side wins doesn't prove a thing. Each side has to represent its own interest, but neither side must be unmindful of the needs of the nation. Who else can point out those needs but the Government?" So the Administration's ploy was obvious: try to get the Chicago-based Inland to hold off. That might firm the spine of the other smaller companies, and in a steel market already pressed by competition, it might tumble the leaders off their price perch.

But would the strategy work? In respect to Inland, there were two things "going" for Kennedy. First, Block was friendly to the Administration, close to Goldberg, and was known to feel that Blough was not the most effective spokesman for the business community. This was his view long before the 1962 fracas over prices. Second, Inland's business was good.

And so, what might be called "the telephone campaign of 1962" got under way, much of it directed by Undersecretary of Commerce Edward C. Gudeman, a former Sears, Roebuck executive from Chicago. On Wednesday morning, back from an emergency White House meeting on steel, Commerce Secretary Luther Hodges called in Gudeman and said:

"Eddie, get on the phone!"

Hodges didn't know that Gudeman, a boyhood chum of Inland vice-president P. D. Block, had phoned him at 7:45 A.M. on his own initiative. Gudeman's approach was low-pressure, with no threats. Had P.D. thought through all of the implications of an industry-wide price boost? Gudeman wanted to know. Later, Gudeman reached Gene Trefethen, No. 2 man at Kaiser, and appealed to him to hold the line. Meanwhile, Goldberg phoned Leigh B. Block, Inland vice-president for purchasing, and Treasury Undersecretary Henry H. Fowler reached Inland President John F. Smith, Jr.

The theme of all the calls followed the Gudeman line: Don't take precipitate action—the President is right—Big Steel is wrong—at least, wait a bit and think it through. "Anybody who knew anybody else got on the horn," explained one participant later. "We called friends, and the people we called called their friends," Gudeman said. The response was at least mildly encouraging. P. D. Block admitted to Gudeman that he had been surprised by Blough's action, and promised that Inland would not make a price boost announcement immediately;

instead, the company would think things over carefully. On Thursday, P. D. reached Joe Block in Japan, and after a long conversation, they agreed that Inland would not raise prices. The announcement was made this way by Joe Block on Friday from Kyoto: "We did not feel that it was in the national interest to raise prices at this time. We felt this very strongly."

In Washington, the Kennedy team could hardly believe the good news. In a calmer moment later on, Goldberg told me: "I never doubted that Joe Block would be shocked by Blough's decision. But you had to have guts to buck Big Steel, and Block had the guts." It was only a battle, and not the war; it would take more than Inland to win, and the telephone campaign was redoubled. Defense Secretary Robert S. McNamara, Undersecretary of State George Ball, White House aide Ralph Dungan, joined Gudeman, Heller, and Fowler in their long-distance efforts. President Kennedy himself phoned Edgar Kaiser of the Kaiser Steel Co.

The real hope for forcing a price rollback rested on dividing Bethelehem Steel Co. from U.S. Steel. But so far as is known, the Administration could devise no personal appeal to Bethelehem. It therefore embarked on a different approach to the No. 2 company, one that brought the FBI into play, and helped to establish the image of a Kennedy Government strong-arming its way through the economy.

From start to finish, there were strange elements to the role played by Bethlehem in the 1962 crisis. Just the day before Big Steel's decision to raise prices, Edmund F. Martin, Bethlehem Vice-President, had told a stockholders' meeting in Wilmington, Delaware, that "there shouldn't be a price rise." He added: "We shouldn't do anything to increase our costs if we are to survive. We have more competition both domestically and from foreign firms."

But as soon as Roger Blough raised prices, Bethlehem dutifully fell in line. Was this collusion? The contradiction between Martin's speech to stockholders and the company action in the space of little more than a day wasn't lost on the Kennedys. After Martin claimed he had been misquoted, Bobby Kennedy set out to get the facts, and the way he did it was typically brash.

At 3 A.M. Thursday morning, an FBI agent phoned Lee Linder, a Philadelphia reporter with the Associated Press who had covered the Bethlehem stockholders' meeting. Although Linder suggested that the matter wait till morning, two agents arrived at his home at 4 A.M., and questioned Linder on Martin's precise words. Another newsman, John Lawrence of the *Wall Street Journal,* was awakened at 5 A.M. At 6:30 A.M. in Wilmington, two other agents were waiting for James L. Parks, Jr., of the Wilmington *Evening Journal,* another reporter who had covered the Bethlehem stockholders' meeting, when he arrived at his office for work.

Parks reported that the agents were polite, and that he—like the others—confirmed the original version: Martin had indeed said there shouldn't be a price increase. But not surprisingly, the Administration was criticized for sending FBI men around in the middle of the night. To the Republicans, it smacked of "gestapo tactics," and they said so loudly. The Administration's tactics were offensive to others, too. For example, columnist Joseph A. Livingston, generally friendly to Kennedy, wrote:

> Persons who regard themselves as "liberals' and even New Dealers had reason to resent U.S. Steel's insensitivity in raising prices. But they also have reason to recoil from the relentless use of power by the President.

Bobby Kennedy's inflexible attitudes helped to shape business's judgment of his brother. For example, in trying to run to earth the rumors of price collusion, Bobby dug deep—even into personal expense account reports by some corporate heads. When one such situation was brought to President Kennedy's attention, he agreed that Bobby had gone too far, and took steps to call him off.

However one assesses the Justice Department tactics—my own view is that the industry was playing a rough game, for keeps, too—they paid off in terms of Bethlehem. The company was caught in a public exposure of its conflicting statements. Coincident with this, McNamara announced that Pentagon policy would be to shift contracts where possible "to those companies which have not increased prices." He added that he would also study the possibilities for substituting other materials for steel. (This was more meaningful than a rather wild estimate by McNamara that the $6 steel increase would increase national defense costs by $1 billion a year.) To drive the point home to Bethlehem—the nation's largest ship-steel supplier—the Pentagon awarded a $5,000,000 armor plate contract to the Lukens Steel Co., which had not raised prices.

Meanwhile, close on the Joe Block announcement from Kyoto, Edgar Kaiser in Oakland, California, said that the Kaiser Steel Corp. "will not raise its mill prices at this time." Armco made no move one way or the other, and the Colorado Fuel and Iron Corp. said it was studying the possibility of selective price changes. So the bandwagon was stalling, and the Administration pressed its advantage. Bobby Kennedy announced a grand jury probe of events, and said that subpoenas for documents had already been served on Bethlehem and other company officials.

On Thursday, April 12, with the outcome far from clear, it was Kennedy's turn to watch Blough handle a televised press conference. His opening statement defended the price increase and denied that there had been "any commitment of any kind" not to raise prices. But the President and his aides got their first inkling of victory when Blough said it would be "very difficult" for Big Steel if some other major producer did not also raise prices. "It would definitely affect us, and I don't know how long we could maintain our position," Blough told a questioner.

By this time, the maneuvering took on an Ian Fleming-ish aspect. Late Thursday night, lawyer Clark Clifford went out to Washington National Airport, where he met secretly aboard one of the U.S. Steel fleet of private planes with Vice-President Robert Tyson. This rendezvous was arranged by Kennedy's newsman-friend, Charles Bartlett. Goldberg had already had several fruitless talks with Tyson, and Kennedy was persuaded that he should try a fresh negotiator. The Clifford-Tyson huddle appeared to have come to a dead end also, but on Friday morning, Blough passed on word that he thought conversations should continue.

Sensing a turning point, Kennedy packed both Goldberg and Clifford onto a military transport plane to meet Blough, Tyson, and other U.S. Steel executives in New York. En route, Goldberg got a radio-phone message: Armco had joined with Inland and Kaiser in standing athwart Big Steel's price boost. In a comfortable suite at the fashionable Carlyle Hotel, the gray-haired Goldberg, his own reputation very much on the line, reviewed all the arguments on the Administration side. The phone rang, for Blough, and then for Goldberg. For both, it was the same message, feared by the one and hoped for by the other: Bethlehem had thrown in the sponge "in order to remain competitive" with Inland, Kaiser, and Armco. According to a participant at the Carlyle denouement, Blough appeared to be "pale and shaken."

Goldberg didn't let up. He listed for Blough some forthcoming ammunition: In a few hours the White House would release a Heller "White Paper," tearing apart the economic justifications Blough had offered in his Thursday statement. Then, on Saturday, Treasury Secretary Douglas Dillon, who had been vacationing at his Hobe Sound, Florida, home, would call in reporters to suggest that the industry was greedy; it could recoup $40 to $45 million in the tax credit and depreciation Kennedy was proposing—or nearly as much as raising prices might yield. The barrage would be continued with an Orville Freeman press conference, in which the Agriculture Secretary would charge that the price increase would cost American farmers $45 million a year. And there would be Congressional harassment, including new hearings under the industry's archfoe, the late Estes Kefauver of Tennessee.

But it was the Bethlehem pullout that did it. Just why Bethlehem backed off as it did and when it did is not completely known even now. It is a reasonable asumption, however, that Bethlehem was embarrassed by its contradictory position on prices, and entertained real worries about competition from Inland and Armco. And it had no taste for any further antitrust matters.

Around 5 P.M., Blough caved in at the Carlyle, and a happy Arthur Goldberg got on the phone to give Kennedy the message. At exactly 5.28 P.M., wire service news tickers clattered with a bulletin, taken from this corporation handout: "The United States Steel Corp. today announced it had rescinded the 3½ percent price increase made on Wednesday, April 11."

Leslie B. Worthington, U.S. Steel president, explained that "the price decision was made in the light of the competitive developments today, and all other current circumstances, including the removal of a serious obstacle to proper relations between government and business." It was a roundabout way for saying the company felt it was under pressure, and had no alternative.

It was a stunning turnabout. The companies that had followed U.S. Steel and Bethlehem up, followed them down. In Washington, after Goldberg's call, Kennedy told Heller to bury the "White Paper," the Cabinet press conferences were canceled, and a date was made for Blough to meet with Kennedy early the following week, prior to the regular Presidential press conference. The President sensed that he would face a difficult period of repairing and restoring relationships, and he told one aide to find areas "where everybody can now work together."

So once again, just a week after he dropped his bomb, Blough walked into the President's office, and this time they talked alone. The victor—a President who had blasted a big steel tycoon while the nation listened in, and then forced him to backtrack on his decision—assured Blough that he held no grudges. He said, also, that he recognized the industry's need to modernize plant facilities, that the Government would help it in this process, and that he would tell the nation so at his next press conference.

They talked for 45 minutes, an uncomfortable session for both men. Kennedy had never been overly impressed with Blough. It was a mystery to him how a man with such a pale personality had become a leading business spokesman. But Blough had been useful in 1961 in re-establishing contact with the Business Council, when Kennedy desperately tried to shuck the "anti-business" tag. And now, for whatever internal turmoil he felt, Blough was willing to keep open a channel of communication to the upper-crust segment of the business world.

Thus, Kennedy happily and sincerely assured Blough that there would be no anti-business vendetta. He promised Blough that he would make this clear to the nation, and that a suitable collection of high Administration officials would be dispatched to the May meeting of the Business Council at Hot Springs. In addition, the Administration would press forward with its plans for a White House Conference on National Economic Issues later in the month, at which JFK would be the principal speaker.

At his next press conference, April 19, Kennedy tried to damp the fires of controversy. He said: ". . . Nothing is to be gained from further public recriminations." He added that he believed firmly in "holding the role of the Government to the minimum level needed to protect the public interest." And without ever suggesting that he had any regrets about his tough attitude and efforts of the preceding week, he promised that his Administration would not proceed from there to engage in broad wage and price fixing. The main thought Kennedy attempted to leave: steel was a very special case, not a guideline for the future.

Kennedy's attempt to bury the hatchet was well received by some. The astute Sidney J. Weinberg, senior partner of Goldman, Sachs, and Co., for thirty years a power in the big business world (and a vice-chairman and founder of the Business Council), told me after the press conference: "Kennedy said exactly what was needed. That's the way a chief executive ought to be—magnanimous at a time of victory. And it's right for the country, very beneficial. Of course, there are scars left, because a lot of people in the business world think that he blew his top a week ago, but his new attitude helps. Believe me, the country would have been in trouble if he hadn't taken steps to smooth things over."

The business community at large, however, was still in a state of shock. It was stunned by the awesome display of Presidential power, embittered by the crack about sons-of-bitches, the use of FBI agents, the rearrangement of Pentagon orders. And it was fearful of the implications of Kennedy's successful intrusion into a basic private decision-making area—the setting of prices. Businessmen who privately confided that Blough's move was "inept" or "bush-league" or "dumb" felt that Kennedy's intervention was hard to justify, even if he did feel Blough double-crossed him.

Above all, what businessmen wondered was: Can it happen again? Through businessmen he liked and trusted—such as Thomas J. Watson, Jr., of IBM and Robert A. Lovett, former Secretary of Defense —and in private conversations with friends and newsmen, Kennedy passed the word along that the unique combination of circumstances was highly unlikely to come up again. For example, there was this exchange in what amounted to a semiofficial interview that Heller gave *Newsweek:*

Q. In what situations or circumstances would the Administration again bring to bear the same weapons it employed in the steel price case?

A. It's hard to conceive of any situation that would call forth the same response. First, steel is a bellwether in its basic role in the economy and as a pace-setter. Second, there were special circumstances, as you well know: there had been a wage settlement in conformity with the national interest, as spelled out in our guidelines for noninflationary wage increases. So steel was a special situation. This is not to deny that the Government will express and assert the public interest in other wage and price decisions having a broad impact on the economy.

To the degree that this word got through, it was encouraging to businessmen. If Blough had been inept, they argued, Kennedy had overreacted. Kennedy may have felt the same way, but—to the end— he never would admit it, even if some members of his team privately concede he went too far. Late in 1962, when he was asked in a television interview by American Broadcasting Co. correspondent William H. Lawrence for a retrospective appraisal, the President said:

. . . Though I don't like to rake over old fires, I think it would have been a serious situation if I had not attempted with all my influence to try to get a rollback, because there was an issue of good faith involved. . . . If I had not attempted, after asking the unions to accept the noninflationary settlement, if I had not attempted to use my influence to have the companies hold their prices stable, I think the union could have rightfully felt that they had been misled. In my opinion it would have endangered the whole bargaining between labor and management, would have made it impossible for us to exert any influence . . . in the future . . . on these great labor-management disputes. So I have no regrets. The fact is, we were successful. . . .

I just think, looking back on it, that I would not change it at all. There is no sense in raising hell, and then not being successful. There is no sense in putting the office of the Presidency on the line on an issue and then being defeated. . . . Given the problem that I had on that Tuesday night, I must say I think we had to do everything we could to get it reversed.

Blough's own backward reflection was that Kennedy's "vehement" reaction did not really stem from fears of inflation, but in order to keep his standing with the labor movement. "His earlier stand against a 35-hour work week had displeased the labor unions," Blough said.

I believe that he and Secretary Goldberg felt an increase in steel prices . . . would be viewed as evidence that the Administration's policies were adverse to labor's interests. . . . It is my opinion that the price increase would not have hurt, but would have helped the American economy. . . . Pricing by political pressure . . . weakens the industrial strength upon which America's very survival may depend in time of crisis.

The truce after battle, in the spring of 1962, left a host of problems. Kennedy's display of power would bring forth the demand that he exert similar pressure on labor unions if they got out of line, and this would be tougher to do. For the steel industry, there was still the problem of finding the right time and the right way to raise steel prices. (As it developed, it was a full year away.) For the President, there was that residue of bitterness, never eradicated.

The widely read *Kiplinger Letter,* for example, said after prices were rescinded that "many businessmen now feel sure that Kennedy is anti-business, even those who have wondered about it in the past or argued against it. Now they tell us that they know it. This even comes from those who feel that the steel companies bungled the whole thing."

Actually, the reaction of the business world was somewhat more subtle. True, the sheer flexing of Presidential muscle was a spectacle. But that was just the external symbol of something that ran deeper. In board rooms and over dinner tables, what businessmen told each other was that the President had abridged a basic right, the right to make business decisions. If business makes the wrong decisions, they feel, those decisions should fall of their own weight, without government intrusion.

In his televised rebuttal to President Kennedy, Blough had stressed that ". . . each individual company in our competitive society has a responsibility to the public, as well as to its employees and stock-holders, to do the things that are necessary, price-wise, however unpopular that may be at times, to keep in the competitive race."

But was competition truly the only factor, as Blough suggested, in establishing prices? The initial grand jury investigation came to an end on March 19, 1963, without arriving at a specific conclusion. This was in the middle of an era, it might be noted, when the Kennedy Administration was still trying hard to eradicate the anti-business stigma. Then in April 1963, the steel industry announced a "selective" price increase, just as the antitrust division began a study of "leads" turned up by the dissolved grand jury.

On October 16, 1963—a month after a second set of increases by the steel industry—a new grand jury was convened in New York, and the major companies were subpoenaed for information on steel sheet, strip, plate, bars, and tin mill products. This panel on April 7, 1964, returned an indictment against eight major companies and two officials accused of illegally conspiring over a six-year period to fix prices for "extras" in the $3.6 billion sheet steel industry. ("Extras" are additional charges for particular sizes, gauges, or quality content of the steel.)

A real shocker in the six-page indictment was the accusation that the huge, supposedly sophisticated steel industry had stooped to the same device that had sent officials in the electrical equipment industry to jail: secret price-fixing sessions in hotel rooms. The Biltmore and the Sheraton-East in New York were specifically named.

The outcome of this indictment—the seventh in two years against various companies—won't be known for perhaps another year or two. But in the public mind, it raises basic questions about steel prices and how they are established. "It's also worth remembering," the New York *Herald Tribune* said in an editorial after the grand jury indictment, "that during the whole steel price hullabaloo [of 1962], one of the companies' principal arguments was that the price rise couldn't have been rigged because competition within the industry was so cutthroat. . . . If indeed, steel executives had been meeting clandestinely in hidden hotel rooms to rig the prices of those 'extras' that figure so largely in their intra-industry competition, then what happens to their argument?"

Just after the companies rescinded the $6 price boost in 1962, the *Wall Street Journal* said: "Let us first of all be clear about just what the Government did. It said that a private company could not change the price of its product, a property right which is obviously basic to a free economy. In other words, the Government set the price. And it did this by the pressure of fear—by naked power, by threats, by agents of the state security police."

This conclusion certainly overstates the facts, but it is typical of the real sense of business jitters that prevailed. When Commerce Secretary Hodges, for example, made a passing reference to aluminum prices, aluminum stocks fell on the New York Stock Exchange. The *Wall Street Journal* notwithstanding, Kennedy had no grand design to change the price mechanisms of American industry. The *Journal* didn't mention the companion pressure that had been brought to bear against the United Steelworkers. And it made no effort to judge whether, in reality, the weakness in the steel marketplace itself was not the dominant reason for the collapse of Blough's attempted push on prices.

The significance of the post-steel-crisis months lies not in the reality of Kennedy's mood—whether he was anti-business or not—but in the fact that much of the business community concluded that he was. Soon, special "S.O.B." buttons showed up in Wall Street, and even Sidney Weinberg sported one on his lapel at the May Business Council meeting at Hot Springs, Virginia. ("It means Sons of Brooklyn," Weinberg joked.)

Kennedy, of course, knew that the business community was hostile, and planned to use a speech scheduled for April 30 to the United States Chamber of Commerce for conciliatory gestures. But business confidence was to prove an elusive goal. The stock market was slipping badly, and historically business has an especially snappish regard for Washington when the bears ride in Wall Street. No one knew it then, but Black Monday's market crash was only a month off, and fair or not, this record-breaking slide would be blamed on the steel flap—and on Kennedy.

Walter Lippmann

Change of Course

A few weeks ago, on the evening of the day when the two Negro students were enrolled in the University of Alabama, President Kennedy took a momentous and irrevocable step. He committed himself to lead the movement toward equality of status and opportunity for the American Negro. No President has ever done this before, none has ever

From Newsweek. *Copyright Newsweek, Inc., July 8, 1963.*

staked his personal prestige and has brought to bear all the powers of the Presidency on the Negro cause.

It is quite clear that the President's recent decision was a sudden change of course. When the Congress met this winter no one in public life foresaw that by the spring the racial crisis would be paramount at home, obscuring all other questions. The Kennedy Administration had no major proposals on civil rights to make to the Congress, and its legislative strategy was to let civil rights lie dormant in order to win back Southern Democrats for the tax bill. All the political calculations were knocked out suddenly when the racial crisis burst into flame.

The President and his brother, the Attorney General, deserve great credit for realizing at once what had happened so suddenly. They understood the magnitude and the temper of the rebellion set aflame by the clash between Martin Luther King's demonstrating Negroes and Bull Connor's fire hoses, dogs, and policemen's clubs. For myself, I count very high the speed, the intelligence, the imagination, and the courage of the Kennedy reaction. Only too often in human affairs do those who reach the highest places leave behind them the capacity to react to the new and the unexpected.

The Hard Part

In order to appraise the impact of the President's change of course we have to realize that while it may be hard to pass laws proclaiming equal rights, that is much the easiest part of what the nation is now committed to do. The hardest part is to provide equal economic opportunity at an adequate level in jobs, housing, and schooling.

For while the right to vote, the right to use public accommodations, the right to be enrolled in schools are of the utmost importance in wiping out the caste system in American life, the emancipation of the Negroes cannot be completed until they have equal economic opportunity at an adequate level. The main obstacle here is not discrimination and prejudice, although they are rampant. The main obstacle is that there are not enough jobs, not enough good housing, not enough good schools.

According to the latest report there are now about 1,150,000 unemployed teen-agers. Of these, 900,000 are whites and 250,000 are Negroes. This is a terrifying situation. Most unemployed youths are not educated and not trained. This makes them unemployable in the better jobs. Quite evidently, equality of rights cannot be made to mean that the 250,000 Negro youths should get jobs ahead of the white youths. There is indeed **no salvation** for the whites *or* the Negroes except to stimulate the American economy to provide many more jobs and to increase very greatly the training programs.

Just as jobs are too scarce, so are good houses. The Negroes get the worst housing. But it would be no solution to the problem to push whites into the Negro slums and Negroes into the white suburbs. The only tolerable, and indeed the only workable solution, is to build more good houses and to wipe out the slums.

Separate, Not Equal

The same condition exists in the schools. It is quite true that by and large the segregated schools, though separate, are not equal. In the North as well as the South, the Negro schools are greatly inferior. But it is also true that the white schools are very often overcrowded, which means not only that there are no empty seats in the classrooms but that the teachers, usually underpaid, are overworked. Equal rights will not solve the problem. For it will be a poor kind of equality which drags down the white children without really raising the Negro children. Again there is no solution except to spend a great deal more public money to expand and develop school facilities.

We can now see why the President's commitment to the Negro cause is so momentous. It brings him and us face-to-face with the conservative coalition of Republicans and Southern Democrats. We are face-to-face with them not only on the hot issues of equal rights but on the issue of using Federal power to expand the American economy and to develop the public facilities of the nation.

For it will prove to be impossible to approach the equality of opportunity for the Negroes without reviving and renewing the progressive movement in American politics, which has been quiescent for some ten years.

T. George Harris

The Competent American

John F. Kennedy managed, for two years, ten months and two days, to keep the country in a state of more or less constant agitation. He was always in a hurry to get on with work that most of us would just as soon put off, or not do at all. He resolved that this nation ought to lower tariffs, rush men to the moon (ticket: $20 billion), produce at full capacity, wipe out unemployment, end racism, and take 50-mile hikes—remember?—to trim its waistline. He didn't just argue in that hacksaw Harvard accent; he nudged us, like none before him, with every power prod in Government.

"He felt that if there was not a certain amount of opposition," recalls Robert S. McNamara, "he wasn't doing as much as he should."

Kennedy recognized the danger in active use of vast authority. Five months before his death, he talked about it with Jesse Unruh, the power-wielding "Big Daddy" of California politics, as the two were chauffeured across the lush abundance of Los Angeles. "Government has grown so far as to be almost beyond comprehension. It gets near this big-brotherness. People have a right to be concerned."

But he saw the deeper threat of inaction. "Congress isn't really out of step with the people," he mused. "They're feeling public sentiment pretty well, and it says don't act. But that's not enough. Somebody ought to see over the hill, even if he risks defeat. If that isn't the President's function, we should never have quarreled with Eisenhower."

He knew the citizen's sense of helplessness in the face of big Government, bigger problems. It leads to paralysis, frantic nostalgia and the fear that any change is dangerous. The real cure, he felt, was for men to seize the jobs ahead, not just in Government, but through the broad range of U.S. institutions. A people confidently driving toward new destiny cannot be trapped by bureaucracy or despair.

Kennedy expected Americans to be ten feet tall. As his Peace Corps sent volunteers, old and young, to patriotic service in the world's dark slums, so his Army Special Forces started in 1962 to send lone green-bereted warriors into Communist jungles. He did little to expand the protective uniformity of the welfare state; he did much through his tax-cut bill and other moves to encourage the vital variety

Reprinted from Look, *November 17, 1964* © Look *magazine.*

of personal effort. He pushed us with such an unrelenting competence that some came to feel a deep resentment.

So what did he do for his country? Historians, the eager undertakers, will decide whether John Kennedy rests among the greats. We know simply that he earned a place in the national memory. The critics who might demand exact measure have been muffled by his death. For now, only the men and women who shared his driving obsessions can—when their views are taken in the context of their work with him—offer strong, if biased, insight from the first year of reflection. Let us begin, then, with[six]of the many Look has interviewed.

Robert S. McNamara

"My personal view—I admit biases—is that he was a major political leader and world statesman," says Robert S. McNamara, the Ford Motor Company president who served Kennedy as Secretary of Defense. "He was least understood by his own people, less than by the rest of the nations. I don't think I've ever gone abroad without being struck by this. You found a tremendous feeling of respect and confidence."

As Englishmen were once too close to Churchill to know his grandeur, McNamara suggests, so Americans were too close to see Kennedy clearly. But they were catching on. Our belated awakening since the assassination has brought about, he believes, "the immense outpouring of not only love, but admiration."

A loyal Cabinet member can be expected to praise. The surprise comes in McNamara's definition of the greatness that he found in Kennedy. "He had wit and humor and style, yes, and with it, he had a more important capacity: moral and ethical insight."

Not many executives talk that way, not about politicians, and it takes a while to get at just what McNamara has in mind. He first sensed Kennedy's moral insight, he recalls, when he read his 1955 book, *Profiles in Courage*. "I was tremendously impressed." Kennedy examined the lives of eight great U.S. senators who, out of conscience, deliberately risked their careers upon unpopular issues. Each had courage, but McNamara found the book's strength in a deeper virtue. Kennedy was concerned with the close calculations by which a man judges what is worth a fight, how much of a fight, and when to risk everything. To back down on a fundamental, he believed, is no more foolish than to go to extremes on the insubstantial. Whether in business or politics, it takes judgment to resolve conflict between the practical and the moral.

McNamara found his boss "always aware" of each man's capacity to judge value, and of his own calculations. If this was a form of moral competence, it was accompanied by another kind. "He was a hard worker, a fast worker and very intelligent," says the Defense chief, himself noted for those traits. "He took a personal responsibility for development of his own views, rather than waiting for a staff study with recommended course of action. But he would change his mind, did so, on the basis of evidence. He thought independently.

"He recognized that the Soviet Union was going through a period of change. We could force it to look inward rather than outward, by not allowing it opportunities to carry on aggression. This could be achieved by building a military force effective at all levels, not just at strategic nuclear war. Further, he associated strong military force with a limited objective. We weren't seeking to overthrow the present Russian regime; we were seeking to limit its sphere of influence."

Here came the ultimate application of the judgment that McNamara calls moral insight. When Khrushchev roared his resolve to seize Berlin, Kennedy saw the evil inherent in a one-button choice between backing down and blowing up civilization. He sought options in between, a range of military responses calculated to handle each struggle on its own level. He did not have them. The Army and Navy had been starved by the massive-deterrence policy. Kennedy ordered McNamara into a crash buildup of conventional forces, plus some highly unconventional guerrillas. "The total program was costly—$30 billion over four years," admits McNamara, "but cheap in terms of risk."

"Not only will it avoid complete dependence on nuclear weapons," McNamara said at the time, "but it will also enhance the credibility to the Soviets of our determination to use nuclear weapons, should this prove necessary." Kennedy, talking with his personal aides about Khrushchev, was less pedantic: "Why, that son of a bitch won't pay any attention to words. He has to see you move."

To avoid the moral bankruptcy of the final war, Kennedy was ready to engage the U.S. in the dirtiest of little wars. "We shall have to deal with the problems of 'wars of liberation,'" McNamara declared. "Their military tactics are those of the sniper, the ambush and the raid. We must help the people of threatened nations to resist these tactics by appropriate means. You cannot carry out a land-reform program if the local peasant leaders are being systematically murdered."

The atmosphere changed. While nuclear war was the fulcrum of U.S. strategy, officers and diplomats used the threat of it in almost any crisis. Once Kennedy found alternatives, he demanded that the Joint Chiefs stop such talk. "Gentleman, I am a civilian," a personal aide heard him say. "Nobody wants to hear the military opinion of an ex-Navy lieutenant, j.g., when they can hear yours. But if I am going to convince the Soviets, our allies and others that we're going to keep the peace, then you can't be rattling your sword every time you get up."

He made his point explicit to the world in the partial ban on nuclear tests. He was not fool enough to expect our troubled species to live without conflict. He sought to settle differences by active, close-in engagement, rather than by ominous gestures with H-bombs.

In the Cuban missile crisis, he found his opportunity to prove his basic principle of calculated military pressure, rather than the desperate yank at the trigger. "He was ready to invade," says an aide, "and the Russians knew it." He forced Khrushchev up against painful options, gave him time to make the right choice.

McNamara, rushing to the White House for the eyeball-to-eyeball evening, found a calm Commander in Chief busy defining options for people. "Caroline!" the President shouted as his small daughter raced across the lawn. "Have you been eating candy?" No answer. He tried again. No answer. "Caroline! Answer yes, no or maybe."

Walter Heller

"How can you move a $500 billion economy with a $5 billion deficit?" rasped candidate Jack Kennedy. "How come the German economy prospered at a 5 percent interest rate, and you fellows want easy money?"

It was October, 1960. Kennedy was, as usual, changing into a fresh shirt when economist Walter Heller walked into his Minneapolis hotel room to be introduced. Instead of palming off the quick handshake, Kennedy instantly let fire with hard, fast questions deep into Heller's field. He concentrated on each answer, tested it and the man behind it. "He just stood there scratching his chest while we talked, and everybody else fell away." Three months later, vouched for by other top pros, Heller became adviser to the new President.

Kennedy wanted knowledge, not advice, and he turned Heller into his teacher. Under three years of drumfire questions, Heller wrote 400 to 500 technical memoranda, often ten pages long, and sent along scholarly documents and books on specific issues. As the President gained command of fact and analysis, he came to his own conclusions, checked them against the views of businessmen and outside economists.

"I was working myself out of a job," Heller says. He watched Kennedy chair one seminar of experts on the gold drain. The dismal science was being absorbed, Heller saw, "into the luster and joy, the crisp, crackling nature of the whole operation. . . . At the time of his death, he was a good orthodox economist."

In economics, as in politics, most people consider themselves born experts, so they learn little about it. Politicians tend to build their policies on catchphrases that please their crowds. Even Churchill and Roosevelt used economic advisers like court magicians, never learned the discipline. Kennedy, first U.S. President to do his homework, sought to make the voters share his study. "I want you to use the White House," he once told Heller, "as a pulpit for economic education."

His know-how led to the boldest political decision of his shortened term. With unemployment hanging high, labor leaders, brain trusters and the popular magazines were near panic over "automation" and its job-kill. Because of private industry's efficient new machines, many believed, only a massive dose of Federal spending could create jobs. Some talked of Government checks for everybody. Almost nobody expected a Democratic President to demand huge tax cuts that would boost business profits, stimulate investment in still more labor-saving machinery. Heller's pupil did just that.

He did not live to see his tax cuts—pushed through by Lyndon Johnson—fire up the economy, eat into unemployment. But he was already setting up the next logical move. The tax cut assumed that private enterprise, not Government, offers most people the chance to better their lives. Yet millions, not all of them on relief, lack the education and confidence to make a good living. They would do even worse when the tax trim speeded up economic change—and also the rate at which workers must educate up to higher skills. "We have to be concerned about those left behind," Heller argued. Kennedy agreed.

In June of 1963, Kennedy gave Heller's staff the go-ahead on research into how people could be helped to fight their way out of poverty. The staff focused on the unemployables not reached by present vocational training and education. Result: "the war on poverty." Late on the night of November 19, Kennedy resolved to push it in 1964. "But I think it's important to make it clear that we're also doing something for the middle-class man in the suburbs," he added. It was his last economic decision before a bullet stopped his capable brain.

Barbara Gamarekian

"I saw him primarily at the time he was playing the role of the President and doing the things that Presidents have to do," says Barbara Gamarekian. This tall girl from upstate New York arranged the White House photography setups. She thus presided over the minor ceremonies in which the Presidency resembles the ritual dances of a tribal chief. As the chief's step and style communicate specific meaning to the watchful tribe, so does the President's manner when he greets foreign dignitaries, pep-talks student groups, endorses charities, and tosses out the season's first baseball. The nation watches him closely through the daily photographs and news reports.

"He hated clichés. Sometimes, he would not say anything new or imaginative, but he clothed it in new words so that sort of an old truth suddenly took on new meaning," says Barbara. "He was especially good with students. He had great rapport, and I think they left with probably a reawakened and perhaps, I hope, a rather changed viewpoint of what the United States was and what they were trying to do."

He fought the clichés where he found them. When Arthur M. Schlesinger, Jr., ghosted the President's annual TV appeal for the United Fund campaign, Kennedy speed-read Schlesinger's words, turned toward the three-network cameras—to deliver his own completely fresh pitch without using a phrase from the prewritten material.

He nearly fell, however, for the Sunday-painter bit. Having learned to dabble on canvas while in the hospital (the wifely influence), he was proud when a magazine tracked down one painting, published it. The press office was deluged with requests from other media. As Barbara passed the President's open door a few days later, he called her into the office. "What do you think of these two paintings?" he demanded. Beside the pictures, two aides stood silent.

"Well, I like the one on the left," she said cautiously.

"Oh, do you?" the President responded in hope. "Do you really like that one?"

"Well, in preference to the one on the right."

Kennedy turned a wry grin upon his aides. "I knew they were no good," he said. He hated a second-rate performance.

One spring, just before he was to throw out the national sport's first ball, Barbara walked briskly past the Rose Garden, suddenly noticed the President of the United States there alone. He was secretly practicing throws with a softball. "Obviously, he felt sheepish," she remembers. "He ducked his head and said, 'Hello.' "

William Walton

"We didn't take him to symphony concerts because we couldn't keep him awake," says William Walton, who was the President's close personal adviser on the arts. "He liked active movies. He loved *Spartacus*. In art, he liked the impressionists—Childe Hassam's *Flags on Fifth Avenue*."

Bill Walton, a muscular man who paints in bold colors, clobbers the notion that Kennedy encouraged pretentious "Culture." Hating the phony in highbrow art as in lowbrow politics, Kennedy went for poetry and painting that made strong, clear statements.

"His specific thing was architecture. You can understand why. It is the expression of our civilization, the most important American art—and we're ahead of the world in it now." More to the point, Kennedy had to make decisions about it. Within a week after he took office, he was expected to give the final go-ahead on two Federal buildings to stand around Lafayette Park, directly across Pennsylvania Avenue. "Stark moderns on either side of the square—it would have been a disaster," says Walton. "We finally fired the architects [two Boston firms] at great expense. When I apologized for taking up so much of his time, he said, 'No, this may be the only mark I leave'."

Once into the subject, brain-first, Kennedy kept going. "He didn't want Pennsylvania Avenue to become a curtain of glass. We must make such complete arrangements, he felt, that they can't change it. His impact won't show for three or four years, when the new buildings start up. He was very Jeffersonian, and Jefferson loved architecture." His eyes rebelled at the bad taste often endemic to public property. Reading an architectural magazine, he once spotted a gaudy design for the U.S. Pavilion at the New York World's Fair. "Do something," he ordered Walton. Landing at Otis Air Force Base, Mass., after his baby died, he dressed down a fighter-pilot commander for dressing his men in "God-awful red jackets with Mickey Mouse shoulder patches."

Mrs. Kennedy's renovation of the White House not only aimed to make it a museum, but a pleasant place to go. Inside it, the Kennedys ended the notion that state dinners, and ancient art form, have to be pompous. "No protocol in the seating," Walton points out. "Jackie would pick out the two prettiest, brightest women—if they were dumb, he would ignore them—and put them on either side of him."

The talk came fast, to the point. At dinner during a Berlin crisis, Kennedy suddenly looked down the table at Walton: "All right, what is the softheaded liberal approach to Berlin?" At another dinner, the President livened things up a bit by doubting that Pope John was all the press pictured him to be. "You Protestants are building him up," he contended. Nor did the Anglican Church, headed by Queen Elizabeth, escape his joyous irreverence. "How can you believe in a church," he asked a guest, "headed by that girl?"

Those lively years may leave as deep a mark on the public mind, Walton believes, as on its buildings. "He gave Americans the vision of what a whole man can be. It's not just the arts. You sail yourself and your wife water-skis, and a great man has his children around him. His eye was always alive, never glazed."

Robert F. Kennedy

Fiercely loyal, Robert Kennedy sees only perfection in the work done while his big brother was Chief Executive. "Mistakes? It's a bad thing to say, but I don't think we made any." His conviction is unshaken by the Berlin wall, Bay of Pigs, two dead men at Ole Miss, and the Vietnamese War. He credits even less the deeper doubt many feel about the way the Administration used concentrated political and economic power.

"Bobby," as fan and foe came to know him, perfected the power tactic. As "Executive Vice-President," armed with White House might, he launched a blitz upon any problem. He thus became the President's most active asset and most visible liability. His every act spoke his brother's hunger for results.

If Bobby threw the FBI into the steel case, he also used the power in less questionable ways. He organized all Federal law enforcers around the FBI for a long-overdue siege of the crime syndicate and achieved a twelvefold rise in convictions (one Chicago hood went to jail for keeping more than the legal limit of doves in his home freezer). For Latin America, he secretly built a civilian counterinsurgency system—U.S. agents in James Bond clothes—that helped local police squelch the Communist revolution in Venezuela. As expediter of civil-rights action, the Attorney General ended the long era of waiting for riot, sending troops. He worked daily on all fronts. Without progress, he knew, "the Negro population would have become completely disenchanted with the American system. You'd have had utter chaos."

By these and other total efforts, Bobby believes, the country was saved from inertia's drift into half-seen dangers. One warm afternoon not long ago, driving out to the gas-lit grave in Arlington National Cemetery, he passionately summed up his case for the man lying there:

"He campaigned to get America going again, and that's what he did. He believed the Presidency to be a position where you could do a great deal. Maybe you couldn't discern movement day to day, but over the months, the change was fundamental. He restored to Americans the confidence in our future, the belief that we are destined for greater things.

"Sputnik had undermined it. Then the shooting down of the U-2. Eisenhower called off his trip to Japan. The stoning of Nixon. Slow economic growth, deficits, unemployment—without any idea of what could be done. No plan.

"He restored the confidence that people from other countries had in the ideals of this country. The President—and his Administration— was the major hope the world had for peace. You can see the change in the feeling of South America when you think of what happened to

Nixon [spit] and what happened to President Kennedy [roses]. The change was just as deep in the feeling of the African countries. They know we have a racial problem, but we're doing something about it."

Martin Luther King, Jr.

Between two resolute Americans, a black Baptist preacher and a white Roman Catholic President, there smoldered a three-year struggle of the will. The two young leaders agreed on principle, but not upon its urgency (Freedom—Now!). The black man won. Near the end, he shaped events so that the white man had to use every resource, his audacity and skill, to avoid national disaster, and to earn his most likely claim on history.

Martin Luther King, Jr., studied John Fitzgerald Kennedy with the cold insight of an enemy and the warm concern of a friend. "The basic thing about him—he had the ability to respond to creative pressure," says King. "I never wanted—and I told him this—to be in the position that I couldn't criticize him if I thought he was wrong. And he said, 'It often helps me to be pushed.' When he saw the power of the movement, he didn't stand there arguing about it. He had the vision and wisdom to see the problem in all of its dimensions and the courage to do something about it. He grew until the day of his assassination."

"Historians will record that he vacillated like Lincoln," King believes, "but he lifted the cause far above the political level."

They first met—a Kennedy invitation to breakfast—only a month before the 1960 Democratic convention. King sensed "a definite concern but . . . not what I would call a 'depthed' understanding." By September, worried about the attitude of Negro voters, Kennedy had King to dinner at his Georgetown home. "I don't know what it is, Senator, but you've got to do something dramatic," said King.

King soon provided by accident the incident for a dramatic move. Back in Atlanta, he was jailed as a probation violator for joining a sit-in. Kennedy, watching for an opportunity, seized it for a substantial act of personal courtesy, the sort that whites seldom extend. He made his famous sympathy call to Mrs. King. "Bobby called the judge," adds King. The gesture inspired record Negro majorities needed to carry close industrial states. "There are those moments when the politically expedient is the morally wise," King observes with a patient smile. "It would have been easy for him to stand by."

A month after inauguration, Kennedy called King to the White House for the first of many visits. The President was going to strengthen the executive order on fair-employment contracts. The move was more important than anybody knew because Vice-President Lyndon Johnson took over the contract-enforcement job, spent as much as half his time nudging industrialists and Federal agencies into all-out Negro recruiting. But, to King's dismay, John Kennedy was putting the civil-rights bill on a back burner. "Nobody needs to convince me any longer that we have to solve the problem, not let it drift on gradualism," he said. "But how do you go about it? If we go into a long fight in Congress, it will bottleneck everything else and still get no bill."

King kept the pressure on, urged Kennedy to shape public opinion in TV fireside chats. He even visited the White House on the day of the Bay of Pigs, again the day Christmas lights were turned on. One night before dinner, when President and Mrs. Kennedy showed King the White House renovations, he walked to the room where Lincoln signed the Emancipation Proclamation. "Mr. President, I'd like for you to come back in this room one day and sit down at that desk and sign the Second Emancipation Proclamation." He followed up, at Kennedy's request, with a 120-page document outlining a total attack.

"He was always ready to listen," says King, who once lectured Kennedy on the nonviolence discipline of the early Christians. "They had practiced civil disobedience in a superb manner," explains King. "But it's a difficult thing to teach a President and his brother, who is a lawyer, about civil disobedience."

The talks convinced King that the President was slowly coming around. Others doubted it. Kennedy sent the troops to Ole Miss to put down the bloody riot and protect James Meredith, but his behind-the-scenes deals with Mississippi Gov. Ross Barnett made Negroes feel like pawns in a white man's political game. He talked only in specifics, they argued, and did not assert the broad moral issue.

"We were puzzled at the anti-Kennedy sentiment among Southern whites," recalls a candid King deputy. "There was almost that much anti-Kennedy sentiment among Negroes in the movement."

Angry activists suspected Kennedy of exploiting King. In the desperate drive to integrate Albany, Ga., Negroes charged that Kennedy men kept King on the telephone for two solid days, when their leader could have turned failure into victory. Next, in Birmingham, King's men were ready to march twice, and twice Kennedy's men persuaded King to hold off. Robert Kennedy called the campaign ill-timed. It was against the Justice Department's hard pressure that the Negro masses marched, May 3, 1963, on the police dogs and fire hoses.

That settled the White House arguments. Next time King went to talk—hours before the President flew to Europe for his triumphal tour —the two spent an hour and fifteen minutes alone. As they walked in the Rose Garden, their ideas were in step. "Birmingham had caused him to revise his legislative agenda. Civil rights, which had been on the bottom of the list, or not there at all, moved to the top. I liked the way he talked about what *we* are getting. It wasn't something that he was getting for you Negroes. You knew you had an ally."

The ally did far more than King knew. After Birmingham, Kennedy began to call bankers, union chiefs, businessmen, churchmen, lawyers, clubwomen, and other leaders to the White House to ask their help in the crisis. A Democratic President was relying on private citizens, many of them Republicans, not only to back a new civil-rights law, but to take action in their own spheres. The Establishment's response was immediate, general, and decisive. "White only" signs fell from most hotel chains, restaurants, and theaters in the South. Negro hiring picked up. Bail money flowed to Negro demonstrators. Businessmen sought out the local Negro leaders. Forced by King, Kennedy learned how strong citizens, given leadership, can be.

The sentiments let loose by Birmingham peaked in the August 28 March on Washington. King brought the jubilee throng of 230,000 to tears with his visionary oration: "I have a dream. . . ." That night, he went with other March leaders to the White House. When the President reached out to shake hands, he said, "*I* have a dream."

"There were, in fact, two John Kennedys," King believes. "One presided in the first two years under pressure of the uncertainty caused by his razor-thin margin of victory. In 1963, a new Kennedy had emerged. He had found that public opinion was not in a rigid mold. He was, at his death, undergoing a transformation from a hesitant leader with unsure goals to a strong figure with deeply appealing objectives."

John Kennedy fought his way to the world's most powerful office while still a young man. He got there before the old pros of his trade could wear down his beliefs into clichés, before he spent the enegry it takes to listen hard, think realistically, and work out a new course. He learned to pace himself, and he lightened the human load each night in prayer. But his ambitions for himself and his country never let him escape the thought that time might run out on him.

One night at the White House, he joined other Administration thinkers—a group called "Hickory Hill School"—in talk with a Civil War historian about Abraham Lincoln. Abe was lucky, somebody argued, to be assassinated before his greatness could be battered by the evil confusions of Reconstruction. Yes, answered the 35th President of the United States, but what if Lincoln had been shot two years earlier? He would have died an uncertain failure and never made known the greatness that was in him.

Rexford Guy Tugwell

The Kennedy Interlude

In domestic affairs nothing of note was accomplished. The single considerable victory in a contest with the Congress was the passage of a bill reducing taxes, and that came after his death. He was a convert to the newer views of the economists he consulted. They believed prosperity and depression were controllable by government policies, fiscal and monetary. They were largely right, of course, except that manipulation of such forces required the collaboration of some five hundred legislators who had other views and other aims and would never do the economists' bidding in time to effect the result wanted. Kennedy was not so naïve as to think that all problems would be solved by higher and more sustained productivity, but he was convinced that this was the source of capability to do what was necessary in society.

In his campaign, Kennedy had made a repeated promise to "get the country moving again" after years of Eisenhower stagnation; and it could only be done by temporarily ignoring conservative prejudice. If the economy was to be stimulated, purchasing power must be increased, and reducing taxes would leave more income for purchasers. The theory would also call for contracting purchasing power when the economy speeded up, in order to avoid inflation; and this was even more difficult. The partisanship in the Congress ought to have been a warning that any accommodation requiring legislation would be slow, and, if the President could not bring pressure to bear, impossible. One of the two Kennedy years was devoted to this struggle, and no considerable progress in more permanent reforms was made while it was going on.

Especially he failed to assess the pressures building up in the cities as a consequence of the massive but unspectacular movement of displaced farm workers—and even farmers themselves—into cities everywhere, but mostly into those of the North. Nothing was done to prepare for this or to prevent it. As a result already overcrowded slums presently held several times as many people as they had held before.

The obvious problems of housing, schooling, and of somehow providing for all this migrating population was immensely complicated by racial strains. Many of the rural workers had been black, and when they

From Off Course: From Truman to Nixon *(1971) by Rexford Guy Tugwell. Reprinted by permission of Praeger Publishers, Inc.*

moved into the cities they were forced to crowd into black neighborhoods. The inconvenienced whites were resentful, and a troubled period began that would not end until genuine national efforts to replan and rebuild were made and until funds were appropriated. The situation had been worsening for years without recognition in Washington. Truman, Eisenhower, and Kennedy were, if not indifferent, neglectful.

Kennedy's was a curiously small achievement considering its spirited beginning and the hopes of those who had been his most prominent associates. In the White House itself were such liberals as Theodore Sorensen, Arthur M. Schlesinger, Jr., Walt Rostow, and Pierre Salinger; the Secretary of State was Dean Rusk, former foundation president; the Secretary of Defense was the brilliant Ford executive Robert McNamara; the Secretary of the Interior was Stewart Udall—so it went. There was the same sort of gathering in Washington of intellectuals anxious to do something in public service as there had been in Roosevelt's time, and actually they did regard themselves as the inheritors of that spirit. For a time it seemed that, after the Eisenhower dullness, the Roosevelt *élan* was again infusing the centers of power. The obstructionism would be overcome; leadership would ignite new fires; and the country would indeed "get moving again."

Almost from the first, however, the brave words of the inaugural "ask not what your country can do for you; ask what you can do for your country"—so inspiring to those who hoped for a renewal of national concern for liberal causes—were emptied of hope by what the country seemed to demand: mostly military service in a doubtful cause.

Attention was fixed on what was happening abroad, and the deployment of forces to meet new crises required energies and funds far beyond any former allocations. What was happening in the cities at home could be taken care of later. Discovery of black wrongs and resentments was perhaps less likely for one who had sprung from Irish ancestry in Boston. As a legislator he had thought first of his own people; it was to them that he owed his early successes. At any rate explosive racial issues were bequeathed to his successors with nothing even begun that would meet the coming crisis.

In the speech to have been made on the day of his assassination, Kennedy was still to have spoken of "manning the walls of liberty." It was a phrase that might have been found in one of the James Bond books he read so avidly; but his preoccupation with communist designs was certainly not so exclusive as Truman's or Dulles'. What was happening closer at home he heard about from his associates; and he may have been concerned; there were evidences of change. He made an eloquent speech at Amherst College about education, for instance, and was negotiating the sale of wheat to Russia when he was assassinated.

In spite of the gracious glow that infused White House entertainment, there was little light in the rest of Washington during the Kennedy years. Especially on Capitol Hill, there was more fog than sun. The informal alliance between Northern and Southern conservatives, ignoring party affiliations, had not been in the least modified by Kennedy's election; anyway, he had beaten Nixon by an infinitesimal margin, and so could not expect any impressive public support for liberal measures. Lacking it, his own Congressional party, dominated by the reactionary Southern committee chairmen, stood in the way; and he had no power to move them.

In retrospect, and considering liberal expectations, there is a melancholy dimness about the Kennedy Administration. The release from Eisenhower and the escape from the Nixon threat had seemed so promising to liberals, and yet so little had been done—except to confront the other superpower in a pointless competition to see which could accumulate the larger store of genocidal weapons that neither could use; and, of course, to offer assistance wherever the conspiracy showed itself. There was a gathering storm at home whose violence was not anticpiated.

Roosevelt had started off with a magnificent array of legislative achievements in his legendary first "hundred days." Kennedy was to finish his "thousand days" with almost no similar accomplishments. The Congress had not listened when he spoke; it had dallied; and he had had no leverage to start it going. When he made the fatal trip to Dallas, there was disillusion among his most faithful supporters and even the possibility of rejection by the party he had blitzed in 1960 and whose older leaders had never forgiven him for it. He was trying desperately to hold the support in the South he had once bought by giving the Vice-Presidency to Johnson. Of course, if he had known that the Republicans would nominate Goldwater and, with him, invite the electorate to approve retreat from governmental responsibilities, he would have had no need to worry; but how could anyone have anticipated such a folly?

If Kennedy had had a longer time in the White House, and if he had had the liberal Congress of 1964–66, he might have done all that Johnson did and have done it in more orderly fashion. He was intelligent, industrious, and dedicated. He might have reached an understanding with the Russians in spite of the past; there were some signs of softening; Khrushchev, with whom he had to deal, was not wholly intractable.

As to the involvement in Southeast Asia, so fatal to Johnson, there is evidence that in 1963 Kennedy considered a complete withdrawal but that it seemed politically impossible without more support than he had. MacArthur told him, in a conversation he took seriously, what he was in for, reiterating the conviction that involvement on the Asian mainland had no advantages worth the costs. If he had lived, been re-elected, and had had a Congress he could depend on, the nation might have been saved the immeasurable agonies of the next decade.

After his assassination, there was more appreciation for Kennedy's quality than there had been while he had been President. It was seen then how distinctive his style had been. His sharp communications had been a striking change from Eisenhower's fusty blandness; it had taken some getting used to; but pride in his grace and style had grown. The Roosevelt agenda that Truman had neither comprehended nor had the power to go on with if he had, and that Eisenhower had regarded as un-American, might have been resumed. What the country needed, after these postwar fumblings, was just the sort of hard, realistic adaptations to the technologized world Kennedy understood and perhaps meant to carry out.

3
Power and Purpose in Foreign Affairs: The Cold War, Cuba Twice, Vietnam

Just as the president's perceptions and philosophy shape and limit his policies in domestic matters, so do they in the realm of foreign affairs also, and often without the salutary checks that are built into the constitutional system for resolving conflicts of domestic policy. Since the powers of the president in the domain of foreign affairs are so vast, and his capacity for leadership in the international community so fraught with consequence for national security and world peace, his predilections can affect the course of nations for years to come.

McGeorge Bundy, Special Assistant to the President for National Security Affairs, said that President Kennedy had a clear view of the Soviet Union but that he rejected the rhetoric of the Cold War, did not insist upon the supposed innate wickedness of Communism, and worked instead to combat its effects. Other views of President Kennedy's outlook on the Soviet Union are, however, more critical. What does seem to be true is that Kennedy's conception of power in relation to the Soviet Union was not supported by the same philosophical foundation as that of John Foster Dulles, President Eisenhower's Secretary of State for most of the 1950's. The Puritan-pietistic conception of power—that it must have some special and particularistic moral justification—encourages demonology in international affairs and inhibits the merely instrumental uses of power to effect necessary results. The reader will recall the distinction made by John Cogley in the Introduction between Catholic and Puritan conceptions of power, a distinction that, in somewhat different terms, is adopted by Bundy. With respect to the Cuban missile crisis in 1962, Bundy is of the view that Kennedy felt free even to risk nuclear war because he did not feel the need for a super-pietistic apology for the use of power, in the manner of Secretary Dulles.

Seyom Brown in his book *The Faces of Power* is concerned throughout with the elements of constancy and change in American foreign policy from Truman to Johnson. In the piece from that book reprinted in this section, he talks, rather, more in military terms of the problem of the world competition with the Soviet Union. Like his predecessors, he thinks President Kennedy accepted the "basic planning premise for the design of the strategic force" (that there should be no deterrent gap) and discovered upon access to the White House that the charges he had made during the campaign that such a gap existed were without foundation. In fact, the United States–Soviet strategic missile balance favored the United States. In the matter of local war capabilities with nonnuclear weapons, what was new in the Kennedy administration, according to Brown, was Kennedy's premise that the competition between the United States and the Soviet Union was a competition for influence in the Third World over the direction of development; and his belief that military initiatives had to be developed and improved in order to make effective "non-military instruments of power" in the vigorous contests that lay before and were yet to come, a principle assumed by Brown to have been validated by Premier Khrushchev's declaration in January 1961 in support of wars of national liberation. From the major premise developed the programs for counterinsurgency that had as their presumed objective the establishment of such security and order in Third World countries as would allow the United States effectively to champion local forces of social change. The reader might wish to consider whether military preoccupations haven't seemed since to precede and impede the sponsorship of social change in Third World countries like Vietnam, Laos, and Cambodia. Brown's thesis is interesting, however, that Kennedy's programs "to get the country moving again" (antirecession measures, trade expansion, and the tax cut of 1963) were "as much required by global balance of power considerations as they were by considerations of domestic economic well-being." This is the other side of the proposition discussed in the Introduction, that the president's power in foreign affairs is only variably and contingently effective, and it suggests that foreign and domestic policies supplement and reinforce each other. What perhaps may be doubted in the Brown statement is the assumption that an antirecession policy needs a global justification. Domestic urgencies would be adequate justification.

William Carleton's conception of Kennedy's position on the Cold War is different from that of Bundy. His argument is that in the first two years, Kennedy's policies seemed to be confused and contradictory but that they were better in the third; that he needlessly fanned the tensions of the Cold War—his inaugural address was alarmist and his first message on the State of the Union was even more so. The Bay of Pigs fiasco occurred in April 1961. In May 1961 Kennedy told the country that it was in the most critical period of its history. In June he met with Khrushchev in Vienna. Upon his return, President Kennedy urged the country to build bomb shelters and called up the reserves, actions which generated a war psychology. Sorensen argues that the crises were real. Professor Carleton thinks that all this was an overreaction to Khrushchev's threat to drive the West out of Berlin, a threat that had been made several times before and from which the Soviet premier had always backed down.

The Bay of Pigs disaster, three months after Kennedy's accession to office, was the abortive invasion of Cuba by anti-Castro Cuban exiles trained by the American Central Intelligence Agency (the CIA) and supported logistically and tactically by American military personnel. Theodore Sorensen's account of this misadventure provides the full chronology and raises questions about the organization and use of the presidential power. As he saw it, Kennedy's luck and judgment were both shown to have limitations. The account is sympathetic to Kennedy's difficulties—he says that there was a gap between decision and execution, between planning and reality; the decisions were made by Kennedy on the basis of the facts and assumptions that were presented to him; and there were three reasons why there was a gap between the assumptions and the facts: Kennedy was new in office, the president could not reverse an inexorable development, and the new administration was not yet organized for crisis planning. The real question, however, may not merely be one of technical proficiency and organization but the more basic political and moral question—whether on the authority of the president of the United States alone, another country with which we were not at war could be invaded for the purpose of producing a change in the regime while our representative in the United Nations was denying American participation at the very moment it was being exposed. Kennedy's reaction to the failure of the invasion seems to have amounted to little more than chagrin that he had listened to the wrong set of advisers, to Adolf Berle and Thomas Mann instead of to Arthur Schlesinger, Jr., and Senator J. William Fulbright.

Major-General Thomas Lane (ret.) too has his own evaluation of the Bay of Pigs failure and also assigns it to technical factors largely, that is, the operation was not poorly planned but it was poorly executed because of failures of Kennedy's leadership. It is argued that, being concerned with his image as a vigorous leader, Kennedy made his office a center of action to control operations rather than a center of policy-making to provide guidance to the operating officials. This difference between personalized and managerial leadership was discussed in Part One. Lane's conception of leadership is basically the military one that President Eisenhower used in the White House— organization is primarily a matter of building blocks. Put a man in charge and let him run things according to policy laid down by the president. This conception, however, may be too rigid a one for the successful operation of the office of president of the United States. On the other hand it does seem to be clear that Kennedy's conception of a personal ministry did lead him to involve himself in tactical and technical details of which he had insufficient knowledge.

The second Cuban crisis by most accounts was a different matter. This was the installation in Cuba of defensive missiles aimed at the United States, supplied to the Cuban government by the Soviet Union. In the month of October 1962 President Kennedy said that a quarantine would be placed around Cuba to prevent the installation of the missiles and after a tense time, Soviet ships turned around, returned to their home ports, and the missiles already in place were removed and shipped out. The threat that the confrontation implied was nothing less than nuclear war.

Hugh Sidey supplies a somewhat adoring account of the action of the president in this crisis, which is represented as a model of cool decisiveness. On the other hand, Dean Acheson, former Secretary of State under President Truman who was drawn into the president's councils during the crisis, was of the opinion that Kennedy had acted on the wrong advice, that he should have ordered the destruction of the missile sites by bombing, and said that an important ingredient in the successful outcome of the blockage had been phenomenal luck, although he did send the president a message of congratulation on his leadership, firmness, and judgment. The Acheson article reprinted here is an answer, published in February 1969, to one published by Senator Robert Kennedy somewhat earlier. One can gather the gist of Senator Kennedy's article from Dean Acheson's statements about it. In July 1971, in an interview published in *Life,* Dean Acheson when asked for his assessment of President Kennedy said, "He was not decisive." When reminded that many thought that Kennedy had been decisive in the Cuban missile crisis, Acheson's reply was that the legend of Kennedy's decisiveness was just that, a legend.

For a criticism of the Cuban missile confrontation from a radical perspective, the collection of pieces in this section includes a statement by David Horowitz from his book *Free World Colossus.* The argument is that the confrontation was unnecessary, that there was no military risk in having missile sites emplaced in Cuba, that the Russian provocation could have been turned off by an ultimatum delivered in private, and that the real stake was not security and military defense but the political balance in the world, which in turn was a question of prestige and appearances, a perilous episode in international public relations. The deed was symbol and the symbol was power.

A presidential decision uncontrolled by other institutions sharing general powers of the president, can lead to a quick disaster like the Bay of Pigs, a quick triumph like that of the missiles, or a long-term disaster that has managed to touch every aspect of American life, like the war in Vietnam. As in so much else, President Kennedy had no strong position on Vietnam when he entered the White House. As Theodore Draper says in the pages reprinted here from his book *Abuse of Power,* the problem before President Kennedy in 1961 was the same problem that President Eisenhower faced in 1954 when the French were overcome by defeat, namely, what to do to stave off a complete collapse of the local regime. There were two solutions, one political and the other military. The political solution was to let the regime collapse and to allow events to reach fulfillment without American intervention. The military solution was to supply military advisers—at the time of the Geneva Accord, the number of military advisers was limited to 685 men, assigned to Saigon. As indicated in the Introduction, President Kennedy violated this international international understanding when in the spring of 1961 he sent 400 Special Forces troops and 100 other military advisers to South Vietnam without public notice. On May 11, 1961, when the Geneva Accord was breached, President Kennedy also ordered the start of a clandestine war against North Vietnam, to be conducted by South Vietnamese

agents, trained and supported by the CIA and some American Special
Forces troops. By the end of 1961, there was, then, a war going on in
which Americans were involved in covert operations against North
Vietnam and Laos, and American ground and Air Force personnel
were being used in the South against the Viet Cong. By the end of 1963,
President Kennedy had 16,732 "advisers" in Vietnam. All of this
was done by the action of the president alone.

Although a distinction was made between the political solution
and the military solution, the second—the violation of the Geneva
Accords by the sending of military personnel above the established
limit—also bore upon and influenced the first, for the security of the
American personnel then required intensified support of President
Ngo Dinh Diem's regime, which was rigid, reactionary, corrupt, and
without substantial support throughout the country. As Draper points
out, the military emphasis appeared to be halfhearted but the political
commitment was not. One of Kennedy's principal advisers, General
Maxwell D. Taylor, who urged in October 1961 that the president
should commit 6,000 to 8,000 ground troops immediately, was of the
opinion that no major land war would result. As was said in the
Introduction, the conclusion of the task force that prepared the
so-called Pentagon Papers is that President Kennedy transformed the
limited-risk gamble of the Eisenhower administration into a broad
commitment to prevent the Communist domination of South Vietnam.

There was also a gamble within the gamble—for the political
commitment to the Diem regime implied in the sending of troops in
violation of the Geneva Accord failed. Diem was finally assassinated
in November 1963 with at least the acquiescence of the United States,
although there is disagreement as to the degree of the complicity
of the United States, as Draper points out.

McGeorge Bundy

The Presidency and the Peace

It is with some sense of temerity that a member of the White House staff undertakes to comment on the large topic of the Presidency and the Peace. Loyalty and affection are so human in such service that detachment is difficult. Nevertheless the importance of the topic and the enforced familiarity of close experience with the Presidential task may justify a set of comments whose underlying motive is to express a conviction that is as obvious as the daylight, in general, and as fresh as every sunrise, in particular: a conviction that the American Presidency, for better, not for worse, has now become the world's best hope of preventing the unexampled catastrophe of general nuclear war.

Moreover, both charity and sorrow can be good lenses for perception, and it may therefore be possible to consider the subject without impropriety by focussing upon the years of John F. Kennedy. The tragedy which has moved his Administration from politics to history may allow to his critics and excuse in his friends some generosity in the assessment of his three years. His death revealed his greatness, and the grief of the world was less for his tragedy than for its own—in that he had shown his spreading grasp of his duty to mankind, as Chief Executive for Peace.

To focus on the Kennedy years is not to forget those before, and still less the firm continuation after November 22. The Presidents of the nuclear age before Mr. Kennedy also made the service of peace the first of their purposes, and the determined commitment of President Johnson to this same end, matured in decades of direct knowledge of our nuclear world, has been made plain in his own words and actions already. Indeed one purpose of a retrospective assessment is to clarify purposes which are as important to the President today as to the President last year.

A President in search of Peace has many powers, but none is more relevant or more effective than his power as Commander-in-Chief. The President is keeping the peace as long as he keeps his own nuclear power in check, and with it the nuclear power of others. This most obvious of his powers, apparently so simple and so negative, can be used for peace in a number of ways.

Reprinted by permission from Foreign Affairs, *April 1964. Copyrighted by the Council on Foreign Relations, Inc., New York.*

The prerequisite, of course, is that this power should exist, and that there should be confidence in its future as well as its present effectiveness. Nothing is more dangerous to the peace than weakness in the ultimate deterrent strength of the United States. In the quarter-century that man has known the atom could be split, each American decision to enlarge its power has been the President's alone. More subtly but with just as great importance, the choices of methods of delivery and their rate of development have also been Presidential.

As important as having strength is being known to have it; and here if anything the Presidential authority and responsibility are still more clear. This is the lesson of Sputnik, and of the "missile gap" which was forecast and feared by responsible and well-informed men both in and out of government between 1957 and 1961. There was ground for doubt and need for rapid action; the ground and the need were recognized, and important steps were taken, but an appearance of complacency led to an appearance of weakness, with considerable costs abroad. These costs would surely have been greater had it not been for the remarkable personal standing of President Eisenhower.

At the beginning of the Kennedy Administration there was need both for further action and for a reestablishment of confidence. The new President himself had feared the missile gap and had pressed his concern in the campaign. It was with honest surprise and relief that in 1961 he found the situation much less dangerous than the best evidence available to the Senate had indicated the year before. His Administration moved at once to correct the public impression, and thereafter, throughout his term, he encouraged and supported policies of action and of exposition which aimed to ensure not merely that American strategic power was sufficient—but that its sufficiency was recognized.

The adequacy of American strategic strength is a matter of such transcendent importance that it must always be a legitimate topic of political debate. "How much is enough?" is a question on which honest men will differ, and interested parties will find room and reason for their claims. Thus it is natural that in the present political year we have ranging shots already from the fringes, some saying that our strength is too little and others that it is too great. Just as it is the responsibility of the Commander-in-Chief to ensure the adequacy of our strength, so it is his task, either directly or through his principal defense officers, to meet and overcome such criticism. The present Administration will not be lax in the exposition of the real situation, and no one who has closely examined the present and prospective balance of strategic strength can doubt that this year any assertion that we are weak will be found wanting to the point of irresponsibility.

There is an equal obligation to meet the arguments of those who

think we are too strong. When these arguments grow out of fundamentally different views on the purpose and meaning of effective strategic strength, it may be necessary to agree to disagree. "Unilateral
disarmament" is a tainted term, but it does embody something of what
is desired by most of those who criticize our present strength as gravely
excessive. The Presidents of the nuclear age have recognized that the
law of diminishing returns applies to strategic missiles as to all other
commodities; they have also agreed with President Johnson's comment
that our nuclear defense expenditures can never be justified as a
W.P.A. for selected towns or states. But they have all rejected the
gamble of limiting our strategic strength in terms of any absolute
concept of what is enough. They have measured our strength against
that of the Soviet Union and have aimed at strategic superiority; that
superiority has had different meanings at different stages, but seen
from the White House its value for peace has never been small.

Yet even in this rejection of the underlying arguments which
move so many of those who find our strength excessive, a President
who cares for peace will respect their general concern. It is entirely
true that nuclear strength can be provocative, that it is full of the
hazard of accident or misuse, and that it imposes upon its commander,
in his own interest as in that of mankind, a passion for prudence. All
the Presidents of the nuclear age have understood this responsibility
and have sought to meet it by insisting on disciplined and responsible
control of this power. In the case of President Kennedy the pressing
need was that as the number and variety of weapons systems increased,
there should be ever more searching attention to effective command
and control. To him this was a better answer to the dangers of accident than some arbitrary limitation of numbers; a thousand well-con-
trolled and safely designed missiles could be less dangerous than a
hundred of lower quality, as well as more effective in deterrence.

A related point was the President's powerful aversion to those
nuclear weapons which could be used effectively only in a first strike.
In 1961 and 1962 he faced a series of judgments on major systems; he
always preferred the system which could survive an attack, as against
the system which might provoke one. In the same way and for related
reasons he preferred the system which was on the high seas or at home
to that which required a base abroad and evoked a real or pretended
charge of encirclement from Moscow.

The Commander-in-Chief must be strong, then, but also restrained. And as his strength must be recognized, so must his restraint.
The doctrine of "massive retaliation" was never as absolute as Mr. Dulles at first made it seem, and its real weakness lay not in the undoubted
fact that against certain kinds of aggression a nuclear response would

be necessary, but in the appearance of a bomb-rattling menace which it created. The Presidency does well to avoid this appearance; in the Kennedy Administration the rule was that statements of strength and will should be made as calmly as possible. The President himself watched constantly to prevent the appearance of belligerence, and when the White House watch nodded—as in one magazine account in which a single phrase out of context was seized upon by Soviet propaganda—he made his dissatisfaction plain.

A similar discipline was enforced throughout the Administration upon both civil and military officials. Those who have read speech drafts for clearance know how seldom there is need for major change, and how often divergence between Presidential purposes and a speaker's draft can be corrected by revision which reconciles the real purposes of both. And again it is not only the act of coordination but the appearance of it which is helpful. The nuclear age multiplies the mistrust that peaceable men must feel toward military men who appear not to be under effective control, and nothing adds more to a President's reputation abroad than recognition that he is Commander-in-Chief in fact as well as in name.

Yet the Kennedy years show again, as the terms of strong Presidents have shown before, that harmony, not conflict, is the normal relation between the Armed Services and the Presidency. The maintenance of clear Presidential control over military policy and over public statements gave rise to some criticism, and intermittently there were assertions that this or that military need was being overridden—this or that viewpoint silenced. Energy and strength in the Office of the Secretary of Defense produced similar worries, and challenges to cherished privileges were not unresisted. But the center of emphasis belongs on the fact that the Presidency has these powers in this country; a President who uses them firmly, with a defensible concept of the national security, can count on the support of the officers and men of the Armed Forces. The American tradition of civilian control is strong and the tradition of loyalty among professional officers high; the services are eager for a strong and active Commander-in-Chief. The armed strength of the United States, if handled with firmness and prudence, is a great force for peace.

II

The President who seeks peace must have a clear view of the Soviet Union. The one great weakness of Franklin Roosevelt was that he did not; he had not the advantage of living, as all his successors have, through the realities of the years after 1945. Nothing is gained for peace by forgetting Czechoslovakia or Hungary or the recurrent menace to Berlin, or Korea or Southeast Asia or any of the dozens of times and places where Communists with help from Moscow have sought to put an end to liberty.

Mr. Kennedy had this clear view. He had it before he became President; he confirmed it in his first state papers; he understood not only the unrelenting ambition and the ruthlessness of Communism, but also the weakness and disarray of much of the non-Communist world. And for almost two of his three years—from the very beginning until the offensive weapons were gone from Cuba—he had an exposure to Communist pressure in Berlin, in Laos, and in the Caribbean which could only confirm the somber estimate with which he entered office.

Against these pressures he was firm, and to meet them more effectively he greatly strengthened the defenses of the United States—not merely in strategic weapons for basic deterrence, but also in forces designed more precisely to meet the hazards of each point of pressure. The reserves who were called up for Berlin never fired a shot in anger, but military service by Americans has seldom made a more effective contribution to the defense of freedom and the keeping of peace. The new kinds of strength deployed to South Viet Nam have not finished that hard job, but they have prevented an otherwise certain defeat and kept the door open for a victory which in the end can be won only by the Vietnamese themselves. And never in any country did President Kennedy leave it in doubt that Communist subversion is always the enemy of freedom, and of freedom's friends, the Americans.

Yet always—and again from the beginning—he put equal emphasis on the readiness of the United States to reach honorable settlement of all differences, the respect of the United States for the reality of Soviet strength, and the insistence of the United States that both sides accept and meet their joint responsibility for peace.

He rejected the stale rhetoric of the cold war; he insisted not on the innate wickedness of Communism but on its evil effects. The Communist world was seldom if ever "the enemy." Characteristically, as in his Inaugural Address, the President used a circumlocution whose unaccustomed clumsiness was proof that it was carefully chosen: "those nations who would make themselves our adversary." Characteristically, too, what he there offered them was a request "to begin anew the quest for peace."

And he pressed in this same direction himself. In Laos, in Berlin, and most persistently of all in the search for a test ban, the President's powers, from beginning to end, were used toward the goal of agreement. Agreement must never be surrender; that would be no service to peace. The firmness of the United States under pressure was made plain both in Berlin and in Southeast Asia. But firmness was a means to honorable settlement, not an end in itself. Harboring no illusion about the difficulty of success, the President nevertheless persevered. He was convinced that at the least it was essential to leave no doubt, in all these issues, of the good will and peaceful purpose of the United States. If there were to be a continued arms race, or a test of strength, it must be plain where the responsibility lay. But the larger truth, as he saw it, was that in these areas of difference there was real advantage to both sides in reliable agreement—if only the other side could be brought to see its own real interests, free of ambition that would be resisted, and of fear that was unjustified.

In 1961 and 1962 the invitation to seek peace together met a thin response. True, the threat to Berlin, so noisy in 1961, and so sharpened by the confession of Communist bankruptcy which was the Wall, seemed slightly milder in 1962. And an agreement was reached on Laos, imperfect in its terms and in its execution, but much better than no agreement at all. It was in Laos above all that one could see the advantage to both sides of even the most incomplete disengagement, as against a tightening and sharpening of confrontation.

But no agreement at all had come in the field nearest the President's heart—that of limiting the nuclear danger. On the contrary, Soviet tests had led inexorably to American tests. It was somehow a measure of the Kennedy temper and purpose that of all the Soviet provocations of these two years is was the resumption of testing that disappointed him most.

III

The Cuban missile crisis was the most important single event of the Kennedy Presidency. As the President himself pointed out afterward, it was the first direct test between the Soviet Union and the United States in which nuclear weapons were the issue.

Although vast amounts have been written about the crisis, we still have no solid account of one half of it—the Soviet side. What is not known of one side limits our ability to assess action on the other, and this limitation should warn us against judgments that this act more than that, or one advantage more than another, was decisive. It does not prevent a more general judgment of the main elements contributing to success.

What is at once astonishing and wholly natural is the degree to which the clear components of this success are precisely those to which the Presidency had been bent and not only in the Kennedy Administration: strength, restraint, and respect for the opinions of mankind.

That strength counted we cannot doubt—though it is typical of the uncertainties of assessment that the partisans of specific kinds of strength remained persuaded, afterward as before, of the peculiar value of their preferred weapons. Believers in nuclear dissuasion as an all-purpose strategy asserted the predominant role of strategic superiority; believers in the need for conventional strength, while not usually denying the role of SAC in the success, were convinced that what mattered most was usable non-nuclear strength at the point of contest. Interesting as this argument may be, it can have no certain conclusion. Prudence argues for a judgment that all kinds of military strength were relevant. The existence of adequate and rapidly deployable strength, at all levels, was the direct result of the reinforcement of balanced defenses begun in 1961.

A further element of strength in this crisis was the firmness and clarity of the Presidential decision to insist on the withdrawal of the missiles. This was not merely a matter of one speech or even of one decision from a week of heavy argument. It was a position clearly stated, and internationally understood, well before the crisis broke. It was reinforced in its power, and the Communist position correspondingly weakened, by the repeated Soviet assertions that no such weapons were or would be placed in Cuba.

The strength of this position, like the strength of the available military force, was reinforced by its disciplined relation to a policy of restraint. That nuclear weapons should not be strewn around as counters in a contest for face was a proposition commanding wide support. Any impulse to discount or disregard the direct threat to the United States, as a problem for the Americans to solve, was deeply undercut by awareness of the difference between American and Soviet standards of nuclear responsibility as revealed in this moment of danger.

More broadly, the strength and restraint of the American position in October stood in striking contrast to the position in which others found themselves. As a first consequence, and to a degree that exceeded predictions, the allies of the United States both in this hemisphere and in Europe were clear in their support, though in public comment, especially in the United Kingdom, there was evidence of the difficulties we should have faced if we had been less clearly strong, restrained, and right.

It can be argued, of course, that in this crisis the opinions even of close allies were not crucial, and it does seem probable that such critical decisions as the turn-around of arms-bearing ships and the announcement that the missiles would be removed were not determined by O.A.S. votes or by world opinion. This particular crisis might have been successfully resolved even in the face of doubt and division among allies whose immediate power at the point of contest was negligible.

But so narrow a judgment neglects two great hazards. Immediately, a serious division among the allies might have provoked action elsewhere, most dangerously at Berlin (and indeed in all the postwar annals of the bravery of West Berlin there is no moment in which the courage and strength of the Berliners—and indeed of all free Germans —have been more important in discouraging adventure). And even if no such adventure had been attempted, the position after the crisis would not have been one in which "the quest for peace" could easily be led from Washington. It was and is the central meaning of this affair that a major threat to peace and freedom was removed by means which strengthened the prospects of both.

The October crisis came out better than President Kennedy or any of his associates had expected. The analysis suggested above would not have been compelling in the discussions of the week of October 15, and the predominant reaction in Washington on October 28 was one of simple and enormous relief. In the weeks after the crisis, attention was diverted, first by backstairs gossip over who gave what advice, and then by a renewal of political debate over Cuba, a problem of another order of meaning than the missile crisis, and one which had rightly been left essentially as it was, while the major threat was removed. And finally, it was far from clear, in the immediate aftermath, that "those who had made themselves our adversary" in such a sudden and shocking way would now be ready for a different relation.

But what is important for our present purposes is that what shaped American action in this crisis—what set and sustained the tempered response, both to danger and to success—was the President. And while the man in the office was Kennedy, with a taste and style of his own, I think it is right to claim that the office as well as the man was embodied in the resolution, restraint, and responsibility that governed in these weeks.

IV

As the great disappointment of 1961 was the renewal of testing, so the great satisfaction of 1963 was the limited test-ban treaty.

The withdrawal of missiles from Cuba did more than end a specific crisis of great gravity. It also signaled an acceptance by the Soviet Government, for the present at least, of the existing nuclear balance. In that balance there is American superiority, as we have seen, but it is a superiority that does not permit any lack of respect for the strength of the Soviet Union. No safer balance appears possible at present. No overwhelmingly one-sided margin is open to either side, and it was one lesson of the Cuban affair—as of many others since 1945—that it was well for peace that Communist strength should be matched with a margin. But the purpose of this margin must still be peace, and the aim of policy must still be to get beyond conflicting interests to the great common need for a safer prospect of survival. This is the meaning of the limited test-ban treaty.

If the missile crisis was the proof of American strength in conflict, the test-ban treaty was the proof of American readiness to work for this common purpose. And whatever the moving forces on the Soviet side, in the non-Communist world the Presidency was the necessary center of action. A special and distinguished role was played by the British Prime Minister, but Mr. Macmillan would be the first to recognize that it was mainly through his close relation to two Presidents that he was able to make the British contribution effective. It is only the American President who can carry the American Senate and the American people in any agreement on arms control, and it is only with American participation that any such agreement can have meaning for the Soviet Government.

Unless a President uses these powers with energy, arms control agreements are improbable. The momentum of the arms race—the power at work to keep it going almost without conscious new decision —is enormous. Military men in all countries find it hard to approve any arms control proposal which is not either safely improbable or clearly unbalanced in their own favor. In the United States only a strong Commander-in-Chief with a strong Secretary of Defense is in a position to press steadily for recognition that the arms race itself is now a threat to national security. Only the President can ensure that good proposals are kept alive even after a first rejection, and that new possibilities are constantly considered—so that there may always be as many proposals as possible on the table waiting for the moment of Soviet readiness. The readiness to meet all threats must be matched by a demonstrated readiness to reach agreement.

In the case of the limited test ban it was President Kennedy himself who reached the conclusion in the spring of 1963 that the United States would not be the first to make further atmospheric tests. That quite personal decision, recognized at the time as fully within the Presidential power, and announced in an address on peace whose power and conviction were immediately recognized, is as likely an immediate cause as any for the announcement, less than a month later, that the Soviet Government would now be willing to sign an agreement which had been open for two years. There followed a period of negotiation and then a debate on ratification, and in these again the Presidency was central. The test-ban treaty, as we have all told each other a hundred times, is only one step, and President Johnson has made clear his determination to seek further steps with all the energy and imagination the government can command. Meanwhile the lesson of the test ban is that no step at all can be taken in this field unless the President himself works for it. A President indifferent to arms control, or easily discouraged by Soviet intransigence or irresponsibility, or inclined to a narrow military view of the arms race, would be a guarantee against agreed limitation of armaments. Conversely, where there is zeal in the search for agreement, refusal to accept initial disappointment as final, a cool and balanced assessment of the risks of agreement against the risks of unlimited competition, and a firm use of the powers of the office, the Presidency can become—as in this case—an instrument of hope for all men everywhere.

V

In concentrating attention upon the great requirements of strength and a love for peace, and in using as examples such very large matters as the missile crisis and the test-ban treaty, I do not pretend to have exhausted the connections between the Presidency and the Peace, even as they showed themselves in the short Kennedy years. There is more in the Presidency·than the special powers of the Commander-in-Chief or the special responsibility for pressing the hard cause of disarmament. There is more, too, than a need for understanding of Soviet realities. The Presidency is a powerful element in the strength or weakness of the United Nations, as every Secretary-General has known. The Presidency remains the headquarters of the Great Alliance, as even the most separated of national leaders has recognized. The Presidency is an indispensable stimulus to Progress in the Americas. The Presidency must make the hard choices of commitment that have brought both honor and difficulty, as in Korea in 1950, or in South Viet Nam in 1954. The White House visit and the White House photograph are elements of democratic electioneering not just in the United States, but wherever the name of the American President can bring a cheer. The death of a President men loved has shown how wide this larger constituency is. Allies, neutrals, and even adversaries attend to the Presidency. When the American President shows that he can understand and respect the opinions and hopes of distant nations, when he proves able to represent the interests of his own people without neglecting the interests of others, when in his own person he represents decency, hope, and freedom —then he is strengthened in his duty to be the leader of man's quest for peace in the age of nuclear weapons. And this strength will be at least as important in meeting danger as in pursuing hope.

The Administration in Washington, led now by President Johnson, will face new problems and make new decisions, and as time passes the new imprint of a strong mind and heart will be felt increasingly—in the Presidency, in the Government, and in the world. President Kennedy would have been the last to suppose that the purely personal characteristics of any President, however loved and mourned, could or should continue to determine the work of the Presidency after his death. President Johnson will conduct the office in his own way. Yet the short space of three months is enough to show plainly that the pursuit of peace remains his central concern, while the effective transfer from one Administration to the next has reflected the fact that loyalty to President Kennedy and loyalty to President Johnson are not merely naturally compatible, but logically necessary as a part of a larger loyalty to their common purpose.

And as we remember John Kennedy, let us separate the essential from the complementary. The youth, the grace, and the wit were wonderful, but they were not the center. There lay courage, vision, humanity, and strength, tested on the path to the office, and tempered by the office itself. It is these qualities, applied to the greatest issues, that belong not only to the man but to the job.

It is my own conviction that this kind of President and this kind of Presidency reflect the general will of Americans. Temperate use of strength, respect for honest difference, sympathy for those in need, and a readiness to go our share of the distance—these qualities, which I have described in phrases borrowed from our new President, are qualities of the American people. They have their opposites in our character too, but these are what we honor; these we expect of our Presidents. In the terrible shock of President Kennedy's death there were many—perhaps too many—who saw the foul deeds of a few days in Dallas, and not the dead President himself, as the embodiment of the real America. They were wrong. As a man, as a President, as a servant of the Peace, he was what we are, and his achievement belongs to us all. Strengthened by his service the Presidency continues, and so does the quest for Peace.

Seyom Brown

Perceived Deficiencies in the Nation's Power

Power is not a matter of arms alone. Strength comes from education, fertile acres, humming workshops and the satisfaction and pride of peoples.

Dean Rusk

The state of the Union leaves a lot to be desired, the new President informed the nation on January 30, 1961. "Our problems are critical. The tide is unfavorable. The news will be worse before it is better." With the help of more than twenty-five specialized task forces, assembled during and after the election campaign, he had been taking a close inventory of "our whole arsenal of tools," and had been discovering serious gaps—gaps which if not corrected would leave the nation with a deficiency of power for meeting the coming challenges to its very survival. And certainly without attention to the neglected components of our national power, we could not hope to advance beyond these immediate security needs and apply our resources to reduce the misery of others.

The New Frontier's initial analysis of the overall power position of the United States and those components of power requiring remedial attention offered little that was new to those who had kept up with the substance of the informed political dialogue in this country. It was essentially an amalgam of the ideas of two sets of Democrats-in-exile: the Truman Democrats and the Stevenson Democrats. What was strikingly new about the New Frontier was the vital fusion of the hardheaded Cold War orientation of the first with the international idealism of the second. To be sure there had been a good deal of cross-fertilization in ideas and personnel between the two groups in the 1952–60 period. But there were tendencies, and a center of gravity which characterized each, particularly when it came to foreign affairs. What united them was the shared psychology of exile status of experienced men in their prime, oriented toward the public service, but excluded for eight years from its highest counsels. Not unnaturally they applauded one an-

From The Faces of Power *by Seyom Brown. New York: Columbia University Press,* 1968. *Reprinted by permission of the author and publisher.*

other's findings that the nation's power under Eisenhower had been sadly neglected. They were not always united, however, on remedial programs, or on which of these should be given priority. But neither were their ideas of what to do sufficiently specific for the new President to accept them as ready-made programs. Out of power, without the vast informational resources of the government at their command, analysts, whatever their previous experience, must confine themselves, relatively speaking, to general propositions. President Kennedy, given his practical frame of mind and wide intellectual grasp, was therefore able to accept the analyses of both groups without offending either and fashion fresh programs in which both could see their views reflected.

The first order of business the new Administration set for itself was to attend to the perceived deficiencies in the nation's power to protect its most vital interests. There, the gaps identified constituted a potpourri of the criticisms leveled at the Eisenhower Administration by various Democratic spokesmen during the last few years.

There was the potential "missile gap" that Congressional Democrats, led by Senators Stuart Symington (Secretary of the Air Force under Truman), Henry M. Jackson, and Lyndon Johnson had been harping on since 1958. Kennedy joined in the charge with a major Senate speech in August of that year, systematically outlining the requirements of strategic deterrence. But the intelligence estimates handed over to the new Administration on the United States–Soviet strategic balance showed the standard Congressional Democratic charge of Republican neglect of the strategic arsenal to have been a vast exaggeration. Revised estimates which were being compiled on the basis of newly received information showed, if anything, a missile imbalance in our favor. Actually, the Kennedy Administration found that its predecessor had done a pretty good job in translating the nation's technological resources into actual and projected instruments for the deterrence of stategic attack. The President's State of the Union message, and his Defense budget message two months later, thus told of decisions to "step up" and "accelerate" the missile program, but no new concept for the strategic forces was advanced. Like their predecessors, President Kennedy and Secretary of Defense Robert McNamara, accepted the planning premise for the design of the strategic force that there should be no *deterrent* gap, by which they meant that the force should be large enough to retaliate with "unacceptable damage" against an attacker or combination of attackers, even under the assumption that we had suffered a surprise strategic attack with all the weapons the enemy could launch. An alternative planning premise—namely, that deterrence of attacks upon other areas, particularly Western Europe, required that the United States maintain a "first strike" strategic force, capable of knocking out the Soviet's means of nuclear bombardment of the United States—appears to have been rejected in these early days and never to have been revived. A more usable means of protecting our vital overseas interests against military attack was thought to lie in the improvement of local defense capabilities.

The charge was frequently made by Senator John F. Kennedy that the Eisenhower Administration had left a gaping hole in the United States arsenal of power by failing to provide adequate local defense capabilities for the non-Communist world. Under the prevailing strategic monism we had been, in the Senator's words:

> . . . preparing . . . primarily to fight the one kind of war we least want to fight and are least likely to fight. We have been driving ourselves into a corner where the only choice is all or nothing at all, world devastation or submission—a choice that necessarily causes us to hesitate on the brink and leaves the initiative in the hands of our enemies.

The perceived deficiency in the nation's ability to fight "limited," or non-nuclear wars was a rallying point for a wide spectrum of Democrats, however they might differ on other matters. The premise that this deficiency was a critical gap in the overall power of the non-Communist world as opposed to the Communist world had been standard with "security"-minded Truman exiles like Dean Acheson and Paul Nitze, both of whom had been pointing since 1949 to the dangers that would face the United States if we did not remedy this gap by the time the Soviets deployed an intercontinental nuclear capability.

The "conventional" capabilities gap had also become a concern of Adlai Stevenson, Hubert Humphrey, and others who were urging greater United States efforts to control the arms race. This group, in the late 1950's was increasingly pessimistic about the prospects for disarmament, but were strongly oriented toward "arms control" concepts that stressed a "stabilization" of the nuclear "balance of terror." They perceived that unless the non-Communist world could balance the capabilities of the Communist nations at lower levels of warfare, the United States would have to maintain an obvious superiority at the nuclear strategic level in order to dissuade the Communists from military adventures. And since the Soviets, it was believed, would never accept a position of strategic inferiority, there would be no end to the ever-more-lethal arms race unless a balance of forces could be achieved at the lower levels. As the Soviets were not about to scale down their local war capabilities, the only recourse for the West, therefore—a proposition reluctantly but realistically accepted by the Stevensonians—was to scale up.

Kennedy, characteristically, chose to sidestep the potential contradiction between the Nitze position, which urged superiority across-the-board, and the arms controllers' position which sought parity at all levels. He chose rather to stress their operational similarities as they came immediately to bear on the improvement of conventional capabilities.

The more precise case for the improvement of capabilities for non-nuclear warfare came by way of the Defense Department after the new Administration had settled in, and it remained for the Secretary of Defense and his deputies to articulate the sharpened rationale.

Analysts with an orientation toward military affairs are prone to pay most attention to the so-called Kennedy-McNamara "revolution" in military policy, as if it were the centerpiece of the Kennedy Administration's foreign policy. But this is to confuse immediacy with high value. At the center of the Kennedy foreign policy was the premise that the competition between the Soviet Union and the United States was shifting to a new arena—the competition for influence over the direction of development in the poorer half of the globe; and it was with respect to this competition that we were in greatest danger of falling behind. Marginal improvements had to be made in our military posture to ensure that the Soviets were not encouraged to try their hand once again in the other arenas of more direct East-West confrontation, such as Berlin. Filling the gaps in our military arsenal, and then vigilance to see that additional gaps did not appear in an era of volatile technology, was the necessary condition for a fundamental retooling in the nonmilitary instruments of power for the vigorous contests in the new arena.

Kennedy's view that the "third world" had now become the decisive field of engagement was shared by most of the Stevensonians, by Senate foreign policy leaders such as J. William Fulbright and Mike Mansfield, and by ever-renewable Averell Harriman. But the Europe-first emphasis remained strong among Truman State Department Alumni, led by Acheson—still the idol of many seasoned top-level career diplomats in the State Department who had survived the Eisenhower-Dulles doldrums. When it came to programmatic expression of the new orientation, the burden of proof would fall on those arguing for allocating a larger proportion of our human and material resources to "containment" in the underdeveloped world. Two weeks before inauguration the supporters of the new orientation received their most effective ammunition from an unexpected source.

Premier Khrushchev, in his historic foreign policy speech of January 6, 1961, displayed the Soviet grand-strategic rationale for focusing Soviet efforts on the underdeveloped areas: due to developments in the technology of warfare, "World Wars" and "local wars" had become obsolete (they would lead to a nuclear holocaust destroying the workers as well as the capitalists), and therefore "unjust." The "just wars" of the contemporary period, the inevitable and necessary wars according to the Marxist-Leninist appraisal of the relation between social and material forces, were "wars of national liberation." The phrase was a catchall for anti-colonial agitations, popular uprisings against established indigenous regimes, and actual guerilla wars. Examples were the campaign of the FLN in Algeria for independence from France, the Castro takeover in Cuba, general efforts to mobilize the leftist forces in Latin America, and the insurgency in South Vietnam. "The Communists support just wars of this kind wholeheartedly and without reservations," said the Soviet leader.

Here, in Kennedy's view, was an eminently realistic appraisal by the Soviets themselves of where their best opportunities for expansion lay. It conformed with the strategy shift attributed to the Soviets by Walt Rostow, particularly—one of the first in Kennedy's circle of foreign policy advisers to make a serious pitch for a major United States counter-insurgency program. Arthur Schlesinger reports that Khrushchev's January 6 speech "made a conspicuous impression on the new President, who took it as an authoritative exposition of Soviet intentions, discussed it with his staff and read excerpts from it aloud to the National Security Council."

The President was familiar with Mao Tse-tung's aphorism that power grows out of the barrel of a gun. But he knew there was more to guerilla warfare than forming new commando-type units. He appreciated and liked to quote Mao's equally important aphorism: "Guerillas are like fish, and the people are the water in which the fish swim. If the temperature of the water is right, the fish will thrive and multiply." It was critically important to tend the temperature of the water —and as far in advance as possible.

The prophylactic aspects of counterinsurgency provided the link between those in Kennedy's advisory entourage who saw the balance of power primarily in terms of the distribution of coercive capabilities and those who emphasized the more benign components of international influence. When put in this frame of reference, Paul Nitze, Generals Maxwell Taylor and James Gavin, Walt Rostow, Roger Hilsman, Chester Bowles, Averell Harriman, John Kenneth Galbraith, and Adlai Stevenson could all agree on the necessity for a much larger program of long-term development aid to the many potential targets for Communist insurgency in Asia, the Middle East, Africa, and Latin America.

Having forged agreement that the purpose of foreign assistance was to affect the "temperature of the water" in the recipient countries —to assure those economic, social, and political conditions that are inhospitable to the growth of Communist movements—the next step was to assure application of foreign aid criteria designed by those with credentials in this type of oceanography. The dominant standard that had prevailed during the Eisenhower period, the degree of overt acquiescence on the part of regimes in power to the anti-Communist orientation of United States diplomacy, was now seen to be hopelessly inadequate. Kennedy accepted the need for a much more "technical"— and complicated—analysis for determining the utility of the kinds and amounts of assistance to go to any particular country. As senator and President-elect he sought the counsel of professionals, and they were not to be found within the Government. He found them, again mainly New Deal–Fair Deal exiles (but professional economists all), encamped along the banks of the Charles River: Galbraith, Carl Kaysen, Edward S. Mason, David Bell, and Lincoln Gordon at Harvard; Rostow, Max Millikan, and P. N. Rosenstein-Rodan at the M.I.T. Center for International Studies. Here, during the 1950's, were developed the propositions on economic assistance that became official government policy in the 1960's: namely, operational criteria for evaluating the worth of any particular foreign aid program must be stated in terms of a concept of the socioeconomic modernization process; and the explicit objective of measures sponsored by the United States should be self-sustaining economic growth for each recipient nation. . . . For the present, it should be noted that the lack of such a concept and objective for determining the flow of foreign assistance to the poorer nations was considered by the new President as probably the most critical deficiency in the arsenal of tools by which we hoped to influence the international environment.

Kennedy's economist friends were contending that modernization and the development of greater constitutional democracy and social justice could go hand in hand; that, indeed, economic development required national planning and reliable administration, and these required the kind of political stability that was best sustained in a constitutional system providing for responsible government according to the consent of the governed. But Kennedy was also sensitive to the potential gap between the rational political-economy of his advisers and their Western-trained counterparts in the developing countries on the one hand, and the combustible character of the "revolution of rising expectations," particularly when exploited by demagogues, on the other hand. He understood that part of the weakness of the United

States in trying to influence the poorer nations from succumbing to totalitarian models for modernization was the lack of passion in our commitment to egalitarian aspects of social justice. We had been only halfhearted in our support for the kind of land reform and tax reform that would bring about the structural economic changes we knew were necessary for modernization. Our excuse, under previous Administrations, had been that an open advocacy of such reform measures would constitute an interference in the domestic affairs of those smaller nations—that it was up to those nations, in their own way, however gradually, to take such social reform upon themselves without outside pressure. The effect of our self-denying ordinance, however, had been to identify the United States with status quo elements in these countries, and to provide social revolutionary elements with confirmation of their suspicion that the State Department was in cahoots with United States private interests who profited from privileges extended them by entrenched local oligarchies. It was from this concern that the Alliance for Progress evolved. As the President put it on the first anniversary of its launching:

> For too long my country, the wealthiest nation on a poor continent, failed to carry out its full responsibilities to its sister Republics. We have now accepted that responsibility. In the same way those who possess wealth and power in poor nations must accept their own responsibilities. They must lead the fight for basic reforms which alone can preserve the fabric of their own societies. Those who make peaceful revolution impossible will make violent revolution inevitable.
>
> These social reforms are at the heart of the Alliance for Progress. They are the precondition to economic modernization. And they are the instrument by which we assure to the poor and hungry, to the worker and the *campesino,* his full participation in the benefits of our development and in the human dignity which is the purpose of free societies.

These were strong words. And there might be a problem in seeing that the expectations they might arouse of United States action in support of social reform did not outrun our ability to influence "those who possess the wealth and power in poor nations." But, in Kennedy's view of where the stakes in the global struggle for power then lay, he had little choice but to reidentify the United States with the rising demands of the poor and the disenfranchised.

The idea that essential power relationships among nations were being transformed by these new expectations, passions, and demands was no new preoccupation of Kennedy's. He was one of the staunchest supporters in the Congress of aid to India, during the years when the Administration and many of his own party in the Congress were suspicious of Nehru's socialism and nonalignment. And in 1959, while most of his colleagues were stepping up their polemics on the presumed missile "gap," he took the opportunity to point to another gap "which constitutes an equally clear and present danger to our security":

> I am talking about the economic gap—the gap in living standards and income and hope for the future . . . between the stable, industrialized nations of the north . . . and the overpopulated, underinvested nations of the south. . . .
>
> It is this gap which presents us with our most critical challenge today. It is this gap which is altering the face of the globe, our strategy, our security, and our alliances, more than any current military challenge. And it is this economic challenge to which we have responded most sporadically, most timidly, and most inadequately.

In order to respond to this economic challenge the people of the United States would have to feel confident enough of their own productivity to allow for a diversion of effort to the needs of others. But, reported Kennedy, in his first Presidential address to the Congress:

> We take office in the wake of . . . three and one-half years of slack, seven years of diminished economic growth, and nine years of falling farm income. . . .
>
> Our recovery from the 1958 recession . . . was anemic and incomplete. Our Gross National Product never again regained its full potential. Unemployment never returned to normal levels. Maximum use of our national industrial capacity was never restored.
>
> In short, the American economy is in trouble. The most resourceful industrialized country on earth ranks among the last in the rate of economic growth.

Not only did this lagging state of our economy reduce our capacity and will to provide direct help to the poorer nations, it also reduced another very important aspect of our influence: our reputation for successful management of a largely free economy for the well-being of all our people. "We must show the world what a free economy can do," admonished Kennedy, in recommending a set of economic measures to take up the slack.

Moreover, the United States was placed in a vulnerable diplomatic position with respect to other industrialized nations by its adverse balance of international payments, which Kennedy felt was partly the result of the sluggishness of our own economy in competition with the dynamically expanding economies in Western Europe. "Our success in world affairs has long depended in part upon foreign confidence in our ability to pay," he said. And to intimates he confided his anxiety that the payments deficit was "a club that DeGaulle and all the others hang over my head. Any time there's a crisis or a quarrel, they can cash in all their dollars and where are we?"

For Kennedy, programs to "get the country moving again"—his anti-recession measures of 1961, the Trade Expansion Act of 1962, and the tax cut of 1963—were as much required by global balance of power considerations as they were by considerations of domestic economic well-being. The continued productive growth of the United States was a value in itself, and to be pursued as part of the basic national interest. But it was also regarded as a means toward the more vigorous exercise of power internationally. Unlike the preceding Administration, which seemed to view the requirements of domestic economic productivity as competitive with, and therefore a constraint upon, our overseas commitments (we could not raise additional conventional forces because that might bankrupt us), the New Frontier felt that any gap between our overseas commitments and the existing domestic economic base needed to sustain them was only an argument for expansion of the domestic economy. It was not an argument for reduced defense spending. A contraction in our commitments or an unwillingness to provide ourselves with the widest array of diplomatic and military tools to sustain these commitments would endanger our security in the long run, and currently would further reduce our ebbing global leadership.

Similarly, a continuance of our reliance on protectionist devices in order to protect the home market from growing foreign competition would have adverse consequences on our overall power on the international scene. "Economic isolation and political leadership are wholly incompatible," asserted Kennedy in urging the Congress to grant him the broad tariff-reducing authority requested in the Administration's trade expansion bill of 1962:

> In the next few years, the nations of Western Europe will be fixing basic economic and trading patterns vitally affecting the future of our economy and the hopes of our less-developed friends. Basic political and military decisions of vital interest to our security will be made. Unless we have this authority to negotiate . . . if we are separated from the Common Market by high tariff barriers on either side of the Atlantic—then we cannot hope to play an effective part in those decisions.
> If we are to retain our leadership, the initiative is up to us.

The revolutionary changes which are occurring will not wait for us to make up our minds. The United States has encouraged sweeping changes in free world economic patterns in order to strengthen the forces of freedom. But we cannot ourselves stand still. If we are to lead, we must act. We must adapt our own economy to the imperatives of a changing world, and once more assert leadership.

Pervading most of President Kennedy's major recommendations to the Congress, for "domestic" no less than specifically foreign programs, was this notion of the power of *movement* itself. The key to leadership on the international scene was a creative exploitation of the currents of change. The surge by the new nations for a place in the sun, the social and economic egalitarianism of the newly enfranchised masses across the globe, and the unconquerable assertion of men that the object of government is to protect and extend the exercise of free choice —this was the very stuff of the new international politics. Leadership in this arena called for a renewal of the dynamics of the American experiment in freedom. Thus, our prestige abroad, our influence upon others—i.e., our power—were seriously weakened by the squalor of our cities, the crime in our streets, the overcrowding and low standards in many of our schools, our shortage of adequate health facilities and medical professionals, and most of all, by the "denial of constitutional rights to some of our fellow Americans on account of race." We had to recapture, Kennedy felt, that pride and nerve to explore uncharted frontiers, without which the nation "would trend in the direction of a slide downhill into dust, dullness, languor, and decay."

As much as to help in the spread of literacy and technical know-how, and to improve the American image abroad, the Peace Corps was directed at improving the quality of life here in the United States. The Peace Corps was typical of Kennedy's integrated and long-term approach to the problem of the nation's power, which would demand from the coming generation of leaders, no less than his own, a willingness to pay a price to secure the blessings of liberty. "A price measured not merely in money and military preparedness, but in social inventiveness, in moral stamina, and physical courage."

President Kennedy's decision, after some hesitation, to stress the competitive nature of the space race with the Soviets, not just the potentials for cooperative scientific exploration, was very much a part of his concern to avoid a flabbiness of the national fiber. The scientific or potential military payoffs from trying to be "first" in space seem to have impressed him less than the intangible effects on the national spirit. Many of the welfare liberals who supported him down the line on other planks in his program cried "Moondoggle." His reply, best articulated in his September 1962 address at Rice University, reflected the New Frontier's intuition of where to probe for that critical vein of adventuresomeness which had once been, and could again be, a special source of national strength:

> But why, some say, the moon? . . . And they may well ask, why climb the highest mountain? Why, thirty-five years ago, fly the Atlantic? Why does Rice play Texas? . . .
>
> We choose to go to the moon in this decade, and do the other things, not because they are easy but because they are hard; because that goal will serve to organize and measure the best of our energies and skills. . . .
>
> Many years ago the great British explorer George Mallory, who was to die on Mount Everest, was asked why did he want to climb it, and he said, "Because it is there."
>
> Well, space is there, and . . . the moon and planets are there, and new hopes for knowledge and peace are there.

William G. Carleton

Kennedy in History: An Early Appraisal

In foreign policy, the first two years of Kennedy were ambiguous. In the third year, there was a clearer sense of direction, one which promised to harmonize American policy with emerging new realities in the world.

At the time of the Kennedy accession, the postwar world was disintegrating. Bipolarization was giving way to depolarization. The Sino-Soviet rift was widening. With the single exception of little Vietminh, all the old European colonies that had recently gained their independence had escaped Communism, although there were Communist guerrilla activities in some of them. The trend was to a new pluralism, a new diversity. The nuclear revolution in war and the American-Soviet nuclear deterrents had rendered an ultimate military showdown unthinkable. The United States was ahead in the nuclear arms race.

Reprinted from The Antioch Review, *Vol. XXIV, No. 3, by permission of the editors.*

In Europe, despite Khrushchev's bluster about West Berlin, the existing arrangements in East and Central Europe were ripening into a more overt *modus vivendi,* by way of tacit understanding rather than formal political agreements. Trade and intercourse between East and West Europe were increasing, the satellites were operating more independently of Moscow, and an all-European economic and cultural cooperation seemed slowly to be replacing the postwar's clear-cut division between the "two Europes." West Europeans were becoming less interested in NATO because they were more and more convinced that there would be no Soviet military aggression in Europe, due to the nuclear deterrent and other reasons. The drive to West European political integration was slackening, owing to the decline of external pressures and to De Gaulle's opposition to the supranational approach. Forces within the Six, composing the Common Market, were honestly divided over whether they wanted an inward-looking European community or an outward-looking Atlantic one.

In short, Kennedy was confronted with a new fluidity, a necessity and an opportunity for a reappraisal of American foreign policy. How much of the old foreign policy was still applicable? What aspects required a new orientation? To what degree was it safe, realistic, and advantageous to strike out in new directions? In some ways this ambiguous situation was more agonizing to decision makers than the obvious crisis situation with which Truman and Acheson had had to deal in the late 1940's and early 1950's. It is no wonder that some aspects of the Kennedy record in foreign affairs seem somewhat confused, even contradictory.

The chief stumbling block to an American-Soviet *détente* continued to be Berlin, the two Germanies, and the territorial arrangements in East and Central Europe. Kennedy rejected explorations of a definitive settlement, and if in the future a genuine American-Soviet *rapprochement* develops, this rejection is likely to be held against him. However, he did move informally in the direction of a more openly tacit recognition of the existing arrangements in East and Central Europe. He deferred less to Adenauer's views than previous administrations had done. In his interview in *Izvestia,* remarkable for its clarity and candor, he agreed that it would not be advisable to let West Germany have its own nuclear weapons. After the Communists built the Berlin Wall, Kennedy resisted all pressures to use force to tear it down.

Nevertheless, during his first two years in office, Kennedy seems needlessly to have fanned the tensions of the dying Cold War. (It may be that "needlessly" is too strong a word; perhaps Kennedy thought he needed to arouse the country to obtain a more balanced military program, more foreign economic aid, the Alliance for Progress; perhaps he thought, too, that a truculent tone was necessary to convince Khrushchev that America would stand firm under duress for its rights in Berlin.) His inaugural address was alarmist, already historically off key, more suited to the Stalinist era than to 1961. His first State of the Union Message was even more alarmist. The nation was told that the world tide was unfavorable, that each day we were drawing near the maximum danger. His backing of the Cuban invasion in April, 1961, further fanned the Cold War. His statement to newspaper publishers and editors gathered at the White House in May—that the United States was in the most critical period of its history—increased the popular anxieties. He overreacted to Khrushchev's Vienna ultimatum in June, for in recent years Khrushchev's repeated deadlines and backdowns over West Berlin had become a kind of pattern. But for Kennedy, Vienna seems to have been a traumatic experience. On his return home he appealed to Americans to build do-it-yourself bomb shelters, and this produced a war psychology in the country and all manner of frenetic behavior, caused right-wingism to soar (1961 was the year the membership and financial "take" of the right-wing organizations reached their peak), and weakened confidence abroad in Kennedy's judgment.

There are no defenders of the Cuban fiasco of April, 1961. Even had the expedition of the Cuban exiles been given American naval and air support and forced a landing, there is scant evidence that the Cubans, at that time devoted to Castro, would have revolted en masse and welcomed the invaders as deliverers. More likely a nasty civil war would have followed, with the Americans, giving increasing support to the invaders, cast in the role of subjugators. The C.I.A. had already rejected the social-revolutionary leadership of the anti-Castro Manuel Rey for a non-leftist leadership, and this would have made the task of overthrowing Castro even more difficult. The world would have looked on with dismay, and outside the United States the whole affair would have come to be regarded as "another Hungary." It is ironical that Kennedy, the generalist with a critical intelligence, the politician with a feel for popular moods, should on this occasion have been taken in by the bureaucrats and the "experts." Prodded by his own anti-Castro stand during the election campaign, Kennedy must have wanted desperately to believe in the reliability of those dossiers of the intelligence agents.

With respect to Western Europe, the Kennedy administration underestimated those forces within the Common Market that wanted a European community rather than an Atlantic community, at first regarded De Gaulle as a kind of maverick without group support for his position, and framed the Trade Expansion Act of 1962 in such a way that the most decisive tariff cuts between the United States and the Common Market would depend upon Britain's inclusion in the Market. Nevertheless, the Act as written still allowed for much liberalization of trade, even with Britain outside the Market, and the responsibility for failure to take advantage of this opportunity must be borne by parochial-minded groups and interests inside the Market.

The Kennedy administration's contributions to national defense were notable. It emphasized a balanced and diversified establishment—both strategic and tactical nuclear weapons, conventional arms, and guerrilla forces—so the nation would never have to make the choice between the ultimate weapons and no other adequate defense. It was realistic in its shift from bombers to missiles as the chief nuclear carriers of the future, and in its dismantling of the intermediate missiles bases in Britain, Italy, and Turkey as the Polaris submarines and intercontinental missiles became increasingly operational. Its attempt to find a formula for a NATO multilateral nuclear force was a way of countering De Gaulle's blandishments to the West Germans and of balancing the possibility of a *détente* with Russia with reassurances to Bonn. Its experiments with massive airlifts of ground troops was in part a response to the desires of many of America's NATO allies for less rigidity, less insistence on fixed ground quotas, and more flexibility. However, NATO was plainly in transition, and while the Polaris submarines and intercontinental missiles were making the United States less dependent on European bases, ways were not yet actually implemented to share America's nuclear weapons with European allies on a genuine multilateral basis and satisfy their desires for less centralized direction from the United States.

There was an honest facing up to the terrible responsibilities inherent in the nuclear deterrent. That deterrent was put under tighter control to guard against accident and mistake, and the "hot line" between Washington and Moscow was set up. A much more determined effort was made to get arms-control agreements and a treaty banning nuclear-weapons testing than had ever been made by Kennedy's predecessors. Negotiations with the Soviet Union had been going on for years, but the Americans now so yielded in their former demands for strict international inspection as to put the Russians on the defensive, making world opinion for the first time believe that it was the Russians and not the Americans who were the obstructionists. Kennedy's administration believed that the United States and Russia had an enormous common interest in preventing the spread of nuclear weapons to other countries, that the Sino-Soviet rift gave Khrushchev a new freedom and a new urge to make agreements, and that the increasing accuracy of national detection systems made the possibility of cheating on a test-ban treaty, even one without international inspection, "vanishingly small."

Kennedy's regime also showed its international-mindedness in its firm support of the United Nations. It defended the Secretariat, the executive, from Soviet attacks, and in practice the activities of the Secretariat were widened. The organization was saved from bankruptcy by American financial aid. The operation of the United Nations military force in the Congo, backed by the United States, showed that the American government had no sympathy for "neocolonialism" as practiced by the Katanga secession, and it added another successful precedent for international enforcement of international decisions.

With respect to the underdeveloped nations, the Kennedy policies paralleled the trend of history. Anti-colonialism and self-determination were more valiantly espoused than in the preceding administrations. The Dulles doctrine that neutralism is "immoral" was abandoned, and neutralism was cordially accepted for nations which wanted it. Neutralism was positively encouraged in Laos and in the Congo. Help to South Vietnam was so hedged as to prevent the guerrilla war there from escalating into another Indo-China war, another Korea. Foreign economic aid was increased. The Food-for-Peace program was expanded. The Peace Corps was launched. The Alliance for Progress, an ambitious economic-aid program in Latin America coupled with domestic reforms, an experiment in "controlled revolution," was undertaken.

However, Kennedy, like his predecessors, did little to make the average American understand foreign economic aid—that it is not only an attempt to raise living standards, prevent Communism, and contribute to the world's economic well-being and stability, but is also a substitute for those obsolete ways in which the old colonialism supplied capital to the underdeveloped areas. Until an American president takes to television and in a series of fireside chats explains to Americans in simple terms the real meaning of the foreign-aid program, that program will be in jeopardy.

The Cuban crisis of October, 1962, provoked by the discovery of secret Soviet intermediate missiles in Cuba, was the high point, the turning point, in the Kennedy administration. Could this crisis have been avoided? This will be debated by future historians. True, Khrushchev could not have declined giving Castro economic aid, technical assistance, and some military help, even had he desired to do so, for to have refused this would have been tantamount to surrendering Communist leadership to the Chinese. But why did he go to the length of planting intermediate-missile bases in Cuba? As an appeasement to the Stalinist and Chinese opposition? As a countermeasure to American missile bases in Turkey (which were soon to be dismantled)? As a means of blackmailing Americans into making a compromise on Berlin? To extract a promise from the Americans not to invade Cuba? Whatever the causes, some future historians will have nagging questions: Might this terrible gamble in nuclear brinkmanship have been prevented had Kennedy previously shown more disposition to come to a *détente* with the Soviet Union by a somewhat clearer recognition of the two Germanies and other *de facto* boundaries and arrangements in East and Central Europe; and if so, did this Kennedy reluctance, coming in part out of regard for West German opinion, represent a realistic appraisal of the world situation?

Anyway, when the crisis came, even neutralist opinion seemed to feel that Khrushchev's attempt to compensate for his own intercontinental-missiles lag and the open and avowed American intermediate missiles in Turkey did not justify the sneaky Soviet operation in Cuba. America's quiet, deliberate planning of countermeasures, both military and diplomatic, was masterly. America's prudent use of force, enough but not more than enough to achieve its objective, won worldwide acclaim. Khrushchev and Castro lost face. The Chinese denounced the Soviet backdown, and Chinese-Russian relations worsened. Most important, the peak of crisis, a spectacular nuclear brinkmanship, cleared the atmosphere like a bolt of lightning. The lunacy of an ultimate nuclear showdown was traumatically revealed. Khrushchev's personal correspondence to Kennedy, reputedly revealing a highly emotional state and a genuine horror of nuclear war, the President had the grace, sportsmanship, and wisdom to keep secret.

Thereafter Khrushchev spoke even more insistently about the need to avoid nuclear war and pursue a policy of peaceful but competitive coexistence. From then on Kennedy gave more public recognition to emerging new international realities, the world's escape from monolithic threats, the trend to pluralism and diversity. In his address at American University in June, 1963, Kennedy spoke as if the Cold War scarcely existed and emphasized the common stake both the United States and the Soviet Union had in world peace and stability. This address, one of the noblest and most realistic state papers of our time, will be remembered long after Kennedy's inaugural address is forgotten.

The new spirit in world affairs expressed itself concretely in the consummation of the limited nuclear test-ban treaty in the summer of 1963, the first real break in the American-Soviet deadlock. After this, Kennedy proposed a joint American-Soviet effort to explore the moon, and he agreed to permit the Soviet Union to purchase American wheat.

By 1963, then, Kennedy had come to much awareness that the postwar world was ending and to a determination to attempt more shifts in American foreign policy in harmony with the emerging fluidity. By this time, too, he had developed close personal relations with a large number of premiers and heads of state the world over. It was felt that after his reelection in 1964 he would be in an unusually strong position to give American foreign policy a new direction, that the test-ban treaty was but a foretaste of more significant measures yet to come, measures which might lead to an American-Soviet *détente,* eventually even to a *rapprochement.* Thus the President's life ended in a tragic sense of incompleteness and unfulfillment.

Every twentieth-century American president with a flair for world politics and in power in time of momentous international decision has been felled by sickness or death before his term was over, before his work was completed. First Wilson. Then Roosevelt. Then Kennedy. For sheer bad luck, this is a record unique among nations.

Theodore Sorensen

The Bay of Pigs

The worst disaster of that disaster-filled period, the incident that showed John Kennedy that his luck and his judgment had human limitations, and the experience that taught him invaluable lessons for the future, occurred on April 17 in the Zapata Swamp at the Cuban Bay of Pigs. A landing force of some fourteen hundred anti-Castro Cuban exiles, organized, trained, armed, transported, and directed by the United States Central Intelligence Agency (CIA), was crushed in less than three days by the vastly more numerous forces of Cuban dictator Fidel Castro. America's powerful military might was useless, but America's involvement was impossible to deny. Both publicly and privately the President asserted sole responsibility. Many wondered, nevertheless, how he could have approved such a plan. Indeed, the hardest question in his own mind after it was all over, he told one reporter, was "How could everybody involved have thought such a plan would succeed?" When I relayed to the President late in 1962 the request of a

From pp. 294–309 in Kennedy *by Theodore C. Sorensen. Copyright © 1965 by Theodore C. Sorensen. Reprinted by permission of Harper & Row, Publishers, Inc., and Hodder and Stoughton Limited.*

distinguished author that he be given access to the files on the Bay of Pigs, the President replied in the negative. "This isn't the time," he said. "Besides—we want to tell that story ourselves."

This is the time to tell that story—at least those parts about which I can speak with confidence. I am limited by the fact that I knew nothing of the operation until after it was over. When I asked the President a few days earlier about the bare hint I had received from another meeting, he replied with an earthy expression that too many advisers seemed frightened by the prospects of a fight, and stressed somewhat uncomfortably that he had no alternative. But in the days that followed the fiasco the President talked to me about it at length—in the Mansion, in his office and as we walked on the White House lawn. He was aghast at his own stupidity, angry at having been badly advised by some and let down by others, and anxious, he said, that I start giving some time to foreign affairs. "That's what's really important these days," he added.

What was really important in the Bay of Pigs affair was the very "gap between decision and execution, between planning and reality" which he had deplored in his first State of the Union. John Kennedy was capable of choosing a wrong course but never a stupid one; and to understand how he came to make this decision requires a review not merely of the facts but of *the facts and assumptions that were presented to him*.

The Eisenhower administration authorized early in 1960 the training and arming of a Cuban exile army of liberation under the direction of the CIA. Shortly before the Presidential election of 1960, it was decided (although Eisenhower was apparently not informed of the decision) that this should be a conventional war force, not a guerrilla band, and its numbers were sharply increased.

On January 20, 1961, John Kennedy inherited the plan, the planners and, most troubling of all, the Cuban exile brigade—an armed force, flying another flag, highly trained in secret Guatemalan bases, eager for one mission only. Unlike an inherited policy statement or Executive Order, this inheritance could not be simply disposed of by Presidential rescission or withdrawal. When briefed on the operation by the CIA as President-elect in Palm Beach, he had been astonished at its magnitude and daring. He told me later that he had grave doubts from that moment on.

But the CIA authors of the landing plan not only presented it to the new President but, as was perhaps natural, advocated it. He was in effect asked whether he was as willing as the Republicans to permit and assist these exiles to free their own island from dictatorship, or whether he was willing to liquidate well-laid preparations, leave Cuba free to subvert the hemisphere, disband an impatient army in training for nearly a year under miserable conditions, and have them spread the word that Kennedy had betrayed their attempt to depose Castro. Are you going to tell this "group of fine young men," as Allen Dulles posed the question later in public, "who asked nothing other than the opportunity to try to restore a free government in their country . . . ready to risk their lives . . . that they would get no sympathy, no support, no aid from the United States?" Would he let them choose for themselves between a safe haven in this country and a fighting return to their own, or would he force them to disband against their wishes, never to be rallied again?

Moreover, the President had been told, this plan was now or never, for three reasons: first, because the brigade was fully trained, restive to fight and difficult to hold off; second, because Guatemala was under pressure to close the increasingly publicized and politically controversial training camps, and his only choice was to send them back to Cuba, where they wished to go, or bring them back to this country, where they would broadcast their resentment; and third, because Russian arms would soon build up Castro's army, Cuban airmen trained behind the Iron Curtain as MIG pilots would soon return to Cuba, large numbers of crated MIG's had already arrived on the island, and the spring of 1961—before Castro had a large jet air force and before the exile army scattered in discontent—was the last time Cubans alone could liberate Cuba. (With an excess of candor during the week prior to the landing, the President revealed the importance of this factor in his thinking when he stated in a TV interview, "If we don't move now, Mr. Castro may become a much greater danger than he is to us today.")

Finally, the President was told, the use of the exile brigade would make possible the toppling of Castro without actual aggression by the United States, without seeming to outsiders to violate our principles of nonintervention, with no risk of involvement and with little risk of failure. "I stood right here at Ike's desk," Dulles said to Kennedy (as Kennedy told me later), "and told him I was certain our Guatemalan operation would succeed,[1] and, Mr. President, the prospects for this plan are even better than they were for that one."

With heavy misgiving, little more than a week before the plan was to go into effect, President Kennedy, having obtained the written endorsement of General Lemnitzer and Admiral Burke representing the

[1] The operation of June, 1954, that restored a non-Communist government to Guatemala. Apparently this should not be confused with a later conversation with Eisenhower, reported in *Mandate for Change,* in which Dulles estimated the prospects of the Guatemalan operation, by then already under way, as "about 20 percent" if aircraft could be supplied.

Joint Chiefs and the verbal assent of Secretaries Rusk and McNamara, gave the final go-ahead signal. He did not regard Castro as a direct threat to the United States, but neither did he see why he should "protect" Castro from Cubans embittered by the fact that their revolution had been sold out to the Communists. Cancellation of the plan at that stage, he feared, would be interpreted as an admission that Castro ruled with popular support and would be around to harass Latin America for many years to come. His campaign pledges to aid anti-Castro rebels had not forced his hand, as some suspected, but he did feel that his disapproval of the plan would be a show of weakness inconsistent with his general stance. "I really thought they had a good chance," he told me afterward, explaining it this way: If a group of Castro's own countrymen, without overt U.S. participation, could have succeeded in establishing themselves on the island, proclaimed a new government, rallied the people to their cause and ousted Castro, all Latin America would feel safer, and if instead they were forced to flee to the mountains, there to carry on guerrilla warfare, there would still have been net gain.

The principal condition on which he insisted before approving the plan was to rule out any direct, overt participation of American armed forces in Cuba. Although it is not clear whether this represented any change in policy, this decision—while in one sense permitting the disaster which occurred—in another helped to prevent a far greater one. For had the U.S. Navy and Air Force been openly committed, no defeat would have been permitted, a full-scale U.S. attack would ultimately have been required, and—assuming a general war with the Soviets could have been avoided—there was no point in beginning with a Cuban brigade in the first place. Once having openly intervened in the air and on the sea, John Kennedy would not have permitted the Cuban exiles to be defeated on the ground. "Obviously," he said later, "if you are going to have United States air cover, you might as well have a complete United States commitment, which would have meant a full-fledged invasion by the United States."

The results of such an overt unilateral intervention, "contrary to our traditions and to our international obligations," as the President said, would have been far more costly to the cause of freedom throughout the hemisphere than even Castro's continued presence. American conventional forces, moreover, were still below strength, and while an estimated half of our available Army combat divisions were tied down resisting guerrillas in the Cuban mountains, the Communists could have been on the move in Berlin or elsewhere in the world. Had such intervention appeared at all likely to be needed, Kennedy would never have approved the operation.

This decision not to commit U.S. forces emphasized the assumption underlying the pleas for the plan by its authors that it would succeed on its own. It also led to other restrictions designed to make the operation more covert and our involvement more concealed, restrictions which in fact impaired the plan's military prospects.

Yet no one in the CIA, Pentagon or Cuban exile movement raised any objection to the President's basic condition. On the contrary, they were so intent on action that they were either blind to danger or willing to assume that the President could be pressured into reversing his decision once the necessity arose. Their planning, it turned out, proceeded almost as if open U.S. intervention were assumed, but their answers to the President's specific questions did not. Could the exile brigade achieve its goals without our military participation? he asked. He was assured in writing that it could—a wild misjudgment, a statement of hope at best. Were the members of the exile brigade willing to risk this effort without our military participation, the President asked, and to go ahead with the realization that we would not intervene if they failed? He was assured that they were—a serious misstatement, due at least to bad communications on the part of the CIA liaison officers. But as the result of these assurances, the President publicly pledged at an April 12 press conference:

> . . . there will not be, under any conditions, any intervention in Cuba by United States armed forces, and this government will do everything it possibly can—and I think it can meet its responsibilities—to make sure that there are no Americans involved in any actions inside Cuba . . . the basic issue in Cuba is not one between the United States and Cuba; it is between the Cubans themselves. And I intend to see that we adhere to that principle . . . this administration's attitude is so understood and shared by the anti-Castro exiles from Cuba in this country.

That pledge helped avoid any direct American attack the following week, thus limited our violation of international law and—despite pressures from the CIA and military—was never reversed or regretted by the President. But he was shortly to realize that he should have instead canceled the whole operation.

Early in the morning of Monday, April 17, 1961, the members of Cuban exile Brigade 2506—some fourteen to fifteen hundred Cubans of every race, occupation, class and party, well trained, well led and well armed—achieved tactical surprise in their place of landing, fought ably and bravely while their ammunition lasted, and inflicted heavy losses on a Castro force which soon numbered up to twenty thousand men. The proximate cause of their defeat, according to the full-scale investigation later conducted under the chairmanship of General Maxwell Taylor, was a shortage of ammunition, and the reasons for that shortage illustrate all the shortcomings of the operation.

The men had ample supplies with them, but, like most troops in their first combat, said General Taylor, they wasted ammunition in excessive firing, particularly upon encountering more immediate opposition than expected. A ten-day supply of ammunition, along with all the communications equipment and vital food and medical supplies, was on the freighter *Rio Escondido;* but that freighter was sunk offshore by Castro's tiny air force effectively led by two or three rocket-equipped jet trainers (T-33's) on the morning of the landing, along with another supply-laden freighter, the *Houston.*

Additional supplies and ammunition were carried by two other freighters, the *Atlántico* and the *Caribe.* But, although the President's rule against Americans in the combat area was violated in other instances, no Americans were on board these freighters or in a position to control their movements. When their sister ships were sunk, these two, ignoring the order to regroup fifty miles from shore, fled south so far so fast that, by the time the U.S. Navy intercepted them, the *Caribe* was too far away to get back in time to be of help. By the time the *Atlántico* returned Tuesday night and transferred her ammunition supplies into the five small boats prepared to run them fifty miles in to the beach, it was too late to complete the run under cover of darkness. Certain that they could not survive another Castro air attack when dawn broke, the Cuban crews threatened to mutiny unless provided with a U.S. Navy destroyer escort and jet cover. With the hard-pressed exiles on the beach pleading for supplies, the convoy commander requested the CIA in Washington to seek the Navy's help; but CIA headquarters, unable to keep fully abreast of the situation on the beach and apparently unaware of the desperate need for ammunition in particular, instead called off the convoy without consulting the President.

That was the only request for air cover formally made from the area, and it never reached the President. Yet that very night, in a somber postmidnight meeting in the Cabinet Room, the CIA and Joint Chiefs were asking him to reverse his public pledge and openly introduce American air and naval power to back the brigade on the beach. The President, still unwilling to precipitate a full-scale attack by this country on Cuba, and mindful of his public pledge of nonintervention and his global responsibilities, agreed finally that unmarked Navy jets could protect the anti-Castro force of B-26's when they provided air cover the next morning. As noted below, these B-26's were capable of providing air cover for no more than an hour. But receiving their directions from the CIA, they arrived on the scene an hour before the jets, who received their directions from the Navy; and whether this tragic error was due to a difference in time zones or instructions, the B-26's were soon downed or gone, the jet mission was invalidated before it started, and without ammunition the exiles were quickly rounded up.

Thus, while the lack of ammunition led directly to disaster, Castro's control of the air had led directly to the lack of ammunition. The landing plan had not neglected to provide for air control. There had been, on the contrary, unanimous agreement that the Castro Air Force had to be removed. But confusion persists to this day about the President "canceling the air cover" that U.S. jets were to have provided. Actually no U.S. Air Force jet participation had even been planned, much less canceled. Nor was there any cancellation of any other combat air cover over the battle front. Instead, the plan was to destroy Castro's air force on the ground before the battle began, and then to provide air support, with an anti-Castro "Air Force" consisting of some two dozen surplus planes flown by Cuban exiles. That plan failed.

The exile air arm, other than transports, was composed solely of lumbering B-26's as part of the covert nature of the plan. These World War II vintage planes were possessed by so many nations, including Cuba, that American sponsorship would be difficult to prove, and the prelanding attack on Cuban airfields could thus be attributed to defecting Castro pilots. No Florida, Puerto Rico, or other bases nearer than Nicaragua were to be used for similar reasons. But the B-26's were slow, unwieldy, unsuited to air cover and constantly developing engine trouble. The fuel used flying between Nicaragua and Cuba restricted them to forty-five to sixty minutes over the island. The limited number of exile crews, exhausted by the long, dangerous flights, and overcome on the final day by fear and futility, had to be replaced in part on that day by volunteers from their American instructors, four of whom gave their lives. Although one reason for selecting the Bay of Pigs site was its airstrip, Castro's superior ground forces and ground fire made it almost completely useless. Supplies dropped from the air blew into the jungle or water, and half of the usable B-26 force was shot down over the beach on the first day by Castro's T-33's.

The failure to destroy Castro's planes on the ground in two strikes before the fight started thus affected control of both the air and the beach. The first strike went off as planned early Saturday morning, April 15. But its effectiveness was limited by the attempt to pretend it was conducted by pilots deciding to defect that day from Castro. Only B-26's were used, no American napalm was used, and the planes had to fly in from Nicaragua and return, except for one flown to Florida to act out the cover story.

The cover story was even less successful than the air strike. It was quickly torn apart—which the President realized he should have known was inevitable in an open society—not only by Castro's representatives but by a penetrating press. Adlai Stevenson's denials that Saturday afternoon at the United Nations were disproven within twenty-four hours by photographs and internal inconsistencies in the story, contrary to all the assurances given the President that the strike could be accomplished without anyone knowing for some time where the attackers came from, and with nothing to prove that they weren't new defectors from Castro. The whole action was much bigger news than anticipated. The world was aroused by this country's deliberate deception. No one would have believed that the second strike, scheduled for dawn Monday after the landing party was ashore, was anything other than an overt, unprovoked attack by the United States on a tiny neighbor. The Soviet Union said American intervention would not go unmet, and our Latin-American friends were outraged.

As a result, the President was urged on Sunday by his foreign policy advisers—but without a formal meeting at which the military and CIA could be heard—to call off the Monday morning strike in accordance with the previous agreed-upon principle of avoiding overt American involvement. The President concurred in that conclusion. The second strike was canceled. The CIA objected strongly but, although given an opportunity, chose not to take the matter directly to the President. All hoped that the first strike had done enough damage to Castro's air power, as had at first been reported. After the events on Monday made clear that these hopes were in vain, the second strike was reinstated for that night, but a cloud cover made this postponement fatal. The last opportunity to neutralize the air over the beach by destroying the T-33's and other planes was gone. In retrospect General Taylor concluded that both in the planning stages and on Sunday the military importance of the air strike and the consequences of its cancellation should have been made more clear to the President by the responsible officers. But in fact the first strike, designed to be the key, turned out later to have been remarkably ineffective; and there is no reason to believe that Castro's air force, having survived the first and been dispersed into hiding, would have been knocked out by the second.

The President's postponement of the Monday morning air strike thus played only a minor role in the venture which came to so inglorious an end on Wednesday afternoon. It was already doomed long before Monday morning, and he would have been far wiser, he told me later, if, when the basic premises of the plan were already being shattered, he had canceled the entire operation and not merely the second air strike. For it was clear to him by then that he had in fact approved a plan bearing little resemblance to what he thought he had approved. Therein lies the key to the Bay of Pigs decision.

With hindsight it is clear that what in fact he had approved was diplomatically unwise and militarily doomed from the outset. What he thought he was approving appeared at the time to have diplomatic acceptability and little chance of outright failure. That so great a gap between concept and actuality should exist at so high a level on so dangerous a matter reflected a shocking number of errors in the whole decision-making process—errors which permitted bureaucratic momentum to govern instead of policy leadership.

1. The President thought he was approving a quiet, even though large-scale, reinfiltration of fourteen hundred Cuban exiles back into their homeland. He had been assured that the plan as revised to meet his criteria was an unspectacular and quiet landing of patriots plausibly Cuban in its essentials, of which the air strike was the only really noisy enterprise that remained. Their landing was, in fact, highly publicized in advance and deliberately trumpeted as an "invasion," and their numbers deliberately and grossly overstated—in part by exile groups and officials hoping to arouse the Cuban people to join them, in part by Castro to inflate first his danger and then his victory, and in part by headline writers to whom "invasion" sounded more exciting than a landing of fourteen hundred men. The CIA even dictated battle communiqués to a Madison Avenue public relations firm representing the exiles' political front. After all the military limitations accepted in order to keep this nation's role covert, that role was not only obvious but exaggerated.

2. The President thought he was approving a plan whereby the exiles, should they fail to hold and expand a beachhead, could take up guerrilla warfare with other rebels in the mountains. They were, in fact, given contrary instructions to fall back on the beaches in case of failure; the immediate area was not suitable for guerrilla warfare, as the President had been assured; the vast majority of brigade members had not been given guerrilla training, as he had been assured; and the eighty-mile route to the Escambray Mountains, to which he had been assured they could escape, was so long, so swampy and so covered by Castro's troops that this was never a realistic alternative. It was never even planned by the CIA officers in charge of the operation, and they neither told the President they thought this option was out nor told the exiles that this was the President's plan.

3. The President thought he was permitting the Cuban exiles, as represented by their Revolutionary Council and brigade leaders, to decide whether they wished to risk their own lives and liberty for the

liberty of their country without any overt American support. Most members of the brigade were in fact under the mistaken impression, apparently from their CIA contacts, that American armed forces would openly and directly assist them, if necessary, to neutralize the air (presumably with jets), make certain of their ammunition and prevent their defeat. They also mistakenly assumed that a larger exile force would land with them, that the Cuban underground or guerrillas would join them and that another landing elsewhere on the island would divert Castro's forces. (A small diversionary landing was, in fact, scheduled but called off after two tries.) Their assumptions were not made known to the President, just as his were not made known to them; and the Revolutionary Council was similarly kept largely uninformed on the landing and largely out of touch with the brigade. Its President, Dr. José Miró Cardona, who believed that only American armed might could overturn Castro, did not pass on the message he received from Kennedy's emissaries that no American military help would be forthcoming.

4. President Kennedy thought he was approving a plan calculated to succeed with the help of the Cuban underground, military desertions, and in time an uprising of a rebellious population. In fact, both Castro's popularity and his police state measures, aided by the mass arrests which promptly followed the bombing and landing, proved far stronger than the operation's planners had claimed. The planners, moreover, had no way to alert the underground without alerting Castro's forces. Cooperation was further impaired by the fact that some of the exiles' left-wing leaders were mistrusted by the CIA, just as some of their right-wing leaders and brigade members[2] were mistrusted by the Cuban underground. As a result, although the brigade was aided after its landing by some defectors and villagers, no coordinated uprising or underground effort was really planned or possible, particularly in the brief time the brigade was carrying the fight. In short, the President had given his approval with the understanding that there were only two possible outcomes—a national revolt or a flight to the hills—and in fact neither was remotely possible.

5. The President thought he was approving a plan rushed into execution on the grounds that Castro would later acquire the military capability to defeat it. Castro, in fact, already possessed that capability. Kennedy was told that Castro had only an obsolete, ineffective air force not in combat condition, no communications in the Bay of Pigs–Zapata Swamp area and no forces nearby. All these reports were wrong:

[2] Whose very presence was contrary to the President's instructions that all pro-Batista suspects be purged from the operation.

expected mass defections did not materialize; Castro's T-33 jet trainers were much more effective than predicted; and Castro's forces moved to the beachhead and crushed the exile force with far greater strength, equipment, and speed than all the estimates had anticipated. Indeed, the jet trainers—which were largely responsible for the ammunition losses and other failures—had been largely overlooked by the planners.

The President, having approved the plan with assurances that it would be both clandestine and successful, thus found in fact that it was too large to be clandestine and too small to be successful. Ten thousand exiles might have done it—or twenty thousand—but not fourteen hundred, as bravely and brilliantly as they fought. General Taylor's subsequent review found the whole plan to have been militarily marginal: there were too few men in the brigade, too few pilots in the air arm, too few seconds-in-command to relieve fatigued leaders, too few reserves to replace battle losses and too many unforeseen obstacles. The brigade relied, for example, on a nighttime landing through uncharted reefs in boats with outboard motors. Even with ample ammunition and control of the air, even with two more air strikes twice as large, the brigade could not have broken out of its beachhead or survived much longer without substantial help from either American forces or the Cuban people. Neither was in the cards, and thus a brigade victory at the Bay of Pigs was never in the cards either.

These five fundamental gaps between what the President actually approved and what he thought he was approving arose from at least three sources:

1. In part they arose because of the newness of the President and his administration. He did not fully know the strengths and weaknesses of his various advisers. He did not yet feel he could trust his own instincts against the judgments of recognized experts. He had not yet geared the decision-making process to fulfill his own needs, to isolate the points of no return, to make certain he was fully informed before they passed, and to prevent preshaped alternatives from being presented to him too late to start anew. Nor were his advisers as frank with him, or as free to criticize each other's work, as they would later become.

2. In part these gaps arose because supposed pressures of time and secrecy permitted too little consideration of the plan and its merits by anyone other than its authors and advocates. Only the CIA and the Joint Chiefs had an opportunity to study and ponder the details of the plan. Only a small number of officials and advisers even knew of its existence; and in meetings with the President and this limited number, memoranda of operation were distributed at the beginning of each session and collected at the end, making virtually impossible any sys-

tematic criticism or alternatives. The whole project seemed to move mysteriously and inexorably toward execution without the President being able either to obtain a firm grip on it or reverse it. Under both Eisenhower and Kennedy it grew, changed and forced decisions without any clear statement of policy or procedure. No strong voice of opposition was raised in any of the key meetings, and no realistic alternatives were presented (consideration was given to putting the action off until a true government-in-exile could be formed to give it a more genuine "civil war" flavor). No realistic appraisal was made of the chances for success or the consequences of failure. The problems of turning back a preconceived project ready to go, supposedly without overt American involvement, seemed much more difficult than permitting it to go ahead.

3. Finally, these gaps arose in part because the new administration had not yet fully organized itself for crisis planning, enabling the precommitted authors and advocates of the project in the CIA and Joint Chiefs to exercise a dominant influence. While not all his associates agreed, Kennedy's own feeling was that—inasmuch as he had personally polled each individual present at the "decisive" meeting—no amount of formal NSC, Operations Coordinating Board or Cabinet meetings would have made any difference. (In fact, this type of operation would never have been considered in a large, formal meeting.) "The advice of every member of the Executive Branch brought in to advise," he commented wryly a year and a half later, "was unanimous—and the advice was wrong." In fact, the advice was not so unanimous or so well considered as it seemed. The Chiefs of Staff, whose endorsement of the military feasibility of the plan particularly embittered him, gave it only limited, piecemeal study as a body, and individually differed in their understanding of its features. Inasmuch as it was the responsibility of another agency and did not directly depend on their forces, they were not as close or critical in their examination as they might otherwise have been, and depended on the CIA's estimates of Castro's military and political strength. Moreover, they had originally approved the plan when it called for a landing at the city of Trinidad at the foot of the Escambray Mountains, and when Trinidad was ruled out as too conspicuous, they selected the Bay of Pigs as the best of the alternative sites offered without informing either Kennedy or McNamara that they still thought Trinidad preferable.

The CIA, on the other hand, although served by many able military officers, did not have the kind of full military staff required for this kind of operation. It was not created or equipped to manage operations too large to remain covert; and both the CIA and the President discovered too late the impossibility of directing such an operation step by step from Washington, over a thousand miles from the scene, without more adequate, direct, and secure communications. The CIA's close control of the operation, however, kept the President and the Cuban exile force largely uninformed of each other's thinking; and its enthusiasm caused it to reject the clear evidence of Castro's political and military strength which was available from British and State Department intelligence and even from newspaper stories.

Both the CIA and the Joint Chiefs were moved more by the necessity of acting swiftly against Castro than by the necessity for caution and success. Answers to all the President's doubts about the military and intelligence estimates came from those experts most committed to supporting the plan, and he had no military intelligence expert of his own in the White House. Instead of the President telling the bureaucracy that action was necessary and that they should devise certain means, the bureaucracy was telling the President that action was necessary and that the means were already fashioned—and making his approval, moreover, appear to be a test of his mettle.

Yet it is wrong now—and was wrong then—to expect the CIA and military to have provided the necessary objectivity and skepticism about their own plan. Unfortunately, among those privy to the plan in both the State Department and the White House, doubts were entertained but never pressed, partly out of a fear of being labeled "soft" or undaring in the eyes of their colleagues, partly out of lack of familiarity with the new President and their roles, and partly out of a sense of satisfaction with the curbs placed on U.S. participation. The CIA and Joint Chiefs, on the other hand, had doubts about whether the plan had been fatally weakened by those very curbs, but did not press them.

Yet nothing that I have set forth above should be read as altering John Kennedy's verdict that the blame was his. He did not purchase, load or fire the gun, but he gave his consent to its being fired, and under his own deeply held principles of executive responsibility only a plea of "guilty" was possible.

Moreover, his own mistakes were many and serious. He should never have believed that it would be arrogant and presumptuous of him, newly arrived on the scene, to call off the plans of the renowned experts and the brave exiles. He should never have permitted the project to proceed so early in his first year, before he knew the men he was listening to and while he was still full of deep-rooted doubts. He should never have permitted his own deep feeling against Castro (unusual for him) and considerations of public opinion—specifically, his concern that he would be assailed for calling off a plan to get rid of Castro—to overcome his innate suspicions. He should have tried to keep the brigade in some other camp in view of the impossibility of keeping it in Guatemala, while considering its future more carefully; and even had he disbanded it, the consequences clearly would have been mild compared to those of the course he chose.

Inasmuch as he was unwilling to conduct an overt operation through the Department of Defense, he should have abandoned it altogether as beyond the CIA's capability. He should have insisted on more skepticism from his staff, and made clear that their courage was not to be questioned by the advocates.

He should have realized that, without wartime conditions of censorship, his hope of keeping quiet a paramilitary operation of this magnitude was impossible in an open society. He should have reexamined the whole plan once all the publicity about a big invasion began appearing. In fact, the Cuban refugee community in Miami, the American press and the Castro government were all talking about the "secret" training camps and invasion plans long before those plans were definite.

Finally, he should have paid more attention to his own politically sound instincts and to the politically knowledgeable men who did voice objections directly—such as Fulbright and Schlesinger—on matters of Cuban and Latin-American politics and the composition of a future Cuban government, instead of following only the advice of Latin-American experts Adolf Berle, Jr., and Thomas Mann.[3] While weighing with Dean Rusk the international consequences of the plan's being quietly and successfully carried out, which they decided were acceptable, he should also have weighed the consequences of the plan being neither quiet nor successful—for those consequences were unacceptable. But for once John Kennedy permitted his hopes to overcome his doubts, and the possibilities of failure were never properly considered.

When failure struck, it struck hard. Tuesday's postmidnight meeting in the Cabinet Room was a scene of somber stocktaking. The President, still in his white tie and tails after the annual Congressional reception, was stunned by each new revelation of how wrong he had been in his expectations and assumptions. He would not agree to the military-CIA request for the kind of open commitment of American military power that would necessitate, in his view, a full-scale attack by U.S. forces—that, he said, would only weaken our hand in the global fight against Communism over the long run. He dispatched Schlesinger and Berle as personal emissaries to the angry exile political leaders who had been held incommunicado by the CIA in Florida. Finally, around 4 A.M., after ordering the ill-fated "air cover for the air cover,"

3 Schlesinger did draft an excellent White Paper on Castro's betrayal of the revolution, but there was too wide a gap between the understanding implicit in that paper and the premises implicit in the landing plan.

and talking halfheartedly with those aides who remained after all officials departed, he walked out onto the South Lawn and meditated
briefly alone.

On Wednesday, in a solid day of agonizing meetings and reports
as the brigade was being rounded up at Zapata, he gave orders for
American Navy and Air Force to rescue as many as possible; and he
talked, at Schlesinger's suggestion, with the exile political leaders flown
in from Florida. He found them remarkably understanding of his resolve to keep the fight between Cubans, and they found him, they
remarked later, deeply concerned and understanding, particularly for
those with sons in the brigade. "I lost a brother and a brother-in-law
in the war," the President told them. "I know something of how you
feel." In truth, words alone could not express how he felt, for I observed in the days and months that followed that he felt personally
responsible for those who had lost their lives—miraculously few compared with Castro's heavy losses—and that he was determined above
all else to prevent the execution and to seek the liberation of the 1,113
men his government had helped send to their imprisonment.[4]

In public and with most of his new associates, the President remained hopeful and calm, rallying morale, looking ahead and avoiding
the temptation to lash out in reproach or recrimination. He asked
General Maxwell Taylor to chair an investigation of the truth, to
determine not *who* was wrong and deserved to be punished but *what*
was wrong and had to be righted. As both mobs and diplomats the
world round decried American imperialism, deception, and aggression,
he remarked privately that many of those leaders most anxious to see
Castro removed had been among the first to assail the U.S. in speeches
for regarding tiny Cuba as a threat. Nevertheless, he held his tongue in
public.

Despite this outward composure, however, so necessary to the
country at that hour, he was beneath it all angry and sick at heart. In
later months he would be grateful that he had learned so many major

---

[4] Some twenty months later, on Christmas Eve, 1962, the prisoners, kept alive by
Kennedy's stern warnings to Castro, were freed in exchange for $53 million in drugs,
baby food, medical equipment, and similar non-embargoed supplies donated without
any use of Treasury or CIA funds under an impressive operation directed by the
Attorney General and negotiated with Castro by lawyer James Donovan representing the Cuban Families Committee. Since mid-1961 various negotiation attempts
had waxed and waned; and while the basic responsibility and financing were kept
private, the President was proud of the assistance his administration provided by
way of tax exemptions, coordination, surplus food, and encouragement. Receiving
the brigade leaders at his Palm Beach home after their release, the President and
First Lady were deeply impressed by their bearing and spirit, and the President
predicted, in an Orange Bowl address two days later to the brigade members and
friends, that its flag would someday fly "in a free Havana."

lessons—resulting in basic changes in personnel, policy, and procedures —at so relatively small and temporary a cost. But as we walked on the South Lawn Thursday morning, he seemed to me a depressed and lonely man. To guard national unity and spirit, he was planning a determined speech to the nation's editors that afternoon and a series of talks with every Republican leader. The Bay of Pigs had been— and would be—the wost defeat of his career, the kind of outright failure to which he was not accustomed. He knew that he had handed his critics a stick with which they would forever beat him; that his quick strides toward gaining the confidence of other nations had been set back; that Castro's shouting boasts would dangerously increase the cold war frustrations of the American people; and that he had unnecessarily worsened East-West relations just as the test-ban talks were being resumed.

"There's an old saying," he later told his press conference, "that victory has a hundred fathers and defeat is an orphan. . . . I am the responsible officer of the government and that is quite obvious." But as we walked that Thursday morning, he told me, at times in caustic tones, of some of the other fathers of this defeat who had let him down. By taking full blame upon himself, he was winning the admiration of both career servants and the public, avoiding partisan investigations and attacks, and discouraging further attempts by those involved to leak their versions and accusations. But his assumption of responsibility was not merely a political device or a constitutional obligation. He felt it strongly, sincerely, and repeated it as we walked. "How could I have been so far off base?" he asked himself out loud. "All my life I've known better than to depend on the experts. How could I have been so stupid, to let them go ahead?"

His anguish was doubly deepened by the knowledge that the rest of the world was asking the same question.

Thomas A. Lane

The Bay of Pigs

It was evident even before President Kennedy took office that one of his first concerns was the public image of himself as a vigorous leader. He had criticized the Eisenhower part-time Presidency, the frequent vacations away from Washington, the delegation of power to subordinates, the drifting in Laos, Cuba, and the Congo. He promised to bring dynamic, forceful leadership to the Presidency.

As members of the Kennedy Cabinet were announced, it was made clear that these men would only be assistants to the President. The Secretary of State would not make foreign policy; he would submit recommendations to the President who would make all decisions. The Secretary of Defense would not make defense policy; he would submit recommendations to the President for decision.

This early trend of image-building might have raised some misgivings among discerning men. It gave the impression that the President-elect regarded his office as a center of action to control operations rather than a center of policy-making to provide guidance to the operating officials. It suggested a misapprehension that the presidential office could be run like a senatorial office.

The buildup of the presidential image carried an unavoidable subordination of the Cabinet images. This seemed unfortunate, given the importance of these officers to the success of the administration. They might really be unimportant men.

The image-building campaign to picture the President as a dynamic, aggressive leader acting continuously in the public interest was very successful in commanding public confidence. It was a workable image for the ordinary routines of politics. But what would happen in time of crisis? Would the leader surrounded by pygmies be capable of living up to the image he had created? Would he know all and judge all and decide all?

The image was beyond human realization. No one could be the leader John F. Kennedy projected because no human being had the knowledge and comprehension to fulfill the role. The astonishing fact is that the President thought he could so manage the office. The lone-wolf financial operations of his father, the experience of the legislator,

From The Leadership of President Kennedy *by Thomas A. Lane. Reprinted by permission of The Caxton Printers, Ltd.*

the uninterrupted success of his political operations, the adulation of devoted followers, the very intoxication of political image-building, all conspired to deceive him.

Great organizations are made with building blocks. The leader does not direct every detail of activity. He places in each block of the organization a lieutenant who can direct its work, inspire its personnel, inform and loyally support the leader. It is the function of the leader to provide all elements of the organization with timely guidance for action, approval of achievement, correction of error, and inspiration. If the leader tries to control each action, he paralyzes the organization. Lieutenants who have no responsibility but obedience will lack the initiative to manage their own offices.

This false concept of his own role and obligation led President Kennedy to attempt detailed control of matters beyond his own comprehension. In doing so he failed to use properly lieutenants who were masters of the operations in progress. The image he had cultivated impelled subordinates to bring him problems, not solutions; information, not answers. Because he was determined to make all decisions, his subordinates hesitated to make any decisions. This, unfortunately, was the command climate to which the Bay of Pigs operation was transferred on January 20, 1961, and under which the invasion of Cuba was executed.

Planning and preparation for the assault on Cuba had been initiated by the United States Central Intelligence Agency with the approval of President Eisenhower during 1960. President Kennedy was informed of these plans and preparations before he took office. State and Defense Departments were informed but entered the planning only at very senior echelons. This was a CIA operation.

Early planning had been aimed at guerrilla warfare to overthrow Castro but later estimates of his strength had changed the attack plan to an assault landing. Organization and training of the participating forces was in progress in Florida, in Guatemala, and in Nicaragua. The invasion fleet would be launched from Caribbean bases. Air support would be provided from Caribbean bases until airfields could be established in the landing area. There was provision for United States carrier-based air support to be used if necessary.

As these plans were revealed to the inner circle of policy advisers in the Kennedy Administration, objections were raised. At a special White House staff meeting[1] on April 5, 1961, called by the President to weigh the final decision to launch or halt the invasion, Senator

---

[1] Those in attendance with the President were: Secretaries Rusk, McNamara, and Dillon; Assistant Secretaries Mann, Nitze, and Berle; Messrs. Dulles, Bissell, Bundy, and Schlesinger; Senator Fulbright and General Lemnitzer.

Fulbright objected to the proposed use of force to topple Castro. He argued that such unilateral use of force would seriously damage United States prestige and foreign policy objectives in the hemisphere and in the world.

After discussion, the President approved the planned invasion but with the proviso that there should be no direct participation of the United States Armed Forces. Since no direct participation of United States forces had been planned, the effect of the decision was to eliminate the contingent provision of United States carrier-based air support. Because the distance to Nicaragua air bases made fighter cover of the invasion force impossible and preinvasion bombardment effects unpredictable, Mr. Bissell, Mr. Dulles, and General Lemnitzer should have protested the presidential change of plan. There has been no evidence that they did so.

The preinvasion bombardment designed to destroy the Castro Air Force began on April 15, 1961. Pilots of the attack bombers who landed in the United States used cover stories that they had fled from Cuba. The planes had been marked with Cuban Air Force insignia. United States government spokesmen denied knowledge of any attack on Cuba.

In the United Nations, however, pressures on the United States increased rapidly. Delegates were becoming skeptical about Ambassador Stevenson's denials, impressed by Cuban and Soviet charges. The situation was reported to Secretary Rusk in Washington.

Secretary Rusk informed the President of the U.N. criticism. According to Attorney General Kennedy, who participated with General Taylor, Admiral Burke, and Mr. Allen Dulles in a still-secret investigation of the Bay of Pigs operation, the President then gave instructions that the D-day morning air strikes in support of the invasion "should not take place at that time unless those having the responsibility felt that it was so important it had to take place, in which case they should call him and discuss it further."[2] Another account reveals that General Charles P. Cabell, Deputy Director of the CIA and Acting Director in the absence of Allen Dulles, made vigorous protest to Secretary Rusk who ordered the cancellation of the air strikes, but was rebuffed. Secretary Rusk seemed to have taken charge of the operation in the absence of Allen Dulles.

The landing force encountered little opposition. It had apparently achieved complete tactical surprise. Initial assault waves quickly moved inland to secure the beach exits and prepare for further operations.

However, the landing force was without air cover or air support.

[2] USN & WR, January 28, 1963.

The preinvasion bombardment of the Castro airfields had left four jet trainers in operation. When these aircraft appeared over the beachhead, they were unhampered in attacking troops and equipment ashore and the supply ships and forces afloat off the beachhead. Destruction of the ships carrying ammunition and supplies for the landing forces placed the whole operation in immediate jeopardy.

As news of this disaster reached the President, he had to consider whether he would commit United States carrier-based planes, within easy striking distance of the landing force, to give it emergency support and destroy the four Castro planes. The clear alternative was to abandon the force to the mercies of Castro. President Kennedy refused to commit United States forces but released the air strikes which had been planned for the morning of April 17 and cancelled on his orders. It was then too late to retrieve the situation with such timorous action. On the eighteenth, the invasion bombers were destroyed and the landing force was overwhelmed.

Although his later action cast doubt on his grasp of the scope and importance of the invasion operation, President Kennedy's initial procedure was sound. When he assembled the National Security Council and White House staff to hear their advice before making his final decision, he was following sound practice. If he had stood firmly behind that decision, he would have fulfilled the exacting demands of his office.

When, however, he weakened his resolve under pressure from the United Nations (which should have been anticipated in the original planning and was forecast by the objections of Senator Fulbright), he betrayed an uncertainty about his original decision. It seemed that an inbred political instinct to move with the pressure caused him to hedge by modifying the invasion plan.

Moreover, he betrayed a lack of grasp of his own organizational arrangements when he communicated his decision to Secretary Rusk instead of giving it directly to General Cabell, Acting Director of CIA, who was in charge of the operation. If the President had given his decision to General Cabell, he would have received a prompt estimate of its implications.

The President should have reconvened the National Security Council which advised him on the original decision before acting to suspend the air strikes. With full consultation, he might have realized the magnitude of the disaster he was risking. He and Secretary Rusk clearly had no personal competence to judge the issue. They had expert advice at their call but they did not use it.

President Kennedy's refusal to use United States aircraft to protect the beachhead and destroy the Castro planes reveals the confusion of his thinking. He was incapable of weighing the relative importance of criticism in the U.N. and disaster to an invasion which he personally had launched. He feared the effect of international criticism but could not comprehend the costs of operational failure. Opposition of Senator Fulbright had weighed heavily on the President, weakening his resolution. His legislative experience was poor preparation for the ordeal.

That he became involved in such tactical details of a military operation betrays the fundamental error of the Kennedy leadership. He had a staff well qualified to handle such details. The presidential question was whether to make such an attack on the Castro regime. If the attack was to be made, it had to succeed; for it was clearly better to make no attack than to fail. If the President had merely approved the operation and insisted on success, he would have provided the guidance necessary for his subordinates.

It is the irony of fate that in his solicitude for international opinion, President Kennedy failed completely to grasp the one essential for that good opinion—a *successful* invasion. The toppling of Castro would have raised United States prestige in the world to new heights. There could be no greater contribution to Castro power and prestige than an invasion *failure*. Castro could not have done better if he had planned the operation himself.

In the light of hindsight, President Kennedy's apologists have argued that the invasion was a poorly planned operation which was destined to fail in any event. The record does not support such a view. Whether by good planning or the grace of God, the invasion was entirely successful, to include the April 17 landing. If the Castro planes had been destroyed by the D-day strikes as planned, the expedition would have had every prospect of success.

It is possible that the D-day strikes originally planned would have failed to destroy the Castro planes. It would then have been necessary to use United States planes for the mission as the Eisenhower plans had contemplated. The U.S.S. *Boxer* had been stationed where it could do the job. The initial presidential decision precluding such use of United States aircraft should have been reconsidered when the essentiality of such support became apparent. Allen Dulles, who should have been at the President's side in that critical hour, was absent in Puerto Rico.

The inescapable conclusion is that President Kennedy failed to grasp the critical values of United States interest in the Bay of Pigs invasion. In this failure, his mistaken image of himself as the all-seeing, all-knowing man of action apparently played an important part. He had been deceived by his own propaganda. He had badly misjudged the nature of presidential power and the prudent methods of using it. He had become a victim of his own illusion.

It would be reasonable to expect this experience of failure to stir in the President new comprehension of the presidential power and of the correct methods of exercising it. Subsequent events indicate that this growth did not occur. Some changes in the White House staff occurred but the established Kennedy approach to the personal exercise of power persisted.

There was no one to show the President his errors. In the post-operation study of the CIA and of the Bay of Pigs failure which is still secret, we may assume that General Taylor, Admiral Burke, and Mr. Dulles were too tactful to point out the presidential mistakes. The Attorney General probably was not even aware of them.

The Kennedy misjudgment of leadership is a common and popular one. It views the leader as a dynamic, driving, intense man-in-motion. That image is false as this event so aptly illustrated. The good leader simply knows what is to be done and does it. There are times for decision and times for action, and times for patience and fortitude. In this event, the good leader would have approved the recommended plan with a single admonition, "You cannot fail in this undertaking!" Then he would have settled back to observe the performance of his staff. When the U.N. criticism arrived, he would have remained serene in the knowledge that the ouster of Castro would win the approval and admiration of the free world.

The illusion that the Presidency must be directed by an omniscient citizen who makes all decisions, large and small, persisted in the administration. It was nurtured by an inexperienced staff which actually believed it. The President and his coterie of neophytes in government could not be shaken out of their dreams even by the reality of disaster.

Hugh Sidey

The Presidency: The Classic Use of the Great Office

On the fifth anniversary of John Kennedy's death the resolution of the Cuban missile crisis stands as his enduring monument, its quieting effect still discernible in the world today. And from details about the crisis that are still coming out from the many retellings of the dramatic story—including that of the late Robert Kennedy—one significant fact emerges. John Kennedy's actions during those days in October 1962 represent an understanding and use of the Presidency that has rarely been equaled in this nation's history. The script John Kennedy followed is a classic text in extracting wisdom from men and injecting it into the affairs of nations.

In its largest dimension, it was an exercise in openmindedness. That morning when McGeorge Bundy, walking on the balls of his feet as he always did, entered the President's bedroom (whether he knocked or not is lost to history, but he probably did not, so extraordinary was the relationship between the President and his close advisers) and told Kennedy that there was unmistakable evidence of nuclear offensive missiles in Cuba, the Celt in JFK stirred first. After a few choice expletives, he, like Bundy, with vision narrowed by shock and danger, declared that armed forces would have to strike Cuba to remove the threat.

From the perilous summit of passion there was a long slope of restraint and deliberation that led to the remarkable solution. Nothing in history held Kennedy prisoner. It was almost as if he were guided by a favorite Lincoln passage:

> The dogmas of the quiet past are inadequate to the stormy present. . . . As our case is new, so we must think anew and act anew. We must disenthral ourselves.

From the start Kennedy cast the challenge as one of communication, not warfare. He never let it get out of that realm. He set his course by his sense of history, a kind of inner road map warning him of human misjudgment and prejudice. The stupidity and breakdown of judgment

From Life, *November 22, 1968.* © *1972 Time, Inc.*

that led to World War I was in his eyes, the result of a total failure of communication. The military men did not overwhelm him, nor did the rather panicky reaction of congressional leaders (including the Senate's foreign relations leader, William Fulbright), nor did the clipped, cold logic of former Secretary of State Dean Acheson, all of whom argued for stronger action. He had often been melancholy about this, and on tired nights around the Oval Office he talked of "Russia stockpiling nuclear weapons and the United States building up and you have all of this and then somebody is going to use them."

He ordered the blockade of Cuba not to stop ships from bringing in missiles—that did not matter in the time which the U.S. had to act— but as a device to send the message of our determination through clearly to Nikita Khrushchev. Language, not just in the letter to Khrushchev but even in the reply to the near-hysterical philosopher Bertrand Russell, was carefully toned to moderation by Kennedy.

Looking back now, men like Bundy are still amazed that in those desperate days Kennedy squeezed so much time out for argument to help distill the decisions. The measured walk through the crisis he insisted upon gave him a remarkable amount of time for thought and planning. Reflection inevitably brought Kennedy to try to view things from the Russian side. If his first reaction was that hostilities were inevitable, was that not likely to be the initial Russian reasoning? Then give them more time to think. The outer perimeter of the blockade, for instance, was reduced from 800 to 500 miles, adding hours to the time in which the Soviets could think over their position.

Kennedy understood what Bundy calls the "shadow of the President." In the inner councils of the White House the presence of the President alters other men's chemistry. Some wait to hear what he says, then agree. Others are intimidated and don't say what is on their minds. Kennedy stayed away from meetings where there were knowledgeable people who reacted in these ways to his presence. He orchestrated other sessions to get the correct mix of personalities—for example, bringing in the acerbic Ted Sorensen to challenge the assumptions of the military men. Kennedy did believe in the net of advisers he had created around himself following the Bay of Pigs, but he did not have unlimited faith in any one man—he even grew grumpy with his brother Bob.

Kennedy understood himself. He knew that frantic all-night meetings not only would exhaust his staff but severely alter his judgment. He hoarded his energy, insisting on an afternoon nap and getting a good night's sleep except at the most critical points. Often he had talked about how the failure to rest enough put him on "the edge of irritability." Some of those around him did not heed that warning.

When in the final hours a U-2 strayed over Soviet territory and one aide came in frantically with the news, Kennedy had him led off and put to bed, then once again asked all of those around him to restrain themselves and think calmly.

Probably most important of all was Kennedy's deep understanding of the impact of the Presidency. He permitted no staging of forces, no phony maneuvers to "show" the Russians that we were serious. He quite rightly reasoned that any contrived actions would do the opposite. And when he ordered mobilization for a possible invasion of Cuba, he allowed no public announcement. Soviet intelligence, he said, would find out about it and would know the meaning instantly.

Dean Acheson

Dean Acheson's Version of Robert Kennedy's Version of the Cuban Missile Affair

On October 28, 1962, when he seemed to be over the hump of the Cuban missile crisis, I wrote a note to President Kennedy congratulating him on his "leadership, firmness, and judgment over the past touchy week." It does not detract from the sincerity of this message to add that I also thought that he had been phenomenally lucky. Senator Kennedy's account of the crisis reinforces both impressions.

As he has written, his and my appraisal of the situation and recommendations to the President differed from the start. What enters into judgment, as distinct from rationalization of it, is difficult to identify or state honestly. Senator Kennedy seemed at the time—a view strengthened by his account—to have been moved by emotional or intuitive responses more than by the trained lawyer's analysis of the dangers threatened and of the relevance to these of the various actions proposed.

Senator Kennedy has described the White House-State Department-Pentagon group that advised the President on this crisis. I was drawn into the group on the second day of its existence, Wednesday, October 17, 1962, by Secretary Rusk, who showed me the U-2 photographs available and described the situation as it was then known. It became fully known only over the next few days as dispersal of hurricane-cloud cover over Cuba permitted more perfect photographs over a broader area. The facts were that the Soviet nuclear-missile installations in Cuba were extensive and formidable. The shorter-range missiles first discovered were soon supplemented by discoveries of longer-range missiles able to cover the continental United States, parts of Canada, and a good part of South America. The missile sites were remote from populated areas and manned and guarded by Russian personnel. When first photographed, only a few missiles were on launching pads—whether operable or not was unknown. Activity around them on all sites was considerable.

The Issue in the Advisory Group

When Secretary Rusk and I joined the discussion, it soon became evident that three views were held by different members of the group: one, that the weapons in Cuba did not change the balance of power and, therefore, no action was required; two, that they were fast becoming an acute danger and should be removed by military action before they became operable; and, three, that a naval blockade against weapons should be established to enforce a demand that the Soviet Union remove the missiles.

As I recall it, the first of these views was put forward with more weight of authority, though not numbers, than Senator Kennedy's account suggests. At any rate, I hit it hard. In the first place, I did not believe for a minute that these weapons, ninety miles from Florida, did not increase our vulnerability above that theretofore existing. They gave shorter-range missiles the same bearing as intercontinental missiles. In the second place, if the United States Government should take a passive position, it would forfeit—and rightly so—all confidence and leadership in the Western hemisphere (also under threat of these Soviet missiles) and in Western Europe. This first attitude was soon abandoned by its advocates.

When the discussion turned to a destruction of the missiles by bombing, Senator Kennedy stated the view expressed in his account. I remember clearly his formulation of it. An attack on the installations, he said, would be "a Pearl Harbor in reverse" and would never be acceptable to his brother. This seemed to me to obfuscate rather than clarify thought by a thoroughly false and pejorative analogy. I said so, pointing out that at Pearl Harbor the Japanese without provocation or warning attacked our fleet thousands of miles from their shores. In the present situation the Soviet Union had installed ninety miles from our coast—while denying that they were doing so—offensive weapons that were capable of lethal injury to the United States. This they were doing a hundred and forty years after the warning given in President Monroe's time that the United States Government would regard an attempt by any European power to extend its "system to any portion of this hemisphere as dangerous to our peace and safety" and as manifesting "an unfriendly disposition toward the United States." Moreover, within the last few months the Congress, and within the last few weeks the President, had reiterated this warning against the establishment of these very weapons in Cuba. How much warning was necessary to avoid the stigma of "Pearl Harbor in reverse"? Was it necessary to adopt the early nineteenth-century method of having a man with a red flag walk before a steam engine to warn cattle and people to stay out of the way?

This dialectical approach was dropped in the group, though in discussion with the President alone, he repeated the "Pearl Harbor in reverse" phrase. I remarked that I knew where it came from and repeated my answer to it.

The more serious discussion of the alternatives—destroying the weapons or pressure for their removal by a naval blockade of the island —convinced me that the former was the necessary and only effective method of achieving our purpose. Yet the narrow and specific proposal, pressed by some of us, constantly became obscured and complicated by trimmings added by the military. To the proposal of immediate and simultaneous low-level bombing attacks on the nuclear installations, some wished to add bombing of airfields, S.A.M. sites, and fighter aircraft; and others, the landing of ground troops to assure that the missiles were destroyed or removed. The former would indeed do what Senator Kennedy—and I, as well—deplored, "rain bombs on Cuba and kill thousands and thousands of civilians in a surprise attack." Attacks on the installations would involve no Cubans but about forty-five hundred Russian technicians and troops preparing for hostile action against our country. While a drill book might call for preliminary attack on Cuban defenses, this was not necessary for the action we recommended. If our action should fail—or if, in the more likely event, the blockade should fail—further military action might be necessary. But we, no more than our colleagues, were proposing killing "thousands and thousands of civilians." The charge was emotional dialectics.

To be sure, our proposal raised dangers of a Russian response against the United States or against an ally, such as Turkey or Berlin. But the blockade created what to my mind were greater dangers without any assurance of compensating benefit. Its effect would in any normal expectation be slow, if ships did not attempt to run through it; or, if they did, would produce the very military confrontation that Senator Kennedy so earnestly sought to avoid. But—most important of all—it would give the Russians time for their technicians to make some or all of the missiles operational. Once this occurred, Cuba would become a combination of porcupine and cobra. My criticism of Senator Kennedy's narrative is that it does not face this possibility—indeed, probability—frankly. It is merely stated and dropped.

The basic point, which both General de Gaulle and Chancellor Adenauer pointed out to me the following week, was that a blockade was a method of keeping things out, not getting things out, of a beleaguered spot. In this case, moreover, it was directed not at the controller of the weapons, but at the host of the controller. It seemed a blunt instrument, ill-adapted to the purpose. To argue, as Senator Kennedy quotes Secretary McNamara as doing, that its pressure "could be increased as the circumstances warranted . . . would be understood and yet, most importantly, still leave us in control of events," seems unworthy of the Secretary's able, analytical mind. The opposite seemed to me to be true: the blockade left our opponents in control of events.

General de Gaulle believed that the Russians would not attempt to force the blockade and asked what we would do in that event to remove the missiles. If the Government had decided upon any course, I had not been informed of it before being sent off to Europe. Improvising, I replied that the Government would immediately tighten the blockade and, if necessary, go further to more positive measures. The General understood.

As I saw it at the time, and still believe, the decision to resort to the blockade was a decision to postpone the issue at the expense of time within which the nuclear weapons might be made operable. The Soviet Union did not need to bring any more weapons into Cuba. The Senator's account reports an intelligence estimate that the nuclear weapons already there represented the equivalent of one half of the Soviet Union's intercontinental-ballistic-missile capacity and were capable of killing eighty million Americans. That was enough.

The consideration that weighed more heavily on the other side with the Senator and the President was that an air attack on the installations alone might drive the Soviet Union to a spasmodic, reflex nuclear attack against the United States or against, say, American nuclear weapons in Turkey. This would be possible, of course; but analysis seemed to show it as unlikely. (Incidentally, General de Gaulle did not believe that the Kremlin would have responded with either action.) One must recall that both the Russian Ambassador and the Foreign Minister were asserting to the President that no offensive nuclear weapons had been installed in Cuba by the Soviet Union. Their representatives at the United Nations continued to repeat this even after Mr. Stevenson had asserted the contrary in the Security Council. So far, then, as the public record was concerned, a sudden air attack by us on nonpopulated areas of Cuba would have been an attack not on the Soviet Union but on something—not people—in Cuba. This would hardly have called for a reflex attack on the United States at the expense of reciprocal destruction of the Soviet Union.

The Russians would have been better advised to stick to their story that no nuclear weapons were in Cuba and charge that we had nervously fired at shadows created by our own fears. This would not have been easy to disprove, for even the evidence of the photographs could be attacked as faked with dummies. The germ-warfare charges against us in 1951 during the Korean war had been widely believed.

Blockade Merely Postponed Confrontation

If one examines the blockade alternative, Senator Kennedy's story makes abundantly clear that it did not offer any greater chance of evading head-on collision with Moscow's prestige, riding like a figurehead on the prows of her ships approaching Cuba. By October 23 Soviet submarines were moving into the Caribbean. Almost as soon as the blockade went into effect, the Government tried, the Senator relates, devices —not too resolute in appearance—for putting off the confrontation. First, the place of challenge was drawn closer to Cuba. Then a tanker was allowed to go through. Then a non-Soviet ship was boarded and passed. What should the Navy do if the Russian ships refused to stop? Shoot off the rudders or propellers? And then take them where? "We could anticipate a rough, fierce fight and many casualties," the President is reported as saying. Meanwhile more photographs of launching pads, missiles, and nuclear storage bunkers "made clear that the work on these sites was proceeding and that within a few days several of the launching pads would be ready for war."

At ten o'clock on Wednesday morning, October 24, a small group sat with the President as Secretary McNamara reported from the War Room two Soviet vessels approaching the U.S.S. *Essex*. A submerged Soviet submarine moved in front of them. "I felt," the narrative states, "we were on the edge of a precipice with no way off." At 10:25 A.M. a message came that the Russian ships had stopped dead in the water. Then came another that several ships in the area were turning around. The Russians, testing us to the last minute, had decided, as General de Gaulle had forecast the preceding Monday, not to attempt to run the blockade. The missiles, however, remained in place.

The Decision to Blockade

To move back a week, discussion within the "Ex-Com" (Executive Committee of the National Security Council, a courtesy title) after a couple of sessions seemed to me repetitive, leaderless, and a waste of time. I was happy, therefore, when the President asked me to meet with him at 3:45 P.M. on Thursday, October 18. He received me alone for about an hour, listening to my views, as he always did, with courtesy and close attention and examining my reasons and premises thoroughly. His questions revealed full knowledge of Attorney General Kennedy's attitude. I could not tell what impression, if any, I had made. When we finished, he walked from his rocking chair in front of the fireplace to the French doors looking out on the rose garden and stood there for a moment. Then, without turning, he said, "I guess I'd better earn my salary this week." I answered, "I'm afraid you have to. I wish I could help more." With that we parted.

The next morning the "Ex-Com" group, as the Kennedy narrative reports, decided to break up into two groups and each write out the steps, diplomatic and military, that the President would need to take to put the respective recommendations into effect.

Going into a room with those who favored the air strike, I asked to be excused from further attendance, saying that it was no place for a person holding no position in the government. For an outsider to give advice and counsel when asked was one thing; it was quite another to participate in writing the most secret strategic and tactical plans of a vital military operation, which might soon be put into effect.

On Saturday night, October 20, Secretary Rusk telephoned me and in a guarded way said that the President had decided a matter about which he had talked with me, though contrary to my recommendation. He wanted me to go to France to convey his decision and reasons to mutual friends, leaving by an Air Force plane the next morning.

In a way I had brought this request on myself. In the talk with the President the importance of informing our European as well as Latin American allies of our problem and enlisting their support before—even if only a split second before—acting and our lack at the moment of an ambassador in Paris led me to suggest that the Vice-President would be none too important a representative to send. The Secretary's request brought to mind an observation of Mr. Justice Holmes that we all belonged to the least exclusive and most expensive club in the world, the United States of America. I told him of it and undertook the obligation of membership he proposed, adding the hope I was enough of a lawyer to do a good job for my client, even though I thought he was making a mistake.

This is not the place for an account of that mission, interesting as it was with its interviews in Paris with General de Gaulle, the American military command in Europe, and the NATO Council, and in Bonn with Chancellor Adenauer and Defense Minister Strauss. Hastily getting together money, clothes, passports, instructions, photographs of the missiles, intelligence officers to interpret them, and an ambassador or two on the way back to his post, we were off early Sunday and home again on Wednesday, October 24. On our return the crisis had been going on for ten days without any progress toward getting the missiles disposed of.

Once More into the Breach

Returning to Washington on Wednesday afternoon, I found that the tension that had temporarily relaxed with the President's decision to impose the blockade was mounting again as realization grew that this was only another road to military confrontation with the Russians. Avoiding group meetings, I reported on my mission to Secretary Rusk on Wednesday afternoon and to the President on Thursday, pointing out again that the missiles remained in Cuba and that a week's collection of photographs showed alarming progress in the work of mounting them. Time was running out. The air strike remained the only method of eliminating them and hourly was becoming more dangerous.

On Friday evening in the State Department we saw the confused, almost maudlin message from Khrushchev, summarized in the Kennedy narrative. It is enough to say here that in its ramblings it admitted the presence of the weapons in Cuba, but denied that they had been put there to attack the United States, which would mean only mutual destruction. They were there only to protect Cuba against American attempts to overthrow its government, as the United States had attempted to do at the Bay of Pigs and earlier to overthrow the Soviet Government soon after its establishment. The suggestion was made that if assurances were given that the United States would not attack Cuba and would abandon the blockade, the removal of the missile sites might be "an entirely different question." The letter then rambled off again on the horror and folly of nuclear war.

At breakfast with Secretary McNamara on Saturday I learned of the second, more formal Russian note conditioning the withdrawal of the Cuban missiles upon our withdrawal of our missiles in Turkey (apparently sent in ignorance of Khrushchev's earlier message), of the shooting down of a U-2 over Cuba on reconnaissance (the S.A.M. sites or some of them were evidently now operational), and the opinion of the Chiefs of Staff that the air strike could no longer in safety be delayed. With this I agreed, but continued to urge that it be restricted to the Soviet nuclear installations only.

Senator Kennedy's paper tells us that on Saturday afternoon, at a meeting I did not attend, "there was almost unanimous agreement that we had to attack early the next morning with bombers and fighters and destroy the S.A.M. sites. But again the President pulled everyone back." And quite rightly, for this proposal would have achieved the worst of both courses. It would have precipitated violence without accomplishing more than the destruction of the surface-to-air missiles, which had shot down the U-2. It would not have touched the source of trouble, the nuclear missiles. " 'We won't attack tomorrow,' he [the President] said. 'We shall try again.' " So the report tells us.

What the President tried again was another message to Khrushchev, another postponement of action while Soviet work on the missiles drove on. It was a gamble to the point of recklessness, but skillfully executed, with ideas contributed by Robert Kennedy. It answered, not the official Soviet note, but Khrushchev's confused one, and accepted what seemed to be a muddled proposal for Russian withdrawal of the nuclear missiles in return for an American undertaking not to attack Cuba. If there were divided counsels in the Kremlin—as there were in Washington—the new message proposed to exploit them.

Meanwhile preparations for an air attack went forward. The amazing result was that by the very next morning this hundred-to-one shot certainly appeared to be paying off.

Reflections

On Luck

It was not enough, Napoleon observed, that he should have good generals; he wanted them to be lucky generals, also. In foreign affairs brains, preparation, judgment, and power are of utmost importance, but luck is essential. It does not detract from President Kennedy's laurels in handling the Cuban crisis that he was helped by the luck of Khrushchev's befuddlement and loss of nerve. The fact was that he succeeded. However, as the Duke of Wellington said of Waterloo, it was "a damned near thing." And one should not play one's luck so far too often.

What, I was asked at the time, was Khrushchev up to? He had, I thought, formed a low opinion of Presidents Eisenhower and Kennedy at the Paris Summit Meeting and Vienna respectively. His aim in Cuba was threefold: first, to increase his nuclear first-strike capacity against the United States by about 50 percent; second, to discredit the United

States completely in the Western hemisphere; and third, to force the United States to pay so high a price for the removal of the Cuban missiles as to discredit us in Europe and Asia. He could with some reason believe that his own prestige was not likely to be damaged beyond what a diversion like the Berlin Wall of 1961 could repair. He went to pieces when the military confrontation seemed inevitable. But he need not have done so. Senator Kennedy's narrative does not convince me that an attack would have been inevitable if Khrushchev had "played it cool."

On Method

"During all these deliberations," Senator Kennedy has written, "we all spoke as equals. There was no rank, and in fact we did not even have a chairman. Dean Rusk, who as Secretary of State might have assumed that position, had other duties and responsibilities during this period of time and frequently could not attend our meetings." One wonders what those "other duties and responsibilities" were to have been half so important as those they displaced. As a result, "the conversations were completely uninhibited and unrestricted. . . . It was a tremendously advantageous procedure that does not frequently occur within the Executive branch of the Government. . . ." One can be devoutly thankful that this is so.

I can testify to the truth of the statement that members of the group did all speak as equals, were uninhibited, and that they had no chairman. But in any sense of constitutional and legal responsibility they were not equal and should have been under the direction of the Head of Government or his chief Secretary of State for Foreign Affairs and his military advisers. One cannot escape the conclusion from reading the Kennedy narrative that the chief advice reaching the President during this critical period came to him through his brother, the Attorney General, out of a leaderless, uninhibited group, many of whom had little knowledge in either the military or diplomatic field. This is not the way the National Security Council operated at any time during which I was officially connected with it; nor, I submit, the way it should operate.

David Horowitz

Showdown: The Cuban Crisis

The United States' response to the Soviet emplacement of missiles in Cuba was clear, vigorous, and decisive. On October 22, President Kennedy went on TV to inform the nation, the Russians and the world, that he had ordered a blockade[1] of Cuba to prevent additional missile equipment from arriving on the island, and that if the preparation of the missile sites did not cease, and the missiles were not withdrawn, "further action" would be taken. This action could either have meant expansion of the embargo to include petroleum shipments or an air strike. By the end of the crisis week, this latter alternative had become a real possibility.[2]

In his address, President Kennedy charged:

> . . . this secret,[3] swift,[4] extraordinary build-up of Communist missiles—in an area well-known to have a special and historical relationship to the United States and the nations of the Western

From The Free World Colossus by David Horowitz. Reprinted by permission of MacGibbon & Kee and Hill and Wang, a division of Farrar, Straus & Giroux. Copyright © David Horowitz 1965.

[1] The President's word was "quarantine," but throughout the planning stages, the action was termed "blockade" by those involved, and this is clearly what it was. For this account, I have drawn on the detailed, day-by-day story of the crisis compiled by the Washington Bureau of The New York Times, and printed in the International Edition, November 6, 1962.

[2] Ibid. This air strike would probably have been against the Cuban anti-aircraft batteries which had shot down one U-2 plane and fired on others.

[3] But cf. the Wall Street Journal, October 24: ". . . the authorities here almost all accept one key assumption: That Mr. Khrushchev must have assumed his Cuban missile sites would soon be discovered. 'The Russians seem almost to have gone out of their way to call attention to them,' said one authority who has studied the photographic evidence." Cf. also, K. S. Karol, New Statesman, November 2, 1962. "Many military men have been astonished by the openness of Soviet preparations in Cuba, under the constant surveillance of U.S. aircraft. It is possible, then, that the dispatch of Soviet missiles should be compared with the reinforcement of the U.S. Berlin garrison at the time of the last crisis there. In Berlin, Kennedy wished to emphasize that American lives would be involved, so making world war certain in the event of a Soviet thrust."

[4] But cf. Hanson Baldwin, New York Times, Int. Edn., November 1, 1962: "Considerable mystery, in the opinion of Congress and military men, still surrounds the Administration's sudden decision to impose a blockade of Cuba after a missile build-up that must have started weeks or months ago. . . . The question that arises . . . is whether the Intelligence data that must have been collected throughout the summer and early fall was accurately evaluated, or whether policy dictated the intelligence estimated or turned them aside." [Emphasis added.]

Hemisphere, in violation of Soviet assurances,[5] and in defiance of American and Hemispheric policy—this sudden, clandestine decision to station strategic weapons for the first time outside of Soviet soil—is a deliberately provocative and unjustified change in the *status quo* which cannot be accepted by this country, if our courage and our commitments are ever to be trusted again by either friend or foe.[6]

Thus did President Kennedy justify the extreme U.S. action in response to the Soviet maneuver, namely, a naval blockade, which was, in fact, an act of war and hence violated the UN charter and the very OAS treaties which the President invoked as bases for United States' concern.[7] The action taken by the United States was even more momentous in that by engaging a test of will with the Soviet Union, it was risking a test of strength, and this test of strength would have involved not only the lives and destinies of the Soviet and American peoples, but hundreds of millions of people in other countries whose governments had no role in the decisions which had led up to, or, afterward, which shaped the crisis.

Therefore, it is of more than passing importance that the nature of the Soviet provocation be understood. For the Cuban crisis provides the first real basis for estimating what the nuclear future may be like without some sort of general disengagement. It is interesting to note in this regard, that the substantive issue involved in the Cuban crisis was not understood at the time and that a general misimpression has persisted in the aftermath. This mistaken view holds that the United States was alarmed because the presence of missiles in Cuba upset or significantly altered the military balance of power, i.e., the nuclear *status quo*.

It would seem that in this case the wish has been father to the thought, that people would like to think that thermonuclear war will be precipitated (barring accident) only when the security of one of the great powers is threatened, or when some similarly clear-cut issue involving self-defense is at stake. In addition to the confusion caused by wishful thinking, Ambassador Stevenson's remarks (October 23) before the UN, may have unintentionally served to mislead many people:

[5] I.e., Gromyko's assurances on October 18, that the missiles were for defensive purposes. This is by no means a clear issue, however, a fact emphasized by the following passage from the above cited Baldwin article: "Military men point out that many Administration officials, including a high State Department official, were emphatically denying the existence of any offensive Soviet missiles in Cuba until just before the President's speech."

[6] *New York Times*, Int. Edn., October 23, 1962.

[7] It has been argued by Arthur Larson and others that because the U.S. move was an act of self-defense, it was in keeping with the principles of the UN Charter. But this assumes that the emplacement of missiles in Cuba altered the nuclear balance of power. Such an assumption is not warranted by the facts. See below.

When the Soviet Union sends thousands of military technicians to its satellite in the Western Hemisphere—when it sends jet bombers capable of delivering nuclear weapons—when it installs in Cuba missiles capable of carrying atomic warheads and of obliterating the Panama Canal, Mexico City, and Washington—. . . this clearly is a threat to the hemisphere. And when it thus *upsets the precarious balance in the world,* it is a threat to the world.

Stevenson avoided saying "upsets the precarious *balance of terror* in the world" or even balance of *power,* just as President Kennedy avoided any reference to a *balance* of nuclear forces in his statement, and with good reason. For if the nuclear background developed to this point in the manner in which we have described it, then the forty-two Soviet missiles in Cuba[8] would have had no effect at all on the overall nuclear balance (except, possibly, to make it more stable).

That this was in fact the case was made clear by Deputy Defense Secretary Gilpatric on a television program November 11. According to *The New York Times* of November 12:

> . . . Mr. Gilpatric made two observations on the over-all missile capability of the United States compared with that of the Soviet Union.
>
> First, he said, defense officials believe that the United States has a measurable margin of superiority in strategic weapons.
>
> Second, in alluding to the Soviet missile build-up in Cuba, he said: *"I don't believe that we were under any greater threat from the Soviet Union's power, taken in its totality, after this than before."*[9] [Emphasis added.]

What, then, was at stake in the Soviet emplacement of missiles in Cuba? What challenge or threat necessitated a U.S. action which not only violated fundamental international law, but risked a general nuclear holocaust as well?[10] It could not have been the mere fact of

[8] Deputy Defense Secretary Gilpatric, quoted in *The New York Times,* Int. Edn., November 12, 1962.

[9] The Institute for Strategic Studies made the following estimates of long-range missile strengths of the two powers for the end of October 1962: Soviet Union 75 ICBM's; U.S. 450–500 missiles capable of being fired more than 2,000 miles. *New York Times,* Int. Edn., November 9, 1962.

[10] The main risk was not simply that of a decision by the U.S.S.R. to engage in such a war, but in the crisis generally getting out of hand. Thus *The New York Times'* account of the crisis reports that on Saturday, October 27, "the possibility of having to knock out hostile anti-aircraft batteries on the island was very real, and *there was doubt about how much longer the crisis could be carefully controlled.* . . . They sat with an over-all confidence in the nation's nuclear superiority over the Soviet Union [*sic*], but this was little comfort if the Russians chose to go

the Soviet build-up, because that had been going on since July.[11] It was evidently not the material presence of "offensive" missiles, since if we are able to believe Deputy Defense Secretary Gilpatric and the evidence of the Institute of Strategic Studies, as well as the previous statements of Gilpatric and McNamara of the relative missiles strengths of the two nuclear giants, the U.S. was under no greater threat from the Soviet's power, taken in its totality, after the emplacement of missiles than before. What then was the nature of the Soviet provocation?

The answer to these questions was revealed by President Kennedy himself during a television interview on December 17, 1962:

> [The Russians] were planning in November to open to the world the fact that they had these missiles so close to the United States. Not that they were intending to fire them, because if they were going to get into a nuclear struggle they have their own missiles in the Soviet Union. But it would have *politically* changed the balance of power, *it would have appeared to—and appearances contribute to reality.*

Thus, it seems it was a *political* balance of power that was actually in danger of being upset, and this political balance was a question of appearances—prestige, presumably—the political consequences of what would appear in the eyes of the world and domestic critics of the Kennedy Administration[12] to be a Soviet act of defiance, perpetrated with impunity. Not to have forced the Russians into retreat would have been appeasement, a sign that the U.S. would not stand up to Soviet power when challenged, and it would therefore have opened the door to further challenges, perhaps over Berlin. This explains why Khrushchev's offer on Saturday, October 27, to exchange

---

to a war that neither side could win. The President gravely remarked that evening that it seemed to him to be touch and go, that it could now go 'either way'." [Emphasis added.]

11 *New York Times*, Int. Edn., November 6, 1962.

12 On October 15, Eisenhower delivered a speech in which he charged that the Kennedy Administration's foreign policy had not been "firm." In the eight years of his own Administration, Eisenhower declared, "We witnessed no abdication of responsibility. We accepted no compromise of pledged word or withdrawal from principle. No [Berlin] walls were built. No foreign bases [i.e., in Cuba] were established. One was ended [i.e., in Guatemala] and incipient wars were blocked." *New York Times*, Int. Edn., October 16, 1962. On the other hand, domestic pressure on Kennedy to do something about Cuba should not be overemphasized. Three separate polls, including a Gallup poll, taken a week before the crisis, indicated that there had been no increase in public support for an invasion of Cuba since April 1961 (or 15 months before the Soviet build-up began). According to the Gallup poll, 24 percent favored invasion, 63 percent were opposed, while 13 percent had no opinion.

the missile bases in Turkey for the bases in Cuba was turned down. And indeed, *The New York Times'* account of the rejection indicates the political-prestige nature of the decision:

> Such a proposal had already been rejected as unacceptable; though the Turkey missile base had *no great military* value, it was of *great symbolic* importance to a stout ally. To bargain Turkey's safety [i.e. to *apparently* bargain Turkey's safety—D.H.] would have meant shocking and perhaps shaking the Western alliance. [Emphasis added.]

The military insignificance of the Turkish missile base and the symbolic importance of not bargaining with the Soviets was emphasized in a front page story in *The New York Times,* less than three months later, on January 21, 1963:

> The Turkish Government has responded favorably to proposals that the United States remove its Jupiter missile bases. . . .
> The removal of these Jupiter missiles was under consideration here *some time before* the crisis last fall over the emplacement of Soviet missiles in Cuba. [Emphasis added.]

The fact that the removal of the Turkish missile bases had been considered *before* the Cuban crisis raises the question as to why there was a crisis at all. Why, for example, was not the Soviet Ambassador given an ultimatum *in private,* before the presence of the missiles was disclosed to the world and the prestige of the United States had been put on the line?[13] Such a move would have been *normal* diplomatic procedure (and was actually proposed by Stevenson).[14] As James Reston wrote on October 27:[15]

> The new Kennedy style of diplomacy is now operating in the Cuban crisis. It is highly personal and national. It is power diplomacy in the old classic European sense that prevailed before the great men worried much about consulting with allies or parliaments or international organizations. . . .
> [The President] did not follow the normal diplomatic practice of giving his antagonist a quiet escape from fighting or withdrawing, but let the Soviet Foreign Minister leave the White

---

13 Since both Cuba and the ships coming to Cuba were under constant surveillance, it would have been simple for the Kennedy Administration to be very precise in framing an ultimatum or deal, and very secure about verifying Soviet compliance.
14 Henry M. Pachter, *Collision Course,* 1963, p. 30.
15 *New York Times,* Int. Edn., October 26, 1962.

House without a hint of what was coming and then announced the blockade on the television.

While generally approving Kennedy's "power play," Reston expressed certain reservations about its wisdom:

> This brisk and sudden diplomacy, however, cannot be pursued without cost. The political reaction within the nation and the alliance has been gratifying to the Administration, but it is misleading because it is not the same as private reaction.
>
> Privately, there are several misgivings. First, many people find it hard to believe that the offensive Soviet missile sites in Cuba suddenly mushroomed over the weekend, and accordingly, there is considerable suspicion either that the official intelligence was not so good as maintained, or the Administration withheld the facts.
>
> Second, many diplomats within the alliance still think it was wrong to confront Khrushchev publicly with the choice of fighting or withdrawing, especially since the security of many other unconsulted nations was involved. . . .

The mysteries attending the discovery of the build-up, the unusual nature of the crisis diplomacy, and the lack of any immediate overwhelming, military threat, all point to the existence of an important dynamic element in the planning of U.S. policy. Further evidence that motives behind the U.S. action in the Cuban crisis were dynamic and not only responsive in character, was offered at the time in a remarkable series of articles by the informed *New York Times* analyst, C. L. Sulzberger (appearing on October 20, 22, and 24).[16] In a retrospective glance, four months later,[17] Sulzberger summarized his previous conclusions in the following way:

> Some weeks before the Cuban confrontation, Washington decided that Khrushchev's cold war offensive, begun in 1957, was petering out. It therefore resolved on a showdown with Russia at a time and place of its own choosing. Khrushchev, with his Caribbean missile game, surprisingly[18] also seemed to seek a test. He chose a time, October, that seems to have suited us. History will judge for whom Cuba was the right place.

[16] International Edition, datelines: Paris, October 19, 21, and 23.
[17] International Edition, February 25, 1963, dateline: February 24.
[18] "Surprisingly" because his power situation was so weak. This suggests that Khrushchev's move was a miscalculation. Cf. James Reston, *New York Times,* Int. Edn., October 24, "Khrushchev's Mistake on Cuba."

In his October 21 article, written from Paris *before* the announcement of the blockade, Sulzberger traced the history of the cold war as seen by the Kennedy Administration and indicated that calculated reasons why a showdown was considered important by the leadership (Sulzberger felt that this showdown would be in Berlin, further indicating the unlikeliness that he knew about the imminent Cuban clash). "Washington," he wrote, "is convinced a moment of truth is approaching over Berlin, and that the West cannot afford to dodge this confrontation; that if we now face and surmount the crisis, the international balance will begin to swing our way." Because of this conviction, Sulzberger observed, Washington "is . . . emphasizing a paramountcy of leadership" that causes some "ripples of disquiet" among the Allies, who wish to avoid a confrontation over Berlin. "Nevertheless, we see this as a chance to turn Russia's second cold war offensive."

Russia's first "offensive" according to Sulzberger, was launched by Stalin in Greece fifteen years earlier, "halted there, blocked in Berlin, and finally checked by 1951 battlefield victories in Korea."[19] Russia's second, or "Khrushchev offensive" dated from the launching of Sputnik, "when Moscow hoped to trade missile prestige [*sic, not* superiority or power] against new real estate." In this offensive, Communism "failed to win the Arab world, Guinea, or the Congo." While these failures were being registered, moreover, "pressures built up inside the Communist world." Khrushchev tried to deal with these pressures—satellite unrest, the split with China, Russia's food crisis—but, as of October 1962, had found "no panacea." "The United States is consequently convinced that Khrushchev is up against vast difficulties and seeking some kind of triumph to advertise. . . . We believe it is necessary to take risks in warning Khrushchev, letting him see clearly what he is up against."

On October 23,[20] Sulzberger concluded his series with an analysis of the Cuban crisis which had begun the day before.

> The new trend in United States policy described in previous columns [he began] has now culminated in a showdown with Russia. That is the real meaning of the Cuban crisis. President Kennedy decided to move against Khrushchev's cold war offensive at a time and place of his own choosing. . . . This calculated risk has presumably been taken for the calculated reasons previously

[19] Sulzberger's reference to 1951 victories indicates that he believes that the Chinese entered the Korean War as part of Stalin's offensive rather than as a result of MacArthur's provocation. As with his statement about Greece, this is untenable before the facts.
[20] *New York Times,* Int. Edn., October 24.

analyzed. Washington seems to feel this is the time to check and reverse Khrushchev's cold war offensive. We have opted to force the issue ourselves without prior approval of our allies and there are going to be uneasy diplomatic moments. . . .

. . . *Some of our leaders have been hinting this for weeks.*[21] *They knew what they were talking about. One must assume it was they who planned the showdown that has started.* [Emphasis added.]

In other words, having built a sizable missile superiority of its own, and having laid the plans for a rapid increase in this superiority in the next few years, the Kennedy Administration had waited for an opportune moment to demonstrate its nuclear superiority to the world, and with the prestige thus gained, tip the scales of the world power balance. The test was expected to come in Berlin, when Cuba presented itself.

Even if Sulzberger weren't as close to the inner circles in Washington as he is, the handling of the crisis by the United States leadership would point to the same conclusion, namely, that once the information about the Soviet build-up was received, the only response considered was one that would precipitate a showdown.[22]

According to official accounts, the key aerial photographs were developed on October 15. On October 16, the President called a meeting of the Executive Committee of the National Security Council.[23] The results of this meeting were summarized in *The New York Times'* account as follows:

At this first meeting the President and his advisors were not yet clear on what was to be their objective to get the offensive weapons out of Cuba. Some talked, rather, about getting Premier Castro out.

---

21 On September 24, Kennedy obtained authorization to call up 150,000 reservists. "General Curtis Le May ordered supplies to be flown to Florida, that mission was to be completed by October 10, and the tactical Air Command was to be combat-ready by October 20. . . . Do these dates indicate that the Chief of Staff of the Air Force expected the crisis at the end of October?"—Pachter, p. 7n.

22 "Most significant [of proposals to avoid a crisis] was Stevenson's proposal to present Khrushchev with a secret ultimatum. . . . The difference between his way of thinking and Kennedy's . . . [is that]: Kennedy and the majority of the Executive Committee felt it necessary to have a public showdown with Khrushchev." —Pachter, pp. 91–92.

23 It was actually an *ad hoc* committee which became known as the Executive Committee. Its members included Vice-President Johnson, Secretary Rusk, Secretary of Defense McNamara, Secretary of Treasury Dillon, Attorney General Kennedy, Under Secretary Ball, Deputy Secretary of Defense Gilpatric, General Carter, Assistant Secretary of State Martin, General Taylor, McGeorge Bundy, and Theodore Sorensen. These were joined by Alexis Johnson, John McCone, Dean Acheson, and Llewellyn Thompson.

The meeting produced two immediate decisions. One was to
intensify air surveillance of Cuba. The second was that action
should await further knowledge, *but should come as close as
possible to disclosure of the Russian bases*—which could not be
long delayed. [Emphasis added.]

In other words, the one point on which all were agreed was that
the Russians should be caught red-handed, faced with a predetermined
show of strength and compelled to retreat. The only question was the
nature of the action to be taken, air strike or blockade.[24] On Friday,
October 19, an air strike was ruled out, and it was decided to use a
blockade:

> Attorney General Kennedy argued against a strike on moral
> grounds. . . . For the United States to attack a small country like
> Cuba without warning, he said, would irreparably hurt our repu-
> tation in the world—and our own conscience.
> The moral argument won general assent. . . .
> The blockade proposal was recognized as one raising most
> serious dangers. As recently as October 6, Vice-President Johnson
> had warned that "stopping a Russian ship is an act of war."
> By the end of the afternoon meeting the blockade was clearly
> the indicated answer.

Fortunately, the immediate danger of precipitating a thermonuclear
war was avoided, and on October 28, the crisis ended, as the Soviet
Union agreed to withdraw its missiles in return for a United States
guarantee not to invade Cuba. In this curious way, the United States
won a prestige victory over its Soviet opponent.

By agreeing to withdraw the missiles, Khrushchev lifted the threat
of nuclear annihilation from millions whose nations were not involved
in the dispute, and hence who tended to view the Cuba base as comparable to U.S. bases in Turkey, as well as from those nations who
were. And though his action of putting the missiles there in the first
place in general drew harsh criticism, his withdrawal of the missiles in
the face of U.S. intransigence[25] gave him an opportunity to demonstrate
moderation and rationality which he would not otherwise have had.

[24] "Invasion was not considered as a possible first action. It would take too long
to mount. Surprise would be impossible. The effect on world opinion was certain
to be unfavourable. The Soviet response might rapidly 'escalate' the affair." "But
the air strike did win significant support. So did a blockade." *New York Times'*
account of events of Wednesday, October 17.
[25] The mediating proposals of UN Secretary General U Thant to stop both missile
preparations and blockade, had been rejected by the U.S. and accepted by the
Soviet Union.

Moreover, the "price" that the U.S. paid to have the Soviets withdraw their missiles, namely, an agreement not to invade Cuba, was surely one of the strangest facets of the whole affair. For it meant nothing less than the United States officially recognized that it would, in fact, contemplate aggression against a sovereign state, and therefore that the Soviet build-up in Cuba had legitimate defensive purposes from the *Cuban* point of view.[26] In retrospect, it would seem that the Soviet Union also gained a "prestige victory."

But Kennedy's triumph, particularly within the Western Alliance and at home, was evident and impressive. From Washington's point of view, the central gain was in dispelling the illusion that the United States would not fight for its vital interests. This was considered to be important not only from the standpoint of the Allies' morale, but from the standpoint of making it clear to Khrushchev, that the United States could not be faced down in areas such as Berlin.

It should further be noted that Kennedy immediately acted to restrain those who might want to see the advantage in the Cuban crisis pressed by further displays of power. After an interview with the President on October 28, the day the crisis ended, James Reston reported:

> President Kennedy is looking at the Cuban crisis not as a great victory but merely as an honorable accommodation in a single isolated area of the cold war. . . .
>
> The President is not even drawing general conclusions from this special case about the tactics of dealing with the Soviet Union in the future. To be specific, while he may be equally bold again in risking conflict in support of vital national interests, he is rejecting the conclusion of the traditional "hard-liners" that the way to deal with Moscow everywhere in the world is to be "tough," as in Cuba. . . .[27]

But if Kennedy was now eager to emphasize the limits of U.S. power in dealing with the Communists, and thus forestall the pressures of his right wing, the months following the Cuban crisis saw him take

26 Cf. the Washington *Star* and Washington *Daily News* of October 29 and 30. The former stated: "Authoritative sources warned today against any feeling that the agreement with the Soviet Union will lead to 'peaceful coexistence' with Fidel Castro's Cuba. . . . Once the first phase of actually dismantling and removing the Soviet weapons is completed, they said that the hemisphere and Cubans can get on with the more 'limited' phase of actually getting rid of the Castro régime. . . . At a forty-five minute briefing in the State Department yesterday, Secretary of State Rusk told the nineteen Latin American Ambassadors . . . not to exaggerate the extent of the U.S. guarantee against invading Cuba." Both articles cited in *I. F. Stone's Weekly*, November 5, 1962.
27 *New York Times*, Int. Edn., October 29, 1962.

an increasingly assertive attitude towards the Western Alliance. In December, the U.S. abruptly announced cancellation of the program to build Skybolt missiles on which Britain had based its long-range plans for maintaining an independent nuclear deterrent. In February, an undiplomatic note accused the Canadian Government of failing to produce a "practical" plan for joint defense. Partly as a result of this note, and the ensuing reaction, the Canadian Government fell.

If there was little question about the vigor of the new post-Cuba diplomacy, however, there were many uncertainties about its direction. As one European observer wrote:

> The series of successes in the last quarter of 1962 has confirmed the Kennedy Administration in its good opinion of its foreign policy. . . .
>
> An intoxicating certainty of power is the prevailing mood. It is only when specific questions of how this power will be used in relations with enemies and allies that there is uncertainty. . . .
>
> In East-West relations there is a new self-assurance, but hardly a sign of new ideas. The Administration which was going out of its way to warn of an impending Berlin crisis, now appears to think Cuba has made a Berlin crisis unlikely, or at least milder when it comes.
>
> But as Mr. Dean Acheson pointed out in the meat of the speech which caused such indignation in Britain, there is now no American policy in central Europe beyond an exhortation to stand firm on Berlin . . . .[28]

As we have seen, however, firmness and the development of power was itself a policy for Kennedy, who believed that strengthening the forces of freedom (to use Acheson's phrase) would induce the Soviets to become reasonable and accept a settlement on "reasonable" terms.

Kennedy's policy after Cuba was, in fact, very consistent with the assumption that only two power centers (East and West) existed in Europe, and that so long as the balance was not tipped heavily against the East, it would not settle for a *status quo* meaning less than domination. For after Cuba, Kennedy moved to give the NATO powers a nuclear force of Polaris submarines under terms that would weld them into unity while integrating them as an arm of U.S. striking power. The net effect would be a stronger "Atlantic" front against the Communist bloc.

Significantly, as the new year began, Kennedy was rebuffed in his design for European economic and military (and eventual political)

[28] Godfrey Hodgson in the London *Observer,* December 30, 1962; cf. also James Reston in *The New York Times,* Int. Edn., December 27, 1962.

unity interdependent with the United States, by de Gaulle, who re-affirmed his intention to build an independent nuclear force for France, and on January 14, vetoed Britain's entry into the Common Market.

Kennedy's reaction to de Gaulle's rebuff was significant, in that he did not emphasize the danger of independent nuclear forces and the spread of nuclear weapons, but rather stressed the threat to the Western Alliance and to the world in any weakening of the power bloc of the West:

> It would be well to remind all concerned of the hard and fast realities of this nation's relationship with Europe—
>
> The reality of danger is that all free men and nations live under the constant threat of Communist advance. Although presently in some disarray, the Communist apparatus controls more than one billion people, and it daily confronts Europe and the United States with hundreds of missiles, scores of divisions, and the purposes of domination.
>
> The reality of power is that the resources essential to defense against this danger are concentrated overwhelmingly in the nations of the Atlantic Alliance. In unity this Alliance has ample strength to hold back the expansion of Communism until such time as it loses its force and momentum. Acting alone, neither the United States nor Europe could be certain of success and survival. The reality of purposes, therefore, is that that which serves to unite us is right, and what tends to divide us is wrong. . . .[29]

Since de Gaulle had not indicated any intention to withdraw from the NATO Alliance, or to make a separate accommodation with the Soviets, Kennedy's picture of the world situation represented a strange estimate both of the balance of forces and the present dangers. For it is inconceivable that Kennedy considered real, or immediate, the danger of a Soviet advance in Europe in any military sense. As of January, the conventional strength of the Western bloc was larger than that of the Soviet bloc by 8.1 million to 7.3 million men.[30] Politically, the Communist bloc was being rent by the Sino-Soviet schism; economically, the East was beset by significant problems. When Kennedy spoke, the general estimate in the West was that Khrushchev's recent statement had indicated the Berlin question would not be pressed. The Russians had been cooperative in tying up the loose ends of the Cuban crisis. Khrushchev had waged a vigorous post-Cuba campaign against

[29] *New York Times*, Int. Edn., January 25, 1963.
[30] P. M. S. Blackett, "The First Real Chance for Disarmament," *Harper's*, January 1963. "The total forces of the Warsaw Pact, including the Soviet Union, number about 4½ million, against 5 million men in the active armed forces of *NATO*." London *Observer*, December 15, 1963.

the militancy of the Chinese and for the policy of peaceful coexistence. Clearly, Kennedy's concern could not have been the weakness of the Western Alliance, but rather the fact that it would not have *enough* strength to force the Soviets into "fruitful negotiations."[31]

On the other hand, all indications pointed to the conclusion that U.S. missile superiority would no more induce a relinquishing of Soviet positions in 1963, than had atomic monopoly or H-bomb superiority before. As in previous stages of the cold war, it would induce, rather, a Soviet move to offset the superiority. Thus, in January it was reported that observers in Washington believed "that the Russians may be attempting to compensate with [a] 'big bang' for their inferiority in missile numbers." A "very few" 50 to 100 megaton bombs "delivered in a promiscuous pattern of nationwide bombing could paralyze any nation, and could destroy or damage all except the most heavily protected military installations. Damage and casualties caused would probably be so great as to be crippling." *"Any President,"* the report continued, *"would hesitate to invoke the threat of nuclear weapons, as we did in the Cuban crisis or even to take extremely strong action if he felt that several giant megaton weapons could be delivered on the United States."* Thus, even a small number of these weapons "mated to the powerful but few Russian ICBM's," though not sufficient to "save" the Soviet Union in a nuclear war, "might well serve, as apparently they are intended to serve, as a means of neutralizing the present superiority of the United States in numbers of ICBM's and in over-all nuclear delivery capacity."[32] And, on February 22, *The New York Times* (International Edition) reported:

> The commander-in-chief of the Soviet strategic rocket forces said today [February 21] the Soviet could launch rockets from satellites at a command from the earth.[33]

[31] For Kennedy's far-ranging optimism about the world power balance at this time, cf. the President's State of the Union Message, January 14, 1963.

[32] Hanson Baldwin, *New York Times*, Int. Edn., January 10, 1963: "I will tell you a secret: Our scientists have worked out a 100 megaton bomb . . . we can use such a weapon only outside the confines of Europe. I am saying this in order that there should be a more realistic appreciation of what horrifying means of destruction there exist. . . . Comrades, to put it in a nutshell, as I have already said during the session of the Supreme Soviet of the U.S.S.R., it is not advisable to be in a hurry for the other world. Nobody ever returned from there to report that one lives better there than here. We do not want a kingdom in heaven but a kingdom on earth, a kingdom of labor. This is the kind of kingdom we are fighting for and without stinting our efforts we shall go on fighting for it."— Nikita S. Khrushchev, to the Communist Party Congress in East Berlin, January 16, 1963; *New York Times*, Int. Edn., January 17, 1963.

[33] For a corroborating account and discussion of the implications of the new weapon, cf. Tom Margerison in the London *Sunday Times*, February 24, 1963.

Henry Kissinger, for one, had warned the previous summer[34] that the time when all of the Soviet Union's missiles could be destroyed by a counter-force blow was limited. Dispersal, hardening of bases, and the development of missile firing submarines would make it impossible in the future to know where all of an enemy's missiles were, and hence to be free from a devastating retaliatory blow.

In the end of January, Secretary of Defense McNamara appeared before the House Armed Services Committee, and made acceptance of the impending stalemate official, declaring that "regardless of what kind of strategic forces we build . . . we could not preclude casualties counted in the tens of millions."[35]

Thus, Kennedy's two-year attempt to gain a decisive lead in the arms race (requiring a 20 percent increase in the military budget) produced the same results as previous attempts: a new stage of the arms race, a further increase in the number of nuclear weapons, and consequently, a more difficult world to disarm. But the Cuban crisis added to the lessons of previous years, by presenting mankind with an unforgettable glimpse into the perils of a nuclear future,[36] a future dominated by the immense gap between man's revolutionary technological means, and his traditional, limited, political and ethical outlook. It was a lesson which underscored the President's own warning to the UN General Assembly, in September 1961, when he said:

> The weapons of war must be abolished before they abolish us. . . . The risks inherent in disarmament pale in comparison to the risks inherent in an unlimited arms race.

[34] Henry A. Kissinger, "The Unsolved Problems of European Defense," *Foreign Affairs,* July 1962.

[35] *Time,* February 15, 1963. The Air Force promptly attacked this "no win" policy of accepting nuclear stalemate as a dangerous one. Cf. *New York Times,* Int. Edn., February 1, 1963.

[36] Consider, for example, what might have happened if the "showdown" had occurred over Berlin.

Theodore Draper

Kennedy's Decisions Regarding Vietnam

Turning Point Number 3 (December 1961)

. . . No sooner had John F. Kennedy been sworn into office than the highest Washington officials were spreading the word among themselves that Diem's regime was on the point of collapse. Kennedy's first appointment as Ambassador to South Vietnam, Frederick E. Nolting, Jr., was sent off to Saigon in April 1961 with this news ringing in his ears. According to John Mecklin, the American Public Affairs Officer in Saigon from 1962 to 1964, Nolting was told in Washington before he left for his post that "it would be a miracle if South Vietnam lasted three months longer." On March 26, 1964, Secretary of Defense McNamara gave a more restrained version of the situation which had forced President Kennedy's hand three years earlier: "When President Diem appealed to President Kennedy at the end of 1961, the South Vietnamese were quite planly losing their fight against the Communists, and we promptly agreed to increase our assistance."

That Diem, who had had the Communists on the run from at least 1955 to almost the end of the decade, should have faced defeat at their hands by early 1961 is inexplicable in terms of the Communists' own strength. It is understandable only in terms of the inner degeneration of Diem's regime and its suicidal estrangement from other non-Communist forces in South Vietnam. The fatal disease was political, not military.

The problem before John F. Kennedy in 1961 was, in essence, the problem that had faced Dwight D. Eisenhower in 1954. What should the United States do to stave off a complete collapse in Vietnam? The most detailed and candid account of Mr. Kennedy's decision appears in Arthur M. Schlesinger, Jr.'s chronicle *A Thousand Days*. It is a veritable case history of how the military submerged the political in action, if not always in intention and thinking.

Kennedy came to the Vietnam problem, as he did to other problems, without a consistent position behind him. Professor Schlesinger cites the speech Kennedy made in the Senate on April 6, 1954, against unilateral United States intervention to bolster an essentially colonial regime which the "great masses" of Vietnamese did not support. Another biographer, Theodore C. Sorensen, even cites the same passage as the "key" to the late President's decision in 1961. (Neither of them recalls the more bellicose, pro-French Kennedy of March 9, 1954.) Professor Frank N. Trager has dug up another speech on June 1, 1956, which was delivered by still another John F. Kennedy. By this time, Diem seemed to have consolidated his rule, and Senator Kennedy hailed it as our "offspring" which we could not afford to permit to fail. Schlesinger and Sorensen do not mention the June 1956 speech, and Trager does not mention the April 1954 speech. The difference in emphasis may be defended on the ground that the situation in South Vietnam had changed markedly in two years, but even so, the conclusion is inescapable that Kennedy was too pessimistic in 1954 and too optimistic in 1956. The ease with which Kennedy can be quoted against Kennedy suggests the dangers and difficulties of evaluating a statesman whose style is considered more important than his substance.

In his first months in office, Kennedy had to make up his mind whether Diem had failed and, if so, what to do about it. As Schlesinger tells the story, his advisers lined up in two camps, the "political" and the "military." Those who put a political effort in Vietnam as the first consideration saw no hope short of a "change of leadership" in Saigon, which meant dropping Diem in favor of some other South Vietnamese leader. Among those explicitly or implicitly urging this course were John Kenneth Galbraith, then Ambassador to India, W. Averill Harriman, appointed Assistant Secretary of State for the Far East in 1961, and the writer Theodore H. White. Schlesinger refers to a "Harriman group" in the State Department which questioned subordinating the political to the military. Vice-President Johnson went to Saigon in May 1961 and was so impressed by Ngo Dinh Diem that he compared him to George Washington, Andrew Jackson, Woodrow Wilson, Franklin D. Roosevelt, and Winston Churchill. Mr. Johnson apparently advocated a substantial increase in all kinds of American aid, short of military manpower, which, he said, was not needed.

This seems to have been Mr. Johnson's second important contribution to America's Vietnamese policy. In 1954, his reluctance to have the United States go it alone without allies had served to restrain Secretary of State Dulles; in 1961, his recommendation for increased aid and all-out support of Ngo Dinh Diem, with no more Allied support than in 1954, served to discourage restraint on the part of President Kennedy.

But the main pressure on Kennedy inside the government came from the military side. A special mission to South Vietnam headed by General Maxwell D. Taylor and Walt W. Rostow of the State Department recommended sending a relatively small American military task force with combat capabilities. Except for the so-called Harriman group, Professor Schlesinger says, the State Department in the person of Secretary Dean Rusk "was well satisfied with military predominance in the formation of United States policy toward Vietnam." General Taylor has revealed that both the introduction of American ground forces and American bombing of Northern military targets were under consideration at least since November 1961, when he presented his report.[1] Sorensen goes so far as to say that "all" of Kennedy's principal advisers on Vietnam favored the commitment of American combat troops.

Finally, Kennedy did more or less at the end of 1961 what Eisenhower had done at the end of 1954. He decided, as General Taylor later put it at the Vietnam hearings of the Senate Foreign Relations Committee, to change the number but not the "quality" of our military advisers. He ruled out combat missions but gradually increased the number of "advisers" from about 800 to 17,000.[2] Schlesinger quotes Kennedy in one of his most appealing, astute, and antic moods, turning down the advice of those who wanted an American combat commitment: "It's like taking a drink. The effect wears off, and you have to take another."

Yet Schlesinger admits that Kennedy's decision at the end of 1961 "was to place the main emphasis on the military effort." This emphasis required renewed and intensified political support of the Diem regime. The new American Ambassador, Frederick E. Nolting, Jr., and the new American military commander in Saigon, General Paul D. Harkins, made Diem's cause their own. Nolting established a relationship with Ngo Dinh Diem similar to that of Ambassador Arthur Gardner with

---

[1] In order to cope with what he called "para-wars of guerrilla aggression," General Taylor wrote in his report of November 3, 1961, "it is clear to me that the time may come in our relations to Southeast Asia when we must declare our intention to attack the source of guerrilla aggression in North Vietnam and impose on the Hanoi government a price for participating in the current war which is commensurate with the damage being inflicted on its neighbors in the south" (letter of President Johnson to Senator Henry M. Jackson, *The New York Times*, March 3, 1967). It should be noted that at the very time of this Taylor report, the State Department's White Paper of December 1961 estimated the full-time regular Vietcong fighting force at less than 10,000 men (pp. 9–10); that it boasted "something close to an economic miracle" had taken place in South Vietnam (p. 5); that, as other sources later admitted, the Vietcong's weapons came almost wholly from the United States via captured South Vietnamese weapons; and the first regular North Vietnamese troops did not allegedly arrive in the south for another three years. Yet General Taylor already projected widening the war to take in North Vietnam, and President Johnson cited his more-than-five-year-old report as justification for turning the full force of American might on North Vietnam.
[2] The exact figures are 773 at the end of 1960 and 16,500 at the end of 1963 (*Congressional Record*, Senate, October 10, 1966, p. 24855).

Fulgencio Batista in Cuba from 1953 to 1957 or of Ambassador W. Tapley Bennett, Jr., with Donald Reid Cabral in the Dominican Republic in 1964 and part of 1965. Thus there was an unmistakable political side to the military decision.

For some reason, Kennedy's military decision, which was half-hearted, has come in for far more attention than its political counterpart, which was not. Ambassador Nolting represented a do-or-die, wholehearted political gamble on the durability and reformability of Diem's regime.

Why did Kennedy do it? Why did Kennedy, as John Mecklin put it, act the way Eisenhower had acted, only "more so"? The answer given by President Kennedy's intimates and biographers is most revealing. Both Schlesinger and Sorensen plead in his defense that past American policy had virtually given Kennedy no other alternative. Kennedy, writes Schlesinger, "had no choice now but to work within the situation he had inherited," and Dulles's policy in South Vietnam had "left us in 1961 no alternative but to continue the effort of 1954." Sorensen strikes the same note. In exculpation, they emphasize that Kennedy's military contribution was still limited. But the principle they accept would make it difficult for a President to refuse to go from a low-level to a high-level limit and, if necessary, to an unlimited effort. Moreover, they neglect to pay enough attention to the fact that, while his military investment in the Diem regime was then limited, he threw in a practically unlimited political bonus in the persons of Ambassador Nolting and General Harkins, and the latter may have been by far the more important of the two.

It is, of course, a truism that no policy is made *in vacuo* and that the past weighs heavily on every important Presidential decision. But if Professor Schlesinger is right that President Kennedy's options were so limited, even in 1961, when he had fewer than eight hundred non-combat military personnel on the scene, the implications are truly frightening. One gets the impression from these memoirs and memorials of Kennedy's associates that they are writing of a man who did what he did not want to do, what he knew or felt he should not do, and what he had little faith would come out right in the end. There is nothing so devastating about our entire Vietnam policy as the sense of fatality, and this is the best argument that Kennedy's friends have been able to muster in his behalf. I rather think that President Kennedy would not have given himself such an easy way out, any more than he did in the Bay of Pigs case. Inasmuch as some of his former aides experienced a partial change of heart in 1966, it is hard to see how, if President Kennedy's options were so limited in 1961 without American combat troops in South Vietnam, they could think President Johnson would have any options with about 400,000 combat troops there. The Vietnam war will go down in history as another "war of lost opportunities," and some of the best opportunities to reexamine and reshape the war were lost in 1961.

Turning Point Number 4 (November 1963)

The fourth turning point came about primarily because John F. Kennedy lost his political gamble on Ngo Dinh Diem.

Diem's regime benefited at first from the increased American military and political support. The military approach seemed to be paying off. Our policy in 1962, writes Professor Schlesinger, was "dominated by those who saw Vietnam as primarily a military problem and who believed that its solution required unconditional support of Diem." When Diem's durability proved to be an illusion, there was nothing to fall back on. Diem's power was based on the demoralization of South Vietnamese political life, and he succeeded so well that we are still living with the political wasteland that he left, not without our cooperation.

What supporting Ngo Dinh Diem unconditionally after 1961 meant has been most intimately described by John Mecklin, whose official duties brought him into contact with the highest officials on both sides. He and other observers agree that we were not even supporting a government; we were supporting a slightly pixilated family's fief. The awesome or awful threesome of this family—Ngo Dinh Diem; his brother, Ngo Dinh Nhu; and the latter's wife, Madame Ngo Dinh Nhu —are most often described in psychiatric terms. Mecklin's bizarre account of their habitual behavior belongs in a textbook of mental pathology. He gently diagnoses the three of them as victims of "blank-wall irrationality." Mecklin relates whimsically that he once had a dream "about an American diplomatic mission that gradually discovered it had been dealing for years with a government of madmen." But when he awoke, he asked himself whether he had been dreaming after all. Shaplen refers to the condition of Nhu, generally considered the power behind the throne, as "seemingly paranoid." Even Professor Trager, always inclined to give the Diem regime the benefit of a doubt, finds it necessary to acknowledge that Ngo Dinh Nhu was "at the end, perhaps crazed."

If the present Premier of South Vietnam, Air Vice Marshal Nguyen Cao Ky, can be trusted, "the collapse of the Ngo Dinh Diem regime was the inevitable consequence of the long treason of a regime deeply engaged in the path of dictatorship, corruption, and brutality. The armed forces could not tolerate the Diem regime, the more so because this regime was deliberately using, while already on the decline, the armed forces as a tool not to protect national freedom and independence against foreign invasion but only to suppress the people's just aspirations." The Communists never denounced Diem in stronger terms than those used by Diem's successor. Either Diem or Ky must have been unfit for the job.

The fall of Diem was not the work of Communists. It was not the result of an imminent military collapse. Secretary McNamara went to South Vietnam in late September 1963 and on his return reported that the military situation was so favorable a thousand American troops could be withdrawn by the end of the year and "the major part of the United States military task can be completed by the end of 1965." General Harkins was quoted on November 1 as saying that "victory". was just "months away" and the reduction of American "advisers" could begin at any time. On that same day Diem's own generals carried out the coup which resulted in his and his brother's assassination. Whether the United States directly connived in the coup is a matter of dispute; but that the United States prepared the way for the coup, knew of it in advance, and did nothing to discourage it, is not.

That Ngo Dinh Diem could not have fallen without American approval is beyond doubt, though the exact measure of the approval is still arguable. At one extreme is Arthur Schlesinger's assurance: "It is important to state clearly that the coup of November 1, 1963, was entirely planned and carried out by the Vietnamese. Neither the American Embassy nor the CIA were involved in instigation or execution." Schlesinger is probably right about the "execution," but "instigation" is a broad word which, in this case, may cover too much ground. The other extreme view is represented by former Ambassador Frederick E. Nolting, Jr., who has publicly charged that the anti-Diem generals were "encouraged by the United States Government." Shaplen, who learned a great deal about the inside story of the coup, says that the coup was executed with the "full knowledge" and "consent" of the Americans. Mecklin reviews the available evidence and clearly believes that United States policy from early October 1963 encouraged and even "led to" the coup. He sums up bitingly: "But to assert that the United States was 'not involved' in the coup was a bit like claiming innocence for a night watchman at a bank who tells a known safecracker that he is going out for a beer." Sorensen states that President Kennedy sent a cable in late August 1963 "indicating that the United States would not block any spontaneous military revolt against Diem" but he denies that the plotters received any "assistance" from the United States, as if the hands-off attitude were not assistance enough. The *coup de grâce* was probably given to Diem on September 2, 1963, when President Kennedy publicly affirmed that the Diem regime had, for the past two months, "gotten out of touch with the people." All that Ambassador Lodge would admit was that the United States wanted Ngo Dinh Nhu out of the government and to see "the behavior of the Government" changed. Lodge also agreed that the Communists had no part in the *coup* and did not even want to see Ngo Dinh Diem ousted because they thought there might be "total disintegration" if he remained in power another month or six weeks—and Lodge thought they were probably right. The upshot seems to be that Shaplen is right in his judgment that the coup "succeeded in the end primarily because it was a genuine homegrown plot that expressed real grievances against a regime that had become totally corrupt and oppressive." But the homegrown plotters needed, if not encouragement, then at least a lack of discouragement from the United States. In the circumstances the latter was almost as positive as the former.

Former Vice President Nixon's view of the complicity of the United States in Diem's overthrow is particularly interesting because he tied it up with the problem of political and military instrumentalities. "Our greatest mistake was in putting political reform before military victory in dealing with the Diem regime," Mr. Nixon averred. "Diem, and more particularly some members of his family, were without question at times hard crosses for America to bear in Vietnam. But when the United States supported a *coup d'état* which led to his murder we set in motion a violent chain reaction not only in Vietnam but throughout southeast Asia."

Factually, Mr. Nixon's analysis left something to be desired. If President Kennedy had put political reform before military victory, he would not—with the encouragement of Vice President Johnson—have given Diem a political blank check in 1961. It is also hard to see how Diem could have obtained any military victory, since Diem had completely alienated his own army leadership, and not a single South Vietnamese general backed him in the showdown.[3] Diem was so much the creation of American policy that the Kennedy administration moved against him with the greatest reluctance, long after it might have made the change with less risk and bloodshed. And the chief wire-puller in bringing about Diem's downfall was a member of Mr. Nixon's own party and a recent candidate for the Republican Presidential nomi-

[3] In the Army newspaper, *Stars and Stripes*, of November 1, 1963, the United States deputy commander was quoted as follows: "The Vietnamese armed forces are as professional as you can get. Sure, they worry about political and religious disputes, but, just like the American soldier, they're loyal to their Government" (cited by Bernard B. Fall, *U.S. News & World Report*, September 28, 1964, p. 59). The South Vietnamese generals showed how "loyal" they were to the government that very day, but at least the *coup* was, if nothing else, "as professional as you can get."

nation, Ambassador Henry Cabot Lodge. But Nixon's strictures, even if they may be wanting in verisimilitude, point to the political-military issue which has bedeviled American policy at every stage. The irony is that there was still time to put political reform before military victory in South Vietnam in 1961, but President Kennedy did not do it and, therefore, paid heavily in 1963. After Diem's debacle, political reform became increasingly more difficult, and Mr. Nixon's predilection for "military victory" as against "political reform" was later satisfied because of the earlier failure.

In any event, Ngo Dinh Diem fell the way Fulgencio Batista had fallen and Donald Reid Cabral would fall. No one cared; no one moved; no one grieved—except possibly those American officials who had staked their reputations and careers on him. When he heard of the deaths of Diem and Nhu, Schlesinger tells us, President Kennedy no doubt "realized that Vietnam was his great failure in foreign policy." Mecklin remarks that the Diem-Nhu raids on the Buddhist pagodas in August 1963, which precipitated the *coup,* "were an act of political bankruptcy, confession of a catastrophic failure of leadership."

It does not really matter what one thinks of the Diem regime, whether it was worth overthrowing or preserving. If Diem deserved his fate, American policy in South Vietnam for at least eight years under two Presidents could not have been more misbegotten and misdirected. If the United States should have opposed the anti-Diem coup, the implicit encouragement given to the plotters was no less wrongheaded. Either way, Diem's downfall represented the political bankruptcy and catastrophic failure of not only his own policy but that of the United States. Kennedy's decision in 1963 not to block Diem's overthrow was the most deadly criticism of Kennedy's decision in 1961 to back Diem to the hilt. The most persuasive argument against Diem's downfall has been that there was nothing better to put in his place. If this is true, it merely indicates how well Diem and his family had done their work of political devastation. In the last few months of Diem's regime it was hard to tell whether he was more anti-American than the Americans were anti-Diem. The ghastly tragedy was not without the overtones of a macabre farce.

No one could blame the Communists for this contretemps. Even Secretary McNamara explained Diem's collapse in political terms: "But this progress [in 1962] was interrupted in 1963 by the political crisis arising from troubles between the government and the Buddhists, students, and other *non-Communist* oppositionists. President Diem lost the confidence and loyalty of his people; there were accusations of maladministration and injustice" (my italics). The same admission is made in the State Department's White Paper of February 1965: "The military and insurgency situation was complicated by a *quite separate internal political struggle* in South Vietnam, which led in November, 1963, to the removal of the Diem government and its replacement with a new one" (my italics).

In the last stage of the Diem regime, the threat of Communist despotism mattered far less than the reality of Diem's despotism. The most scathing indictment of the political failure was probably pronounced by the responsible and experienced Australian correspondent Denis Warner, who wrote that "the tyranny the West allied with in Saigon was in many ways worse than the tyranny it was fighting against."

The eight lost years of Ngo Dinh Diem were, then, the Vietnamese equivalent of Batista's seven years in Cuba and Reid Cabral's sixteen months in the Dominican Republic.

4
Power as Knowledge and Symbol

It was Francis Bacon who said that knowledge is power, and it has been pointed out in the Introduction to these essays that symbol is also power. It is about power as knowledge and symbol that this last section deals. Although knowledge and symbol may seem to refer to different aspects of human comprehension and sensibility, they do come together in a study of Kennedy's presidential leadership, for the "intellectuals" were one of the links between the two concepts, being both a source of knowledge and a symbol of cultural virtues that deserve celebration—learning, sensitiveness, courage, excellence, and commitment of self to unselfish purposes—and that President Kennedy admired. But Kennedy himself was a symbol, and attention will be given to this facet of his power after a consideration of his relations with intellectuals, which were not tranquil and trustful.

It has to be admitted at the outset, that one of the difficulties in discussing intellectuals and politics is the imprecise and wobbly meaning of the key word "intellectual." The generic sense of the term implies mental ability put to use, most often through the use of words and phrases and writing and talking, as opposed to physical and manual activity. It suggests the life-style of the literary or philosophical person, perhaps, imaginative and creative in verbal

expression, critical, skeptical, cool or impassioned, but somewhat
unmaterialistic. In the plural form—"intellectuals"—the term begins
to take on certain class and political connotations. That is to say,
it suggests a small elite of cultural influentials with something like
a common identity and a common critical stance against the prevailing values of the society. In this sense of the term, "intellectuals"
are somewhat set off from the professional classes generally, the
lawyers, the scientists, and the doctors. A tributary trickle of historical
reference from Russia helps to expand this contemporary understanding. The Russian intelligentsia was a small cultural elite in the
middle of the nineteenth century who had received a Western European education either in Russian universities or abroad, and who
(because all free political expression had been forbidden in Russia
until 1905) were, as a specially educated class, politically hostile to
the Czarist regime. Thus, intellectuals and the intelligentsia (the
words mean the same) were reformers and radicals of the left.

The historian Christopher Lasch has written a book that honors
this connection between the intellectual and the left in America
(*The New Radicalism in America, 1889–1963: The Intellectual as a
Social Type,* 1965) and Arthur Schlesinger, Jr., does the same in
The Thousand Days when he talks about two strains in the history
of American progressivism—the pragmatic and the utopian. For
Schlesinger the difference lies in their respective attitudes toward
power, with the pragmatists accepting the responsibility of power
and risking corruption. In this usage, it is common to suppose that
there are no intellectuals of the right; the right is simply designated
as "reactionary." The implication that intellectuals of the left eschew
power, however, is hard to square with the positions stated by
theorists of Communism in its various cults and denominations—
Stalinist, Titoist, Maoist, Trotskyite (certainly all left intellectuals)—
who do not reject power, but look forward to the apocalyptic time
when it will all be brought into the service of the revolution. It is
perhaps only the anarchist inspiration that entirely fulfills Schlesinger's
dictum that utopians refuse complicity with power. On the other
hand, not all left intellectuals who refuse such "complicity" are
anarchists, and so the ambiguities persist.

The historical fact is that intellectuals (that is, those in the
singular as well as the plural senses) have often been associated with
and been bemused by power. Eric Hoffer has remarked that the art
of antiquity often shows the overseer with the whip (the man of
power) and beside him the scribe (the intellectual). Edward Shils
in an encyclopedia article has spoken of the historic role of many

intellectuals as tutors, agents, counselors, or friends of the sovereign: Plato in Syracuse, Aristotle and Alexander, Alcuin and Charlemagne, Milton and Cromwell, Hobbes and Charles II before the Restoration, and, in modern times, the "brain trust" of Franklin Roosevelt. John Kennedy, as has been said, drew a notable number of able men into his administration. What is to be remarked in American history, however, is the fact that although literary and philosophical men sometimes graced public positions, scholars and other intellectuals in the seats of power in Washington generally had little or no vogue between the administrations of Andrew Jackson and Franklin Roosevelt. Even Woodrow Wilson who had been a professional scholar, and was an "intellectual," did not draw upon the resources of the knowledge community but from the worlds of law, commerce, and politics.

Knowledge is power, and intellectuals were both sources and agents of power for President Kennedy, but there was some ambivalence in him about them and the experts; and the literature on Kennedy contains contradictory judgments about his relations with them. In the opinion of certain writers, some intellectuals (almost by vocation alienated from politics) became involved in polictics and policy-making because of Kennedy's special attractiveness for them. The academic advisory group that was formed for him when he decided to run for the presidency contained such names as Arthur Schlesinger, Jr., John Kenneth Galbraith, Jerome Wiesner, Carl Kaysen, Paul Samuelson, McGeorge Bundy, Abe Chayes, Archibald Cox, and eventually scores of others, many of whom had been supporters of Adlai Stevenson. But there were also many intellectuals outside the fold, and some were severely critical of President Kennedy. Alfred Kazin represents the critical position that some took of Kennedy, suspecting him of affecting the "intellectual" stance because it was *chic* to be intellectual, and mistrusting the sincerity of his openness to the intellectual community.

The three other judgments that follow Kazin's piece also suggest some distance between Kennedy and the intellectual community, although he was a favorite with liberal press writers. The first is the essay by Joseph Alsop, the principal theme of which is the unconventionality of Kennedy's values, which should have endeared him to the intellectual community; but Alsop is of the view that Kennedy neither liked nor admired most leading liberal intellectuals. Joseph Kraft is of the opinion that Kennedy used intellectuals for clear political purposes; he took aim at the egghead liberals in the Democratic Party for votes and money but he was never able to establish real rapport with the Democratic reformers. Finally, John Cogley is of the opinion that Kennedy was a man of ideas and used intellectuals, but that he did not trust them.

In addition, there is the interesting speculation by a conservative writer as to why Kennedy had such vogue with intellectuals abroad, especially those in the underdeveloped countries. The argument is that they, like their counterparts in the United States, are in a love-hate tension with America. They profess hatred of materialism, middle-class prosperity, and populist politics that have no room for intellectuals. They perceived Kennedy to be the tamer of the beast, one with whom they could identify.

When we turn more directly from power as knowledge to power as symbol, we are truly in the domain of the intangible, although it can at least be said that symbol has both a representative and a creative dimension. In its representative dimension it stands for a sum of attainments. In its creative aspect, it inspires action.

As to attainments some have said that Kennedy's presidential leadership achieved relatively little. Such a one was Rexford Guy Tugwell, as we have seen. Another was Dean Acheson, who was of the opinion that President Kennedy's reputation is greater because of the tragedy of his death than it would have been had he lived out two terms in the White House, although no one, of course, can ever prove such a proposition, or its opposite.

What the record shows is that although President Kennedy was not richly informed in economic matters before reaching the presidency, he changed from economic conservatism to economic liberalism in his three years in office; that although he was not a strong civil rights supporter when he entered office, had become so by the time of his death; that he was not very successful in working with a Congress that contained a predominant number of members of his own party; that the months of April, May, and June 1961 were extremely unfortunate for the course of American foreign policy, the springtime of his administration in which he sponsored the Bay of Pigs misadventure, made a secret commitment in Vietnam, and met with Khrushchev in Vienna; that he employed Cold War rhetoric in 1961 but had dropped it by 1963, one byproduct of the change being the desirable and beneficial test-ban treaty with the Soviet Union; that he tended to center decision-making powers in his own hands in the fulfillment of a personal ministry in office, and so on. On the other hand there were many other events in the busy three years of President Kennedy's active administration, positive and energetic moves, along the broad and distant range of public affairs, as preceding sections of this book have indicated.

But one may ask whether history will appraise the Kennedy administration entirely in terms of its success in this or that policy or whether it will do so on some other basis. Will the reader of this book appraise his handling of presidential power on the basis of statistical calculations only? We come then to the creative aspect of Kennedy as symbol.

President Kennedy's brother Robert doubtless would have had a successful career in national politics had he not met an untimely death, in part because of his positions on various issues, but also in incalculable part because of his association with his brother John. His brother Edward may have a national career in politics in part because of *his* position on various issues, but also in incalculable part because of his association with his brother John. But what is true of the brothers is not necessarily true of anyone else associated with John Kennedy. Pierre Salinger, his press secretary, failed to win his contest for a seat in the United States Senate from California; Theodore Sorensen failed to win the Democratic nomination for United States Senator from New York on the appeal that John Kennedy trusted him; Kenneth O'Donnell, President Kennedy's Appointments Secretary, failed more than once to win the Democratic nomination for Governor of Massachusetts; Sargent Shriver, President Kennedy's brother-in-law, failed to win the Democratic nomination for Governor of the State of Maryland. However, although these men failed to develop political careers on the basis of their real association with John Kennedy, there are numerous others who hope that they resemble him in ways attractive to voters. He has thus become a model, a paragon, a creative symbol to many people, able to evoke feelings, provide meanings, and control and direct behavior.

What may some of these meanings have been? First, he meant something special to young people. At the time of the assassination many parents had the experience of a call from their children in school, in tears over the death of a beloved public figure, one with whom they identified even though they were innocent of any concern with or even knowledge of affairs of state. He stirred the interest of the young in politics, made it seem to be a refreshing enterprise after the fustian of traditional politics that seemed to be impenetrable, or boring when comprehended. He seemed young—and of course by presidential standards *was* young—only Theodore Roosevelt having achieved the eminence of the White House at an earlier age than he. In a sense then it can be said that he presaged the incursion of young people into politics that has climaxed with the eighteen-year-old vote, guaranteed by constitutional amendment. An exemplar whose activity succeeds in making politics interesting and in adding to the size of the active electorate is a symbol of powerful pull.

Second, Kennedy was a symbol of the accession to the highest office by a Catholic candidate, thereby dispelling forever the inhibition that had led political strategists to debar candidates for religious reasons, and leading the way eventually—there is no doubt—for the accession of others than white Protestants to the highest office in the years to come. He was not the Catholic candidate; he was the candidate who was a Catholic.

Third, although he seems not himself to have been a devotee of high culture, he and Mrs. Kennedy in fact made of the White House a center of high culture to a greater degree than any president since Thomas Jefferson. President Kennedy never felt, whatever his level of taste, that he had to be "just folks." The city of Washington, governed as it has been since Andrew Jackson by small-town congressmen for over a hundred years reflected small-town tastes unworthy of the capital of the most powerful nation in the world. Although it may never rival New York as the capital of high culture, the Kennedys in the White House did something to move the city out of the small-town ambiance where the nightlife was to be found in the drugstores and soda fountains, and the drugstores closed at ten. It is altogether fitting that in 1971 a new center for the performing arts was created in Washington in his name.

Fourth, perhaps the greatest symbolic value of all was the feeling that President Kennedy imparted (certainly to the young, but also to ethnic and other minority groups) that there was excitement in the exercise of personal energy, in the fulfillment of self through action, in the rescue of the individual from both the *douleurs* and *longueurs* of routine, in the refusal to accept anything less than excellence. He was a model of a life-style that others have come to imitate. It is charisma, personal magnetism, attractiveness as an individual, whatever it may be called, that made him a culture hero, and this symbolism has had an important political impact.

The last two pieces in this section set out different views about Kennedy as symbol. The first, by Norman Mailer, discusses the Kennedy symbol as representation. The piece by Mailer is a review of a book by Victor Lasky titled *JFK: The Man and the Myth,* which was published in 1963, and was intended to disparage the president. (It was withdrawn from circulation after his death). Mailer however goes far beyond the necessities of a review to offer his own interpretation of Kennedy and it, like much that other intellectuals wrote about Kennedy, is ironic, suspicious, and a little dismissive, but richly suggestive. Mailer is of the opinion that the contradictions in the national character are so considerable that no single symbol of authority could satisfy the country. His central theme is that politics is much like movie-making, with leading men taking various roles, and it is his view that Kennedy's impulse to re-create himself (consider the changes in political position on the Cold War and civil rights, for example) was his dominant passion, and that in so doing, he was really the fulfillment of the movie culture. The reader may wish to recall two things in the preceding pages. First, a similar or at least not unrelated view was expressed by Kazin in his essay on "The President and Other Intellectuals," where he said that Kennedy was the "final product of a fanatical job of re-modeling." Second, in the Introduction, reference was made to the art of representing reality, called there, "political mimesis."

The last piece is the concluding part of the essay by William Carleton, a portion of which was set out in Part Three. Here, Professor Carleton is considering the creative dimension of Kennedy as symbol, what he calls the "beau ideal." It is of interest, however, that he also connects Kennedy with the movie culture in his references to the former president as promoter and impresario, with the "glamorous videographic personality favored by Hollywood and TV."

Perhaps all of these interpretations are wrong. What *was* the reality John Kennedy represented? Or did the creative power of the symbol establish a new reality?

Arthur Schlesinger, Jr.

The Politics of Modernity

The Kennedy message—self-criticism, wit, ideas, the vision of a civilized society—opened up a new era in the American political consciousness. The President stood, in John P. Roche's valuable phrase, for the politics of modernity. "Liberalism and conservatism," Kennedy remarked one night, "are categories of the thirties, and they don't apply any more. . . . The trouble with conservatives today is that most of their thinking is so naïve. As for the liberals, their thinking is more sophisticated; but their function ought to be to provide new ideas, and they don't come up with any." His effort was to dissolve the myths which had masked the emerging realities in both domestic and foreign affairs. His hope was to lead the nation beyond the obsessive issues of the past and to call forth the new perceptions required for the contemporary world.

1. The Presidency of the Young

It was no accident therefore that he made his most penetrating appeal precisely to those who were coming of age in this contemporary world and who were most free of the legacies of historic controversy. Indeed, nothing in the Kennedy years was more spectacular than the transformation of American youth.

In the fifties the young men and women of the nation had seemed to fall into two groups. The vast majority were the "silent generation," the "uncommitted generation," the "careful young men," the "men in the gray flannel suits"—a generation fearful of politics, incurious about society, mistrustful of ideas, desperate about personal security. A small minority, rejecting this respectable world as absurd, defected from it and became beats and hipsters, "rebels without a cause." Pervading both groups was a profound sense of impotence—a feeling that the social order had to be taken as a whole or repudiated as a whole and was beyond the power of the individual to change. David Riesman, hearing undergraduate complaints in the late fifties, wrote, "When I ask such students what they have done about these things, they are surprised at the very thought they could do anything.

They think I am joking when I suggest that, if things came to the worst, they could picket! . . . It seems to me that students don't want to believe that their activities might make a difference, because, in a way, they profit from their lack of commitment to what they are doing." This was November 1960.

Probably it was all beginning to change; but the coming of Kennedy certainly made it change very much faster. He was the first President since Franklin Roosevelt who had anything to say to men and women under the age of twenty-five, perhaps the only President with whom youth could thoroughly identify itself—and this at a time when there were more young people both in the population and the colleges than ever before. His very role and personality, moreover— his individuality in a homogenized society, his wholeness in a special- ized society, his freedom in a mechanized society—undermined the conviction of impotence. If the President of the United States seemed almost a contemporary, then political action—even picketing—no longer appeared so ludicrous or futile.

The New Frontier gospel of criticism and hope stirred the finest instincts of the young; it restored a sense of innovation and adventure to the republic. The silent campuses suddenly exploded with political and intellectual activity. Young people running for office explained that Kennedy had made politics respectable; what perhaps they more often meant was that he had made it rational. The Civil Service Com- mission reported a great increase in college graduates wanting to work for the government. The Peace Corps was only the most dramatic form of the new idealism. Some of the energy Kennedy released moved rather quickly beyond him and against him, subjecting his administra- tion to unsparing, often deeply emotional, criticism; but it was none- theless he who had struck off the manacles.

The very qualities which made Kennedy exciting to the youth made him disturbing to many of his contemporaries and elders. For his message was a threat to established patterns of emotion and ide- ology. When he would say, as he did to William Manchester, "We simply must reconcile ourselves to the fact that a total solution is impossible in a nuclear age," he was affronting all those on both the left and the right who had faith in total solutions. The politics of modernity was intolerable for the true believers. This accounts, I believe, for the ambiguity with which the radical left regarded Kennedy and the hatred which the radical right came to concentrate on him.

2. Kennedy and the Left: Ideas

From the start of the republic American progressivism had had two strains, related but distinct. The pragmatic strain accepted, without wholly approving, the given structure of society and aimed to change it by action from within. The utopian strain rejected the given structure of society, root and branch, and aimed to change it by exhortation and example from without. The one sprang from the philosophy of Locke and Hume; its early exemplars were Franklin and Jefferson. The other sprang from the religion of the millenarians; its early exemplars were George Fox and, in a secularized version, Robert Owen. The one regarded history as a continuity, in which mankind progressed from the intolerable to the faintly bearable. The other regarded history as an alternation of catastrophe and salvation, in which a new turn of the road must somehow bring humanity to a new heaven and a new earth. The one was practical and valued results. The other was prophetic and valued revelations. The one believed in piecemeal improvements, the other in total solutions. Both were impatient with established complacencies and pieties. Both recognized that the great constant in history was change. But the problem of power split them. The pragmatists accepted the responsibility of power—and thereby risked corruption. The utopians refused complicity with power—and thereby risked irrelevance.

Both strains were much alive in the Kennedy years. The administration itself expressed the spirit of liberal pragmatism; and the other liberal pragmatists in Congress and elsewhere urged only that it do so with greater audacity and force. Hence mild tensions sometimes existed between the administration and its logical allies. Kennedy and much of the White House staff retained a suspicion of the ritualistic liberal as someone more intent on virtuous display than on practical result; moreover, criticism was harder to take from friends than from enemies. As for the liberals on the Hill, they were sometimes hurt and resentful, as their predecessors had been toward Roosevelt a quarter-century earlier, when the President seemed to be compromising too much and sticking too close to the southern Democrats in the leadership. Hubert Humphrey was our most effective liberal in Congress; after one bitter debate he said wearily to me, "It's hard for us down here to keep on defending the things we think the White House believes in when the White House seems to spend its time saying nice things about the other side."

But the pragmatic liberals, if they often wished the administration to move faster, had no doubt that it was *their* administration. Humphrey worked closely with the White House, where he was liked and valued, and Paul Douglas's attitude toward Kennedy reminded one of George Norris's attitude toward Roosevelt—a large and serene faith in the President's basic purpose and therefore an unwillingness to draw drastic conclusions from temporary tactics. As for Kennedy, despite occasional annoyance over the refusal of some liberals to understand the constraints on presidential action, he knew at bottom that over the long run pressure from the left increased his freedom of maneuver. In 1963, when I prepared a message for him to the annual convention of Americans for Democratic Action, describing the ADA as having contributed an indispensable ferment to the American politics, the President took out his pencil and scrawled an insert: "and looking back you can take satisfaction that on the whole time has confirmed the rightness of your judgments."

The liberals who did not like power constituted a different problem. Their mood was that of the political philosopher of old Virginia, John Taylor of Caroline, who wrote James Monroe on the eve of his Presidency, "The moment you are elected, though by my casting vote, carried an hundred miles in a snow storm, my confidence in you would be most confoundedly deminished, and I would instantly join again the republican minority." The nuclear age had given the recoil from power new intensity. Since Hiroshima many liberals and intellectuals had been reluctant to identify themselves with anything done by government.

Such people now viewed the Kennedy administration with deep suspicion. The President in their mind was the Tempter, using the allurements of power, charm, wealth, and flattery to seduce their brethren into betraying their vocation and becoming the tools of what C. Wright Mills had called "the power elite." Kennedy's air of interest in ideas and the arts seemed only the latest and most diabolical Establishment ruse to defeat dissent by absorbing it. Those who succumbed to the temptation, the critics argued, would pay a heavy price both in weakening that principled opposition to power which was the duty of an intellectual community and in debasing themselves. Some critics, like Mills, were inordinate in their reaction; his companion in the last months before his death reports Mills as "ashamed to be an American, ashamed to have John F. Kennedy as his President." Others, less rabid, felt, as Sidney Hyman wrote, that it was "a poor exchange to trade in first-class intellectuals for second-class politicians," or, as Alfred Kazin concluded in a piece not without some highly perceptive passages, "Kennedy's shrewd awareness of what intellectuals can do, even his undoubted inner respect for certain writers, scholars and thinkers, is irrelevant to the tragic issues and contributes nothing to their solution. To be an 'intellectual' is the latest style in American success, the mark of our manipulable society."

Kazin had told me one July day at Wellfleet that he was planning this article, and I suggested that he might want to meet Kennedy first. When I mentioned it to the President, he proposed that I bring the eminent literary critic down for luncheon. I thought it a lively and agreeable occasion, the talk ranging from Cooper and Malraux to Khrushchev and Chiang Kai-shek. We chatted a bit about the role of the writer in American society. Kennedy said that in the United States the trouble was that success was construed in individual terms and thus was ultimately unsatisfying. On the other hand, in Castro's Cuba, people had the higher satisfaction of working together in a group; but, since the writer was in the end a "single individual," he would be even more thwarted in a collective society. Frustration, the President concluded, was evidently the writer's destiny. Finally, in a remark which Diana Trilling later reported was passed around New York literary circles, he said, "But what has all of this to do with the papers waiting for me on my desk?"

Kazin manfully resisted seduction. A few months later he came to dinner and announced that the New York intellectuals considered Kennedy slick, cool and empty, devoid of vision, an expert and calculating pragmatist. When I observed that the same people had thought the same things about Roosevelt, Alfred replied, with admirable consistency, that he thought they were right then too. (As for Kennedy, he was very funny about Kazin's essay when it appeared in *The American Scholar*. "We wined him and dined him," he said, "and talked about Hemingway and Dreiser with him, and I later told Jackie what a good time she missed, and then he went away and wrote that piece!")

Kazin's application of John Taylor's principle expressed a wholly legitimate belief that one role for intellectuals was that of unremitting hostility to power. But was that the only role? It seemed to me that there was also a strong case for intellectuals so inclined to take part in government if only to provide a link between the political and the intellectual communities. The process of mediation might well give the intellectual community more impact on the political process than if it remained in solid and permanent opposition. It seemed hard to argue, moreover, that serious intellectuals were inexorably corrupted by public responsibility; this had hardly happened to Keynes or to MacLeish or to Berle in the thirties, to Murrow or Galbraith or Heller now. That was not to say that intellectuals made a great deal of difference to government, or that intellectuals in government always kept faith with their own ideals. Ted Sorenson, describing government meetings with mordant accuracy, once wrote, "The liberal may seek to impress his colleagues with his caution; idealists may try to sound tough-minded. I have attended more than one meeting where a military action was opposed by military minds and supported by those generally known as peace-lovers." Nonetheless, if intellectuals decided to abandon government to non-intellectuals, they would have only themselves to blame for the result. If John Taylor of Caroline had a right to his position, Thomas Jefferson had an equal right to his.

3. Kennedy and the Left: Policies

Where the utopian left felt more than a generalized mistrust of power, it objected to both the foreign and domestic policies of the administration. In foreign affairs, some regarded the cold war as the invention of the military-industrial complex and supposed that, if only Washington changed its course, Moscow and Peking would gladly collaborate in building a peaceful world. This had been somewhat the Indian view—or at least until the Chinese crossed the Himalayas and reality broke out. Others, while seeing communism as a problem and the cold war as a reality, felt that resistance involved too great a risk and were gloomily prepared to endure a communist world if that would avert a nuclear holocaust: better red than dead. Both groups condemned the policy of nuclear deterrence. Both identified themselves a bit self-righteously with "peace" as if everyone who disagreed with them wanted to blow up the world. Both yearned for total solutions. And for both the proper United States policy was unilateral disarmament and neutralism.

Thus Professor Stuart Hughes, the Harvard historian, advised the United States in his book *An Approach to Peace* to seek "a new model for foreign policy in the experience of Sweden or of Switzerland, or even of India." He added that he had "toyed" with the idea that the United States should unilaterally declare itself first among the neutrals; but "in reality we do not need to go that far. The events of the next generation will doubtless do it for us." The mission of the American intellectual, as Hughes saw it, was to do what the Asians and Africans had thus far failed to do and define neutralism "as a faith and a way of life." In the meantime, the United States should renounce nuclear weapons (by stages), close down most overseas military bases and rest national safety on "a territorial-militia or guerilla-resistance type of defense."

In domestic affairs, the contribution of the utopian left was unimpressive, except in the civil rights effort, in which its members played a brave and valuable part. Some, like Hughes, called themselves socialists but refrained from specifying what they meant by socialism. Obviously if they meant the supersession of the mixed economy by state ownership of the means of production and distribution, they were committed to a gospel which was politically irrelevant and technically obsolete. If they only meant a change in the mix, they had stopped being socialists. Others, like Paul Goodman, were anarchists,

who wrote vaguely of diversifying and decentralizing the economy.
Goodman thus summarized his program:

> An occasional fist fight, a better orgasm, friendly games, a job of
> useful work, initiating enterprises, deciding real issues in manage-
> able meetings, and being moved by things that are beautiful,
> curious, or wonderful.

Norman Mailer's "existential politics" was more drastic. Existential
experience, he said, was

> experience sufficiently unusual that you don't know how it is go-
> ing to turn out. You don't know whether you're going to be dead
> or alive at the end of it, wanted or rejected, cheered or derided.
> . . . The hoodlum is more likely to encounter existential experi-
> ence than the university man. . . . When violence is larger than
> one's ability to dominate, it is existential and one is living in an
> instantaneous world of revelations.

Apart from the whimsy of Goodman's manifesto and the hysteria of
Mailer's, one could only say that, as serious programs for a high-tech-
nology society, they simply would not do. And on the more relevant
issues the left made few original contributions. They acted as if they
were crying out great ideas in the wilderness which the political leaders studiously ignored. In fact, the political leaders themselves were
begging for usable ideas—and not finding any. Even Michael Harring-
ton's book on poverty came along half a dozen years after Averell Harriman had begun a poverty program as governor of New York.

The utopian critique still had value perhaps in its sheer intransigence, though nothing more infuriated the utopians than to be
patted on the shoulder and told that society needed their noncon-
formity. The crime of "incorporating the critic into the consensus"
was quite naturally regarded as the dirtiest trick of all. Thus Goodman wrote bitterly, "I myself have been urged, by one who has access,
to continue my 'indispensable role of dissent.' That is, we are the
Jester." The undertone was almost a longing for the good old days
of McCarthy when heresy was at least taken seriously enough to war-
rant persecution. One could sympathize with Goodman's chagrin but
still wonder whether he was not offering a heads-I-win-tails-you-lose
proposition. If dissent was punished, terrible; if embraced, worse.

The Bay of Pigs had quite understandably thrust the utopian
left into bitter opposition; and a curious episode later in 1961 turned
its members even more bitterly against the administration. This was
the furor which followed the President's request, made originally in

May and repeated with emphasis in his July speech on the Berlin crisis, for a fallout shelter program. The proposal was sensible enough. Any President, living in a world of possible nuclear war and knowing that things could be done to save the lives of twenty or thirty million people if war came, would have been plainly delinquent if he had declined to ask for them. Earlier both Truman and Eisenhower had urged civil defense measures, only to have the nation regard the problem with supreme boredom. Now in the Berlin context it acquired, or seemed to acquire, a frightening reality. Before anyone was aware what was happening, a condition of national panic seemed to be boiling up. Get-rich-quick shelter manufacturers arose on every side. Father L. C. McHugh, a Jesuit priest, suggested that shelter owners had the moral right to repel panicky neighbors by "whatever means will effectively deter their assault." The civil defense coordinator of Riverside County, California, warned his constituents to arm themselves in order to turn back the thousands of refugees who might flee their way from Los Angeles. In Las Vegas a civil defense official similarly wanted the Nevada militia to repulse invaders from California. ("In suburban civil defense," said an air-raid warden in a Feiffer cartoon, "our motto is: If you can't get yourself a Russian, settle for an American.") Many on the utopian left feared that the program, if it were not actual preparation for a surpise nuclear attack on the Soviet Union, would at the very least give the American people a false sense of security and therefore encourage them in reckless foreign adventures. Within the United States itself they perceived it as an incitement to vigilantism if not a means by which the radical right could seize control of local communities. The program, in short, became in their minds a portent of preventive war and fascism.

Civil defense policy, in the meantime, was in a state of unjustifiable confusion. As the Defense Department had first conceived the problem, each family was to dig for itself. To advance the cause the Pentagon hired Madison Avenue specialists to prepare a shelter instruction booklet intended for distribution to every householder. This was a singular document. In the draft submitted to the White House, it did not make clear that American policy was to avoid a holocaust; and it offered a relatively sanguine picture both of life in the shelter and of the world into which people would emerge after the attack. Moreover, it seemed to be addressed exclusively to the upper middle class—to people owning houses with gardens or basements; there was nothing in it for those who lived in tenements. When the President asked Galbraith to take a look at it, he responded, "I am not at all attracted by a pamphlet which seeks to save the better elements of the population, but in the main writes off those who voted for you. I think it particularly injudicious, in fact it is absolutely incredible, to have a picture of a family with a cabin cruiser saving itself by going out to sea. Very few members of the UAW can go with them." Moreover, the tract assigned the protection of the population to private enterprise. "The anticipation of a new market for home shelters," it even said, "is helpful and in keeping with the free enterprise way of meeting changing conditions in our lives."

Kennedy, while unshaken in his belief that defense against fallout was a necessary form of national insurance, was dismayed both by the booklet and the public reaction. He remarked ruefully that he wished he had never said the things which had stirred the matter up and wanted to diminish the excitement as expeditiously as possible. Carl Kaysen and I, who were following the problem for the White House, concluded that the do-it-yourself family shelter theory was a disaster and that the only fair and rational policy would be one of public community shelters. The Defense Department itself was reaching the same conclusion. The issue went before the President at the defense budget meeting at Hyannis Port the Friday after Thanksgiving 1961. It was a dark, sullen day, interrupted by pelting rain. When I discoursed on the demoralizing effect of the private shelter approach with its *sauve qui peut* philosophy, the Attorney General said grimly, "There's no problem here—we can just station Father McHugh with a machine gun at every shelter." The President speedily decided in favor of the public program. The Defense Department rewrote its pamphlet and, instead of putting it in every mailbox, left copies at post offices for concerned citizens. Thereafter the shelter panic subsided. Under the calm direction of Steuart Pittman in the Defense Department, and despite mounting congressional resistance to bills offering matching funds to non-profit institutions for including shelters in new construction, some progress was quietly made in marking existing buildings as shelter locations and stocking them with food and equipment.

This episode, following too soon after the Bay of Pigs, seemed to many on the left a further horrible revelation of the inner essence of the administration. Stuart Hughes, announcing his candidacy for the Senate in Massachusetts in 1962, attacked "the deadening similarity of the two major parties" and declared it time for "a *new kind of politics* in America." When I talked with him on the Cape that summer, he said he expected this would be the beginning of a nationwide third party dedicated to peace. The apparent response to his candidacy and to similar candidacies in other states gave the radical left a few moments of genuine hope.

Kennedy was well aware of this disaffection among the radical intellectuals. He used to say that Adlai Stevenson could still beat him in Madison, Wisconsin, or in Berkeley, California—even perhaps in Cambridge, Massachusetts. Yet, most of the radicals, even at their most critical, felt a sense of reluctant kinship with the President. Kennedy was too bright, too attractive, too *contemporary* to be wholly disowned. He had fortified their own feelings of self-respect. He had made them feel in some way more at home in some way more at home in their own country. "For the first time in our literary life," Mailer told an English interviewer, "it was possible to not only attack the President, you see, but to attack him as a younger brother, with the intensity of a family quarrel."

4. Kennedy and the Radical Right

There was no question of a family quarrel with the radical right—and the fury of the right-wing response to Kennedy was a measure of his impact on the nation. If the intellectuals did not always recognize a friend, the reactionaries lost no time in recognizing an enemy.

The burst of right-wing activity in the early sixties was a predictable historical phenomenon. In conservative periods, like the fifties, the radical right was characteristically disorganized and dormant. Its members were soothed by the eternal hope that a conservative administration might do something they would like. The existence of friends—or at least of nodding acquaintances—in Washington restrained them from major organizational efforts on their own. Thus McCarthy faded away quickly after the end of the Korean War; and the publication of Robert Welch's *The Politician* in 1958, with its concise characterization of President Eisenhower as "a dedicated, conscious agent of the communist conspiracy," and the formation the same year of his John Birch Society passed unnoticed.

But the election of a progressive administration generally has a galvanizing effect on the radical right. It grows desperate, convinced that the nation is in mortal danger, that it is five minutes before midnight, that it must rally and resist before it is too late. This happened in the early thirties under Roosevelt. It happened again under Kennedy in the sixties.

I first heard of the John Birch Society in an early-warning letter in December 1960 from that fine old progressive Republican Alfred M. Landon. One heard a great deal more of it and similar groups in the months following. The radical right appealed especially to the incoherent resentment of the frightened rich and the anxious middle class. It flourished particularly in states like California and Texas, overflowing with raw new money; in states like Arizona and Florida, where older people had retired on their pensions; and in small towns in the mountain states, where shopkeepers felt themselves harassed by big business, big labor and big government. The mood was one of longing for a dreamworld of no communism, no overseas entanglements, no United Nations, no federal government, no labor unions, no Negroes or foreigners—a world in which Chief Justice Warren would be impeached, Cuba invaded, the graduated income tax repealed, the fluoridation of drinking water stopped, and the import of Polish hams forbidden.

In domestic policy the philosophy of the radical right was well stated by Senator Strom Thurmond in a speech vindicating the right of the military to conservative political utterance: "If the military teaches the true nature of communism, it must necessarily teach that communism is fundamentally socialism. When socialism, in turn, is understood, one cannot help but realize that many of the domestic programs advocated in the United States, and many of those adopted, fall clearly within the category of socialism." The social changes of the last generation were thus—"objectively," as the communists themselves would have put it—a communist plot. In foreign policy the radical right, like the radical left, derived much of its early impetus from the Bay of Pigs, though it drew the opposite conclusion. It now rallied behind Senator Barry Goldwater, echoing his opposition to a "no-win" policy and his call for "total victory."

As Senator Thurmond's declaration suggested, an early issue was the existence of right-wing views in the military establishment. This aroused attention in the spring of 1961 when Major General Edwin A. Walker was relieved of his division command in West Germany after having propagandized his troops with ultra-conservative political materials and suggested that Mrs. Roosevelt, Edward R. Murrow, and others were under left-wing influence. Though reprimanded, Walker was not discharged; instead he was about to be reassigned to Hawaii as assistant chief of staff for training and operations when he resigned from the Army. Subsequently Senator J. W. Fulbright prepared a memorandum reporting the formation of an alliance between Army officers and right-wing groups under the imprimatur of a National Security Council policy statement of 1958 instructing military personnel to arouse the public to the menace of the cold war. This led to prolonged hearings by the Senate Armed Services Committee in which Fulbright was denounced for trying to "muzzle the military." In the meantime, Secretary McNamara quietly reorganized the military education program and terminated the relations between the program and private groups.

President Kennedy felt deep concern at the spread of extremism, right and left. This concern was related, I feel sure, to his sense of the latent streak of violence under the surface of American life: the sun o'ercast with blood, the nation torn asunder and dismembered. "We are a frontier country," James V. Bennett, the federal director of prisons, told the Senate Subcommittee on Juvenile Delinquency, "and we have certain elements in our background and culture that incline us to the use of weapons more than some other countries in the world." The tension and anonymity of urban life had further sharpened the impulse to violence. Every day the television industry instructed the children of the nation how easily problems could be solved by revolver shots. Fortifying the Gunsmoke ethic was a mood of national self-righteousness—the happy conviction of American uniqueness, which smoothed out and washed away the cruelties and sins of the past and which now licensed for Americans acts which, if performed by Russians or Chinese, would have seemed instinct with evil.

It all culminated in an image of free-talking, free-shooting national virility. E. M. Dealey, chairman of the board of the *Dallas Morning News,* said furiously to the President that he was a weak sister; "we need a man on horseback to lead this nation, and many people in Texas and the southwest think that you are riding Caroline's bicycle." (When the editor of the evening paper in Dallas, the *Times Herald,* sent the President a note saying that Dealey did not speak for Texas, Kennedy scrawled a postscript on his acknowledgment: "I'm sure the people of Dallas are glad when afternoon comes.") Early in November 1961 the President chatted in his office about the points he planned to make on a trip to the West Coast. An age of insoluble problems, he observed, breeds extremism, hysteria, a weakness for simple and passionate solutions. "There are two groups of these frustrated citizens," he soon said at the University of Washington in Seattle, one group urging the pathway of surrender, the other the pathway of war.

> It is a curious fact that each of these two extreme opposites resembles the other. Each believes that we have only two choices: appeasement or war, suicide or surrender, humiliation or holocaust, to be either Red or dead.

Against the left he urged the indispensability of strength; against the right, the indispensability of negotiation. But the challenge to the right was the main burden of the speech. "At a time when a single clash could escalate over night into a holocaust of mushroom clouds, a great power does not prove its firmness by leaving the task of exploring the other's intentions to sentries."

Two days later in Los Angeles he returned to the theme. "In

the most critical period of our Nation's history," he said, "there have always been those on the fringes of our society who have sought to escape their own responsibility by finding a simple solution, an appealing slogan or a convenient scapegoat." Today such people

> look suspiciously at their neighbors and their leader. They call for "a man on horseback" because they do not trust the people. They find treason in our churches, in our highest court, in our treatment of water. They equate the Democratic Party with the welfare state, the welfare state with socialism, socialism with communism.

Kennedy delivered his reply. "Let our patriotism be reflected in the creation of confidence in one another, rather than in crusades of suspicion. . . . Above all, let us remember, however serious the outlook, however harsh the task, the one great irreversible trend in the history of the world is on the side of liberty."

5. The Politics of Resentment

A few days later 1800 delegates attended a meeting of the National Indignation Convention at the Memorial Auditorium in Dallas, Texas. One speaker, to the delight of the crowd, complained that the chairman of the meeting had turned moderate: "All he wants to do is impeach Warren—I'm for hanging him."* General Walker himself had now retired to Dallas to advocate the cause of the John Birch Society. Other right-wing organizations were trundling their wares across the country, like the Christian Anti-Communism Crusade of Dr. Fred Schwarz and the Christian Crusade of the Reverend Billy James Hargis. Even further to the right the Minutemen were drilling their members in guerrilla tactics to deal with Soviet invasion or other unspecified contingencies. In the outskirts of Washington itself, George Lincoln Rockwell was recruiting pimply youths for an American Nazi party.

The spectrum of the right ran all the way from the amiability of Barry Goldwater to the lunacy of the outer fringe. The press reported much of this with surprising solemnity. In the summer of 1962 New York right-wingers, convinced that Nelson Rockefeller and Jacob Javits were beyond redemption, organized the Conservative Party; like Hughes in Massachusetts, though on the opposite side, they hoped to prepare the way for a national movement. When *Life* ran a skeptical story about Fred Schwarz, the outcry from Schwarz's backers, some of

---

* The speaker was J. Evetts Haley, whose book, *A Texan Looks at Lyndon,* was one of the more scurrilous contributions to the 1964 campaign.

whom were national advertisers, induced *Life*'s publisher, C. D. Jackson, to fly to a Schwarz rally in the Hollywood Bowl and offer a public apology. "I believe we were wrong," Jackson said, "and I am profoundly sorry. It's a great privilege to be here tonight and align *Life* magazine with Senator Dodd, Representative Judd, Dr. Schwarz, and the rest of these implacable fighters against communism."

Aided by such reverent treatment, the right wing grew, if not more popular, at least richer. Careful analysis by Group Research, Inc., indicated that the expenditures of the thirty basic groups rose from $5 million in 1958 to $12.2 million in 1962 and $14.3 million in 1963; nor did this estimate include groups for which no figures were available, such as the very active youth organization Young Americans for Freedom. (The annual national office budget of Americans for Democratic Action in 1962 and 1963 was about $150,000.) A large amount of the right-wing finances, Group Research added, had "some sort of privileged status under the tax laws," and the contributors included a number of leading industrial families and their family foundations.

The more frenetic right-wing agitation focused more and more directly on the President and his family. Every President, of course, provokes his quota of more or less good-natured jokes, and so did Kennedy. In Texas businessmen passed out cards saying "I MISS IKE" and then, in lower case, "Hell, I even miss Harry." The Kennedy cocktail? Stocks on the rocks. "Caroline Kennedy is certainly a nice kid. But that's the last time we should let her plan a Cuban invasion." The Kennedy rocking chair as the symbol of the New Frontier: you get the feeling of moving but you don't go anywhere. If Jack, Bobby, and Teddy were on a sinking boat, who would be saved? The country. "Truman showed that anyone can be President, Ike that no one could be President, Kennedy that it can be dangerous to have a President."

But in the domain of the radical right it all became much sicker and nastier. Not since the high point of the hate-Roosevelt enthusiasm had any President been the target of such systematic and foul vilification. Everything about Kennedy fed resentment: his appearance, his religion, his wealth, his intelligence, his university, his section of the country, his wife, his brothers, his advisers, his determination to de-emotionalize the cold war, his refusal to drop the bomb. A widely mimeographed letter called for contributions to erect a Kennedy statue in Washington. "It was thought unwise to place it beside that of George Washington, who never told a lie, nor beside that of F. D. Roosevelt, who never told the truth, since John cannot tell the difference." It went on:

Five thousand years ago, Moses said to the children of Israel: "Pick up thy shovels, mount thy asses and camels, and I will lead you to the Promised Land." Nearly five thousand years later, Roosevelt said: "Lay down your shovels, sit on your asses, and light up a Camel; this *is* the Promised Land." Now Kennedy is stealing your shovels, kicking your asses, raising the price of Camels, and taking over the Promised Land.

In Georgia, it was said, a movie house showing the film of Robert Donovan's *PT-109* inscribed on its marquee: "See how the Japs almost got Kennedy." Southerners repeated with smacking relish a story about Kennedy's seeking out a medium in order to interview the spirit of Abraham Lincoln. "I need your help on this question of civil rights," Kennedy was represented as saying. "What is your advice?" "The only thing I can tell you," Lincoln replied, "is to go to Ford's Theater." Other stories, often of an unbounded obscenity, must be left to specialists in political pornography. All this crystallized and disseminated the pose of national virility, the Gunsmoke stance; it encouraged the unthinking and the vicious to cherish their threats and hatreds. In the two years after November 1961 the Secret Service investigated thirty-four threats against the President's life from the state of Texas alone.

Kennedy, who disliked the very thought of an "age of hate," mobilized the weapons of reason to fight the spreading hatreds of his own land, beginning his education of the public before his first year was over. But he knew that reason by itself could not be enough. Once again, he fell back on his most powerful weapon—himself; on his own willingness to attest by example his faith in American rationality and decency, on his own determination, as Norman Mailer said in a flash of insight, to define "the nature of our reality for us by his actions." Kennedy was in this sense the existential hero, though the term would have amused or depressed him. So in November of 1961 he chose to carry his attack on extremism into the city of Los Angeles where four weeks before the publisher of *Life* had publicly apologized to Fred Schwarz. So in the future he never hesitated to define America by his presence and courage in the heart of the enemy's country.

6. The Trial of 1962

In this swirling mood of emotion Kennedy prepared to confront his first national electoral test—the congressional elections of 1962. The radical right, despite the Conservative Party of New York, constituted, of course, a tiny minority of the electorate and the radical left, despite Stuart Hughes, a tinier still. The great majority of the voters remained in the orbit of conventional politics. But the probabilities were always against the party in power in a mid-term election. In 1954 Eisenhower, for all his popularity, had lost control of both houses of Congress. Indeed, in the entire century only Theodore Roosevelt in 1902 and Franklin Roosevelt in 1934 had been able to prevent opposition gains in off years. The average loss of House seats by the party in power in mid-term elections, leaving out 1934, had been forty-four; the average in the Senate since the First World War, again excepting 1934, had been seven or eight.

These statistics were gloomy. "History is so much against us," Kennedy mused at a press conference. "[Yet] if we can hold our own, if we can win five seats or ten seats, it would change the whole opinion in the House and in the Senate." No one thought this likely. In August the Gallup poll reported that twenty-four of the thirty-five marginal Democratic seats were in danger. Meanwhile Kennedy pondered his own role in the campaign. A letter from Thomas Storke, the venerable Santa Barbara editor, saying that Wilson had intervened disastrously in the 1914 campaign and hoping that Kennedy would not follow this example in 1962, prompted the President to ask me to check the record on presidential intervention in mid-term elections. Storke's memory was inaccurate about 1914, a contest in which Wilson had taken no part; but the historical inquiry seemed to sustain his general point. I reported back that, while presidential intervention had steadily increased in the course of the century, there was no evidence that it had ever played a significant role. Roosevelt, for example, had made only "non-political" speeches during the great Democratic triumph of 1934; while Eisenhower's campaigns of 1954 and 1958—the most extensive ever undertaken by a President in mid-term elections—had not succeeded in staving off Democratic victories. My memorandum suggested that "the most fruitful form of presidential participation" was the non-political tour, quoting Theodore Roosevelt: " 'The most effective political speeches are often those that are nominally not political speeches at all.' History," the memorandum concluded, "suggests that it would be a mistake . . . to turn the 1962 mid-term election into a test of personal confidence by actively intervening in the form of personal endorsement or advocacy of (or opposition to) individual candidates."

Kennedy wisely ignored both the memorandum and history. He already planned a non-political tour to dedicate dams in mid-August, and he undertook another in early September. But he plainly felt under wraps. Given his sense of the politics of modernity, he may subconsciously have perceived that he himself was the best argument for his issues and that the best hope was to turn the mid-term election precisely into a test of personal confidence. Campaigning, moreover, was a refreshing experience; he always returned cheerful and rejuvenated. I can remember his coming back enormously invigorated from New Jersey after his last-minute entry into the gubernatorial campaign in 1961, saying that the crowds lining the streets reminded him where his support really lay—and that most of them couldn't care less whether the budget was balanced or not. He acknowledged that in the past "fate usually didn't seem to be affected" by what Presidents had done; but "I've never believed that precedents really mean anything in politics. From my own personal experience as well as for other reasons, just because it happened this way in the past doesn't mean anything. The question really is, can we interest enough people to understand how important the congressional election of 1962 is? And that is my function."

In the end he traveled more miles in the campaign of 1962 than Eisenhower had in 1954 and 1958 put together. His central theme was to establish the difference in domestic policy between the two parties. "We have won and lost vote after vote by one or two or three votes in the Senate, and three, four or five votes in the House of Representatives," he would say, "and I don't think we can find jobs for our people, I don't think we can educate our younger people, I don't think we can provide security for our older citizens, when we have a party which votes 'no.'" He would conclude with sharpening voice and stabbing hand: "And that's why this election is important."

Alfred Kazin

The President and Other Intellectuals

Some years ago, when Sherman Adams was still grand vizier of the Eisenhower administration, a famous American poet and long-time friend of Adams's, while sitting in his office in the White House, expressed a desire to meet the President. Adams went in and came out again and tactfully explained that the President was not curious to meet the famous poet.

That same poet, however, was prominently displayed at the inauguration of John F. Kennedy. And although many of us who admire Robert Frost's poetry and enjoy Robert Frost's conversation and have not shared his political views may well be surprised to hear that he has *returned* to the Democratic fold, Frost's enthusiasm says a good deal about Kennedy's charm for some of the most interesting minds in the United States. During the campaign and afterwards, Kennedy certainly never hid his allegiance to the fundamental principles of the New Deal—which Robert Frost has always detested. Yet no sooner did the New Frontier get itself named (somewhat mechanically) than Robert Frost heralded "an Augustan age of poetry and power, with the emphasis on power."

For Robert Frost even to think of himself as Virgil to Kennedy's Augustus in this new age of American power shows how deeply Kennedy not only affected some writers but encouraged them to feel a new confidence about America's role in the world. During the campaign, the very literary and "socialist" columnist of the *New York Post,* Murray Kempton, confessed that although he was pledged to vote for Norman Thomas, his heart belonged to Kennedy, while Walter Lippmann must have carried many votes for Kennedy by certifying his faith in Kennedy as a thinking politician who promised to be a statesman.

It was particularly on the more intellectual and liberal correspondents with him that Kennedy seemed to make the greatest immediate impression. At Los Angeles, watching his first press conference before the nomination, Norman Mailer thought that Kennedy did not seem too popular with the general run of reporters; he was "too much a contemporary, and yet difficult to understand." But Richard Rovere in the *New Yorker* not merely testified with increasing warmth and affection to Kennedy's abilities, but that July was able to say "with a fair amount of certainty that the essence of his political attractiveness is his extraordinary political intelligence. . . . The easy way in which he disposes of the question of Church and State . . . , suggests that the organization of society is the one thing that really engages his interest." In his recent book on the campaign, *The Making of the President, 1960,* Theodore H. White describes Kennedy on tour as one

> who enjoys words and reading, is a Pulitzer Prize winner himself and a one-time reporter; he has an enormous respect for those who work with words and those who write clean prose. He likes newspapermen and their company. Kennedy would, even in the course of the campaign, read the press dispatches, and if he particularly liked a passage, would tell the reporter or columnist that he had—and then quote from its phrases, in an amazing effort of memory and attention.

Norman Mailer at Los Angeles, preparing the article that *Esquire* was to insist on calling "Superman Comes to the Supermart," was staggered on interviewing Kennedy when the candidate said he had read *The Deer Park . . . and the others.*" The conventional remark on meeting Mailer is, of course, that one has read *The Naked and the Dead . . . and the others.*" But Kennedy, happily, was not conventional. The man who was very possibly the next President of the United States had read the scandalous hip novel about Hollywood doings in Palm Springs that had enraged and disgusted so many publishers and critics. Mailer's brilliant if overwritten article expressed the same hope for Kennedy that in their different ways Lippmann and Rovere and Kempton and even Robert Frost had openly felt. Given the "vacancy" in American life, as Lippmann had put it during the last days of the Eisenhower administration, the increasing divorce between private thought and the public realm, could it be that here at last was one of the "creative innovators" in politics, one man with brains and vision enough to pull our people to world reality, away from business as usual? Could it be, dared one hope, that with this rich, handsome, literate and courageous young man the sickening cycle of underground life and public insanity had at last been cut? *Esquire,* more hip than Mailer himself, advertised his article as "The Outlaw's Mind Appraises the Heroes' Dilemmas." But what Mailer said, with moving hope as well as concern, was that perhaps, with Kennedy, there might at last be some positive awareness of the ever-growing disrespect of intellectuals for politics. Too long, as he said, had politics quarantined us from history, and too long had we left politics to those who "are in the game not to make history but to be diverted from the history which is being made." Although the convention at Los Angeles was actually dull, full of seedy machine politicians, "The man it nominated was unlike any politician who had ever run for President in the history of the land, and if elected he would come to power in a year when America was in danger of drifting into a profound decline."

Mailer was stirred enough to romanticize Kennedy with faintly derisory analogies to Marlon Brando. Yet whatever Mailer's personal symbol of an American hero, what he said was no more than what so many intellectuals felt.

> It was a hero America needed, a hero central to his time, a man whose personality might suggest contradictions and miseries which could reach into the alienated circuits of the underground, because only a hero can capture the secret imagination of a people, and so be good for the vitality of his nation. . . .

And just recently there has come to hand the most moving expression of the wretchedness and the positive sense of unreality that political alienation can suggest to a sensitive mind. It is the brilliant excerpt, recently published in *Esquire,* from Saul Bellow's new novel, *Herzog.* The hero is a university teacher and writer, racked by the collapse of his marriage and by his spiritual loneliness, who wildly scribbles in his notebook letters to public leaders as well as to private individuals. At the end of this excerpt, he suddenly writes a letter to President Eisenhower, and this defines not only the ground of his private unhappiness but his feeling that it has a public source:

> . . . it seems a long time since chief executives and private citizens had any contact. The President is briefed by experts or informed by committees on the problems of the nation. That is too bad. Sometimes obscure citizens are wildly intelligent, without the disabilities of special training. But we have to recognize that intelligent people without influence have a certain contempt for themselves. This partly reflects the contempt the powerful have for them, but mainly it comes from the contrast between strength of mind or imagination and social weakness or political impotence. . . . It seems to them that society lets them think everything, do nothing. The private resentment and nihilism that result are due to a private sense of failure which possibly comes from the intellectual's faulty definition of himself and his prospects. What should his thought do? What power ought he to have from it?

The Russians speak of many disaffected and silent people in their country as "internal *émigrés*"; increasingly it has become natural for many American writers and scholars and intellectuals to think of themselves as "internal *émigrés.*" In the very Thirties that now seem to some young people an unrecapturable time of *engagement* and public responsibility, Nathanael West said that we have no outer life, only an inner one, "and that by necessity." By the 1960 Presidential campaign, it was perfectly possible for writers like Robert Frost and Norman Mailer (who, whatever the outer life, are not so hilariously divergent as they seem) to herald, with varying tones of enthusiasm and private distrust, what Frost called "a new Augustan age" and Mailer an end to the "alienated circuits of the underground." I grant that writers welcome an audience in high places, that "the new Augustan age" is pure rhetoric—much more so (whatever the phrase) than Mailer's felt and even obsessive feeling that now there are "alienated circuits of the underground." But if the writer is good, even his egotistical affections are intelligent. And of course one reason for this pro-Kennedy feeling was the contrast he made with the General and the General's Westerns and the General's sentences—to say nothing of the General's party, which a year after the campaign announced a major new campaign to enlist "the specialized knowledge and experience of the nation's intellectuals," which has now drawn plans in every state "to facilitate the utilization of friendly academicians in party affairs at all levels."

Truman, even more than Eisenhower, showed himself to be intemperate in denouncing "advanced" American pictures that had been selected by museum officials for exhibition abroad, while F.D.R., whatever his spontaneous shrewdness in answering to immediate situations, had the landed gentleman's repugnance to excessive intellectual labor. No wonder that so many writers and scholars have felt that they can at least *talk* to Kennedy. He reads, he reads endlessly, his reading is constantly an amazement in a country where the strongest minds often on principle declare a positive contempt for the reading of serious books. Addressing a newspaper publishers' convention, the President of the United States recalled that Karl Marx had been correspondent for the *New York Tribune*. Before leaving for his talks with De Gaulle and Khrushchev, the President at his birthday dinner in Boston quoted William Lloyd Garrison's famous thunder-cry from the opening number of the *Liberator*. When he was welcomed to Paris by De Gaulle, the President graciously replied by invoking Jefferson's love for France and Franklin's popularity in the *salons*. When Hemingway died, the President quickly issued a tribute in which he made reference to Paris in the 1920's, the lost generation, and the fact that Hemingway had helped to end the old provincialism of American letters. The President, as James Reston has said, takes printer's ink for breakfast, and by now his bookishness and intellectual sophistication are so well known that one is no longer surprised to hear that C. P. Snow has been invited to the White House and that E. E. Cummings has been in to tea, or that at a certain juncture Kennedy alone, of all his intellectual entourage, knew the title of Churchill's first book. It did not seem at all pretentious to me that the First Lady, interviewed on her plans for redecorating the White House, should have spoken of her interest in antique furniture as natural to the wife of a "historian." Not only has "history" been the President's strongest intellectual interest, but so far as he has been trained to any profession, it has been to the study and the writing of "history." The son of the American Ambassador to Great Britain in 1940 had positive reasons to remember that during the Civil War the son of the American Ambassador to Great Britain was Henry Adams, and there learned a great deal that was to be important to the life of politics and the writing of history. President Kennedy, who before the war thought of becoming a newspaperman, reminds me, in the range of his sophistication, of a great many "intellectual" newsmen and editors. The author of *Why England Slept* and *Profiles in Courage,* the President whose favorite book has been given out as Lord David Cecil's *Melbourne* and favorite novel as Stendhal's *The Red and the Black* is in his personal interests alone far more of a "historian" than many who teach history rather than learn it.

Now it is also true that President Kennedy's anecdotes from American history tend to be trotted out rather irrelevantly to formal occasions, and that the punch line quoted in Paris from Samuel Adams is unaccountably accredited in Vienna to someone else. And if he cited a little-known detail from Karl Marx's biography to an audience of publishers, it was to joke that Marx had vainly asked the *New York Tribune* for a raise—look, said the President, what you fellows may get us all into by not giving a correspondent a raise! William Lloyd Garrison's "I will not equivocate and I will be heard!" is in excess of what a birthday dinner among Massachusetts politicians, even on the eve of his going to Europe to meet Khrushchev, seems to call for. And *Profiles in Courage,* perhaps because it was indubitably *written* by the author himself (as he replied to reviewers who doubted it), is certainly far more interesting for its personal emphasis on "courage," courage by *anybody* in the United States, whether Taft or Norris, than for any significant political ideas of his own. *Profiles in Courage* always reminds me of those little anecdotes from the lives of great men that are found in the *Reader's Digest,* Sunday supplements, and the journal of the American Legion. It is the kind of book that reads like a series of excerpts even when you read it through; and indeed it seems composed of excerpts—excerpts of reading, excerpts of anecdote. Nor, quite apart from his conventional public statements, am I impressed with the tales of a voracious reading that seems to be concerned largely with getting the "facts," the highly separable material and statistical facts that can be shoveled into the executive mind. And with everything that has been said about Kennedy's being a Catholic, almost nothing, so far as I can tell, has emerged about the personal and intellectual side of his Catholicism. Unlike Senator Eugene McCarthy and other American politicians whose thoughtfulness and sense of philosophical principles owe so much to the traditional teachings of their church, John F. Kennedy seems to have been more aware of Catholics as a source of political support than of the Church as a source of intellectual inspiration. And although Kennedy's narrow victory, which owes so much to Catholics, has caused many Catholic writers and intellectuals to rally almost defensively around him, some of them, before Kennedy was nominated, were positively bitter about his political exploitation of Catholic support.

Yet with all these limitations and conventionalities and sales tricks, it is interesting to see how much of an "intellectual" Kennedy wants to be and how eagerly his bookishness, his flair and sophistication, his very relish for the company of intellectual specialists, have been advertised to the public without any fear that it might dismay a people so notoriously suspicious of these qualities in others. Obviously in Kennedy's case an "intellectual" taste does not suggest a fastidious withdrawal from anything—not even normal passion. Adlai Stevenson in his two campaigns seemed to be running not only against the bluff, smiling General, but against the General's philistine supporters. It is interesting to learn from the autobiography of T. S. Matthews that when Matthews warned Stevenson against "Ohio" (meaning the Yahoos), Stevenson's advisers just stared at him, while Stevenson smiled and went back to work. The extraordinary identification that so many American intellectuals make with Stevenson has often struck me as loyalty not to a lost cause but to lostness as a cause. I have never been sure just how much of an "intellectual" Adlai Stevenson is, but he has certainly been cherished among intellectuals more for his obvious sensitivity than for the strength of his ideas. In 1956 even more than in 1952, and at Los Angeles in 1960 even more than in 1956, he seemed the peerless leader of intellectuals who boasted that they had never had a candidate before—and who warned that if he were counted out for positively the last time, they could never be that much concerned again: they would have suffered just too much. And since Stevenson's public style seemed to combine self-demeaning wit and vulnerability to such a degree that some of his closest friends condoled with him on having to face the public at all, perhaps it is no wonder that the candidate who publicly yearned that the cup might pass from him was defeated by the General who listens with particular respect to the head of any large American corporation.

By contrast, of course, Kennedy has not only surrounded himself with many of the liberal historians, economists, and political scientists who were reputedly such a liability to Stevenson, but despite certain necessary political favors to be paid back he has made a point of appointing as Ambassador to Japan a professor of Japanese history, as Ambassador to India a John Kenneth Galbraith, as Secretary of the National Security Council the former dean of the Faculty of Arts and Sciences at Harvard, as one of his immediate advisers the author of a scholarly study of Presidential power, as another adviser a young man in his twenties who was first in his law class at Harvard. Although the Secretary of State obviously was chosen to be one of a team, it is interesting that his last previous job should have been as president of the Rockefeller Foundation; although the Secretary of Defense was president of the Ford Motor Company, he came to Ford and rose at Ford because he was a brilliant statistician; although the Secretary of the Interior necessarily comes from the West, the present one really is crazy about Robert Frost. Even the Postmaster General in this administration has written a novel; even the new Military Adviser to the President has written a superb book on American defenses. No wonder that Arthur Miller and John Steinbeck and W. H. Auden were asked to the inauguration as publicly declared assets of the Republic; that even the Kennedys' French chef is felt to be a compliment to their good taste rather than to their wealth—to say nothing of the *fête champêtre* thrown for the Pakistan President at Mount Vernon, which (it is safe to guess) irritated some congressmen not because of its reputed cost, but because, with its announced links to classic entertainments in the past, it represented a bit of intellectual swagger that not all Americans are likely to admire.

In short, the President has gladly let it be known that he is in fact a highbrow, an intellectual, an omnivorous reader. There was once a Tammany mayor of New York who, in private, talking with a favorite magazine reporter, confided that he indeed knew and enjoyed Joyce's *Ulysses*. But this was a secret, not a boast. President Kennedy's acquaintance with some minor details in the life of Karl Marx is rather more a boast than a secret, like his open espousal of Robert Frost, his invocation of William Lloyd Garrison in Boston and of Jefferson in Paris; all these and more are attempts to form his public style. As has often been said, Kennedy is the most "intellectual" President since Woodrow Wilson—some even say since Theodore Roosevelt. Hoover may have been a brilliant mining engineer on three continents and with his wife he did translate a medieval Latin treatise on mining; but in public he gave the appearance of suffering fools miserably, and stimulated no one. Wilson had been a political scientist and had written books; but he, too, tended rather to patronize and to moralize, and at Versailles in 1918 was hopelessly outclassed in wit and learning, to say nothing of his not knowing a single blessed word of French. (President Kennedy's French is primitive, but even on a state visit to Canada he was able to make a virtue of his limitations by likening it to Prime Minister Diefenbaker's.) Like Theodore Roosevelt (also trained to no profession but that of "historian"), Kennedy has cultivated as his public style the bookman-in-office. Although Kennedy has not yet publicly found jobs for poets (as T.R. did for Edwin Arlington Robinson), he, like Roosevelt, has praised the strenuous life as if he were promoting a historical revival and, like T.R. again, he lets his literary opinions be known. He has helped to establish taste. And it is just this cultivation of the highbrow world as an executive taste and Presidential style, his turning the poor old suffering American egghead into something better than a martyr to popular culture, that I find most suggestive about Kennedy-as-intellectual. If during the campaign he grew on many thoughtful observers who distrusted his family background and despised his failure to say a single word about McCarthy, so in his first weeks, at least, he was able to persuade many cool observers that his was the necessary style of administration in these times —like Churchill, like De Gaulle. Before Cuba, one English joke was that Kennedy talked like Churchill but acted like Chamberlain; even after Cuba, it was said that there had been an *unaccountable* lapse of his dominant executive style. But Cuba apart for the moment, it is obvious that Kennedy's reputation as an "intellectual" has been an asset to him at a time when government operates on a scale of such complexity, requires so deft an ability at least to show a nodding acquaintance with many subjects. It has often been said that Kennedy turned the tide in his first television debate with Nixon by the precise answers he was able to supply to questions raised from so many different fields. Before his nomination, says Theodore H. White in *The Making of the President, 1960,* Kennedy astonished his own staff by analyzing without notes his chances in every single state of the union, and, in the "honeymoon" weeks of the administration, Vice-President Johnson let it be known that he was positively awestruck by the President's ready handling of so many different subjects.

This smooth and easy assimilation of fact, this air of overall sophistication, is what Americans have learned more and more to admire in journalism, in business, in conversation, and on television quiz shows—whether the man in the dock is Charles Van Doren or the President of the United States being questioned mercilessly (and pointlessly) about everything from Laos to Tammany. The quiz show did not die out with the exposure that the contestants had been briefed; the candidates in the 1960 campaign were also briefed, as is the President of the United States today, and the show goes on. If the reporters sometimes act as if they wanted to trip the President up, the President knows that he can impress the country by way of the reporters. This overall style, so much like the division of even the arts and sciences into departments of *Time* magazine, became a "research" style among the military during the war, and it has now invaded the big universities and "scientific research and development." It is our national style, *intellect-wise*. We now admire it—when it comes unaccompanied by personal stress. A recent article in a liberal weekly on "The Mind of John F. Kennedy" turns out to be an entirely admiring study of Kennedy's range as an administrator. This vocational or psychological use of the word "mind" is so typical of our time and place that it probably never even occurred to the author to extend the word to cover "beliefs." Instead we are told that Kennedy's "marshaling of related considerations" defines Kennedy's mind "as political in the most all-encompassing sense. The whole of politics, in other words, is to such a mind a seamless fabric, in which a handshaking session with a delegation of women is an exercise directly related to hearing a report from a task force on Laos." And this ability to assimilate on the jump necessary quantities of fact, to get statements of a problem that carry "action consequences"—this is what we have come to value as the quality of intellectual all-roundedness or savvy. It is a style that depends always on research done by other people, on a swift and agile reaction to the statement of the problem *set* by other people, on the professional politician's total recall for names and faces, the professional communicator's ability to wham the effective phrase right down the mass media to the great audience. The more complex and insoluble the problems become, the more intellectuals are needed to pile up research on them; the incoming trays are piled higher, ever higher, with Freedom Riders, Latin American poverty, education bills, recalcitrant congressmen, the Congo, obstinate Englishmen and offended Nigerian diplomats who were refused a cup of tea in a Maryland restaurant. The professors who coasted along on two courses and one committee now work from eight-to-eight before they go out to the big dinner every night: "I don't have time to put my shoes on in the morning." Since the boss is the man who takes his problems home with him, the boss proves that he is the boss by a certain air of tense vigilance and unsleeping physical resiliency and readiness. Never in any administration have we been told so constantly how little sleep the President gets.

The boss nowadays does not have to be an expert himself; in the normal course of nature he cannot be one and boss too. But he has to know who the experts are. So much is this executive style—with its dependency on batteries of advisers, experts, "researchers"—the admired "intellectual" style because it works with intellectuals, that the President of this nation of boastful pragmatists, in a public tribute to Robert Frost, told the story of a mother's writing the principal of a school, "Don't teach my boy poetry; he's going to run for Congress"—and affirmed: "I've never taken the view that the world of politics and the world of poetry are so far apart." No wonder that some who suffered with Stevenson in 1956 for being too good for the American public felt with Kennedy in 1960 that intellect was at last in touch with power. He had read the essential books; and the essential names, the principal formulae, the intellectual shorthand, were at his disposal. No wonder that, conversing with certain Kennedy advisers in March, one felt about them the glow of those who have not merely conceived a great work but are in a position to finish it. The boss *understood;* he was just as savvy as anyone else, but less "sensitive" (meaning destructible). It took half the time to explain highly technical problems to Kennedy that it had to Stevenson, and it turned out, too, that Stevenson actually wasn't much of a reader. During the Eisenhower administration, I heard a famous scientist say with some satisfaction that the President was "actually very intelligent." And Robert Frost, when he finally did get to an Eisenhower stag dinner at the White House, made a point of saying afterwards that President Eisenhower was extremely intelligent. I understood. When a really good mind, suffering from the natural loneliness of really good minds, gets the ear of a man smart enough to make his way to the very top, even to make the topmost pinnacle an attribute of himself, there is a natural sense of satisfaction. For when all is said and done, action *is* the natural sphere of a mind sane and hopeful, eager to revive the classic center of man's public activity. To real intellectuals, power means not Caesarism but right influence; and it must be said that the type of Henry Adams, who wants to be near power so that he can deride it but feels that he is too intelligent to influence it, is really the prisoner of his own despairing rationality. Adams did not want his private obsessions interrupted by any new dimension of experience. And while the *quality* of mind is not necessarily better among those who are more "healthy-minded," it is a fact that the capacity of certain intellectuals to wield influence, the belief that they not only can but that they should, is interpreted maliciously by those who are so alienated from the body politic (to say nothing of politics) that they must explain everything as self-seeking.

2

I would suggest that what drew certain historians, political scientists, economists, and lawyers to Kennedy was the fact that he, too, was outside the business community, had grown up independent of the main influence, and that Kennedy's very adroitness and eagerness of mind, his sense that there were deeper sources which he could employ, pleased them as the style of a politician no more limited by the business ethos than they are. In many ways the current intellectual style brings together people who have nothing in common but their indifference to the conventional values. It is the style of labor lawyers from immigrant families; of university administrators with a family tradition of diplomacy and liberal Republicanism in the tradition of Stimson, not the shabby rhetoric of "free enterprise" set up by professional demagogues; of professors themselves brought up in professors' families; of economists who remember with bitterness what young men with brains had to fight in the way of prejudice and snobbery when they first made their way up the university ladder. Such figures, whether their background was too patrician or too scholarly or too radical or too foreign for the majority view, represent the accelerating war of the "specialists" (or the "engineers," as Veblen called them) with the "price system." They have grown up on ideas, they have made their way up on ideas, they live on ideas. And in some way that must be both exciting to them and yet frustrating, Kennedy is also not limited to business and by business. He shares with his advisers a certain intellectual freedom from the dominant prejudices and shibboleths. But what for them is often a positive article of belief may, for him, be only freedom from vulgar prejudice—and it is exactly here that Kennedy's use of his advisers has already proved so much more significant than their influence on him.

About Kennedy one *has* to make psychological guesses, for unlike his advisers, one does not know what he thinks by reading him—nor even by talking to him. His most essential quality, I would think, is that of the man who is always making and remaking himself. He is the final product of a fanatical job of self-remodeling. He grew up rich and favored enough not to make obvious mistakes or to fall for the obvious —he has been saved from the provincial and self-pitying judgments that so many talented Americans break their teeth on. He has been saved, not merely from the conventional, but from wasting his time on it. Even now there is an absence in him of the petty conceit of the second-rate, and a freshness of curiosity behind which one feels not merely his quickness to utilize all his advantages, but also his ability to turn this curiosity on himself. He turns things over very quickly in his own mind; he gets the angle. Yet all the while he stands outside, like a sculptor surveying his work. He is what a certain time has made, has raised highest, and he can see himself in perspective in a way that perhaps only Americans can—since only they have *made* so much of themselves. The father made a killing in liquor and even as ambassador managed to sound like a district boss; the son has as many European "connections" as royalty. The father worked it so that each of his children would have at least a million dollars; the son, starting out high above the economic motive, asked advice of fatherly gentlemen in New England as if he had all the world to choose from. The grandfathers in Boston still had to look at *No Irish Need Apply;* their grandson, as the Attorney General of the United States said with grim pride when he urged Negroes to fight more for their *political* rights, is now President of the United States. He is President of the United States, he is a millionaire, he has the sex appeal of a movie hero, the naturalness of a newspaperman, and as much savvy as a Harvard professor—and whereas you and I would be scared even to imagine ourselves taking on such responsibilities as face him every moment of the day and night, the highest office is what he wanted, this is what he went straight for, this is what he has. He has learned so continuously, so brilliantly, even so greedily, that one observer, noting that the author of *Profiles in Courage* didn't show his profile on the McCarthy issue, dryly wonders "if the book didn't, on some very private level, instruct him in what to avoid." The determination to succeed, the guardedness against vulnerability of any sort, the constant vigilance not to show himself wanting (his health has been the only admitted "weakness")—this is so sharp that another writer has brilliantly compared Kennedy to the type of Whig who in the eighteenth century entered the rising House of Commons:

> of large and comparatively recent fortune, intelligent, elegant, tremendously determined to make a place for himself, desiring above all to be effective and to succeed, contemptuous of the aristocratic condescensions and concerned not to be condescended to.

But unlike those Whigs, it is to be doubted that Kennedy represents a definite social interest. What has given him his influence, even over the "brain power," as he describes this resource passingly in *The Strategy of Peace,* is his sophisticated freedom from conventional prejudice. When one adviser, submitting a memorandum on Latin American problems, noted that certain recommendations could be highly irritating to American business, Kennedy waved the hypothetical objection aside. This elasticity makes him exciting to work for, and to pass from so detached a mind to the endless analysis of itself that Washington goes in for might well make an intellectual in Washington feel that "brain power" is at the center of things again, that the few have again the chance to do well by the many.

3

Yet as this is being written, nothing stands out so clearly about the Kennedy administration as its frustrations. The occasion is piled higher with difficulty than ever before, and "the most intellectual and idea-seeking President since Woodrow Wilson" must find it as hard to remember some of the ideas he came in with as it is to promote some he has acquired since. Only in the White House, it may be, will Kennedy know the "contradictions and miseries" that other men have always lived with. And perhaps it is only in the White House, too, that the intellectual advisers who have gone smoothly from academic success to academic success may for the first time experience rebuff, defeat, obloquy. The "decisions" get more and more "educated," to use the President's interesting word, but they do not grow more decisive. And when I think of the increasing ugliness of American "conservatives," the political stalemate that Kennedy is faced with by Russia, the impossible difficulty of getting Americans to limit their smallest economic privileges enough to create a new social sense in this country, the conflicting views of so many different groups of advisers who were meant to counteract each other but who can produce administrative chaos, I anticipate that so restless and so ambitious a man as Kennedy will want to cut through the ever-deepening morass.

The most striking side of the Cuban disaster, to me, was the virtually official apologia that since Kennedy inherited the invasion scheme from Eisenhower and found that the C.I.A. had been arming and training an invasion army that could no longer be "contained," the technical approval by the Joint Chiefs of Staff and the approval of a majority of his advisers were enough to make him approve not merely an immoral but an impractical scheme to invade Cuba. Even a literary man reading up on Castro and his revolution could guess that Castro was much too popular to be overthrown from a small landing at the Bay of Pigs. Yet, faced by so many conflicting and in a sense mutually canceling bodies of advice, Kennedy allowed the gun to go off. And nothing has been said by him since, or by his advisers, that indicates it was anything but the *failure* of the Cuban invasion that they regret. It has given a "bad mark" to the administration that wants so much to succeed. What is immoral and downright stupid about the invasion, what represents not merely faithlessness to our traditions but an executive temperament restless, tricky, irritable—this has not been understood by the administration and its advisers. And seeking out Hoover and MacArthur at the Waldorf in an effort to make a show of national unity at the first sign of national dismay! The only defense that I have heard against the frightening impatience displayed in the Cuban adventure has been that so-and-so wasn't in on the decision, and that intellectuals on the outside never recognize how many important decisions are improvised and uncalculated. Where, then, is the meaningful relation of intellectuals to power? Is it only to write memoranda, to "educate" the decisions that others make? History will not absolve them that cheaply. What troubled me about the Cuban adventure was that although its failure was attributed to "erroneous" advice, the essential philosophy behind it was perhaps uttered by the adviser who, when asked for a show of hands, said "Let 'er rip," and by another who said pompously that it was time to come to a power confrontation with Communism in this hemisphere. (Stewart Alsop reporting.) In short, actions may be excused as "improvised," but is the essential philosophy a longing to come to a power "confrontation" in this hemisphere? Is it possible that the very freedom from conventionality that I interpret as the essential mark of Kennedy's intellectuals and of his receptivity to them—that this may yet create an abstract and virtually ideological conception of American power?

The famous State Department "White Paper" on Castro, published before the invasion attempt, listed many distinguished Cuban liberals, democrats, intellectuals, who had fled from Castro after being part of the 26 July revolutionary movement against Batista. Various pro-Castro "progressives" in this country noted that the White Paper quite conveniently omitted mention of any of the privileges lost by American business in Cuba. But although it is not for me to prove this, I suspect that in the mind of the author of the White Paper was not so much the desire to overlook the resentment of American business against Castro as the intellectual bitterness of an American liberal democrat against a political adventurer (Castro), who began as a "reformer" and has since shown himself a cynical and dangerous ally of totalitarianism. Perhaps business just did not come into it for the principal author of the White Paper. Hard as it is for pro-Castro intellectuals in this country to take this, I believe that economic determinism seems to explain as little of our bellicosity as it does Russian bellicosity. Anyone who has studied Castro's political development can see that his gravitation toward totalitarianism has had nothing whatever to do with American economic policies in Cuba. Khrushchev's stated belief to Walter Lippmann that Kennedy takes orders from "Rockefeller" is as mechanical a piece of Communist rhetoric as Stalin's stated belief that Hitler's policies were dictated by German capitalists. Indeed, the Russian Revolution itself, launched entirely by intellectuals whose historic dissociation from the great mass of the Russian people explains the very structure of the Communists as a party of intellectual managers, offers the most devastating proof that, especially in our times of centralization, history is made not for material interest but out of intellectual fanaticism often divorced from the most elementary social interest.

After the invasion attempt against Cuba, Kennedy replied to Khrushchev's professed indignation by cautioning him not to support Castro militarily. He ended his message with this emphatic burst: "I believe, Mr. Chairman, that you should recognize that free people in all parts of the world do not accept the claim of historical inevitability for the Communist revolution. What your government believes is its own business; what it does in the world is the world's business. The great revolution in the history of man, past, present, and future, is the revolution of those determined to be free." This is stirring language quite different from the usual muddle of Eisenhower's public statements. But I find it hard to believe that for Kennedy the Soviet government's philosophy is "its own business"; I find it also hard to believe Khrushchev when he says (on alternate Tuesdays) that he himself does not plan to attack the socially backward nations and explains that the well-known law of Marxist development will take care of that. Of course Kennedy is not driven by a fanatical creed of political messianism that is taken as the only universal law of history; nor is he as driven as Russians have been by a profound resentment of the creeds and relative good fortune of the West. But to the extent that Kennedy has been liberated by his own good fortune from the intellectual torpidity of American business, he may have been thrown back on the intellectual's natural outlet in causes. And the most significant side of Kennedy-as-intellectual seems to lie, not in his public cultivation of the "intellectual" style that is now admired in the highest echelons, but in the fact that, as a would-be intellectual who happens to be President of the United States, his natural tendency may be to identify the United States with a crusade, a cause, with "liberty." It was exactly this accessibility to causes that now constitutes, retrospectively, the disagreeable and even false side of Theodore Roosevelt. Similarly, what one fears about Kennedy is the other side of what one admired and was prepared to admire more in him—that he has been left free by his immense power to adopt a cause forged out of his energy and the depths of his restless ambition. Hard as it is for most of us to imagine ourselves arguing the fate of humanity with Khrushchev, it does not seem to bother Kennedy. And when I ask myself, as I increasingly must, what it is in Kennedy's ambition to be an "intellectual" statesman that steels him for his awesome responsibility, what in his *convictions* can carry him over the sea of troubles awaiting all of us, I have to answer that I do not know. At this juncture, Kennedy's shrewd awareness of what intellectuals can do, even his undoubted inner respect for certain writers, scholars, and thinkers, is irrelevant to the tragic issues and contributes nothing to their solution. To be an "intellectual" is the latest style in American success, the mark of our manipulatable society.

Joseph Alsop

The Legacy of John F. Kennedy:
Memories of an Uncommon Man

A year has gone by since the shots in Dallas put the world in mourning. For most of us the passage of these twelve eventful months has not so much as blurred the edges of the vivid vision of John F. Kennedy. We can see him still in our minds' eyes, almost as he was in life—tall, slender, graceful, quick-striding; now gay, now genially ironical, now sternly serious, and never, in whatever mood, untrue to himself; always full of zest for the countless problems that the Presidency brought each day, always carrying his heavy burden with mingled humor and high purpose, and above all, always full of pride in the country that he led and loved.

The angular, ruthlessly honest George Orwell once remarked, in a critical essay, that you could not "definitely prove" Shakespeare was a great writer, or even "definitely prove" that the worst, most cheaply sentimental mass-producer of best sellers was a bad writer. "Ultimately," said Orwell, "there is no test of literary merit except survival, which is in itself an index of majority opinion." Orwell, of course, meant a kind of cumulative majority opinion, registered by successive generations over a long period. The same rule that Orwell laid down for writers also applies to public men.

The nation mourned for Warren Harding, thinking his death a genuine loss. Yet we now remember him as the worst President in the long American line, with hardly a redeeming feature except a certain blowzy amiability. The nation mourned for Abraham Lincoln. We now remember him as the unique American saint; yet we also regard his earthiness and humor and unpresidential humility as vital ingredients in Lincoln's saintliness, whereas these were just the qualities that sadly shocked many of Lincoln's ablest contemporaries. Nor you nor I can tell, therefore, how John F. Kennedy will survive (in Orwell's sense) in the memory of generations still to come. Yet I myself believe that he will be remembered as one of the great Presidents. It seems to me that his time in office, for all its tragic shortness, was nonetheless a time of renovation and renewal, when our country found a new and better course after long years of search.

I offer this forecast, however, with a personal reservation of some significance. Kennedy the President was particularly hard to judge, even for those who knew him best, because Kennedy the man was so enigmatic and complex.

The broad outlines of the portrait are easy enough to sketch. He enjoyed pleasure. He read deeply, and he was the first American President since Theodore Roosevelt to care greatly for learning for its own sake. He was sometimes slow to decide, often grumbling when he had a hard decision thrust upon him; but once his decision was taken, he never looked back. He believed, perhaps too completely, in the power of reason; and he was both astonished and annoyed when he made what seemed to him a logical case, yet failed to persuade his hearers. He had an enduring horror of any public show of strong emotion, which led foolish persons to say that he was cold and unfeeling. Even on occasions when other men might be tempted to tear a passion to tatters, he would often be self-mocking and ironical, and irony and light self-mockery were the twin essences of the wry wit that illuminated all his discourse, whether public or private. Between the flashes of wit his talk was solid and nourishing, yet racy and to the point. In conversation he liked to learn about every imaginable subject, from the techniques of Greek sculpture (which he began to collect toward the end of his life) to the intricate squalor of a local political problem. And when he played the leading conversational role himself, he invariably dealt in facts, not theories, in salty human realities, not moral generalities. Whether in private talk or on public parade, his beautifully good manners never failed him; he was singularly considerate of others, whether they were great or humble. With this considerateness went an unfailing interest in the concerns of other people; and this interest extended to honest enjoyment of a good gossip. But although he liked to be amused by this world's follies and oddities, he was never harsh or unkind, for he was singularly generous-hearted. All the countless persons within his ever-widening orbit could turn to him in need. To his close friends, he was strongly attached. He loved his brothers and sisters with a tribal intensity. He adored his wife and children, and his pride in them, though half the time expressed in gentle teasing, was something to delight an onlooker.

The surface portrait shows a favorite of fortune, blessed with such good gifts of heart and mind as fate brings to few men in a generation. Yet what lay beneath this smiling surface? What made John Kennedy tick? What were his private values, what were his inner standards and his ultimate goals? Here the enigmas lie. Here the questions become difficult to answer with assurance, mainly because the President's standards and values were so obviously very different from the average American values and standards.

Consider, for example, his total lack of reverence for the kind of success in business that is the goal, or at any rate the envy, of most Americans. This was perhaps a weakness, for ours is a business society, after all. Yet the fact remains that big businessmen, simply as big businessmen, most emphatically did not command Kennedy's liking and admiration. To put it bluntly, he held their success cheap; and he did not value them as individuals unless they had proved themselves in other arenas, in the manner of Robert S. McNamara and Douglas Dillon, Robert A. Lovett and John J. McCloy. For just this reason, although the Kennedy Administration was brilliantly successful in promoting business expansion, the vast majority of big businessmen detested Kennedy.

Or consider, again, his conspicuous lack of rapport with many leading figures at the other end of the American spectrum. He neither liked nor admired most of our liberal intellectuals; and he was even given, on occasion, to making fairly hilarious fun of the liberals' special hero, Adlai E. Stevenson. The trouble was that the American liberals too often struck Kennedy as sterile in their prescriptions, and he always suspected them, too, of being more eager to demonstrate their own ineffable righteousness than to get done the things that needed doing. For just these reasons, although he found the ideal outlet for Stevenson's undoubted talents at the U.N. and also gave important opportunities to numerous others in this group, many American liberals always cherished an ill-concealed dislike for Kennedy while he was alive; and even now, when he is dead and they loudly proclaim their posthumous admiration, they still vent their lingering spleen on his partner-brother, Robert Kennedy.

These failures of sympathy may seem to balance. They may seem to situate Kennedy in the American center—halfway, so to say, between the Texas oilmen and the Stevenson coterie. Yet nothing could be more misleading. Kennedy's style and outlook were not merely foreign to the styles and outlooks of our liberals and our businessmen; his style and outlook were also singularly foreign to the outlook and style of central, average, day-to-day America in the mid-'60s. No one could have differed more sharply from the good, average American, who watches television in his off-hours, is content if his is a two-car family, and does not mind bulging a bit in middle age.

Even about those bulges, Kennedy was almost un-American. Our wealth and our machines have made us, as a nation, just a bit soft and fat, and most of us do not mind this in the least. But Kennedy minded. All Kennedys have an obsession about physical fitness, and the President, like the rest of them, was decidedly repelled by softness and flabbiness. Then, too, in modern America the old, almost primitive,

concern for physical courage, functional in ruder times, has now become exceedingly uncommon. But for Kennedy, courage, whether physical or moral, was the first and most essential of the virtues. In judging
another man, courage was the first quality he looked for. Finally, and
above all, the hankering for intensity of experience is close to an eccentricity in our easy, prosperous, homogenized, anonymous modern
America. Yet this hankering, I am sure, came close to being Kennedy's
strongest drive. The routine, the ordinary, the merely average displeased and bored him. He wanted to live intensely, meaningfully, to
the utmost limit of his powers. It was almost as though he wished to
personify the dictum of Justice Oliver Wendell Holmes, who said,
"Man is born to act; to act is to affirm the worth of an end; and to
affirm the worth of an end is to create an ideal." The citizens of the
Athens of Pericles may perhaps have been able to claim with justice
that their lives "created an ideal," but horribly few of us nowadays
could put forward such a claim without falling into ridicule. Such
were the reasons why Kennedy, in his mature years, always struck me
as a man set apart, even a bit remote, from his era and his environment.
From this remoteness he was rescued, if that is the right word, because
he loved his country with the kind of daily felt, unquestioning patriotic love that is, once again, a bit old-fashioned nowadays. Yet his
divergences from the American average were so great that I sometimes
wondered how Kennedy managed to win the votes and hearts of so
many Americans.

His success is rendered still more remarkable by another fact
that most people have forgotten. Although he went so far so fast, John
F. Kennedy was a late starter as a serious politician. He was far from
serious, and I am confident he had no notion of making a great political career in his early years in Congress when I first met him. Perhaps
that first meeting is worth recalling here, if only to illustrate the chanci-
ness of political handicapping when the new entrants are very young.
It must have been in 1946 or 1947, when Kennedy's sister Kathleen,
the Marchioness of Hartington, paid a visit to Washington. "Kick"
Hartington was a friend of mine; and so I was asked to dinner by the
younger sisters, who were then keeping house for their Congressman
brother. When I arrived at the hour named, not a soul was anywhere in
sight. At first, in fact, I thought I must have mistaken the day; for a
half-eaten sandwich decorated the living-room mantelpiece; as a result
of some sort of recent competitive feat of strength, the whole room appeared to have suffered from a hurricane or tornado, and the usual
preparations for hospitality had all too plainly not been made. Eventually, however, the sisters began strolling vaguely into the room, appearing one by one, each looking more beautiful than the last. The

maid at length announced that dinner was ready, with an air of well-justified astonishment that this should be so; and after a further wait the Congressman brother unobtrusively joined us. It was a cheerful evening, after that, for the brother and the sisters composed an entertaining tribal act in which the brother was the central figure. His young good looks were striking. He had great charm. But I must confess I went home thinking that he would not last long in politics, and doubting whether he wished to do so.

Later I got to know him a bit better, but the next Kennedy characteristic that I clearly remember noticing was the occasional greenness of his complexion. From time to time, in those early days, his face would literally turn a dull grayish-green, which made an odd contrast with his thick reddish hair. It made me so curious that I ventured to ask him the reason for it. He replied that this greenness was caused by periodic injections the doctors made him take, and then he added, almost as an afterthought, "The doctors say I've got a sort of slow-motion leukemia, but they tell me I'll probably last until I'm forty-five. So I seldom think about it except when I have the shots."

The cool courage, the complete absence of self-pity when he made this admission of a delayed sentence of death, were deeply moving and impressive. This was when I first began to think of him as someone out of the ordinary. But I still thought him essentially unambitious.

Others tell me that I am mistaken in believing he had no great ambitions at the outset. But really ambitious budding politicians always study every aspect of the political process with absorbed attention, whereas Kennedy quite clearly paid very little attention to the real business of Government in his years in the House of Representatives. One could tell how little he had noticed then, by how much he had forgotten later on. When he was President, he no longer remembered even the most prominent features of the Truman Administration, such as the dominant role of the State Department in the secretaryships of George C. Marshall and Dean G. Acheson. How, then, can one explain this initial lack of ambition?

The key to the puzzle, I think, most probably lies in that moving but surprising remark about his green face. I never dared, either then or later, to ask him for further explanations. One does not, after all, ask for details of a potentially fatal illness; one must wait for the victim of the illness to speak first. Hence I know only that he came back from the Pacific in exceedingly bad health; that the damage he suffered on the fighting line, from unusually severe malaria as well as exposure and fatigue, was quite seriously misdiagnosed by his doctors; and that this error in diagnosis was not corrected for a good many years. His resulting belief that he had Addison's Disease or whatever it may have been was, of course, combined with the crippling bouts of pain recurrently inflicted by his bad back. Therefore, I suppose, he did not think he had much time allowed to him and he could not imagine reaching the summit of the White House with so little time to climb so high. No contest ever interested him unless he could aim for the very highest place. For just this reason, no doubt, he was content for a long while to go through the motions of politics, albeit with all his usual efficiency and grace. He must have begun to change with his election to the Senate in 1952; and three even more important things then happened to him, in rapid succession.

First, he married, in 1953. Second, in 1954, he grimly chose the considerable risk of death on the operating table, as preferable to the continuous torture his back was by then inflicting on him. He came so close to death that extreme unction was twice administered. But the back was much improved, although not cured; and the doctors also corrected the postwar misdiagnosis. Third, he therefore went to the Democratic convention of 1956 as a man no longer under sentence, with thoughts of a great career already forming in his mind; and these new thoughts were naturally encouraged at Chicago when he came within an ace of winning the vice-presidential nomination. It was a strong spur, and it set him on his final course.

Thenceforward he made the Presidency his goal. I like, nowadays, to recall how I finally learned what his real goal was. From December, 1956, until March, 1958, I lived and worked abroad. When I came home again, I was at once struck by the great change in Kennedy. Quite suddenly he had matured. The inward seriousness was now easy to detect beneath the surface wit and charm. The old casualness had now given way to a passionate absorption in every national problem; and his detailed knowledge of our problems was now combined with an equally detailed knowledge of the national political map, such as every serious politician needs. In sum, he had ripened into fitness for a very big role. As was natural, I was much impressed. He scented this, and was pleased. So we became friends, and fell into the habit of talking together about politics and other things as often as once or twice a week when we were both in Washington. Yet it is not easy to imagine a President of the United States much younger than oneself. At first, I did not realize that he meant to try for the Presidency in 1960, and he said nothing about it. Then one summer afternoon in 1958 we happened to talk about the Democrats' need to win back the Catholic voters. With this subject on my mind, as I was seeing him to the door of my house, I said casually, "Of course, the vice-presidential nomination would be yours for the asking next time; but surely you can't want the damn job."

"Let's not talk so much about vice," he replied with a quick grin. "I'm against vice, in all forms." And with that he ran down the steps and drove away, leaving me a bit popeyed on the doorstep.

The chapters that were then beginning—the triumphant drive for the 1960 nomination, the hard-fought election, and the years in the White House—belong to the public annals. But it is important to remember that before the public annals began, John F. Kennedy, like Franklin D. Roosevelt, passed through the valley of the shadow on his road to the White House. For this experience, surely, helped to give him his special fund of patience, humaneness, and seriousness about serious things.

When one attempts to assess Kennedy the President, it is first of all necessary to define the nature of the task that confronted him, and to suggest how he approached his task at the outset. I think it is fair to say that his task was one of the heaviest and most taxing that has ever confronted any newly elected President. A period of very great and rapid changes, both at home and abroad, had created correspondingly great and complex problems for the United States. Yet the importance and urgency of these problems were largely veiled from the eyes of the American people by the new affluence which made most of us sluggishly contented with things as they were. Franklin Roosevelt took office in a time of desperate national crisis, when the whole nation begged to be shown the way. John Kennedy took office in a time of huge but hardly noticed challenges, when there was much to be done, yet few Americans were eager to be up and doing.

Furthermore, it is pretty clear that John F. Kennedy brought to the White House a rather serious underestimate of the burdens he would have to bear and the difficulties he would have to overcome. Who can blame him? It was then an axiom of our political folklore that a strong President could move the nation to any necessary deed—although this is only true in special circumstances which did not exist in 1961. Furthermore, when Kennedy took office, the youngest Administration that this country has ever had abruptly succeeded the oldest; and an Administration that was the most talented in our history, man for man, also succeeded an Administration that was at least a bit tired and lackluster. This novel combination in Washington—youth at the prow and brilliance at the helm, so to say—at first dazzled the country. The country's dazzlement in turn tended to bedazzle the new President and many of those around him. Anything seemed possible. All seemed within easy reach. The first disillusionment, and very bitter it was, was the disaster at the Bay of Pigs.

Yet I think that even the Bay of Pigs did not quite make Kennedy feel the full weight of his presidential burden. The yoke of the Presidency, the heavy, heavy yoke of an American President in the H-bomb age, only settled on those youthful shoulders when he went to Vienna to meet Nikita S. Khrushchev, and was directly threatened with war over Berlin. I can see, as though I were still there, the very instant when he revealed Vienna's impact on him.

The true nature of the confrontation with Khrushchev had not emerged at Vienna, and I followed the presidential party to London without a hint of what had happened. In London the Kennedys were to attend the christening of their Radziwill niece, to which my wife and I were also invited. The afternoon of the christening was gloriously sunny. The house of Prince and Princess Radziwill made an enchanting setting. The scene itself, if encountered in a novel, would have seemed quite ludicrously overdrawn—so many famously beautiful women and men with great names and great positions had gathered to compliment the baby's parents and to meet the President. He came in a little late, looking strangely preoccupied. By chance, I was standing near the door, so that mine was the first ear of an old friend to present itself, as it were. To my considerable astonishment, he took me aside for a few minutes; and he poured out in swift, strained sentences what had really happened at Vienna, and how he had answered Khrushchev's arrogant threat.

"We'll stand firm," he ended. "By God, we'll stand firm. We'll never surrender—no matter what it costs."

Against the general gaiety and glitter of the occasion, the somberness of the brief episode was as poignant as it was unforgettable. It meant, unless I am mistaken, that Kennedy had at last been forced to face the choice that is always inherent in the modern Presidency—the ultimate, dire choice between final surrender and open-eyed acceptance of the risk of H-bomb war. Before Vienna, his faith in the power of reason had led him to believe that this choice could always be avoided by rational men. But Khrushchev at Vienna had thrust this choice upon him. No doubt the Soviet leader was falsely encouraged by the pattern of the Bay of Pigs. No doubt he expected the President to quail and give way. The President did not give way. He went home to order partial mobilization.

Thereafter he lived—we all lived, although many of us hardly knew it—under the lingering menace of a Third World War, a thousand times more terrible than its two precursors, until the second

Cuban crisis revealed that the menace was empty. The point about this period, of course, was that no one could be dead sure of the emptiness of the menace until the Soviet bluff had been decisively called. The rest of us could console ourselves by saying, "The Soviets are only bluffing"; but the President, the solitary man with ultimate responsibility for meeting the final test, had to ask himself, "What if the Soviets aren't bluffing?" The strain on him must have been very great, although he never made the smallest reference to it. The severity of the strain was certainly underlined by the sole sign that was ever given to me. He was dining with my wife and me. That morning, as we later learned, he had got the first grim news of the Soviet missiles in Cuba. That evening, however, no one else in the little party except Ambassador Charles E. Bohlen had the slightest inkling of what was afoot. We were downright jolly at table. After the meal the talk ran on history and its unforeseeable chances. Historic odds, for and against, was the sort of subject the President liked. Yet he offered no comment for a while; then he merely remarked, in a dry tone, "Of course, if you simply consider the mathematical chances, the odds are even on an H-bomb war within ten years."

Hearing this from him in these circumstances was a bit like draining a glass of champagne, and abruptly seeing doom reflected in the bottom of the empty glass. But as it fortunately turned out before many days had passed, the emplacement of those missiles in Cuba was the last great bluff. No one, I must repeat, could be sure it was a bluff until it had been called; but the call was made, with extreme toughness, with philosophic coolness, and with careful prudence and a wise sense of limits. So the time of seeming menace ended, and a quite new era opened. Always hoping for such a moment, he had doggedly, pragmatically made his preparations to profit from a better climate throughout the whole time when the strain on him was heaviest. Always he had worked to keep open, and to widen, all avenues that might lead to saner dealings between the two hostile halves of the world. His farsighted, patient preparations have now begun to produce their first results. These results can be simply summarized. Before Kennedy's Presidency and, indeed, throughout his Presidency until the end of the second Cuban crisis, the odds governing our future seemed to be as he stated them that evening at dinner. Now, in contrast, although courage, wisdom, vigilance, and strength are as needful as ever, even the sternest realist can see good grounds for hope. That is a difference one can hardly overestimate. Maybe the difference will be lessened by the changes in the Kremlin; the mere beginning of this sort of difference is still the achievement of a great President.

In our home affairs, too, I am persuaded that Kennedy's Presidency has made a very great difference, although a difference even harder to gauge. For purposes of measurement at least two rather complicated sets of facts must first be understood. On the one hand, our power, our population and our wealth had grown apace through the years after the Second World War; but this growth had been uneven. It had largely failed to benefit one tenth of our people. It had created all sorts of wholly novel problems, such as the problem of the sprawl of the suburbs and the decay of our great cities at their centers. Above all, by accentuating the contrast between the affluent Americans and the inhabitants of the "other America" of poverty and racial discrimination, the growth of our wealth, while enriching so many, had also inflamed the ancient, shameful, agonizing problem of injustice based on a color bar. For all these reasons a shocking backlog of unfinished business—of business not even begun in many cases—awaited Kennedy when he entered the White House. On the other hand, in the many years while this backlog was accumulating, there had been no proportional accumulation of ideas about the best ways to handle all this unfinished business. On the left, the American liberals were still repeating the same slogans that they had used since 1948 when they ceased their mystic postwar chant of "Revive the OPA!" And these slogans, about indiscriminately unbalancing the budget, for instance, were hardly more applicable, in the America of 1961 than the drive to revive wartime price controls in the America of 1947. On the right the American businessmen were also using slogans still more out of date, about rigidly balancing the budget in good times and bad, for instance. Almost all of the businessmen were still paying their customary lip service to all the shibboleths Kennedy attacked in the famous, highly conservative Yale speech that so offended so many self-styled conservatives.

In short, there was a great deal to do; no one had any very clear idea of how to do it; and a good many people were still saying that any attempt to do anything at all would be wicked, unconstitutional, and fraught with sinister risks. There was so much to do, in fact, that John F. Kennedy was only able to make a start in his short years in office. He was cut off too untimely to liquidate the backlog of unfinished business. The greatest steps forward were actually taken after his death, when the Congress, whipped on by Lyndon B. Johnson, enacted the Civil Rights Bill, the tax cut, and a long series of other measures Kennedy had initiated. Yet I suggest that if we look back to the time when Kennedy became President, we find that although he was killed too soon to see more than the first fruits of his efforts, his brief years in office nonetheless transformed the American domestic scene. From the beginning he was like a brisk young judge who inherits a calendar intolerably crowded with long-neglected cases. Crowded court calendars are not cleared overnight, but the great thing is to go to work with a will to succeed; Kennedy's will to succeed was iron-strong. Thus the outstanding problems began to be boldly tackled. This, in itself, was a renovating new departure. But the true renovation that Kennedy wrought was more important still. He not only tackled problems long neglected; he also set us the invaluable example of a new style of attack on our problems—a style that should influence us for many years to come.

As the oldest nation with a written constitution, whose founding fathers were farseeing and highly articulate political thinkers, we Americans have always been much more given to ideology than most of us suppose. But in the swiftly moving era in which we now live, the consecrated ideologies of the past need constant adaptation to retain real meaning in the present. Yet both the programs of the left and the programs of the right have long been parroted without adaptation; and thus both sets of programs have come to seem equally silly to anyone who looks at the facts. Faced with this seeming dilemma, Kennedy simply brushed all the ideological programs aside with splendid unconcern. "To hell with ideology," he seemed to say. "Let us have the courage to face the facts. And let us have the energy to deal with the facts. And let us have the common sense to deal with the facts without prejudice, taking them as they are, and doing the best we can to make things better." Courage, energy and common sense, clear-mindedness, practicality, a hearty dislike for slogans of whatever kind, and a flat refusal to admit defeat—these were the characteristics of John F. Kennedy in action. They comprised his pragmatic yet hopeful style, which he offered as an example to us. He indulged in no flimflam. He promised few palliatives. He never attitudinized. He was not rhetorical or falsely folksy or cheaply grandiose. But he had a vision of this nation's greatness, which he somehow conveyed to the rest of us. And so, on that snowy day in January, 1961, which now seems so tragically long ago, he said to the people of America, "Let us begin"; and begin we did.

To this assessment of Kennedy as President, I must add one further fact—a fact that only became entirely clear to me on the day before the President's funeral, when the long lines of sorrowing Americans, old and young, rich and poor, white and black and yellow, many from neighboring Washington but just as many who had come from afar, were still filing by the bier in the Capitol rotunda with bowed heads and tear-filled eyes. The fact is that Kennedy was loved. Furthermore, he was not merely loved as Franklin Roosevelt was loved, by the millions he led and sought to serve. Great leaders, with a true concern for their people, are always loved in this way. But Kennedy was loved

in quite another way too; and for this I can think of no recent precedent. Even Roosevelt did not command the love of his closest col-
laborators, who saw the real man behind the public personage. They
admired him; they believed in him; they sought to aid him by all means
in their power; but Harry Hopkins himself, who was F.D.R.'s closest
friend, cannot quite be said to have loved his chief. Yet on that day
before Kennedy's funeral, when I spent an accidental hour with one
of the toughest-minded members of the Kennedy team, I found a man
who was truly heartbroken, as one might be heartbroken by the loss
of a beloved elder brother. In the days and weeks and months that followed after, I found the same thing again and again, in all the
memorable company of outstandingly able, coolly intelligent men
whom Kennedy had brought into the Government.

One man who had served the President daily, and must have
taken the bad with the good, quite simply said, "I minded more than
when my father died, and I loved my father." Another said, "It is the
worst thing that has ever happened to me, and that is how I shall
remember it as long as I'm alive." It is curious, if you think about it—
this power that Kennedy had over these men who daily saw the lines
and faults and blemishes that show on every politician's private face.
This reverent affection for him breaks the rule that no man is a hero
to his valet. I have thought about it long and often, and I think I
have arrived at the reason for it, which was also the reason for my own
feeling for him. To all the qualities that made him a leader of men,
Kennedy added yet another quality that had little to do with leadership but much to do with his impact on those close to him. As an
English poet long ago wrote of a very different sort of lost leader:

> He nothing common did, or mean,
> Upon that memorable scene.

Joseph Kraft

Kennedy and the Intellectuals

Some of the brains which were corralled for the New Frontier
have gone back to pasture, and most of the maverick reformers
have never been roped in ... but the trained draft horses are pulling
an impressive load.

Back in the palmy days when the Kennedy Administration was being
put together, a professor at the Harvard Law School turned down an
important appointment, chiefly in order to work on a history of the
Supreme Court. "I am sorry," the President told him. "I had hoped
you would prefer to make history rather than write it." But have the
intellectuals in the Administration had a chance to make history?

Certainly there are enough of them. According to one tabula-
tion, nearly half (seventeen out of thirty-five) of the President's top
appointments were men who had previously taught at universities.
Like Richard Nixon during his campaign for the Presidency, Senator
Goldwater never ceases to attack the dominant influence of Arthur
Schlesinger, Jr., and John Kenneth Galbraith. Robert Frost, before
he died, hailed the Kennedy era as a "new Augustan age."

But if so, a good part of the intellectual community bears false
witness. Professor Henry Kissinger of Harvard has resigned as a special
consultant to the President, and become a special consultant to Nelson
Rockefeller. Something less than perfect good feeling attends the return of George Kennan to Princeton from his post as Ambassador to
Yugoslavia. Harsh criticisms have come from the novelists Norman
Mailer and James Baldwin, the playwright Gore Vidal, and the political scientists Sidney Hyman and Louis Halle. "Where," the critic Alfred Kazin asked in a notable essay, "is the meaningful relation of
intellectuals to power?"

The answer is that there are two meaningful relations. One is
public and political; the other obscure and bureaucratic. Each, in its
own way, is important. But neither is recognized as a familiar function
of the intellectual in our society. Hence the misgivings in the ranks of
the intellectuals, and the criticism.

The public role of the intellectual has probably been more em-

Reprinted from Profiles in Power *by Joseph Kraft by permission of the author
and New American Library.*

phasized by John Kennedy than by any other President. His speeches bristle with poetic and historical allusions. He made a special point of having Frost perform at his inauguration. He is restocking the White House library. He has established a government coordinator of cultural affairs—first August Heckscher, now Richard Goodwin. Writers, painters, scientists, and musicians dot the White House guest lists. Chiefly to do them homage, the President instituted an annual civilian honors list.

Undoubtedly the President's respect for intellectual achievement is heartfelt—something of a piece with a general pursuit of excellence apparent in Mrs. Kennedy and in his approach to clothes, sports, and education. He took off time from a particularly heavy schedule, the day after he returned from his last European trip, to work on the design for the Presidential Medal of Freedom. He personally insisted that an award go to Edmund Wilson, who had been bypassed by the medal committee because of writings critical of the Administration. Still, if the emphasis on brains is genuine, it also has a political purpose—as plain as the appointment of a Negro judge or a Polish Postmaster General. It is aimed, to be specific, at the egghead liberals within the Democratic party, a source of votes and, even more, of money throughout the industrial states—and notably in New York and California, where they are organized in reform clubs.

For various reasons, the Kennedy clan has never been able to establish true rapport with the Democratic reformers. The reformers count as principal hero the man Kennedy beat out for the Democratic Presidential nomination—Adlai Stevenson. They count as principal villains political bosses whom the Administration has chosen to favor, chiefly Jesse Unruh of California and Charles A. Buckley of the Bronx. They remember bitterly the President's failure to take a stand, when he was a Senator, against the late Senator Joseph McCarthy. And where Kennedy politics tends to be pragmatic, reform politics tends to be ideological and programmatic.

Cultural Patronage

But one avenue of harmony between the Administration and the reformers is open. The reformers constitute the nation's principal consumers of books, plays, art movies, concerts, and educational TV. They care about culture. And much as it offers judgeships to some, and post offices to others, so the Kennedy Administration dispenses culture to enlist the support of the Democratic liberals. It has made of culture, in other words, a form of patronage.

That is why, when the civilian medal of honor was instituted, there was going round the White House a *mot* attributed to Napoleon: "With enough ribbon, I could conquer the world." That is how it happened that as his 1960 campaign leader in New York, the President picked not a political pro, but his artist friend, William Walton. That is why, at the express direction of Attorney General Robert Kennedy, the 1962 gubernatorial campaign in New York was put in charge of a former magazine writer and Syracuse University faculty member, Assistant Secretary of Labor Daniel P. Moynihan. And there lies the explanation of the famous Washington mystery: What does Arthur Schlesinger do in the White House? Just as Kenneth O'Donnell handles White House relations with the Democratic organizations across the country, just as Lawrence O'Brien handles relations with the Democrats in the Congress, Schlesinger handles relations with the Democratic reformers. It is no mean assignment.

But to say that some intellectuals are political figures is not to say that none have influence over substantive policy. There are notable instances to the contrary. By drawing on the planning staffs at the State Department and the Pentagon, McGeorge Bundy, the former Harvard Dean who became the President's Special Assistant for National Security Affairs, has made himself a principal architect of all foreign policy. With a nod to the tax staff at the Treasury, Professor Walter Heller, the chairman of the Council of Economic Advisers, can, and does, take credit for the tax-reduction program. The Pentagon Whiz Kids—Research Director Harold Brown, Comptroller Charles Hitch, Deputy Comptroller Alain Enthoven, and Deputy Assistant Secretary Henry Rowen—are all former professors; and they have provided Secretary McNamara with the conceptual tools he has used to get a grasp on the complex of uncertainties that is the defense effort. And then there is the extraordinary and almost unknown success story of Carl Kaysen, Bundy's former deputy who, after accompanying Averell Harriman to Moscow for the test-ban talks, has returned to the economics department at Harvard.

Kaysen's Influence

As much as anyone, Kaysen drew together the scattered forces inside the Disarmament Agency, the State Department, the Pentagon, and the Atomic Energy Commission, which kept pushing inside the Administration for a test-ban treaty; in the pinch he arranged that the chief American negotiator be Averell Harriman, not a more cautious diplomat. He was the main White House contact for the State Department hands who favored the Congo policy which eventually bore fruit with the liquidation of the Katanga secession and the decline of its leader,

Moise Tshombe. He organized the drive of officials in the State Department, the Council of Economic Advisers, and the Bureau of the Budget which produced, over the resistance of the Treasury, the moves made through the International Monetary Fund meeting to revise the world's monetary mechanism. He has been, in short, one of the really influential figures inside the Administration.

Kaysen's effectiveness was not unconnected with his relative obscurity. Like the achievements of Bundy, of Heller, and of the Whiz Kids, Kaysen's achievements, in every instance, involved good relations —not only with the President—but with the staff of one of the great Departments. If he was one of the President's men, he was also a man of the bureaucracy. And that slow, silent, but indispensable force tends to react negatively to fame. As Richard Neustadt once put it: "You can get a lot more done more easily in Washington if you're not a celebrity."

On the other side of the medal, those intellectuals who supposed they could work closely with the President, and thus shake off the bureaucratic trammels, have tended to be disappointed. As a part-time adviser, dealing almost entirely with the President, and remote from the daily flow of bureaucratic business, Henry Kissinger found that his advice was chiefly honored in the breach. George Kennan failed in what was largely a one-man effort to have Yugoslavia brought within the most-favored nation terms of the 1962 Trade Act. And here is John Kenneth Galbraith's view of the intellectual's hard time in government, as expressed in a commencement address made before he resigned as Ambassador to India:

> As compared with twenty-five years ago, the federal government now lays a much stronger restraining hand on the individual who has a clear view of what he would like to accomplish and a strong desire to do it. The abrasive controversy which characterized the Roosevelt bureaucracy has all but gone. So has the art of broken-field running by the man who knew precisely where he wanted to go and who was skilled at finding holes in the formidable phalanx composed of those whose mission in life is to resist action and, where possible, also thought. Instead we have much greater emphasis on order, discipline, and conformity.

The Loneliness of the Broken-field Runner

The fact is that not even the most artful broken-field runner, inside or outside of government, can expect to have the kind of influence Galbraith is talking about—the kind that Felix Frankfurter commanded when he was a professor at the Harvard Law School dispatching students and ideas to Washington in the New Deal days. Almost all the important problems of government go beyond the range of individual knowledge. Even to know what to think, much more to convince others what to think, about the problems of government requires mountains of detailed information that can only be produced by large staffs. But staff resources do not exist at the White House, or even in the small advisory agencies: Walter Heller, for example, has to write almost all his own stuff, because the Council of Economic Advisers is too thin on staff even to give him first drafts. The true capacity for providing information and analysis on the problems of government lies with the old-line Agencies and Departments. They have the staff resources, and these they have recently supplemented with their own "house" intellectuals.

A striking illustration of the point arises in the area where intellectuals have in the past enjoyed probably the greatest influence on government—the area of relations between the scientific community and the defense program. Under Roosevelt, the atomic bomb was built as a result of a suggestion to the President by a handful of scientists casually grouped around the figure of Albert Einstein. Under Truman and Eisenhower, scientists were able to shape the defense program through special advisory committees, *ad hoc* groups such as the Gaither Committee, and, after 1958, the Office of Science and Technology. But with the Whiz Kids, intellectuals have entered the defense program itself, in regular bureaucratic jobs. Whoever would influence the program must deal through them. Even the President's scientific adviser, Jerome Wiesner, has a weekly meeting with one of the Whiz Kids.

For better or worse, just as it encompassed private economic power in the New Deal, government has engrossed private brain power in the postwar era. In the process of policy formulation, there is more room than ever for the trained intellectual bureaucrat. But the kibitzing intellectual celebrity has no place. The sun has set on one of the familiar figures of the political landscape. The long line of semi-official advisers from Aristotle through Keynes who combined intellectual genius with favor in high places to exert a dominant influence on the course of events has had its day.

John Cogley

JFK—A Final Word

From the beginning, I was an almost scandalously faithful supporter of John F. Kennedy. Sometimes it was a source of personal embarrassment, for I realized that it looked to others like a manifestation of tribal loyalty at its worst. Here was Kennedy, Irish-American and Catholic, and here was I, ditto, and what could be more natural, etc., etc.

I remember that back in 1959 *Esquire* magazine polled a certain number of people about their hopes for the 1960 Presidential winner. I was one of those polled, and I replied to all the other queries but left blank the space for the actual choice of candidate. Since I knew the results would be published I did not want to name Kennedy because I felt it might hurt him by suggesting that he was the "Catholic candidate." In replying to the questions of what I hoped from a new Administration, though, it was John F. Kennedy I had in mind.

There were times when I wished Kennedy were a Baptist and the son of Swedish immigrants so I could feel less self-conscious about the all-out support I was prepared to give him. All my life I had written and spoken against Catholic clubbiness and "our own kind" thinking. Then, when the first Irish-Catholic President came along, I found myself his ardent supporter. It was unsettling.

Still, now, as the Kennedy years are already fading into memory, I think I can honestly say that it was neither his Irish inheritance nor religious faith that really won me but a cast of thought, a characteristic political approach and certain personal traits.

For me, the Kennedy appeal had something to do with intellectuality, though I never regarded JFK as an "intellectual" in the usual sense of the word. He was, rather, a man of action, and that was all right with me. He used ideas but was never enthralled by them. This meant, on the one hand, that his Administration was uncommonly friendly to intellectuals; but, on the other hand, it meant that the totally dedicated intellectuals never quite trusted him, probably because they knew instinctively that he never quite trusted them. Their accustomed indifference to the necessary, and sometimes grubby, means to get good things done and their habit of practicing politics-by-proclamation was the President's bone of contention. His cool acceptance of the present reality as the starting point for the thousand-mile journey

From Commonweal, *May 8, 1964. Reprinted by permission of Commonweal Publishing Co., Inc.*

to the future in turn bothered them. Leaps rather than single steps are the only way to advance in the fast-moving age we live in, the intellectuals insisted; and they felt that Kennedy was too concerned with the techniques of politics and not enough with its goals to make such leaps of thought and of leadership.

My sympathies were notoriously with JFK here, even though my associations were much more intimate with the critical intellectuals than with him and his New Frontiersmen. This meant that I found myself defending the President in the area where he was most vulnerable and his critics most just, and again those nearest and dearest to me.

But the tension between the practicing politician and the intellectual strikes me as inevitable, like the perennial helpful struggle between priest and prophet, and it seemed that John F. Kennedy accepted this too as a fact of life and cherished the intellectuals for what they had to offer, while still realizing that in itself intellectuality is not enough for political leadership. This, to me, meant that though he did not identify with the intellectuals, he had the good sense to be, on the whole, for the intellectuals and to accept their contribution for its full worth. I believe he could not have honored them more, nor should he have honored them less.

Then my sympathy for the President had something to do with style, the most enduring of his qualities. It may be true, as one national columnist recently pointed out, that a preference for style over substance is a deadly political weakness. However in Kennedy's case I never thought of style in such terms. The style of Kennedy was the man Kennedy, and, I believe, it had a great deal to do with the substance of his leadership.

The Cuban confrontation, for example, depended mightily on his style. Any suggestion of either unsureness or bellicosity on his part could have been fatal. Making Khrushchev's capitulation possible, saving the loser's face, so to speak, was another exercise of the Kennedy style which proved to have great substantial significance: though the President tested the limits of deterrence, he did not try to test the limits of human perversity.

The Kennedy style, which at first seemed incomprehensible to some otherwise percipient commentators (remember all that silly talk about the cold, hard-eyed, humorless young man" in early 1960?) did not get across immediately. But, had JFK lived (and how often we find ourselves repeating that phrase!) it would, I believe, have been turned into more political, cultural, and educational capital with every passing month—and the whole nation would have benefited.

The sudden realization of what this style had affected us as a people, and how we would miss it, accounted, I believe for the phenomenal sense of loss at the time of his death.

It's no use trying to say what I mean by the Kennedy style. Style is not something one can define exactly, or prescribe for another. It is a gift of the gods and JFK had it in abundance. It has something to do with taste, something to do with restraint and control, and something to do, finally, with grace and gallantry. A rich, powerful, maturing and still uncertain nation needs all the example of it one who is so gifted can offer—as we realized when it was suddenly taken from us.

Finally, my loyalty to JFK had a great deal to do with his modernity.

I know there are many reasons why one might think of the present era as a totally undesirable period to live in. No generation of men has been witness to evil on a more colossal scale. None has had to bear with such uncertainty about the very future of the human race. None has had to live with problems so complex and failure to solve them so awesome. But, for all that, Kennedy seemed to say, it is a good time to be alive; maybe even because the challenges appear so stupendous, it is a good time to be alive.

John F. Kennedy communicated this sense of sane *joie de vivre* to the whole world and particularly to the young. Perhaps it was a result of his own comparative youth in a position usually filled by older men, but I don't think so. I think, rather, that it had something to do with his disdain for whimpering; his cool (that word keeps coming back) acceptance of contemporary reality and not because it was contemporary either but because it was presently real; his lack of fear of any idea and unspoken insistence that an idea, after all, is only an idea and not the stuff of life itself; and, finally, his abiding sense of history—the frantic contemporariety which many mistake for modernity did not mar his appreciation of the present.

Now, months after the assassination, like many others, I still wake up in the middle of the night and try to convince myself that it did not happen. The sense of loss is more present than ever—and the sense of utter tragedy, too. For I do not believe that John F. Kennedy will go down now as being among the great Presidents. And that is the heart of the tragedy. He needed more time and maturing and the time was taken away from him. What was still promise will now be forever no more than promise. And after our generation is gone, it will take unusual imagination to grasp what might have been, but now will never be.

There is the tragedy that keeps spelling itself out again and again in the lonely night.

As the months since Dallas stretch into years, the slow, historic death of John F. Kennedy will finally be complete. But it is not so long ago now that one cannot write once more of what his brief hour meant to some who lived through it, though this is the last time for such writing on my part.

What JFK meant ultimately is what he *could* have meant, and in that potentiality even the historians will have only a mild interest. So one settles finally for the tragic explanation, and as time goes on, it explains more and seems less tragic. And that in itself is tragedy of another sort, isn't it?

Cecil Osbaine

Kennedy: The Making of a Myth

On a late fall afternoon, returning from lunch to UN headquarters in New York, I was told by my shocked friends of the death of President Kennedy. I can see their faces now—grave and worried, reflecting minds struggling to adjust to a sudden and completely unforeseen change in our political environment.

A few minutes later I was in the crowded Delegates' Lounge of the General Assembly. And I saw and heard things there which didn't make sense to me—things which aroused my curiosity and which I am not sure I fully understand even today. Delegates from India, Nigeria, and even Sweden were literally grief-stricken. One of my Indian friends told me, with tears streaming down his cheeks, that the death of President Kennedy was a greater and more painful tragedy than was the death of Gandhi.

This kind of empathy with Americans at a moment of national tragedy led me to believe that perhaps America was, after all, the second homeland of all educated men. Perhaps the grief I saw reflected an unspoken admiration and affection for the United States, for its culture and its people. But this didn't fit another fact which fairly leaped out at the casual observer. Among foreign delegations (except for the Communists, of course) the symptoms of near-hysterical grief

From National Review, *November 5, 1968. Reprinted by permission of* National Review, *150 East 35th Street, New York, N.Y. 10016.*

were evident in inverse proportion to the degree of friendship and cooperation which each delegation had been showing for the United
States. And within particular delegations, the grief-stricken individuals
were the very ones who had in the past weeks been least cooperative
with the American delegation, the ones who had been most ready to
run errands for the Russians, the ones most eager to stick pins in the
United States. A closer analysis showed that cosmopolitan, sophisticated
"pros" among the foreigners at the UN tended not to be deeply affected
by the death of an American President. It was those who were new
to the trade of diplomacy or those who didn't pretend to be diplomats
but were rather teachers, lawyers, or politicians who took Kennedy's
death as a personal blow.

       During the next week I could observe, through the funeral and
the killing of Oswald, two more phenomena which didn't seem to be
predictable. One was that those foreigners who were so deeply affected
by Kennedy's death seemed to leap, as did Chief Justice Warren, to
the conclusion that the President was killed by ultra-conservative
forces personified by Dallas and Texas. Unlike the Chief Justice, but
like *most* American intellectuals, my grief-stricken friends continued
to assume that a conservative conspiracy must have been behind the
assassination.

       These observations left me puzzled and troubled. During the
next two years in Washington and the following three years in India
and Pakistan, I made a hobby of analyzing the reactions of foreign
intellectuals, particularly those of the underdeveloped countries, to
the death of President Kennedy and to related events and patterns of
events.

       It was soon evident that non-intellectuals abroad tended to react
in normal, predictable patterns except insofar as they were influenced
by the non-standard and unpredicted reaction of the intellectuals. The
reaction of the non-intellectuals was in general not intense and did not
involve personal values. Inquiry should obviously be concentrated on
those who defined themselves as members of an educated minority.

       I found that most foreign intellectuals were eager to talk to
Americans about their reactions to the death of Kennedy, but there
was a qualitative change in their disclosures as individual discussions
went deeper. These qualitative changes were remarkable in their extent, and I was never able, in an individual case, to reach a level of
inquiry and response which seemed to represent a stable emotional
level. This characteristic was so marked that I would often observe
reactions of an individual to a remark about Kennedy as a method of
determining whether he could be expected to react as an intellectual
to other events and situations.

What was John F. Kennedy in the mind of a typical under-developed intellectual? It seems almost certain that a kind of identi-fication with Kennedy lay at the bottom of these easily observed and deep emotions. But why should a Nigerian schoolteacher or a junior of-ficial in Pakistan choose John F. Kennedy as an object of identification?

The John F. Kennedy they identified with was not the real Kennedy—their image of Kennedy bore hardly more than a coinci-dental resemblance to the real Kennedy. They had not been "sold" a false image of Kennedy, although some of the Madison Avenue tech-niques used in American political campaigns may have given the initial impetus and even some of the direction to the process of enlarging Kennedy much bigger than life. The Kennedy they saw in their hearts was, first and foremost, a self-aware intellectual, even as they them-selves. There is no doubt whatever that Kennedy to them represented a creative academic intellect. His *Profiles in Courage,* for example, is regarded by his foreign admirers as an intellectual landmark; it is fervently believed that he wrote his own speeches just as Lincoln did. Many foreign intellectuals have memorized parts and even entire texts of Kennedy speeches. By a remarkable exegesis, they interpret some of Kennedy's more vapid and meaningless public utterances as clarion calls against racial persecution, social injustice, and the philistine mores of the middle class.

Kennedy is further regarded as being so "progressive" as to be revolutionary. He is, in myth, rapidly becoming a doctrinaire socialist, his squabble with the steel companies an Armageddon against capital-ism, his American University speech a valiant effort to call off the cold war.

Kennedy's wealth is recognized, but it is emphasized that John Kennedy himself never made the money. The senior Kennedy (who appears on the stage only for this purpose) had presented him with great wealth. But the Kennedy of the myth is above all an aristocrat—his social standing is beyond the reach of his detractors; his is the self-confidence which comes of casual, careless certainty of superiority, of supreme self-confidence.

But the Kennedy of myth is also a "fun" person who, when he relaxes, can be identified with the sophistication of the American entertainment industry—with the blasé film hero in a nightclub. His adoring, beautiful, wealthy wife, who is also an intellectual and a pro-gressive, is his feminine mirror image. They complement each other, figures of power, grace, beauty, and confidence.

It is not difficult to see why a foreign intellectual could identify deeply with such a figure. But why should the individual chosen for this glorification be an American?

Here one must turn to Eric Hoffer's analysis of the non-creative intellectual as a class, with class interests and class aspirations which are international in scope. The underdeveloped intellectual is caught in a love-hate relationship to the United States. He is awed by the material achievements of the United States, but horrified by our mass culture and our mass-oriented pluralistic political and economic systems. The U.S., if he looks at it dispassionately, forces upon him the necessity for choice between material achievement without class barriers or the retention of a compartmented social structure with poverty and weakness as its price. The very fact that his traditional orientation as an intellectual is antithetical to the prosperity, pride and power he lusts for is too devastating an idea to be faced. It must be shunted aside, and the minds of intellectuals the world over are cluttered with shunting mechanisms, operable and inoperable.

Identification with the mythical construct of John F. Kennedy was a most efficient shunting device. Here is John Kennedy—here is what *I* would be if I were an American! Here am I, the proud, self-confident tamer and shaper of this powerful but mindless beast, hitherto guided by middle-class morality and middle-class politics. Though the American people be ever so stubborn, though populist politicians be ever so noisome and clever, though the Pentagon warmongers and the racists and the forces of capitalism be ever so strongly entrenched— yet will I slay the dragon, yet will I win the people to a proper respect for their intellectual superiors! And I will do it all with grace and beauty!

Only thus can we comprehend the general correlation between hatred of American mass culture and love for a President of the United States. Only thus can we comprehend the worldwide genuine grief over the death of John Kennedy. But—the depth of that grief was not a measure of affection for the United States. It was a measure of hatred for the United States.

And with the hero of myth dead, what then? The next step is quite necessary, of course—death cannot come to the mythic hero by a casual accident. The hero was overcome by the dragon, which dared not face him in the open. And what is the dragon? The dragon is everyday, Main Street America—the mass-culture America which regards intellectuals with amused contempt instead of the reverent awe which is their due, the America which can't respect its betters! John Kennedy *had* to be killed by an America which is represented in its striking arm by the armed forces, the CIA, the FBI, lynch mobs, Texas millionaires, and gangsters. Kennedy in his death proved the unregeneracy of the American mass culture—it killed its own savior.

Did Oswald Exist?

Therefore, we can predict that our foreign intellectual friends would tend to believe in all kinds of conspiracy theories about the assassination and reject the Warren Report. I have not talked to a single foreign intellectual who does not believe that in some way or other, directly or indirectly, Lyndon Johnson stands as the symbol of that conspiracy, as the symbol of capitalism and racism and militarism, and, worst of all, as the symbol of a mass culture which is powerful and successful and hence triply unfair and intolerable.

One other element is required to fill in the blank spaces of this great delusion—one other unpredictable symptom requires explanation. We can from the foregoing understand why foreign intellectuals must hold to conspiracy theories of the death of President Kennedy. But in my conversations another aspect gradually came into the foreground—a strong tendency to refuse to accept the reality of Lee Harvey Oswald at all! I have repeatedly had foreign intellectuals pretend that, though they knew all the other details of the assassination through one or another conspiracy theory, they had forgotten the name of the man who was killed by Jack Ruby, even though they knew Ruby's name. Others, who do know his name but believe him to be a dupe or martyr, pretend to be utterly ignorant of his life history and background. There is a strong tendency for a foreign intellectual to shift his eyes, change the subject, to even terminate the interview when he is confronted with a picture of Lee Harvey Oswald. What can be the reason for this widespread refusal to look in Oswald's eyes, to relive poor Oswald's miserable nightmare of a life?

Who is this Oswald who exists only as an unhealthy wraith, flitting around the edge of the epic tapestry? Why is he, poor wretch, denied even his true value as a human being while the mythic hero, blown up and blazoned, is magnified beyond reality? Kennedy is the projection of the better part, the dreams and the pseudo-idealism, of our typical foreign intellectual. But when our foreign intellectual looks at Oswald, he sees himself—he sees the bitterness and false pride, the shoddy imitation of creativity, the urge to destroy the measuring rods which make him seem petty. He tries to dodge away from the horrid truth—America didn't really kill the epic hero. He himself killed the glorious ideal. The perverted instincts which drove Oswald are the same instincts which drive the underdeveloped intellectual to try to destroy, if he cannot tame, the mass culture of America, and anything else which symbolizes a threat to his status and hopes.

So, the thought that there even might have been a Lee Harvey Oswald who might just possibly have killed the glorious symbol is something which must be smothered in the subconscious. The look in Oswald's eyes must be forgotten while the look in Kennedy's eyes must be glorified into something that never was.

Those tear-stained faces in the General Assembly Delegates' Lounge represent a complex of the lies that men tell themselves—the lies in which they enmesh themselves. There is a symmetry in the interlocking circles of deception. It may be that there is some variant of this pattern among American intellectuals. One would doubtless have to dig very deep to find out.

Norman Mailer

The Leading Man
A Review of J.F.K.: The
Man and the Myth

Co-author of *Seeds of Treason,* a book on the Hiss-Chambers case, Victor Lasky has now written a giant political biography of John Fitzgerald Kennedy. It is a thoroughgoing performance which begins with the career of Joseph Kennedy, Sr., then moves from Jack Kennedy's first political musings in college on through the separate stations of his career all the way into the first years of the Presidency. A considerable number of vignettes are offered as well of other members of the Kennedy family and such figures in the New Frontier as Theodore Sorensen, Arthur Schlesinger, Jr., and John Kenneth Galbraith. It is close to being a monumental study of Jack Kennedy's stops and starts, dips and swoops, turns to Right and Left as he advanced along his political life, and the work becomes an indispensable if not altogether trustworthy reference to anyone who would study the peculiar logic of political success, the practical details in the art of the possible.

Lasky has done an impressive amount of work. He has hunted down a thousand anecdotes in newspapers and magazines (half of them sufficiently apocryphal to be worthless, we can suspect), he has talked to everyone who knew Kennedy and would agree to talk to Lasky, he

From Cannibals and Christians *by Norman Mailer. Reprinted by permission of the author and the author's agents Scott Meredith Literary Agency, Inc., 580 Fifth Avenue, New York, N.Y. 10036.*

has come up with much of the goods and a hundred goodies. Did Jack Kennedy ever kiss a baby in the congressional campaign of 1946 and turn to a friend to say, "Kissing babies gives me asthma"? Well, you may be certain Lasky has found the item and put it in. *J.F.K.: The Man and the Myth* is a book which will give pleasure to every Kennedy-hater who reads it—they will feel as if they are dipping into a box of creamy chocolate. Indeed, at his best and worst, Lasky is reminiscent of Lait and Mortimer—he could have called his job *John F. Kennedy— Confidential.*

And there is value in such an undertaking: a man *is* responsible for his past. It is not fitting that Jack Kennedy should get away with all of it. The Republicans will employ these pages as a running hand-book for the '64 campaign, and it will be of inestimable use to them, good use and dirty use, but ideally the book can be worth even more for liberal Democrats, since their chronic disease is hero worship, and Lasky's pages are effective antitoxin. For example:

> In 1950, John F. Kennedy made a personal contribution to Richard M. Nixon in his Senate campaign against the California Congresswoman [Helen Gahagan Douglas]. . . . Like any other contribution it was turned over to the Nixon Senate Campaign Committee in California.

On the preceding page is one of numerous references to the President's not unfavorable attitude toward McCarthy in the early Fifties: "he thought he 'knew Joe pretty well, and he [McCarthy] may have something.' "

But then the Kennedy of 1948 was making these sorts of headlines in the Boston *Herald:* "Kennedy says Roosevelt sold Poland to Reds." F.D.R. had done this "because he did not understand the Russian mind." So had gone a modest speech Congressman Kennedy had given to the *Polish*-American Citizens Club in Roxbury.

Lasky is unrelenting. A letter from the President to his father, written in 1937 when he was 20, goes in part (note the fence straddling):

> . . . while I felt that perhaps it would be far better for Spain if Franco should win—as he would strengthen and unite (sic) Spain —yet at the beginning the government was in the right morally speaking as its program was similar to the New Deal.

A little later, in his undergraduate thesis, "Appeasement at Munich," he was defending the Munich Pact: "The state of British opinion and the condition of Britain's armaments . . . made 'surrender' inevitable."

But these, after all, were the somewhat Right Wing views of a very young man. The embarrassment for liberals is that the attitude persisted almost up to his nomination. Calculated, in retrospect, seems J.F.K.'s courtship of President Eisenhower, his announcement in 1955 that he was only in "moderate opposition" to the White House, and Lasky's evidence that all through the late Fifties Jack Kennedy was doing his best to seduce the South. "Georgia loves him," reported the political editor of the Atlantic *Constitution*.

This catalogue of Right Wing sins and stances does, however, a violence to the balance. Kennedy's real political art—Lasky's documentation is more than adequate here—came from his ability to occupy the political Center yet move simultaneously to the Right and to the Left. He committed himself, for example, to the legislative programs of Walter Reuther and George Meany while engaging at the same time in an all-out attack on Dave Beck and Jimmy Hoffa. Thus he could nail down the support of the most powerful sectors of organized labor in the Democratic Party for his nomination while advancing himself in the public eye as a militant crusader against union rackets. At the junction of these two prongs is pure political sugar. The instrument of his attack on Hoffa had been the McClellan Labor Rackets Committee; Jack and Bobby Kennedy dominated the committee to the point where other senators would arrive for hearings to find witnesses called without their knowledge. Lasky's explanation is that the brothers were able to attain this exceptional power over a committee only because they possessed "the blessing of the Majority Leader of the Senate, Lyndon B. Johnson." It was Johnson's notion presumably to bind Jack Kennedy over to the idea of a Johnson-Kennedy ticket for President. The shade of Frankenstein falls dark on the shoulder of a politician.

Barry Goldwater once remarked bitterly that the Kennedys had nothing working for them but "money and gall," and when one thinks of the devoted work Bobby Kennedy gave to the McCarthy committee as a lawyer on McCarthy's staff, quitting finally only because he refused, according to Lasky, "to play second fiddle to Roy Cohn," there is either high comedy or the suspicion of horror in Bobby Kennedy's subsequent attack on Hubert Humphrey's tactics as McCarthyite during the West Virginia primaries seven years later.

The political point, of course, is that one can usually get away with it. For every man who would remember that Bobby Kennedy was once a McCarthyite, there would be a dozen others who would forget and call the first man a liar. A speech made in one city does not have the same magic when it is read about in another city. A promise made in private to a politician will not interfere with a contradictory promise made to another politician. When the time comes to fulfill the promise, one can reward the man who did the most for you, or is strongest, or indeed one can break both promises and make a deal with a third politician. One can promise the Negro his rights in the North while giving intimations to the South that one is secretly sympathetic to their fears. The art is to practice duplicity and double-dealing with a sense of moderation, taste, and personal style; the secret is to remain alert to the subtler shifting realities of mass communication: what sort of news in this season is likely to become national, which oratory will happily or unhappily remain local.

These are some of the lessons to be elucidated from the political career of John Fitzgerald Kennedy. If Lasky's work had been an objective study, if Kennedy had been considered merely the first among equals, if it had been understood that such men as Barry Goldwater, Hubert Humphrey, and Dick Nixon are all in their way equally adept as political operators—if Lasky's work had risen into an unbiased exploration of political mendacity in general and President Kennedy in particular, there might have been a hard remaining substance to the book. He could have left us with a classic in political biography. (A badly written classic, be it said—the prose is left without comment.) Instead, Lasky's pretense to be objective, which keeps the first half of his book interesting, begins even as pretense to disappear about the time Jack Kennedy begins to work for his nomination. Lasky's bias shows itself. He is, we discover, a Nixon man, an all-out Nixon man. The moral judgments slide over into propaganda. Nixon is invariably presented as honest, self-effacing, put upon, unjustly rejected; Kennedy grows into a villain of the first proportions. So a work which might have reminded us that we take the politician too seriously is replaced by Lasky's more specific objective—which is to stitch up a campaign flag for the return of Richard M. Nixon; so a work which could have reminded Jack Kennedy that there is still a public conscience becomes instead a campaign tract to be overpraised by Republicans and damned by Democrats. That is the crime of commission in *J.F.K.: The Man and the Myth.*

The void of omission is more grave. For, with all his documentation of Jack Kennedy's political life, the large disappointment in the book is that Lasky has no intimation of the curious depths in the President's nature. J.F.K. is a divided man, and only half his nature is political. Even through the lenses of his bias, Lasky understands that half very well—that half-man comes through the pages as one of the most consummate political animals in the history of America. But the half omitted is more crucial. For Jack Kennedy is a new kind of political leader, and a study of his past political sins will not help us to comprehend his future. The likelihood is that our President is a new kind of Commander-in-Chief. He is not a father, nor a god, nor a god-figure, nor an institution, nor a symbol. He is in fact—permit the literary conceit—a metaphor. Which is to say that Jack Kennedy is more like a hero of uncertain moral grandeur: is his ultimate nature tragic or epic? Is he a leading man or America's brother? A symbol is static. It exists eternally, immutably. It is the circle of the sun or the wave of the sea. But a metaphor is a relation. It changes as our experience changes. We say for example: the sun was burning with hate. A day later the meaning alters and we say to ourselves that it is only our own hatred we perceived in the sun; in a week the metaphor has come to mean something else again, something deeper perhaps—between the sun and ourselves is a celestial terrain of hatreds which alter our understanding of the sun at every moment.

These poetic mechanics are of course far indeed from Victor Lasky's prose, stance, and intention. But *J.F.K.: The Man and the Myth* is an irritating, frustrating, and finally disappointing book because it offered the promise of becoming a first-rate job, and was spoiled—this spoliation being a first-rate loss—by Lasky's incapacity to entertain a poetic concept of his subject. Jack Kennedy is somewhat more and considerably less after all than a hero or a villain—he is also an empty vessel, a man of many natures, not all of them necessarily rooted in granite. He is, it must be said, a Kierkegaardian hero. One can assume that in the private stricken moments of his life, those moments all of us know at rare and best-forgotten times, it is impossible for him to be certain of his moral bedrock. Kierkegaard was probably the first Western mind to have an intimation that either the nature of man was changing or had never been properly understood, that it was just as natural for man to be flooded with sensations of goodness when he was most evil as it was for him to taste his evil, and that a man in the act of being good could equally be depressed with an awareness of his profound evil. In this sense one did not have a nature which was formed already—on the contrary, one created one's nature by the depth or power of one's act. Kierkegaard had divined that there was probably no anguish on heaven or earth so awful as the inability to create one's nature by daring, exceptional, forbidden, or socially impossible acts.

This impulse—to create and forever re-create his nature—has been the President's dominant passion. There is no other way to comprehend him. From the Hairbreadth Harry of his P.T. boat exploits through the political campaigns with their exceptional chances (who could beat Cabot Lodge in Massachusetts in 1952?) through the lively bachelordom, through the marriage to the impossibly beautiful and somewhat madcap wife, the decision to run for President, a decision worthy of Julien Sorel, the adventure in Cuba, the atomic poker game with Khrushchev last October when the biggest bluff in the history of the world was called—yes, each is a panel of scenes in the greatest movie ever made.

The President is not a great mind, and it may be that he will prove ultimately not to be a good man—those who are forever re-creating their personalities can end with a mediocre nature even more naturally than a great one—but he had genius in one respect. Jack Kennedy understood that the most important, probably the only dynamic culture in America, the only culture to enlist the imagination and change the character of Americans, was the one we had been given by the movies. Therefore a void existed at the center of American life. No movie star had the mind, courage, or force to be national leader, and no national leader had the epic adventurous resonance of a movie star. So the President nominated himself. He would fill the void. He would be the movie star come to life as President. That took genius. For Jack Kennedy grew up in the kind of milieu which was so monumental with finance and penurious with emotion that everybody's breath smelled like they had been swallowing pennies and you were considered mentally disturbed if you did not bet on the New York Yanks. He had a character thus created of the most impossible ingredients for his venture: overweening ambition and profound political caution—he had been taught never to commit himself to a political idea since ideas often pass, weaken, and die long before the men who believed in them.

Yes, John F. Kennedy was without principles or political passions except for one. He knew the only way he could re-create the impoverished circuits which lay between himself and the depths of his emotions was to become President. *He* was his own idea, and he had the luck to have a powerful father who agreed entirely with his venture. So he combined the two halves of his nature, the Faustian adventurer and the political opportunist, and behind him left a record of deceits, evasions, broken promises, Congressional absenteeism, political pusillanimities, after-dinner clichés, amoral political negotiations and a complete absence on the record of a single piece of important legislation. Or the utterance of a single exciting political idea. He didn't have to. He was on the trail of something else and the people who gathered to his support were in quest of something else.

His impulse, that profound insight into the real sources of political power in America, came from a conscious or unconscious cognition that the nation could no longer use a father; it was Kennedy's genius to appreciate that we now required a leading man. The contradictions of our national character had become so acute that no symbol of authority could satisfy our national anxiety any longer. We had become a Kierkegaardian nation. In the deep mills of our crossed desires, in the darkening ambiguities of our historic role, we could know no longer whether we were good or evil as an historic force, whether we should prosper or decline, whether we were the seed of freedom or the elaboration of a new tyranny. We needed to discover ourselves by an exploration through our ambiguity. And that precise ambiguity is embodied in the man we chose for our President. His magnetism is that he offers us a mirror of ourselves, he is an existential hero, his end is unknown, it is even unpredictable, even as our end is unpredictable, and so in this time of crisis he is able to perform the indispensable psychic act of a leader, he takes our national anxiety so long buried and releases it to the surface—where it belongs.

Now we must live again as a frontier nation, out on a psychic frontier without the faith of children or the security of answers. So the country, for better or for worse, is now again on the move, and the President is the living metaphor of our change. It is this power in him to excite—whether he desires it or no—our change, our discord, and our revolt, which Victor Lasky has failed most resolutely to comprehend. He does not see that Kennedy is the agent of our ferment and that we now go forth into the future ignorant of whether the final face of the Presidency and America shall prove to be Abraham Lincoln or Dorian Gray.

William G. Carleton
Kennedy in History: An Early Appraisal

Because of the vividness of his personality and the shortness of his tenure, Kennedy will be known more for the intangibles—a tastemaker, a symbolic embodiment of the values of his time, a romantic folk hero—than for his achievements in statesmanship.

Government requires pageantry, and rulers are expected to put

Reprinted from The Antioch Review, *Vol. XXIV, No. 3, by permission of the editors.*

on a show. The Kennedys put on a superb one. Never before, not
even under Dolly Madison, was the White House the scene of such a
dazzling social life, one which combined beauty and intelligence, radi-
ance and creativity. There were, to be sure, crabbed Mrs. Grundys
who derided "peacock opulence" and looked back longingly to the
decorous days of Lucy Webb Hayes. But most Americans were fascinated, pleased as punch that even Elizabeth and Philip appeared a
bit dowdy in contrast to those two young American thoroughbreds in
the White House. They figuratively crowned Jacqueline Queen of
Hearts. This aspect of the Kennedy reign has been inimitably described by Katherine Anne Porter, and no historian will ever record
it with more grace, insight, and tenderness.[1]

   Kennedy's contributions to the cultural life of the nation also
belong to the intangible, and they are difficult to measure. Now of
course President Kennedy did not engage in as wide-ranging an intellectual life as President Jefferson or President Theodore Roosevelt.
He did not carry on a voluminous and polemical correspondence with
American and foreign intellectuals as these men had done, even when
they were in the White House. And Kennedy himself realized that
his "little promotions" did not help young and struggling artists and
writers in the direct and material way the New Deal works projects
had done.

   But never before Kennedy's time had the White House paid so
much personal and social attention to the nation's writers, artists,
musicians, scientists, and scholars. At first some of the public was
inclined to take a snidely skeptical view of all this. Was not this
celebrity-hunting, highbrow name-dropping, a further drive to presidential glamour? The recipients of these attentions did not think so.
Only William Faulkner, in bad-tempered petulance, rebuffed the
President. For the rest, a chat with the President or an invitation to
an event in the White House was an occasion of a lifetime, and these
felt that Kennedy was not merely honoring them but the creative work
they represented. As Richard Rovere has pointed out, Kennedy was
tremendously concerned that the American society become a good,
even a brilliant, civilization. He thought of himself as a promoter, an
impresario, of excellence in every phase of American life, and he hoped
that future presidents would emulate him in this.[2]

   To latter twentieth-century Americans, Kennedy will be a kind
of beau ideal reflecting what they consider admirable in the politician—

[1] Katherine Anne Porter, "Her Legend Will Live," *Ladies' Home Journal,* March
1964.
[2] See Richard Rovere, "Letter from Washington," *The New Yorker,* November 30,
1963.

a shunning of corniness and hokum, an accent on youth and wealth, the glamorous videographic personality favored by Hollywood and TV, a contrived casualness in dress and manner, the sophistication and urbanity of the ivy league, direct and clear speech sprinkled with wit, an avoidance of doctrine and dogma, a pragmatism just emotionally enough involved to be effective, the capacity for using expertise and Madison Avenue techniques, the ability to create and sustain an "image." In these, most of them externals, Kennedy will have many imitators.

The Kennedy elan will not be easy to imitate. Even more difficult of imitation will be the Kennedy mind—rational and balanced thinking, objectivity, the ability to see all around a question, resilience, elusiveness, the capacity for keeping judgment in suspense, a detachment reaching to one's self and one's own image, an avoidance of absolute commitment combined with genuine intellectual involvement, a general critical intelligence brought to bear on the findings of the specialists. The Kennedy magic lies in its combination of the various elements: the externals, the verve with which the externals were carried off, and the cast of mind.

There is still another Kennedy intangible, perhaps the most important, one which belongs to the non-rational. Kennedy is becoming a folk hero, a subject of myth and legend, one of those few in history who capture the poetic imagination and affection of the masses. Solid achievement may have something to do with arriving at such a place in history, but very often it has little or nothing to do with it. Indeed, the titans who have wrought most mightily and in the end been felled by tragedy inspire awe and reverence more frequently than they do folk affection. They are too mature, their lives too devoid of colorful gallantries and foibles, their achievements too overwhelming for the average man to identify himself with such figures. To this class belong Caesar, William the Silent, Lincoln. Increasingly Lincoln has become a father image and "the martyred Christ of the democratic passion play."

The folk hero in the affectionate, indulgent sense is one who leaves behind him an overall impression of elan, style, beauty, grace, gaiety, gallantry, bold and light-hearted adventure, valor—mingled in one way or another with the frail, the fey, the heedless, the mystic, the tragic. This is the romantic tradition, the tradition of Achilles, David, Alcibiades (despite his damaged soul), Arthur, Roland, Abelard, Richard the Lion Hearted, St. Francis, Bayard, Raleigh, Henry of Navarre, Gustavus Adolphus, Byron. Alexander the Great is often put in this tradition, but his exploits were so dazzling, so epoch-making, that he became more a god than a hero.

Kennedy's death has in it the touch of religious epic, of man pitted against fate. Here surely was one favored by the gods, one possessed of power, wealth, youth, the aura of manly war heroism, zest for living, personal charm and beauty, glamour, imagination, keen insight, intelligence, immense popularity, the adoring love of family and friends. Great achievements were to his credit, and even greater ones seemed in store. Then in the fullness of his strength, he was cut down in a flash. History has no more dramatic demonstration of the everlasting insecurity of the human condition.[3]

Was Kennedy himself a romantic? In some ways, mostly in appearance and manner. There are photographs of him, for instance several public ones taken in Tampa five days before his assassination, which reveal him in a kind of narcissistic euphoria. (Those who understand how wondrously flexible human nature can be will see nothing damaging in this.) James Reston once observed that the effect Kennedy had on women voters was "almost naughty." In his personal relations—and this is a matter not of appearance but of substance—Kennedy had an outgoing freshness and (there is no other term for it) a sweetness of temper. But basically Kennedy was not a romantic. He was a rationalist with a critical intelligence, a realist who knew the hard and subtle uses of power.

However, one need not be a romantic to become a romantic hero of history. Many romantics miss it—sometimes for a variety of reasons just barely miss it: Bolívar, Garibaldi, Gambetta, Jaurès, Michael Collins. In modern times romantic heroes have become rare. Kennedy is the first in this tradition in a long time, and he is the only American in its top echelon. Strange that he should have come out of the America of the machine and mass production. Or is it? People in our prosaic age, particularly young Americans, were yearning for a romantic hero, as the James Dean cult among our youth revealed. Now they have an authentic one.

---

[3] Although the folk think of Kennedy as a child of fortune, actually he suffered much physically. He seems never to have been robust; the state of his health often concerned his father; in my own brief Kennedy files are letters from the elder Kennedy which speak of Jack's poor health in periods prior to World War II. Following his service in the war, Jack was plagued with malaria and his serious back injury. Even after the successful operation on his back, it would appear that he was rarely free from pain. When this comes to be realized, Kennedy's pace as president will appear even more gallant.

1 2 3 4 5 6 7 8 9 10